STORIES *from* THE STACKS

Writers: Ang Seow Leng; Chung Sang Hong; Gracie Lee; Goh Yu Mei; Jan van der Putten; Janice Loo; Jessie Yak; Joanna Tan; Juffri Supa'at; Kevin Khoo; Kong Leng Foong; Lee Meiyu; Lim Tin Seng; Liviniyah P.; Makeswary Periasamy; Mazelan Anuar; Michelle Heng; Mok Ly Yng; Nadia Ramli; Nadirah Norruddin; Ong Eng Chuan; Seow Peck Ngiam; Sundari Balasubramaniam; Timothy Pwee; Vladimir Braginsky; Yosuke Watanabe; Zoe Yeo

Publication Project Team: Amanda Chan; Ong Eng Chuan; Wong Siok Muoi; Sharon Koh; Stephanie Pee; Veronica Chee

Editorial Consultants: Francis Dorai; Jimmy Yap

Design and Production: Marshall Cavendish International (Asia)

Printer: Oxford Graphic Printers Pte Ltd

Published by:
National Library Board, Singapore
100 Victoria Street
#14-01 National Library Building
Singapore 188064
Email: ref@nlb.gov.sg
www.nlb.gov.sg

National Library Board, Singapore Cataloguing in Publication Data
Names: Singapore. National Library Board, collector.
Title: Stories from the stacks : selections from the Rare Materials Collection National Library Singapore.
Description: Singapore : National Library Board, Singapore : Marshall Cavendish Editions, [2020] | Includes index.
Identifiers: OCN 1201501796 | ISBN 978-981-14-4499-9 (hardcover)
Subjects: LCSH: Singapore. National Library Board--Catalogs. | Rare library materials--Singapore--Bibliography--Catalogs. | Rare books--Singapore--Bibliography--Catalogs.
Classification: DDC 016.95957--dc23

STORIES *from* THE STACKS

SELECTIONS FROM THE RARE MATERIALS COLLECTION
NATIONAL LIBRARY SINGAPORE

CONTENTS

INTRODUCTION

Collecting, preserving and making accessible Singapore's documentary and published heritage is a key mission of the National Library. There is no better expression of this than our Rare Materials Collection.

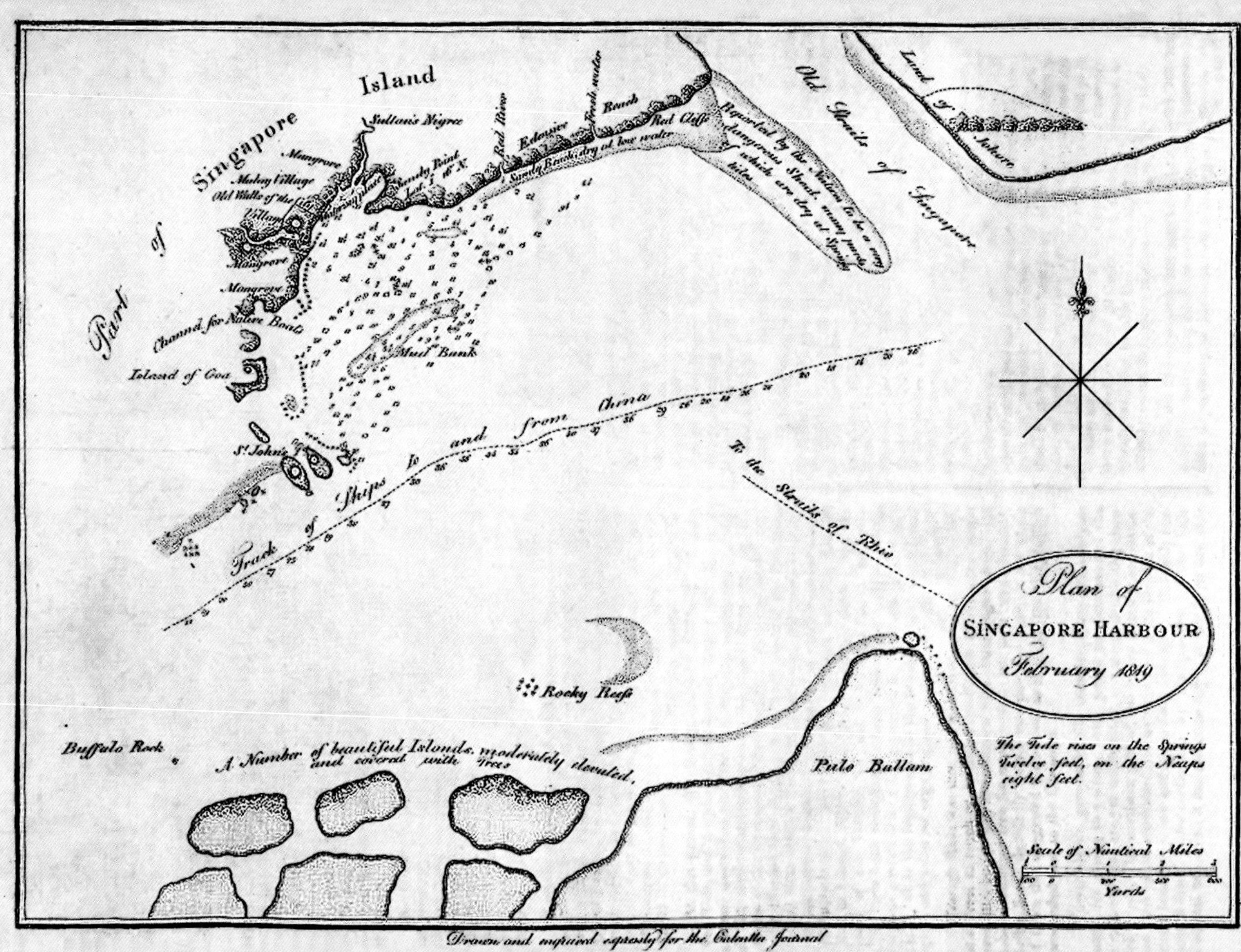

This first map of Singapore's harbour was borne out of a cartographic survey conducted in 1819 by Captain Daniel Ross, a hydrographer with the British East India Company's (EIC) Bombay Marine, the India-based naval fleet set up to protect British trading routes in the Far East.

Comprising more than 19,000 items, the Rare Materials Collection includes books, periodicals, manuscripts, maps, photographs, art prints, handwritten letters, documents, and other forms of paper ephemera. Some of these artefacts are centuries old and they represent our nation's patrimony.

For preservation purposes, the items are carefully stored in a climate-controlled room at the National Library Building in Victoria Street. Those interested in consulting these items can examine the microfilmed version. For ease of access, many of these have also been digitised and can be accessed at our BookSG website.

To raise the profile of these artefacts, we published *The Rare Materials Collection: Selections from the National Library, Singapore* in 2017. It was so well received that we reprinted it two years later. However, that book only scratched the surface of what we have at the National Library, hence this follow-up work, *Stories from the Stacks.*

Stories from the Stacks showcases 48 artefacts from the Rare Materials Collection as well as a sprinkling of items from our other collections. It is a diverse selection comprising everything from a 15th-century copper-engraved map of Southeast Asia to the handwritten manuscripts of contemporary Singaporean writers. All the items are accompanied by essays written by a team of librarians from the National Library and invited researchers. These provide a detailed description of each artefact as well as highlights of its history.

This volume features the oldest artefact in our collection – *Vndecima Asiae Tabvla.* Printed in Rome in 1478, this European map was based on the ancient work, *Geographia*, by the astronomer and geographer Claudius Ptolemaeus (c.100–170 BCE) and depicts Southeast Asia flanked by India and China.

Stories from the Stacks also covers several early Dutch publications and manuscripts relating to the early history and maritime trade of Southeast Asia. These include Isaac Commelin's monumental compilation of 21 accounts of Dutch expeditions to Asia between 1594 and 1642; a treaty signed by the Sultan of Banten and the Dutch East India Company in 1691 to establish a Dutch trading monopoly in the region; as well as two 18th-century Dutch manuscripts on the Malay language.

The core of this volume, however, are the Singapore-related materials from 1819 onwards. Of particular interest is a sketch of Singapore based on the hydrographic surveys conducted by Captain Daniel Ross in early 1819. This map was instrumental in the decision to make Singapore a British outpost in the Far East. The map also contains the first known appearance of the Anglicised spelling of "Singapore" on a chart or map, eschewing variants used previously.

Of interest too is one of the earliest publications related to the greening of Singapore – Nathaniel Cantley's *Report on the Forests of the Straits Settlements* (1883), which tells us how Singapore's nature reserves came to be. On a lighter note, football fans will be intrigued to learn that the sport was so popular in colonial Singapore that an 1895 Jawi rulebook (*Inilah Risalat Peraturan Bola Sepak yang Dinamai oleh Inggeris Football*) was published by Dar al-Adab, one of the island's earliest Malay-Muslim recreation clubs.

Insights into life in 19th- and 20th-century Singapore can be gleaned from the wide range of documents featured in this book. The development of photography in the 19th century made it an important tool for capturing Singapore's rapidly changing physical and social landscapes. The earliest photographic material in the library's collection is *Views and Types of Singapore, 1863*, an album of photos produced by Sachtler & Co., a photographic studio established in Singapore around 1863. Alongside images from the Edwin A. Brown Collection (Brown was a prominent public figure in colonial-era Singapore), these images evoke a sense of a bygone era.

Glimpses of Singapore's entertainment scene are offered through items such as issues of *The Magic Fan* (1938–39), the official magazine of the Malayan Magic Circle; while one of the oldest scrapbooks in the collection, *Repertory Players 1937–1948*, illuminates aspects of Singapore's English-language theatre scene. On a more sombre note, this volume includes pre-war Japanese reconnaissance maps and documents from the Lim Shao Bin Collection as well as 火焰樹 (*Kaenju*; The Flame Tree), a magazine produced by Japanese prisoners-of-war while they were incarcerated in Woodlands after Japan's surrender in 1945.

This book also celebrates the accomplishments of notable figures. It features Penang-born Dr Wu Lien-teh (伍连德) who was nominated for the Nobel Prize in Medicine in 1935,

The Magic Fan was the official magazine of the Malayan Magic Circle. Shown above are six issues which were published between 1938 and 1939, with covers designed by the group's resident illustrator L.A. Duckworth.

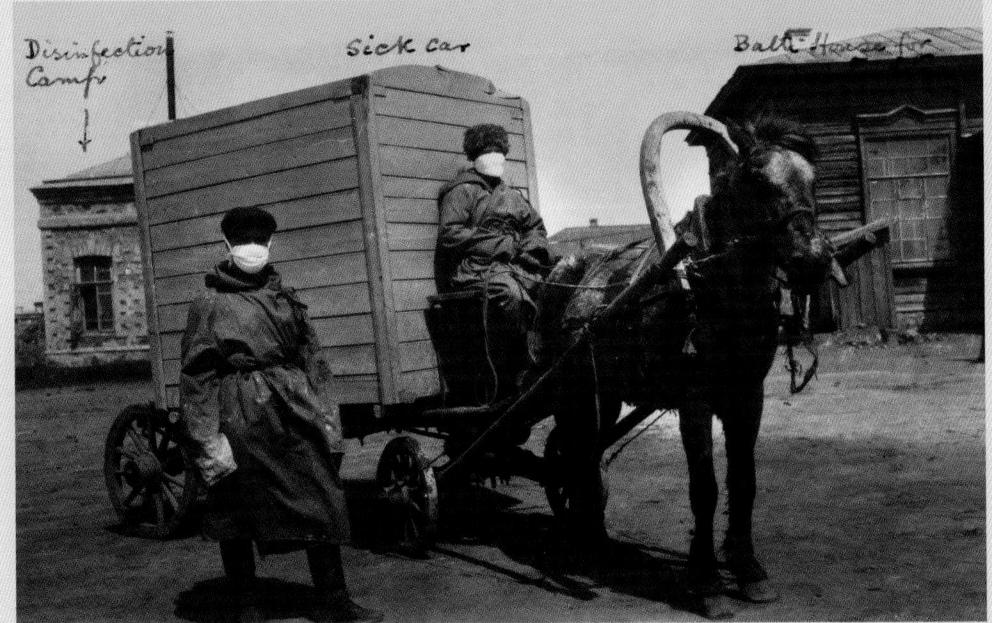

(Left) Photographs such as this from one of Dr Wu Lien-teh's albums attest to measures which helped to stem the pneumonic plague in Manchuria in the early 20th century. Dr Wu played a key role by implementing preventive actions such as the wearing of face masks. Shown in the foreground of this image dated 1921 are masked medical workers and a horse-drawn wagon which was used as a "sick car" to transport patients. The building on the left in the background is a disinfection camp, while the one on the right is a bathhouse where people who had come into contact with the sick were disinfected.

thanks to his pioneering work in fighting the pneumonic plague that afflicted Manchuria from 1910–11 and again from 1920–21. Our collection includes two albums containing black-and-white photographs documenting Dr Wu's efforts in battling these epidemics. We also have the personal diaries of Professor Hsu Yun Tsiao (许云樵), a distinguished Chinese scholar in Nanyang studies, which bear testimony to his reflections on his early years in Southeast Asia.

Literary enthusiasts will be pleased to learn that local authors are well represented. Items include *F.M.S.R.: a poem* (1937), which has been called "the first notable work of English poetry produced by a Singaporean writer".[1] Besides published material, we also have handwritten and typed drafts, many of which bear the writer's edits and notes, thus providing an insight into the creative process. These include drafts of Edwin Thumboo's five-part poem "The Cough of Albuquerque"; Muhammad Ariff Ahmad's illustrated note-books; drafts penned by Masuri S.N.; the manuscripts of Fang Xiu (方修); and eight poems composed by Ka Perumal (கா பெருமாள்). Art aficionados will be drawn to the notes and photographs of Liu Kang (刘抗), one of Singapore's foremost pioneer artists.

Born of the triumphs and tragedies that have shaped Singapore and the region, the diverse materials in this book are a product of a unique sociocultural mix. The National Library will continue to collect and preserve important documents relating to Singapore's history and heritage as they arise, for the sake of current and future generations.

Ong Eng Chuan
Senior Librarian (Collections – Rare Materials)
National Library, Singapore

Notes

1 Ogihara-Schuck, E. (2015). Introduction (p. 8). In E. Ogihara-Schuck & A. Teo. (Eds.), *Finding Francis: A poetic adventure*. Singapore: Ethos Books. (Call no.: RSING S821 NG)

PTOLEMY'S MAP OF SOUTHEAST ASIA

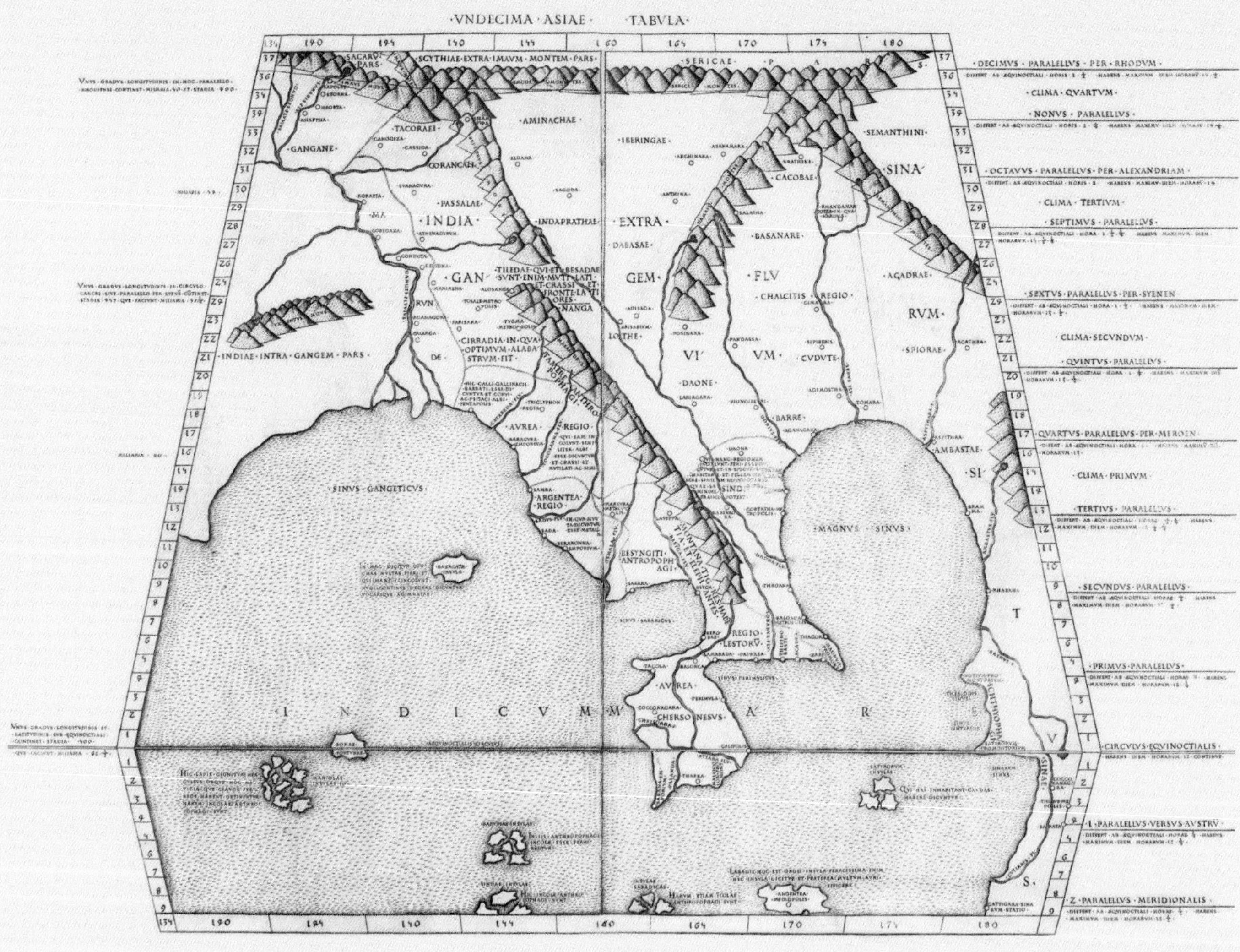

The 1478 Rome edition of *Vndecima Asiae Tabvla* is the first edition to use the trapezoidal projection.

Title: *Vndecima Asiae Tabvla (Southeast Asia, China and India)*
Creator: Claudius Ptolemy
Year published: 1478
Printer: Arnold Buckinck (Rome)
Publisher: Domitius Calderinus
Language: Latin
Type: Map; 41 cm x 55.5 cm
Call no.: RRARE 912.54 PTO
Accession no.: B26055962B

The oldest item in the National Library's Rare Materials Collection is a 1478 copper-engraved Ptolemaic map of Southeast Asia, flanked by India and China. Measuring 41 cm by 55.5 cm, it was printed in Rome by Arnold Buckinck, a printer originally from Cologne, Germany.

This map is one of the six incunable[1] editions of maps based on Claudius Ptolemy's geographical text, *Geographia* (also known as *Cosmographia*). Written in ancient Greek, the text is a compilation of what was known about the geography of the world in the Roman Empire during the second century.

Claudius Ptolemaeus (c.100–170 BCE), better known as Ptolemy, was an influential philosopher, astronomer and geographer of the ancient world. He was also considered the father of cartography. Ptolemy compiled his work, *Geographia*, based on earlier geographical works available at the Library of Alexandria at the time, and reports of contemporary travellers and traders passing through Alexandria. Although Ptolemy was not the first to write about geography and cartography, he was the first to use a rigorous scientific method to gather, organise and present his data. In *Geographia*, Ptolemy introduced a system of coordinates with latitudes and longitudes for about 8,000 places in the world.[2]

Ptolemy divided the Asian continent into 12 parts (*tabvlae*), and dedicated the 11th (*vndecima*) part to Southeast Asia and China (*Sinae*). On Ptolemy's map, Southeast Asia is depicted as "India beyond the Ganges" or "Further India".[3]

The 1478 Rome edition of *Geographia* is the second European printed edition to contain maps based on the Latin translation by Jacopo d'Angelo in 1406. It contains 27 unsigned maps, 12 of which are on Asia. The Bologna edition was printed in 1477, a year before the Rome edition, even though work on the latter began earlier. However, it has been noted that the quality of the Rome edition is better than the Bologna counterpart, in that the inscriptions on the 1478 edition are consistent and the lettering more elegant. According to Tony Campbell, former map librarian at the British Library, "the uneven quality of the engraved lines and the frequently crowded inscriptions [of the 1477 Bologna edition] do not make for ready comprehension."[4]

Although Arnold Buckinck's name is stated in the colophon in the 1478 edition, credit should be given to Conrad Sweynheym, a German printer. The latter began engraving the maps in 1474 and continued to improve on the copper-plate method of printing maps until his death in 1477. Sweynheym, together with Arnold Pannartz (a German engraver and publisher), was responsible for introducing printing in Italy in the 15th century.[5] As Sweynheym's partner, Buckinck took it upon himself to complete the 1478 work.

The 1478 Rome edition is the first edition to use the trapezoidal projection, unlike the earlier 1477 Bologna edition. The trapezoidal projection renders the meridians as straight lines that converge towards the poles, thus creating a trapezoid. This was due to the influence of Donnus Nicolaus Germanus, a 15th-century cartographer and printer.[6] Maps from the 1478 *Geographia* also contain punched lettering (letters and numerals punched from a set of dies rather than engraved), a method perfected by Sweynheym.[7]

On the map, the leaf-shaped region called Aurea Chersonesus (Golden Peninsula) is usually[8] associated with the Malay Peninsula as Ptolemy believed it to be a land abundant with gold and thus regarded it as an important place. It is depicted as extending into the southern hemisphere; this could have been a result of Renaissance-era European cartographers misinterpreting Ptolemy's *Geographia* – they believed that Sumatra is joined with the Malay Peninsula, ignoring the Melaka Straits that separates them.[9]

The map features various places in Southeast Asia identified by Ptolemy who usually marked the coastal cities as "emporiums" or port cities. The ports of Baracura, Barabonna and Bsyga are sited at the area where Myanmar (Burma) is currently. Along the Malay Peninsula, one can see the ports of Tacola and Sabana, the latter sited at the southernmost tip. Tacola has been identified as the area along the western coast of the Malay Peninsula while Sabana (also spelled Sabara or Sabang) has been variously identified as being Selangor, Singapore or the Strait of Sabam (Kundur). However, there is no consensus among scholars regarding the actual identity of both ports.[10]

The map also refers to precious metals and spices found in places that are now located in present-day Myanmar, such as the kingdom of gold (Aurea Regio), and the kingdom of silver (Argentea Regio), further down the coast. Above Aurea Regio lies Cirradia, which Ptolemy claimed had the finest cinnamon then.[11]

The map shows various topographical features of the region, such as the Sinus Perimulicus (Gulf of Siam), Sinus Sabaricus (Gulf of Martaban) and Magnus Sinus (Gulf of Tonkin and South China Sea), as well as the mountain range running through present-day Myanmar and northern Thailand, which Ptolemy described as being inhabited by tigers, elephants and wild men in caves.[12]

Ptolemy's descriptions of the local inhabitants on various islands dotted along the region appear on the map too. For instance, he noted that naked natives known as Agmatae lived on Bazacata Insula, which is located west of the peninsula, and most likely refers to the Nicobar Islands. The map also depicts a group of islands, which he referred to as Satyrorum, situated to the southeast of the Malay Peninsula. Ptolemy believed that natives with satyr-like tails lived on Satyrorum. This area might refer to the northern Anambas Islands in present-day Indonesia.[13]

Although Ptolemy's work was a major contribution to the knowledge of geography and map-making, there were several mistakes in it that were perpetuated by European cartographers for many years. One such error depicted in the 1478 Rome edition is Ptolemy's idea that the Indian Ocean was an enclosed body of water. He believed that a land bridge connected Southeast Asia with Africa, which ran southwards from southern China, making Southeast Asia inaccessible by sea from Europe.[14]

The 1478 edition of *Geographia* was re-issued three times, in 1490, 1507 and 1508, with a few changes each time.[15]

♦ **Makeswary Periasamy**

Notes

1 An incunable publication is a book or ephemera (such as pamphlets or broadsides) printed in Europe before 1501.

2 Campbell, T. (1987). *The earliest printed maps, 1472–1500* (p. 122). London: British Library. (Call no.: R 912.09024 CAM)

3 Suarez, T. (c. 1999). *Early mapping of Southeast Asia* (pp. 82, 84). Hong Kong: Periplus Editions. (Call no.: RSING 912.59 SUA)

4 Parry, D. (2005). *The cartography of the East Indian Islands [Insulae Indiae Orientalis]* (p. 28). London: Country Editions. (Call no.: RSING 912.59 PAR); Campbell, 1987, pp. 126, 131.

5 Campbell, 1987, pp. 126, 132.

6 Stefoff, R. (1995). *The British Library companion to maps and mapmaking* (p. 234). London: British Library. (Call no.: R 912.03 STE); Campbell, 1987, p. 123.

7 Campbell, 1987, pp. 126, 223.

8 The term "Aurea Chersonesus" has been interpreted by various scholars as referring to Southeast Asia or Sumatra or Malay Peninsula or Malaya. In some of the early Ptolemy maps, "Aurea Chersonesus" is written on the peninsula that seems to contain both Malaya and the countries below it (Sumatra, etc.) which are now separated by the Malacca Straits. Suarez (p. 84) says that the "Golden Chersonese is generally accepted to be Malaya".

9 Gerini, G. E. (1909). *Researches on Ptolemy's geography of Eastern Asia (further India and Indo-Malay Archipelago)* (p. 77). London: Royal Asiatic Society. (Call no.: RCLOS 950 GER-[JSB]); Parry, 2005, p. 31; Suarez, 1999, p. 84.

10 Suarez, 1999, p. 85; Gerini, 1909, pp. 85, 92, 100; Colless, B. E. (1969, March). The Ancient history of Singapore. *Journal of Southeast Asian History, 10*(1), 1–11, p. 11. Singapore: Dept. of History, University of Malaya in Singapore. (Call no.: RCLOS 959.05 JSA)

11 Suarez, 1999, p. 84.

12 Suarez, 1999, p. 85; Gerini, 1909, pp. 70, 761; Parry, p. 31.

13 Suarez, 1999, p. 85, 86; Gerini, 1909, pp. 707–709.

14 Suarez, 1999, p. 86; Parry, 2005, p. 31.

15 Campbell, 1987, p. 132.

FROM THE ROYAL COURTS TO THE PEOPLE

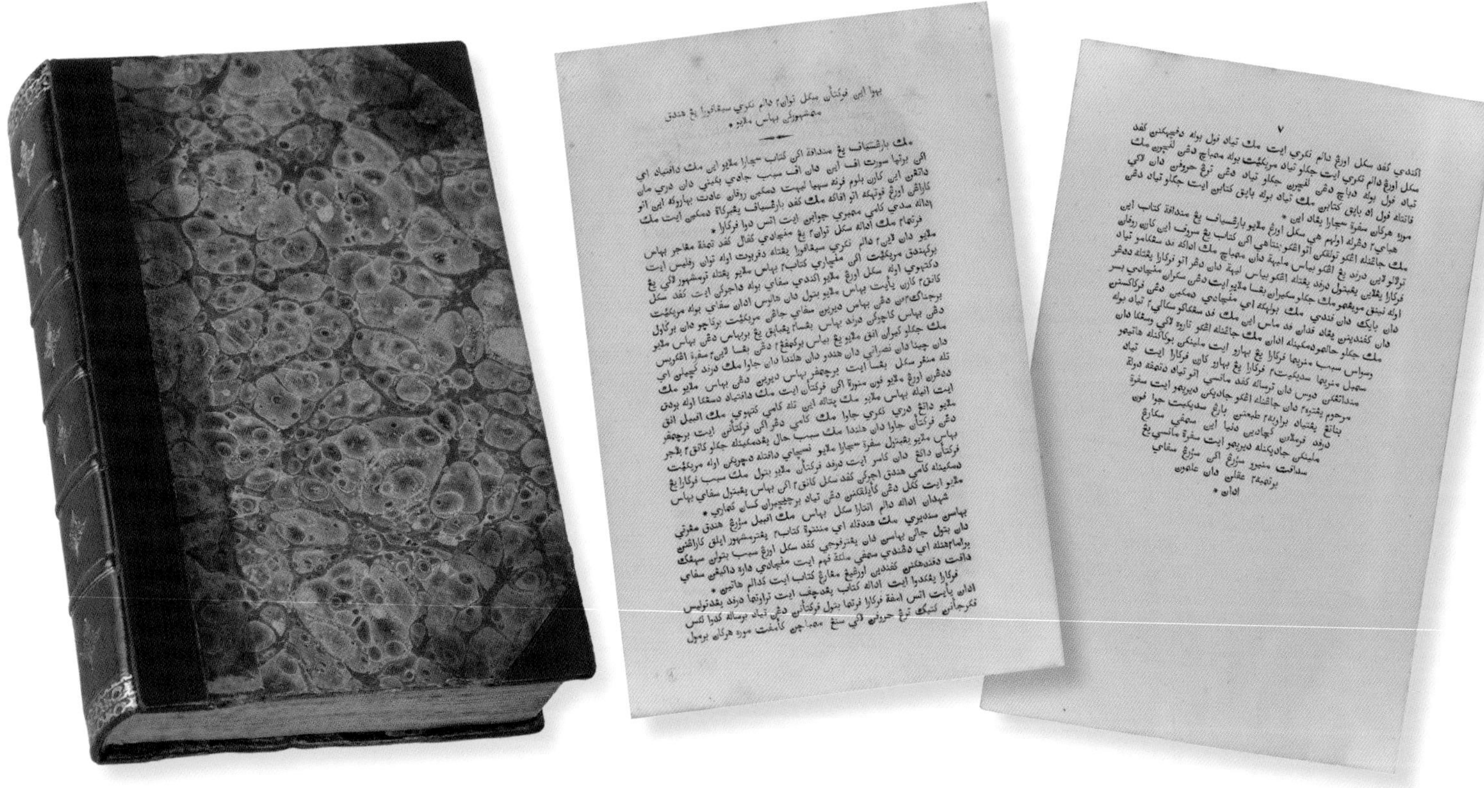

[Above] The National Library's copy of Munsyi Abdullah's *Sejarah Melayu* is one of the few known copies held in libraries today.
[Above right] The extensive preface comprising seven pages primarily details Abdullah's intentions for printing the court text.

Title: *Sejarah Melayu* (Malay Annals)
Editor: Abdullah bin Abdul Kadir
Year published: c.1840
Publisher: Singapore Institution
Language: Malay (Jawi script)
Type: Book; 368 pages
Call no.: RRARE 959.503 SEJ
Accession no.: B31655050CC

This printed copy of the *Sulalat al-Salatin* (Genealogy of Kings), one of the most profound works in the history of Malay literature, was published in Singapore around 1840. Spanning 34 chapters in Jawi (Malay written in modified Arabic script), it was edited by the acclaimed scholar Abdullah Abdul Kadir (c. 1797–1854), more popularly known as Munsyi Abdullah.

The *Sulalat al-Salatin* was likely composed in the 17th century by Tun Sri Lanang, the Bendahara (Prime Minister) of the Johor Sultanate. This court text traces the genealogy of the Malay kings to Sang Nila Utama, the 13th-century Srivijayan prince from Palembang who founded Singapura on the island of Temasek. His fourth generation descendent Iskandar Shah, who fled Singapura to escape invading Majapahit forces, subsequently established the powerful Melaka Sultanate (c. 1400–1511).

The text also describes in detail the traditions and customs of the Malay kings (*yakni peristiwa dan pertuturan segala raja-raja Melayu dengan istiadatnya*)[1] as well as Malay statecraft and extolls the unbreakable covenant between ruler and subject (*wa'ad*). Despite being several centuries old, the *Sulalat al-Salatin* continues to have an important place in the modern world as its themes of justice, loyalty and treason are timeless and universal.

The title *Malay Annals* (or *Sejarah Melayu*) was coined by the Scottish linguist John Leyden when he translated the *Sulalat al-Salatin* into English in the early 19th century. Leyden's printed version of his work was published posthumously in 1821.

Today, some 32 known variants of *Sulalat al-Salatin* are found in the collections of regional and international institutions, the earliest being the Raffles M18 (dated 1612) version held by the Royal Asiatic Society of Great Britain and Ireland.[2] The different versions of the *Sulalat al-Salatin* emphasise different events and issues, being coloured as they were by the motives and perceptions of their respective patrons or editors.

Abdullah was a prolific scholar as well as editor and translator of Malay and English who became involved in the printing of numerous works in the 19th century, including religious tracts, textbooks and periodicals. The printing of the Jawi edition of the *Sejarah Melayu* was likely a much anticipated event as the precious manuscripts of the text had hitherto been used only in court settings.[3]

Under the supervision of the American scholar and missionary Alfred North (1807–69), Abdullah is believed to have referred to six different manuscripts to produce his printed Jawi edition of *Sejarah Melayu*.[4] Abdullah's *Sejarah Melayu* was endorsed by the Trustees of the Singapore Institution (present-day Raffles Institution), whose objective was to "collect scattered traditions and literature of the country ... that are instructive to the people",[5] and used as a text in government-run schools.

Abdullah's depiction of the eventual demise of the Melaka court and the incompetency of the Malay sultans in his *Sejarah Melayu* was used by the British to their advantage, who saw themselves as the colonial saviours of the Malay world. These elements of the *Sejarah Melayu* along with the various contexts in which the text was used throughout history to either reinforce or undermine power are invaluable in the study of the evolving social, political and cultural realms of the Malay world.

Abdullah wrote a lengthy preface in his *Sejarah Melayu* outlining five reasons why he produced a printed version of the text:[6] first, he was of the view that printing creates authoritative texts; second, a single printer could produce what it would take 200 scribes to accomplish; third, printing produces clear and legible texts; fourth, printing encourages people to learn how to write; and fifth, printed texts are an efficient and relatively economical way to disseminate knowledge.

Abdullah was driven by his mission of making Jawi manuscripts more accessible to the common people. Prior to the 19th century, manuscripts were mainly read aloud in court settings; the opportunity to read for pleasure was a privilege that only wealthy elites could enjoy. The printed version of the *Sejarah Melayu* marked a breakthrough as it was aimed at an indigenous readership. With the printing of the *Sejarah Melayu*, a manuscript tradition that was the preserve of Malay royalty was now made available to everyone.[7]

Equally important was Abdullah's desire, as stated in his preface, to "spread the knowledge of Malay language" (*Bahawa ini perkataan segala tuan-tuan dalam negeri Singapura yang hendak memasyhurkan bahasa Melayu*) through this monumental work.

Generations of scholars have regarded the *Sulalat al-Salatin* as a paragon of "good Malay" with its lively narrative style and vivid descriptions. Abdullah believed that printing a work of such literary merit would spark people's passion for reading and help inculcate knowledge of Malay history and heritage among a new generation of readers.

In the decades since it was first printed, Munsyi Abdullah's edition of the text was considered the standard reference text for scores of students and scholars studying Malay history. In his 1849 French translation of the *Sejarah Melayu*, Édouard Dulaurier referred to the Singapore imprint as "our text" (*notre text*), suggesting that Abdullah's version was his source material.

When the scholar and missionary W.G. Shellabear (1862–1948) produced a romanised Malay (*rumi*) edition of the *Sejarah Melayu* in 1896, he adopted the same spelling and grammar forms as those used in Munsyi Abdullah's 1840 edition. In fact, Shellabear credited Abdullah's *Sejarah Melayu*, which he had consulted at the Logan Library in Singapore, as one of the sources for his work.

The National Library's copy of Munsyi Abdullah's *Sejarah Melayu* is one of five known copies held in libraries today. Abdullah's desire to disseminate knowledge through modern printing methods contributed to the survival and lasting popularity of a landmark text in Malay literature. Its influence extends far and wide, as witnessed by subsequent editions of the *Sejarah Melayu*, that are still read and studied to this day.

♦ Nadirah Norruddin

Notes

1 The usage between *pertuturan* (conversation) and *peraturan* (rules) has been a point of contention between some scholars. It is believed that in Batak-Toba language, *pertuturan* refers to relatives and kinship ties which would correspond with the narrative of *Sejarah Melayu*.

2 Cheah, B.K. (1998). *Sejarah Melayu: The Malay Annals* (p. xi). Kuala Lumpur: Malaysian Branch of the Royal Asiatic Society. (Call no.: 959.5 SEJ)

3 Ming, D. (1987). Access to Malay Manuscripts. *Bijdragen Tot De Taal-, Land- En Volkenkunde, 143* (4), 437. Retrieved from JSTOR.

4 Rony, A. (1991). Malay manuscripts and early printed books at the Library of Congress. *Indonesia, 52*, 123–134, 131. Retrieved from Cornell University Library website. Three of the six manuscripts Abdullah collected are extant manuscripts currently residing in the collection of the Royal Asiatic Society of Great Britain and Ireland: Raffles 80, Farquhar 5 and Maxwell 105.

5 Neilson, J.B. (1927). *A history of Raffles Institution* (p. 3). Singapore: Raffles Institution. (Call no.: RCLOS 373.5957 NEI)

6 These five reasons were also printed in one of Abdullah's works for students, *Ceritera Ilmu Kepandaian* (1855) that was published in collaboration with Keasberry.

7 Before the 19th century, manuscripts were not traded and only loaned sparingly. They were kept at the court or with feudal chiefs, and access depended on social relationships. It has been argued that the increased accessibility of *Sejarah Melayu* through mass production may have devalued its significance and meaning as a court text. However, it was observed in the 19th century that a copy of *Sulalat al-Salatin*, wrapped in yellow silk, was kept as part of the regalia of the Riau court. It was read aloud during certain court ceremonies.

Contested Waters

Title: *Mare Libervm: sive, De ivre qvod Batavis competit ad Indicana commercia dissertatio* (*Mare Liberum*, or Freedom of the Seas)

Author: Hugo Grotius

Year published: 1609

Publisher: Lugduni Batauorvm: Ex officina Ludovici Elzevirij

Language: Latin

Type: Book; 65 pages

Call no.: RRARE 343.096 GRO

Accession no.: B29251735A

A gift from: Agnes Tan Kim Lwi in memory of Tun Tan Cheng Lock

MARE LIBERVM SIVE DE IVRE QVOD BATAVIS COMPETIT AD INDICANA COMMERCIA DISSERTATIO.

CONCORDIA

LVGDVNI BATAVORVM, Ex officinâ Ludovici Elzevirij. ANNO CIↃ. IↃI. IX.

Mare Libervm, written by the Dutch jurist Hugo Grotius, is an argument for the navigation and trading rights of a state trying to penetrate the rich emporia of the East.

Oceans and seas make up a whopping 70 percent of the Earth's surface, and this vast expanse is today governed by the United Nations Convention on the Law of the Sea (UNCLOS), an international treaty signed in 1982. The roots of this modern law can be traced back to a 1609 treatise written in Latin: *Mare Libervm* (Freedom of the Seas). This is a slim, albeit highly influential, booklet on the freedom of navigation and trade in the seas. Incidentally, the catalyst for the creation of this landmark legal doctrine was an event that occurred off the northeastern coast of Singapore in 1603: the Dutch hijacking of the Portuguese merchant vessel *Santa Catarina*.

On 25 February 1603, an expedition of the Vereenigde Oostindische Compagnie (VOC, or United East India Company), led by captain Jacob van Heemskerk, seized the *Santa Catarina* near Changi, with the help of the Johor-Riau sultanate. The Dutch looted and then sold the valuable cargo on board the ship, which yielded tremendous profits, doubling the wealth of the VOC.[1] This attack took place against the backdrop of a long-running war between Spain and the Netherlands, in which the latter sought independence from Spain. At the time, Portugal was under the dynastic rule of the Spanish monarchy.

[Above] A portrait of Hugo Grotius by Dutch painter Michiel van Mierevelt in 1631 after Prince Maurice's death allowed Grotius to return to the Netherlands. *Courtesy of Rijksmuseum Amsterdam.*
[Below] The slim booklet's 13 chapters argue against the monopoly claims of the Portuguese and Spanish, and assert the right of the Dutch to trade in the East Indies.

To deflect accusations of piracy, in the following year, the VOC engaged Dutch jurist Huig de Groot, better known as Hugo Grotius, to write a defence of van Heemskerk's actions.[2] In 1608, when it seemed that peace with the Spanish could come at the cost of the Dutch losing their East Indies trade, Grotius was pushed to publish one section of the justification he had been preparing. This section became the 65-page *Mare Libervm*, comprising 13 chapters.

Originally published anonymously, Grotius argued that all states should have the freedom of navigation and trade in the seas, and, specifically, that the Dutch had the right to participate in the East Indies maritime trade. In *Mare Libervm*, Grotius challenged the claims by the Portuguese that they had a monopoly over the East Indies, the sea, and the right to free navigation. He claimed that the Dutch had an equal right to trade with the East Indies and had to maintain that right "*qua pace, qua induciis, qua bello*" (by peace, by treaty, or by war). But the publication may have come a little too late to influence the negotiations. The Treaty of Antwerp concluded in 1609, thus bringing about the Twelve Years' Truce, during which the Dutch were able to continue expanding their trade in the East Indies.[3]

Unfortunately for Grotius, his patron, Johan van Oldenbarnevelt, who favoured renewing the Truce in 1621 when it was due to expire, fell afoul of Maurice, Prince of Orange, the commander of the Netherlands' military forces. In 1619, van Oldenbarnevelt was executed as a traitor and Grotius was imprisoned in the military fortress of Loevestein. Two years later, Grotius escaped to France by hiding inside a book chest.[4] Grotius eventually published his magnum opus on international law, *De Jure Belli ac Pacis* (On the Law of War and Peace), in 1625 in Paris.[5]

The principle of free seas displeased the English, who wanted control of the seas around Britain, particularly the English Channel. They countered Grotius' treatise with *Mare Clausum* (The Closed Sea) by English jurist John Selden, published in 1635. *Mare Clausum* articulated Britain's contention that the seas ought to be territories owned and controlled by individual states.[6] A compromise between these two opposing positions evolved into today's concept of territorial coastal waters.

The principle of *Mare Libervm* came to dominate maritime conduct and is today enshrined in UNCLOS. It is all too fitting that Singapore – now a leading global port – was the site of the historical moment that triggered the creation of *Mare Libervm*. It is a principle that is as relevant as ever today in the face of increasing maritime disputes.

♦ **Timothy Pwee**

Notes

1 Borschberg, P. (2010). *The Singapore and Melaka Straits: Violence, security and diplomacy in the 17th century* (p. 68). Singapore: NUS Press. (Call no.: RSING 911.16472 BOR)

2 Borschberg, P. (2011). *Hugo Grotius, the Portuguese and free trade in the East Indies* (p. 43). Singapore: NUS Press. (Call no.: RSING 341 BOR)

3 Gordon, E. (2008). Grotius and the freedom of the seas in the seventeenth century (p. 256). *Willamette Journal of International Law and Dispute Resolution, 16*(2), 252–269. Retrieved from JSTOR; Kennedy, J. C. (2017). *A concise history of the Netherlands* (p. 142). Cambridge: Cambridge University Press. (Call no.: R 949.2 KEN)

4 Kennedy, J. C. (2017). *A concise history of the Netherlands* (p. 155). Cambridge: Cambridge University Press. (Call no.: R 949.2 KEN)

5 Borschberg, 2011, p. 34.

6 Ziskind, J. (1973, October). International law and ancient sources: Grotius and Selden. *The Review of Politics, 35*(4), 537–559. Retrieved from JSTOR.

CAPITA DISSERTATIONIS.

Cap.I. Iure gentium quibusvis ad quosvis liberam esse navigationem.
Cap.II. Lusitanos nullum habere ius dominij in eos Indos ad quos Batavi navigant titulo inventionis.
Cap.III. Lusitanos in Indos non habere ius dominij titulo donationis Pontificiæ.
Cap.IV. Lusitanos in Indos non habere ius dominij titulo belli.
Cap.V. Mare ad Indos, aut ius eo navigandi non esse proprium Lusitanorum titulo occupationis.
Cap.VI. Mare aut ius navigandi proprium non esse Lusitanorum titulo donationis Pontificiæ.
Cap.VII. Mare aut ius navigandi proprium non esse Lusitanorum titulo præscriptionis, aut consuetudinis.
Cap.VIII. Iure gentium inter quosvis liberam esse mercaturam.
Cap.IX. Mercaturam cum Indis propriam non esse Lusitanorum titulo occupationis.
Cap.X. Mercaturam cum Indis propriam non esse Lusitanorum titulo donationis Pontificiæ.
Cap.XI. Mercaturam cum Indis non esse Lusitanorum propriã iure præscriptionis, aut consuetudinis.
Cap.XII. Nulla æquitate niti Lusitanos in prohibendo commercio.
Cap.XIII. Batavis ius commercij Indicani, qua pace, qua induciis, qua bello retinend...

AD PRINCIPES
POPVLOSQVE LIBEROS
ORBIS CHRISTIANI.

ERROR est non minus vetus quam pestilens, quo multi mortales, ij autem maxime qui plurimum vi atque opibus valent, persuadent sibi, aut, quod verius puto, persuaderi conantur, iustum atque iniustum non suapte natura, sed hominum inani quadam opinione atque consuetudine distingui. Itaque illi & leges & æquitatis speciem in hoc inventas existimant, ut eorum qui in parendi conditione nati sunt dissensiones atque tumultus coerceantur: ipsis vero qui in summa fortuna sunt collocati, ius omne aiunt ex voluntate, voluntatem ex utilitate metiendam.

The Market by the Sea

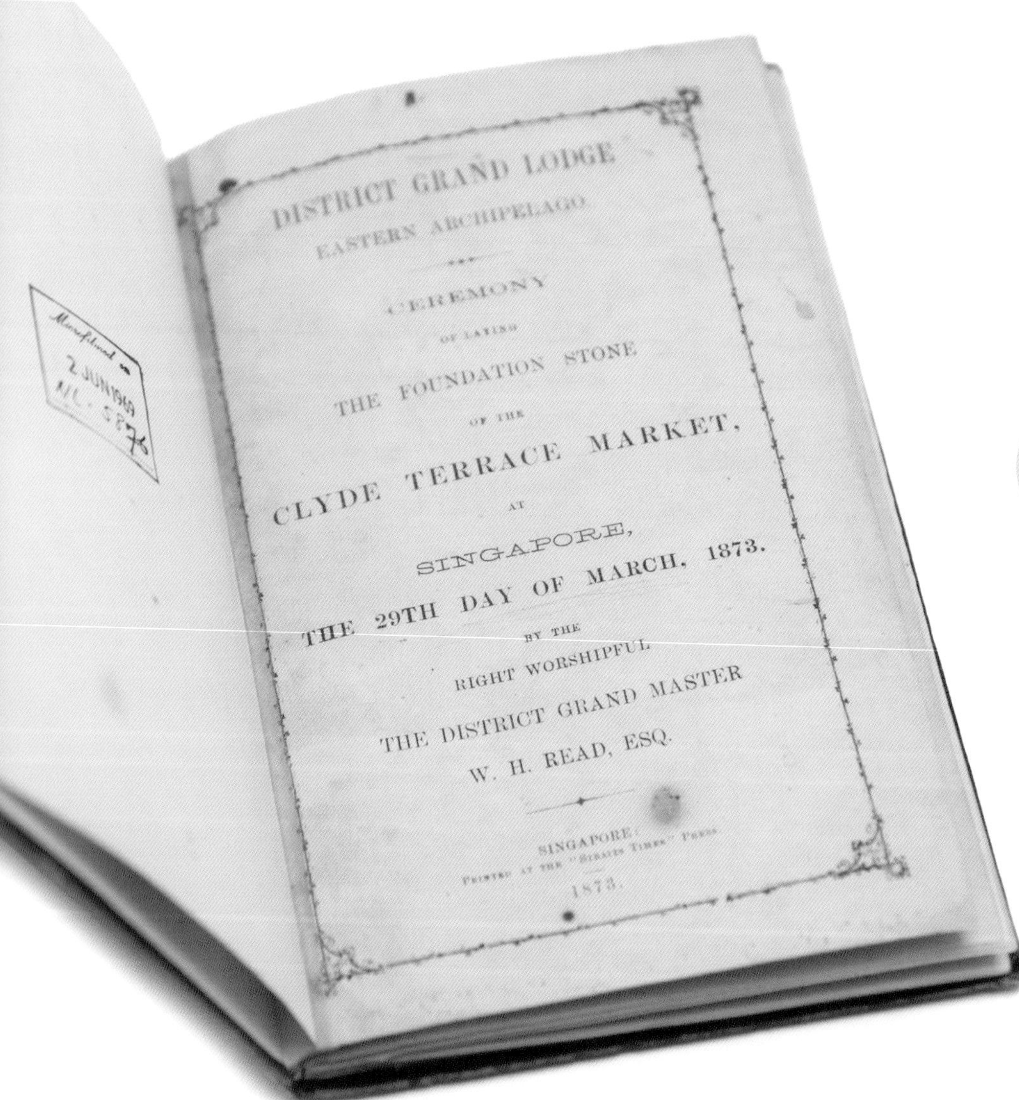
DISTRICT GRAND LODGE
EASTERN ARCHIPELAGO
CEREMONY
OF LAYING
THE FOUNDATION STONE
OF THE
CLYDE TERRACE MARKET,
AT
SINGAPORE,
THE 29TH DAY OF MARCH, 1873.
BY THE
RIGHT WORSHIPFUL
THE DISTRICT GRAND MASTER
W. H. READ, ESQ.
SINGAPORE:
PRINTED AT THE "STRAITS TIMES" PRESS.
1873.

Title: *Ceremony of Laying the Foundation Stone of the Clyde Terrace Market, at Singapore, the 29th day of March, 1873 by the Rt. Worshipful, the District Grand Master, W.H. Read Esq.*
Author: Theodore Heinrich Sohst
Year published: 1873
Publisher: Straits Times Press
Language: English
Type: Book; 23 pages
Call No.: RRARE 959.51
Accession no.: B17796298E

Clyde Terrace Market's beginnings as one of Singapore's first purpose-built markets is documented in the National Library's copy of *Ceremony of Laying the Foundation Stone of the Clyde Terrace Market at Singapore, the 29th day of March, 1873.*

This 23-page booklet features the proceedings, speeches and names of personnel involved in what was, curiously, a Masonic ceremony. Freemasonry, whose members are known as Freemasons, is a fraternity of men that traces its roots to the medieval period in European history. In Singapore, Freemasonry was introduced in 1845 with the establishment of a lodge where members of the fraternity would meet.[1]

The ceremony booklet was prepared by a Freemason named Theodore Heinrich Sohst, Grand Secretary of the District Grand Lodge of the Eastern Archipelago that was based in Singapore. The document is a reminder of the now-defunct market, but sheds little light about the Freemason community in the Straits Settlements.

In the early 1800s, markets in Singapore were invariably makeshift places with vendors laying out their produce or wares on the ground or in baskets, either in open areas or under a shed.[2] Clyde Terrace Market[3] used to be so – a cluster of tiled sheds at Campong [Kampong] Glam Beach. A news article dated 26 August 1871 describes the market as "disgraceful" and "reeking with filth", and hints at the government's plan for a "project of erecting a brick or iron building" to improve it.[4]

Preparations for the new and much larger market started in 1872, with iron pillars, roofing and other building materials ordered and shipped from England. To be located near Clyde Terrace (present-day Beach Road) on the reclaimed stretch of land facing the sea, the new market would sell fruits and vegetables. It would also function as a fish market, since its seaside location would allow fishermen to pull their boats right up to the steps leading to the market and unload their catch.

In the booklet, Sohst reports that as the public were looking forward to the new market, Sir Harry St. George Ord – the first Governor of the Straits Settlements – ordered that a ceremony "as impressive as possible" be held before construction commenced. Although the choice of a Masonic ceremony was left unexplained (and we do not know if Governor Ord was a Freemason himself), it was not unusual for Masonic rituals to be held for important official occasions, such as the laying of the foundation stone for the Raffles Lighthouse in 1854.[5]

[Facing page] The title page of the ceremony booklet.
[Far left] The officiator of the ceremony, William Henry Macleod Read. *Courtesy of the National Museum of Singapore, National Heritage Board.*
[Left] Sir Harry St. George Ord, first Governor of the Straits Settlements under the Crown Colony system, who requested that a foundation stone laying ceremony be held for Clyde Terrace Market. *Courtesy of the National Museum of Singapore, National Heritage Board.*

An "imposing spectacle", an occurrence not commonly seen in this part of the world – was how Sohst described the ceremony held on 29 March 1873 in a pavilion erected over the site where the new Clyde Terrace Market would be built. Individuals from elite colonial society in Singapore attended the ceremony. They

Freemasons in Singapore

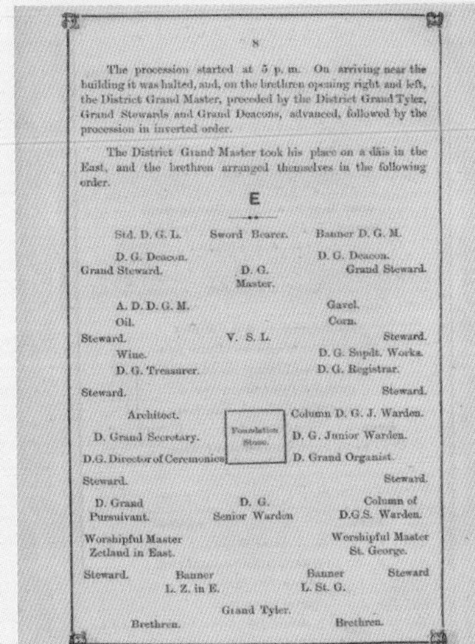

8

The procession started at 5 p.m. On arriving near the building it was halted, and, on the brethren opening right and left, the District Grand Master, preceded by the District Grand Tyler, Grand Stewards and Grand Deacons, advanced, followed by the procession in inverted order.

The District Grand Master took his place on a dais in the East, and the brethren arranged themselves in the following order.

E

Std. D. G. L. | Sword Bearer. | Banner D. G. M.
D. G. Deacon. | | D. G. Deacon.
Grand Steward. | D. G. Master. | Grand Steward.
A. D. D. G. M. | | Gavel.
Oil. | | Corn.
Steward. | V. S. L. | Steward.
Wine. | | D. G. Supdt. Works.
D. G. Treasurer. | | D. G. Registrar.
Steward. | | Steward.
Architect. | | Column D. G. J. Warden.
D. Grand Secretary. | Foundation Stone. | D. G. Junior Warden.
D.G. Director of Ceremonies | | D. Grand Organist.
Steward. | | Steward.
D. Grand Pursuivant. | D. G. Senior Warden | Column of D.G.S. Warden.
Worshipful Master Zetland in East. | | Worshipful Master St. George.
Steward. | Banner L. Z. in E. | Banner L. St. G. | Steward
Grand Tyler.
Brethren. | | Brethren.

This diagram from page 8 of the ceremony booklet shows where the participating Freemasons stood around the foundation stone.

Freemasonry has its roots in a guild of stone-workers in 16th-century England. Historically known to be involved in charity work, they promote three main principles: society, charity and morality.

The first two Freemason lodges in Singapore were Lodge Zetland in the East No. 748 E.C. (consecrated on 8 December 1845), and Lodge of St. George No. 1152 E.C (consecrated on 24 June 1867). Both were overseen by the District Grand Lodge of the Eastern Archipelago.[6]

During a procession at the ceremony on 29 March 1873, Freemasons from both lodges stood in the order shown in this diagram. Those who were also public figures included:

District Grand (D.G.) Master William Henry Read, who led the ceremony. Read was the second member to be initiated when Freemasonry was introduced in Singapore. He was also the first District Grand Master when the District Grand Lodge of the Eastern Archipelago was formed in 1858. Read was an honorary police magistrate and Justice of Peace in Singapore from 1862 to 1885. He came to be known as the "Father of the Colony" for his contributions to the Straits Settlements.[7]

Acting Deputy District Grand Master (A.D.D.G.M.) Felix Henry Gottlieb, a distinguished lawyer, served in the Straits Settlements from 1846 to 1882 before going into private practice. He was Founding Master of the Lodge of St. George in Singapore. The Gottlieb Lodge of Mark Master Masons No. 382 E.C. in Penang was named in his honour.[8]

District Grand (D.G.) Senior Warden Thomas Braddell was appointed the first government lawyer in the Straits Settlements in 1864, and was the first Attorney-General when the Straits Settlements became a Crown Colony in 1867. He reportedly held all key appointments associated with Freemasonry, with the exception of the position of District Grand Master.[9]

District Grand (D.G.) Deacon, John James Greenshields was a member of the Legislative Council, and a partner at Guthrie & Co, a prominent British trading company established in Singapore.[10]

District Grand (D.G.) Director of Ceremonies James Wheeler Woodford Birch served as Colonial Secretary of the Straits Settlements from May 1870. He came to be appointed the first British Resident in Perak in November 1874.[11]

District (D.) Grand Secretary Theodore Heinrich Sohst, who wrote the booklet, described it as "a memento of an interesting ceremony". Sohst, a well-known German businessman, was listed as a shareholder of the Tanjong Pagar Dock Company Limited in 1872, and a member of the Singapore Exchange in 1873.[12]

Architect, Captain W. Innes, R.E. obtained his commission in the Royal Engineers in 1858, having topped his cohort at the Royal Military Academy. He was Acting Colonial Engineer of the Straits Settlements in 1872.[13]

Front view of Clyde Terrace Market, 1963. *Courtesy of National Archives of Singapore.*

include: Sir Ord; his wife Julia Graham (Lady Ord);[14] members of the Legislative Council – such as Lieutenant-Colonel Crowe, V. C.[15] and Chief Justice Sir Thomas Sidgreaves; as well as several Freemasons from the District Grand Lodge of the Eastern Archipelago who were also active in commercial and public affairs.

A prominent Freemason businessman named William Henry Read – District Grand Master of the Lodge of the Eastern Archipelago, and a Justice of Peace[16] – led the ceremony. The foundation stone was laid together with the same-day copy of *The Straits Times*, a plan of the building and currencies from England, Australia, India, Mexico, Hong Kong and the Straits Settlements. These served as records of the point in time when the stone was laid. Masonic symbols of "prosperity and abundance" – kernels of corn, wine and oil – were then poured over the stone to seek blessings from the Supreme Grand Architect of the Universe.[17]

The new market was functioning by 1874.[18] It came to be locally known *thih pa sat* (铁巴刹) in Hokkien, or *pasar besi* in Malay, both of which translate as "Iron Market".[19] This was an apt description as most of its structure consisted of ironwork. Over time, the market also functioned as a wholesale market and distribution centre where vendors purchased fresh produce and then sold these in rural villages and smaller markets.[20] Unfortunately, Clyde Terrace Market developed a notorious reputation from the 1950s onwards with gangsters extorting money from hawkers.[21] Smugglers also used the market as a transit point, unloading cartons of liquor and cigarettes from ships anchored in the sea near Nicoll Highway onto little wooden boats that brought the goods down a canal leading to the market where buyers waited.[22]

In 1980, it was announced that the site housing Clyde Terrace Market would become part of a land parcel used for office development.[23] Consequently, some 64 wholesalers were relocated to the new Pasir Panjang Wholesale Centre, which would centralise the distribution of fruits and vegetables in Singapore. Clyde Terrace Market was eventually demolished in 1983. Today, The Gateway office complex stands where the market once stood.[24] ♦ **Zoe Yeo**

Notes

1 Wan, M. H. (2009). *Heritage places of Singapore* (p. 77). Singapore: Marshall Cavendish International Asia. (Call no.: RSING 959.57 WAN-[HIS])

2 National Heritage Board. (2013). *Community heritage series II: Wet markets* (p. 5). Retrieved from National Heritage Board website.

3 Clyde Terrace Market was named after Sir Colin Campbell, Baron Clyde (*b. 1792–d. 1863*), a British soldier who was commander in chief of the British forces in India during the Indian Mutiny of 1857. See S. Ramachardra. (1954, October 10). Telok Ayer – The Oldest Market in Singapore. *Sunday Standard*, p. 9. Retrieved from NewspaperSG; Colin Campbell, Baron Clyde. (2019, October 16). Retrieved from Britannica website.

4 From the Daily Times, August 22nd. The Campong Glam Beach. (1871, August 26). *Straits Times Overland Journal*, p. 3. Retrieved from NewspaperSG.

5 Untitled. (1854, May 23). *The Straits Times*, p. 4. Retrieved from NewspaperSG.

6 History of the District Grand Lodge of the Eastern Archipelago. Retrieved from District Grand Lodge of the Eastern Archipelago website.

7 Buckley, C. B. *An anecdotal history of old times in Singapore 1819–1867* (pp. 437, 367–369). Singapore: Oxford University Press, 1984. Death of Mr. W. H. Read. (1908, June 4). *The Straits Times*, p. 7. Retrieved from NewspaperSG.

8 Khoo, S.N. (2006). *More than Merchants: A History of the German-speaking Community in Penang* (p. 24). Pulau Pinang: Areca Books (Call no.: RSE305.73105951 KHO)

9 From the Straits Times, April 19th. Short-hand report of the proceedings of the Legislative Council, Straits Settlements. (1873, April 24). *Straits Times Overland Journal*, p. 6; Death of Mr Thomas Braddell. (1891, September 21). *The Straits Times*, p. 3; Retrieved from NewspaperSG.

10 Messrs. Guthrie & Company. (1927, September 12). *Malaya Tribune*, p. 2. Retrieved from NewspaperSG.

11 Mr. Birch. (1975, November 27). *The Straits Times*, p. 2. Retrieved from NewspaperSG; Consecration of Royal Prince of Wales's Lodge, No. 1555, Penang, Straits Settlements. *The Freemason and Masonic Illustrated*, 22 January 1876 (p. 41). (Not available in NLB holdings)

12 The Tanjong Pagar Dock Company Limited. (1872, September 7). *Straits Times Overland Journal*, p. 3; Untitled. (1873, August 9). *Straits Times Overland* Journal, p. 14. Death of Mr. T. H. Sohst. (1912, January 10). *The Straits Times*, p. 7; The Late Mr. T. Sohst. (1912, January 11). *The Singapore Free Press and Mercantile Advertiser (Weekly)*, p. 30. Retrieved from NewspaperSG.

13 Legislative Council. (1872, October 7). *The Straits Times*, p. 2; The late Captain Innes. (1875, December 18). *The Straits Times*, p. 5. Retrieved from NewspaperSG.

14 Boyce, P. (1974). Ord, Sir Harry St. George. Retrieved from Australian Dictionary of Biography website.

15 Legislative Council. (1873, March 27). *Straits Times Overland Journal*, p. 6. Retrieved from NewspaperSG.

16 Death of Mr. W. H. Read. (1908, June 4). *The Straits Times*, p. 7. Retrieved from NewspaperSG.

17 *Ceremony of laying the foundation stone of the Clyde Terrace Market at Singapore, the 29th day of March, 1873* (pp. 13–17). The Supreme Grand Architect of the Universe represents a conception of a deity in whatever form and name each member may believe in. See Freemasonry. Network. *Great Architect Of The Universe*. Retrieved from Freemasonry.network website.

18 Retrospect. (1874, January 15). *Straits Times Overland Journal*, p. 3; Local. *Straits Observer* (Singapore). (1875, January 14). p. 2. Retrieved from NewspaperSG.

19 Savage, V. R., & Yeoh, B. S. (2013). *Singapore street names: a study of toponymics* (p. 69). Singapore: Marshall Cavendish Editions. (Call no.: RSING 915.9570014 SAV-[TRA])

20 Kiang-Koh, L. L. (Interviewer). (2016, May 9). *Oral history interview with Phua Him Ko* 潘鑫构 [Accession Number 004050, Reel/Disc 1 of 5]. Singapore: National Archives of Singapore.

21 Perkins, J., & Lim, S. T. (1984). *Kampong Glam: spirit of a community* (pp. 27–28). Singapore: Times Pub. for Kampong Glam Citizens' Consultative Committee. (Call no.: RSING 959.57 PER-[HIS])

22 Dorai, F. (2012). *South beach: from sea to sky* (pp. 42–43). Singapore: South Beach Consortium. (Call no.: RSING 959.57 DOR)

23 Ng, E. (1980, August 7). End of the beach road market is in sight. *The Straits Times*, p. 10. Retrieved from NewspaperSG.

24 Malay Heritage Centre. (2016). *Kampong Gelam: beyond the port town* (p. 69). Singapore: Malay Heritage Centre. (Call no.: RSING 305.8992805957 KAM)

A Book of Early Dutch Expeditions to the East Indies

Volume 1 of Isaac Commelin's *Begin ende Voortgangh* (1646) includes a map showing parts of Southeast Asia, Nova Guinea (New Guinea) and China, as well as locations key to the spice trade in Southeast Asia, such as Sumatra, Amboina (Ambon) and the Banda Islands. The Dutch captured Amboina from the Portuguese in 1605, thus gaining control of the clove trade.

Title: *Begin ende Voortgangh, van de Vereenighde Nederlantsche Geoctroyeerde Oost-Indische Compagnie* (Origin and Progress of the United Netherlands Chartered East-India Company)
Compiler: Isaac Commelin
Year published: 1646
Publisher: Joannes Janssonius (Amsterdam)
Language: Dutch
Type: Book (two volumes); 2,426 pages
Call no.: RRARE 910.9492 BEG
Accession nos.: B20031948E (v. 1); B20031949F (v. 2)
Donated by: George Hicks

The first half of the 17th century saw the Dutch breaking into the Portuguese-controlled East Indies trade, which culminated in the Dutch taking Melaka from the Portuguese in 1641. Just a few years later, a compendium of the various Dutch expeditions to the East Indies appeared: *Begin ende Voortgangh, van de Vereenighde Nederlantsche Geoctroyeerde Oost-Indische Compagnie* (Origin and Progress of the United Netherlands Chartered East-India Company), henceforth referred to as *Begin ende Voortgangh*.

First published by Dutch historian Isaac Commelin in either 1644 or 1645 (sources differ on the precise year), it was a compilation of 21 travel accounts of expeditions that took place between 1594 and 1642. The work was popular and subsequently went through several reprints and new editions. The National Library's Rare Materials Collection has the 1646 version that comes in two volumes with 2,426 pages and 231 illustrations.

As a travel compendium, *Begin ende Voortgangh* was a pioneering work in Dutch literature. Although some of the accounts were reprints, many were published in their entirety for the first time. Prior to the publication of *Begin ende Voortgangh*, only brief manuscript reports were publicly available and these were only circulated among officers of the Oost-Indische Compagnie and the Dutch government.[1] The accounts that were published in full for the first time include the voyages of the 1599–1601 fleet under Pieter Both and Paulus van Caerden, as well as the 1599–1601 fleet that started out under Steven van der Hagen's command.[2] Both undertakings were led by various Dutch companies before the Dutch East India Company (Vereenighde Nederlantsche Geoctroyeerde Oost-Indische Compagnie, or VOC) was formed in 1602.

The accounts include that of Cornelis Matelieff de Jonge's voyage from 1605 to 1608. The 11 vessels of Matelieff's fleet reached Johor in 1606 and his journal recorded observations about the politics of the Johor sultanate. Among other things, this account is significant because it contains evidence that Singapore was of some importance in the early 17th century. The journal describes a meeting with the *shahbandar* (harbourmaster) of Singapore who had been dispatched by the Sultan of Johor to meet Matelieff and the fleet.

Translated, the entry reads: "On the fifth of that month [of May, 1606], some entrenchment baskets were brought to Pulau Melaka from Pulau Besar. Toward the evening, two *perahus* from Johor joined the fleet; the King [of Johor, Alauddin Riayat Shah III] has dispatched them from there five days earlier. The commander was the *shahbandar* of Singapore, called Sri Raja Negara. Admiral [Matelieff] welcomed them as they were coming from the king of Johor, our ally, and let them navigate through the fleets and view the ships."[3]

As a *shahbandar* is a high ranking official in the Malay court – with the responsibility of mediating between foreign merchants and royalty – his presence in Singapore implies that the island was not a neglected backwater in the early 17th century.[4] His title, Sri Raja Negara, also suggests that the *shahbandar* was also head of the Orang Laut, who served in the armada of the Johore rulers.[5] This is more evidence of Singapore's importance during this period.

10 Scheep-vaert op Ooſt - Jndien

1606. welck al naer binnen ghewecken was/ende datter in de Stadt v el koopmanſchap was. Des morgens daer aen ſtierf de ſelve Furtado, ende wert terſtont over boort ghewopen.

2. Prauwen van Iohor komen in de Vloot. Den 5. ditto werdender eenighe Schanſkorven van 't groot Eylant gebracht op Pulo Malacca. Ende tegen den avont zijnder in de Vlote gekomen 2. Prauwen van Iohor, die de Coning over vijf daghen van daer ghesonden hadde. Den Overſten was de Sabander van Sincapura, genaemt Seri Raya Nugara. Den Admirael hiet'ſe wellekom/als komende van den Coning van Iohor onſen bontgenoot / ende lietſe door de Vloot varen / ende de Schepen beſien. Seyden hem / dat de Coning haer geſonden hadde / om te beſien offer Schepen van Hollandt waren / want hy tijdinghe ghekregen hadde van Pera, datter eenige Schepen naer Malacca waren gevaren die ſy vermoeden Hollanders te weſen/ Onſe afgeſonden Chaloup ſeyden ſy over 3. dagen geſien te hebben over geen zijde van de helft van Iohor, ende dat ſoo haeſt de Coningh van ons komſte ſoude veradvertéert menden 2. Fuſten eñ eenige andere Prauwen vol volcks 1606. die naer de ſtad roepden/doch hoe ſeer d'onſe haer daer tegen ſtelden/quamen ſy niettemin behouden inde ſtad/ waer over ſy van binnen groote triumphe bedreven overmits ſy nu ontſet hadden gekregen. Deſe Fuſtẽ waren over eenigen tijt in ambaſſade uytgeſonden na Pahan, om eenige Portugeſen / die daer van een gebleven ſchip waren/te verloſſen/ ſo datter nu 80. witte Portugeſen eñ over de 100. ſwarten inde ſtad quamen/ waer doorſe eens ſo ſterck waren geworden als te voren.

Den 13. ditto is de chaloup van Iohor weder ghekomen tijding brengende dat de Coning binnen 4. daghen ſoude volgẽ met ſo veel volcx als hy konde/ ghelijck hy dan alrede boden over al ſijn Lant geſonden hadde om volc ende Ammunitie te vergaderen. Den 14. is den Admirael een brief van den Coning van Iohor behandicht/ by de duytſche aldaer woonende in onſe ſpraeck overgeſet/ende by hem ondertekent/luydende als volcht:

De Coning van Iohor ghenaemt *Radja Sabrang*, (dat is *Brief des* Coning van de Over-ſyde)wenſcht dẽ Admirael geluc ende *Coninck van*

Detail from Matelieff de Jonge's account in volume 2 includes a mention of him meeting the *shahbandar* or harbourmaster of Singapore. Included in the chapter is an illustration titled *Malacca*.

[Left] *Afteeckeninghe, hoe den Vice-Admirael Sebaldt de Weert met dan fijnen door den Coninck van Candy vermoort warden.* [Vice-Admiral Sebaldt de Weert killed by the King of Candy]. This engraving in volume 1 of *Begin ende Voortgangh* was copied from volume VII of Johann Theodor de Bry's *Petit Voyages*.

[Above] Commelin was a Dutch historian who also served as Regent of the Huiszitten House – he was one of Amsterdam's appointed leaders who oversaw the distribution of alms. *Courtesy of Amsterdam Museum.*

Matelieff's secret orders were to attack the Portuguese and to this end, he formed an alliance with Sultan Alauddin Riayat Shah III (Sultan of Johor from 1597–1615) and laid siege to Melaka in 1606. The siege failed and Matelieff lost two ships at the subsequent Battle of Cape Rachado (today's Tanjong Tuan).[6] It would be another 35 years before Melaka would fall to the Dutch.

The first volume of the *Begin ende Voortgangh*, which runs into 1,066 pages, also contains interesting travelogues such as Gerrit de Veer's *Voyages to the North* which he had written in the 1590s when he joined the failed expeditions of Dutch navigator and Arctic explorer Willem Barentsz in search of a sea route from Europe to the East Indies via the Arctic.

Other highlights in the same volume include a description of the first Dutch voyage to the East Indies, which took place between 1595 and 1597 under Cornelis de Houtman of the Compagnie van Verre. This is followed by an account of the second East Indies expedition from 1598 to 1600, led by Jacob Corneliszoon van Neck and Wybrand van Warwijck, in a joint venture between Compagnie van Verre and Brabantsche Compagnie. The fleet reached the Spice Islands and the vessels returned laden with spices whose sale netted a fortune for the investors.

This volume also has a description of the first voyage made by a VOC fleet (1602–07). The VOC was formed by uniting all the existing Dutch companies leading expeditions to the East Indies in an effort to reduce excessive competition. Commanded by Wybrand van Warwijck, the fleet journeyed to Ceylon, Sumatra and as far as the Pescadores Islands, an archipelago in what is now known as the Taiwan Strait just off the southern coast of China.[7]

The second volume spans 1,360 pages and leads with a description of the second VOC voyage (1603–06), which was led by Steven van der Hagen. The account had previously been published in German with a brief version in Dutch.[8] It covers the capture of Ambon from the Portuguese in 1605, in what was a major VOC victory as Ambon was then the centre of the Moluccan (Malukan) clove trade. Matelieff de Jonge's voyage is also part of the second volume.

Commelin's compendium followed in the tradition of travel accounts popularised in the 16th century by *Della Navigationi et Viaggi* (Navigations and Travels) published by a Venetian, Giovanni Battista Ramusio (1485–1557) in the 1550s.[9] In its judicious use of engraved illustrations, *Begin ende Voortgangh* was also similar to accounts published by Levinus Hulsius (1546–1606) and Johann Theodor de Bry (1561–1623), both in Frankfurt am Main.[10] Indeed, some chapters and engravings were copied from de Bry and other publishers.[11]

A healthy demand for travelogues led to the publication of *Begin ende Voortgangh*. A subsequent expanded edition by another Dutch publisher, Joost Hartgers, was released in 1648.[12] This was followed by other Dutch travel anthologies and translations of *Begin ende Voortgangh*.

At the time it was published, *Begin ende Voortgangh* would have been useful to the mercantile, political and academic circles of the Netherlands for its detailed accounts of these voyages and intelligence about the East Indies. These accounts are still important to researchers today, as well as being a landmark of early travel writing. Our copy of Commelin's valuable compilation is part of the economist and author George Lyndon Hicks' extensive personal library on Asia, which he donated to the National Library in 2013. ♦ **Timothy Pwee**

Notes

1 Boxer, C. R. (1988). Isaac Commelin's 'Begin ende voortgangh': Introduction to the facsimile edition. In *Dutch merchants and mariners in Asia, 1602–1795*, pp. II 1–17. London: Variorum Reprints, p. II 3. (Call no.: RSING 382.094920598 BOX)

2 Boxer, 1988, pp. II 1–17.

3 Borschberg, P. (2016). *Admiral Matelieff's Singapore and Johor (1606–1616)*, pp. 87–89. Singapore: NUS Press. (Call no.: RSING 959.503 MAT)

4 Borschberg, 2016, pp. 20–21.

5 Borschberg, 2016, pp. 21–25.

6 Borschberg, 2016, pp. 100, xxxii.

7 Lach, D. F. & van Kley, E. J. (1993). *Asia in the making of Europe (Vol. III Book I)* (p. 465). Chicago: The University of Chicago Press. (Call no.: RCLOS 901.0 LAC-[GH])

8 Lach & van Kley, 1993, pp. 444–445.

9 Lach, D. F. (1965). *Asia in the making of Europe (Vol. I Book I)* (p. 204). Chicago: The University of Chicago Press. (Call no.: RCLOS 901.0 LAC-[GH])

10 van Groesen, M. (2008). *The Representations of the Overseas World in the De Bry Collection of Voyages (1590–1634)* (p. 371). Leiden: Brill. (Not available in NLB holdings).

11 van Groesen, 2008, pp. 371–372.

12 van Groesen, 2008, p. 372.

GLIMPSES INTO LIU KANG'S ARTISTIC JOURNEY

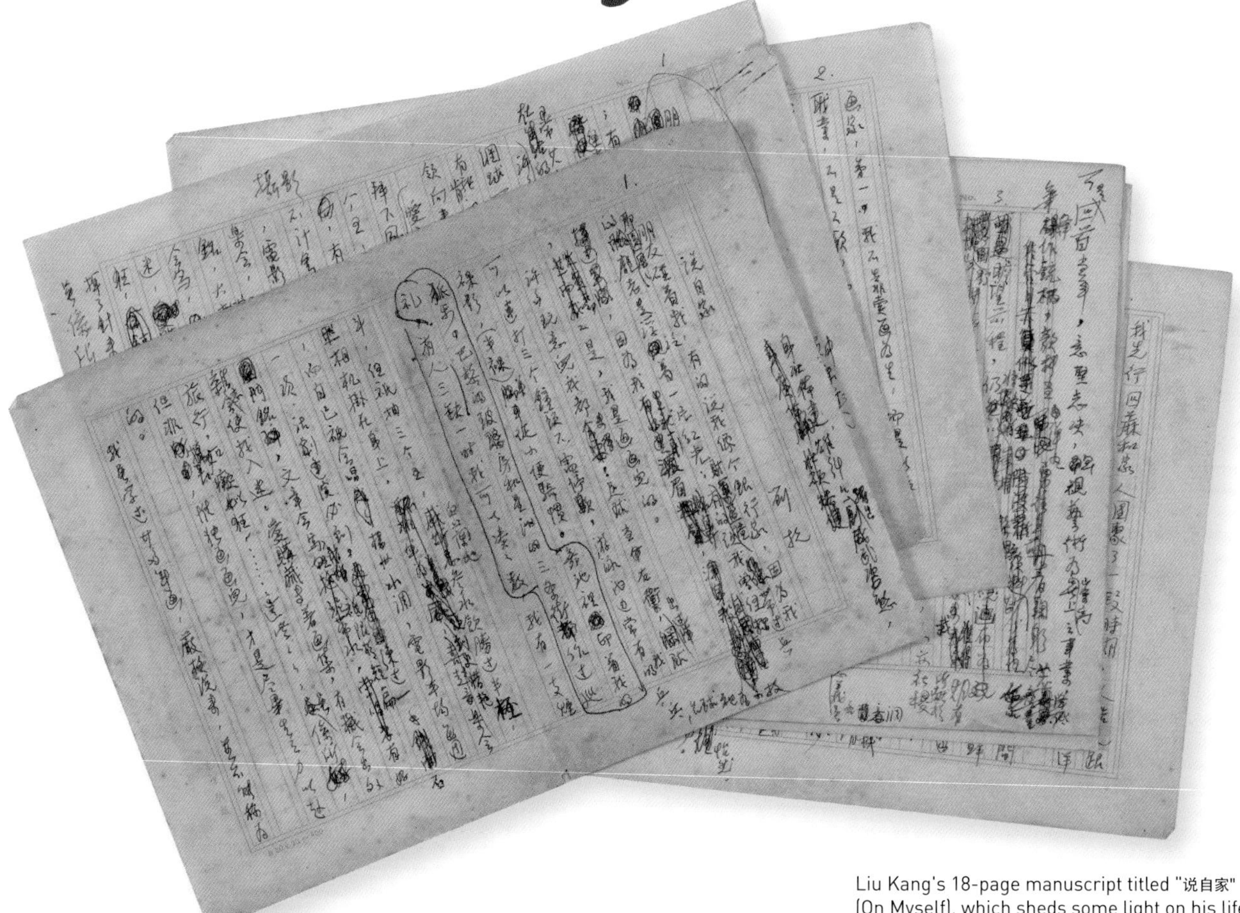

Liu Kang's 18-page manuscript titled "说自家" (On Myself), which sheds some light on his life between ages 6 and 22.

Title: Liu Kang Collection
Year created: 1930s–2000s
Language: Chinese and English
Type: Manuscript; photograph
Call no.: RCLOS 759.95957 LKC-[LK]
Accession nos.: B31818584E–B31818589J (manuscripts); B31818590B–B31818619D (photographs)
Donated by: Family of Liu Kang

Delving into the rich array of documents, photographs and publications belonging to the pioneering artist Liu Kang (刘抗), one learns so much about how his life experiences shaped his art. A central figure in the development of the Nanyang style of painting in Singapore, Liu Kang travelled widely; and his collection is an important physical embodiment of his reflections as well as what he had encountered.

A case in point is Liu Kang's 18-page manuscript titled "说自家" (On Myself). Written in Chinese around the late 1940s or early 1950s,[1] it sheds some light on Liu's life between ages 6 and 22, that is, up to the point when he returned to Shanghai from Paris in 1933. It cannot be ascertained if this was ever published though.

This document is possibly one of Liu Kang's earliest attempts at describing him-

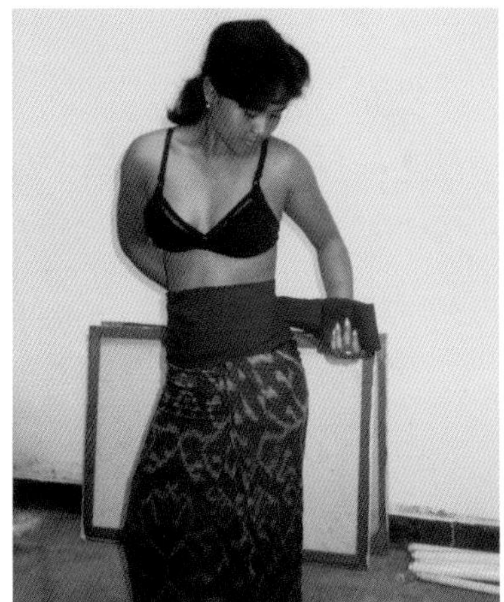

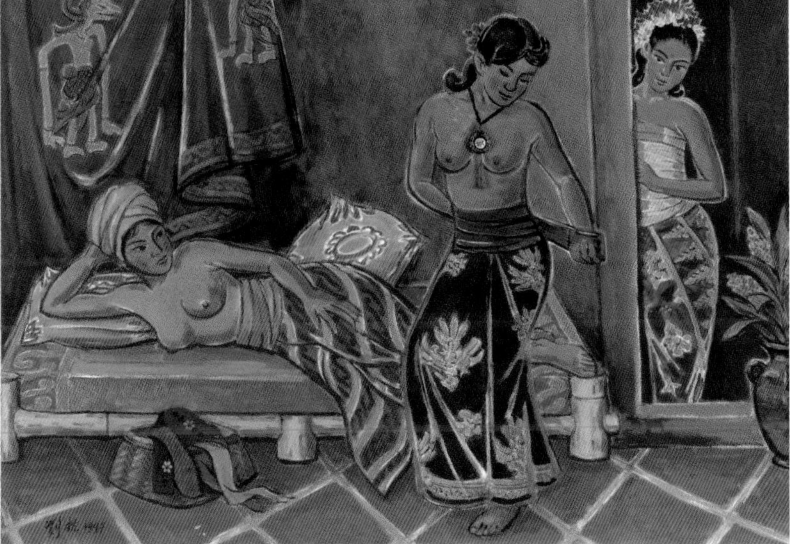

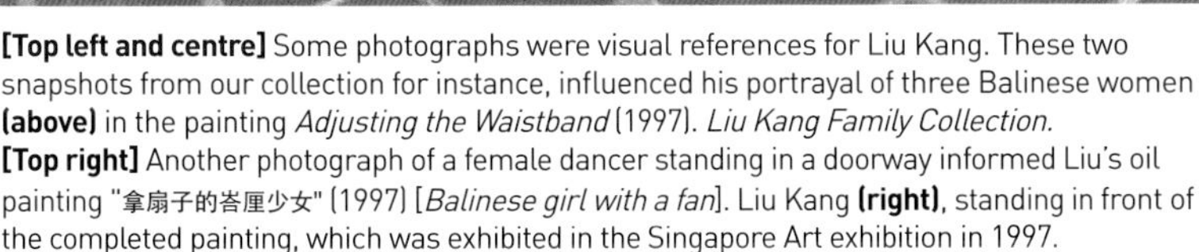

[Top left and centre] Some photographs were visual references for Liu Kang. These two snapshots from our collection for instance, influenced his portrayal of three Balinese women **(above)** in the painting *Adjusting the Waistband* (1997). *Liu Kang Family Collection.*
[Top right] Another photograph of a female dancer standing in a doorway informed Liu's oil painting "拿扇子的峇厘少女" (1997) [*Balinese girl with a fan*]. Liu Kang **(right)**, standing in front of the completed painting, which was exhibited in the Singapore Art exhibition in 1997.

self. At the time it was written, Liu was probably in his late 30s or early 40s and living in Singapore. The essay gives us an idea of how Liu Kang saw himself at that point in time. A translation of his words reads:

> Although I have studied art for more than 20 years, strictly speaking, I cannot call myself an artist. Firstly, I do not sell my artworks for a living; instead I work as a teacher. It is not that I am unwilling to do so, but I am unable to do so, as I would have difficulties bringing bread to the table if I make art my main source of income. For most part of my life, I was either studying or teaching in school, and I have spent very little time on my own art. Thus, I have very few accomplishments in this field. The most important mission of an artist is to have new and correct theories (on art), to have outstanding achievements in his artistic work, and to contribute his extraordinary energy to humanity. In my opinion, I do not fulfil the aforementioned points, so how can I be considered an artist? Thirdly, an artist must have an artistic temperament and lead the way of life of an artist, which is totally different from that of a teacher's. For example, an understanding of the soul, independent thinking and the freedom from worldly connections are the basic criteria of being an artist. This is the exact opposite of a teacher who must be prim and proper, and follow the school's schedule. It is ironic that I would like to follow the way of an artist but I have lived the life of a teacher.

Liu also recounted his time in France. He attended the Académie de la Grande Chaumière in Paris between 1928 and 1933; and in his essay, he recalled how Paris offered serious art students wonderful learning opportunities, as they were surrounded by artworks such as those exhibited at the Louvre, the Rodin Museum and various commercial galleries.

Interestingly, on one of the first pages of the draft, Liu Kang substantially edited his description of himself. Where he described

Liu Kang (second artist from right) during an outdoor sketching session at the artists' village in Bali in 1987. Liu was doing a pastel drawing of the model.

the activities he engaged in, he added "摄影" (photography) at the top margin of the paper. He then rewrote the description to say "照相机挂在身上，到处猎艳", which expresses how he brought a camera with him wherever he went to capture beautiful sights.

This would certainly be borne out by the many photographs in the collection, which span from the 1930s to 2000s. While some photographs may have been taken by him, many more were sent to him, or shot during events or trips, and showed Liu Kang in action. These photographs document his life visually — his work as an art teacher, the exhibitions he helped to organise and those he visited, his visits to local collectors' homes, his meetings with artists and others, activities of art societies he was active in, sketching demonstrations he took part in, as well as overseas trips.

Liu Kang believed that personal experiences of places and cultures are essential to producing vivid art.[14] Bali, for

Tracing the Footsteps of Liu Kang

Liu Kang (刘抗; 1911–2004) was an artist, an art educator and a critic who contributed greatly to Singapore's art scene.[2]

Born in Yongchun, Fujian province, China, Liu moved to Muar at the age of six, where his father owned a rubber plantation.[3] He attended Chung Hwa School in Muar, and the Chinese High School (present Hwa Chong Institution) in Singapore, before joining the pre-university section of Jinan University in Shanghai.[4]

During the summer break, he took a two-month course at the Shanghai Art Academy (上海美术专科学校), which deepened his interest in art. After he completed the summer course, he decided to enrol in the school. Here, he met Chen Jen Hao (陈人浩), who became his close friend and future brother-in-law, and studied under renowned modern Chinese artists such as Wang Chi-yuan (王济远).[5]

In 1928, Liu Kang went to Paris and studied at the Académie de la Grande Chaumière. In France, he was exposed to the works of different masters, in particular those of Vincent van Gogh and Henri Matisse. The experience left a deep impression on him.[6]

Liu Kang returned to Shanghai in 1933 and became a lecturer in his alma mater. He stayed there until 1937 when the war forced him to move back to Muar.[7] There, he taught art at Chung Hwa School and joined the activities of the Society of Chinese Artists in Singapore.[8] After the Japanese Occupation, he set up a studio in Singapore, taught art in various Chinese schools, and was actively involved in various art societies and activities, contributing to the local art scene in various capacities.[9]

Leadership positions held by Liu Kang include his appointment as vice president of the Society of Chinese Artists in 1952 and again from 1957–58. A founder of the Singapore Art Society in 1949, he also served as its president from 1968–79. Additionally, he was the chairman of the National Day Art Exhibition Committee for eight years (1969–77).[10] Among the awards he received are the Bintang Bakti Masyarakat (Public Service Star) in 1970, the ASEAN Creative Art Award in 1993, and the Pingat Jasa Gemilang (Meritorious Service Medal) in 1996.[11]

Liu Kang is one of the key figures in the development of the Nanyang style of art in Singapore.[12] The Nanyang style is one of the most significant and distinct art directions in the history of Singapore and Malaysia, particularly in the 1950s and 60s.[13] Although there are varying definitions of this style, two main characteristics are: an association with Chinese artists who had migrated to Southeast Asia between the 1930s and 50s; and a depiction of local subjects using a combination of Eastern styles such as ink painting and Western art styles such as Cubism.[15]

Liu Kang.

[Above] An undated photograph of Liu Kang (on the extreme right) with Chinese ceramics expert Han Wai Toon (韩槐准) (seated in the foreground) and others, possibly taken during one of the artists' visit to Han's rambutan orchard, Yu Qu Yuan (愚趣园), in Upper Thomson Road. Han was known to have hosted many literati (artists included) in his orchard[16] and Yu Qu Yuan was a popular spot among artists.[17]
[Right] Liu Kang was awarded the 1970 Public Service Star award. This photograph, possibly taken in June 1971, shows Liu receiving his award from then-President Benjamin Sheares.

one, was an important source of inspiration, as its vibrancy, culture and scenery shaped the Nanyang style he came to be known for. Liu Kang also commented in an interview in 1997 that Bali was his favourite location.[18]

Amongst numerous snapshots capturing Liu Kang's overseas visits, a few photographs taken in 1987 during his visit to Bali featured models who were the likely muses for his paintings, such as *Adjusting the Waistband* (1997). The resemblance between the models and the final painting is unmistakable, down to their pose and hairstyles. Another snapshot depicts a female dancer standing in a doorway; her pose and outfit closely mirror Liu's depiction in the oil painting titled "拿扇子的峇厘少女" (1997) [*Balinese girl with a fan*].

These are part of the more than 7,000 documents, photographs and publications (including exhibition catalogues of local artists) donated by Liu Kang's family to the National Library, Singapore in 2017. The materials date from the 1920s to 2000s, although the majority are from the 1970s to 1990s. Mostly written in Chinese, with some in English and a small minority in French, Liu Kang's drafts, notes, correspondence, awards and appointment certificates are an inspirational source for scholars, artists and art lovers seeking to study his work.

♦ **Goh Yu Mei**

Notes

1 Liu mentioned in his essay that Chen Jen Hao, whom he befriended while studying in Shanghai, was the principal of Chung Hwa High School in Muar at that time. Chen was the principal of the school from September 1945 to December 1954. See 蔴坡中化中学 (2018). 历届校长. Retrieved from Muar Chung Hwa High School website.

2 Choy, W. Y. (1981). Introduction. In *Liu Kang Retrospective*. (unpaged). Singapore: National Museum. (Call no.: RSING 759.95957 LIU)

3 Tan, B. L. (Interviewer). (1982, April 9). Oral history interview with Liu Kang [Transcript of Cassette Recording No. 000171/74/1, pp. 3, 8]. Retrieved from National Archives of Singapore website.

4 Tan, B. L. (Interviewer). (1982, April 9). Oral history interview with Liu Kang [Transcript of Cassette Recording No. 000171/74/2, pp. 19–20]. Retrieved from National Archives of Singapore website; Tan, B. L. (Interviewer). (1982, April 9). Oral history interview with Liu Kang [Transcript of Cassette Recording No. 000171/74/3, p. 29]. Retrieved from National Archives of Singapore website.

5 Tan, B. L. (Interviewer). (1982, November 16). Oral history interview with Liu Kang [Transcript of Cassette Recording No. 000171/74/6, pp. 50–51, 56]. Retrieved from National Archives of Singapore website.

6 Gu, S. (2000). Reflections on the paintings of master Liu Kang. In *Journeys: Liu Kang and his art*. (p. 24). Singapore: National Arts Council, Singapore Art Museum (National Heritage Board). (Call no.: RSING q759.95957 LIU)

7 Kwok, K. C. (2010). Foreword. In *Liu Kang: colourful modernist*. (pp. 8–9). Singapore: National Gallery Singapore. (Call no.: RSING 759.95957 LIU)

8 Tan, B. L. (Interviewer). (1982, December 7). Oral history interview with Liu Kang [Transcript of Cassette Recording No. 000171/74/21, pp. 188–189]. Retrieved from National Archives of Singapore website.

9 Tan, B. L. (Interviewer). (1983, January 13). Oral history interview with Liu Kang [Transcript of Cassette Recording No. 000171/74/37, pp. 341–343]. Retrieved from National Archives of Singapore website.

10 *Liu Kang at Ninety*. (2000). (p. 88). Singapore: Liu Kang. (Call no.: RSING 759.95957 LIU-[LK]); *新加坡艺术协会画家名鉴 1949–2009* [Singapore Art Society artists' directory 1949–2009]. (p. 16). (2010). 新加坡：新加坡艺术协会. (Call no.: RSING Chinese 759.95957 SIN)

11 *Liu Kang at Ninety*, 2000, p. 88; The Society of Chinese Artists. (2017). *About SOCA*. Retrieved from The Society of Chinese Artists website.

12 Kwok, K. C. (2000). Liu Kang and Singapore art. In *Journeys: Liu Kang and his art* (p. 15). Singapore: National Arts Council, Singapore Art Museum (National Heritage Board). (Call no.: RSING q759.95957 LIU)

13 Sabapathy, T. K. (1983). "Modern art in Singapore: pioneers and premises". *Asian Culture*, Issue 1, 42; Kwok, 2000, p. 15.

14 Tan, B. L. (Interviewer). (1983, January 3). Oral history interview with Liu Kang [Transcript of Recording No. 000171/74/42, p. 387]. Retrieved from National Archives of Singapore website.

15 Tan, L. K. (2011). *Defining the Nanyang style in painting* (pp. 18–29). M.A. thesis, LaSalle College of the Arts, Singapore. (Call no.: RART 759.95957 TEO)

16 Lai, C. L. (2011). Rambutans in the Picture: Han Wai Toon and the Articulation of Space by the Overseas Chinese in Singapore. In Heng, D. & Syed Muhd Khairudin Aljunied (Eds.). *Singapore in global history*. (p. 161). Amsterdam: Amsterdam: Amsterdam University Press. (Call no.: RSING 959.57 SIN -[HIS])

17 Yeo, W. W. (Ed.). *Liu Kang: colourful modernist* (p. 25). Singapore: The National Art Gallery. (Call no.: RSING 759.95957 LIU))

18 吴启基 (Wu, Q. J.). (1997, September 22). 画遍美景最爱峇厘 [Painted numerous places and Bali is his favourite]. 联合早报, p. 27. Retrieved from NewspaperSG.

POEMS IN PRAISE OF LORD MURUGA

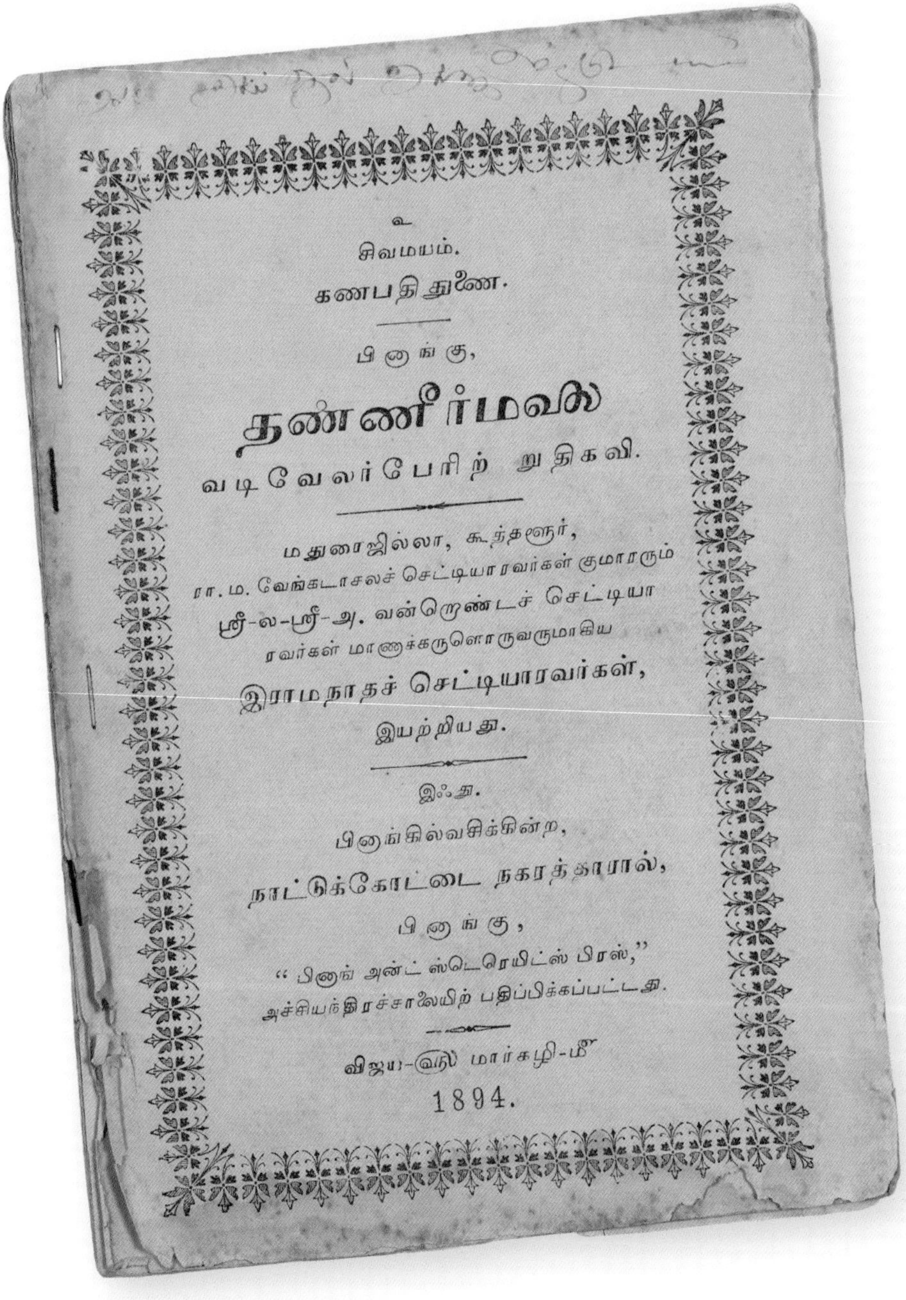
உ
சிவமயம்.
கணபதி துணை.
பினங்கு,
தண்ணீர்மலை
வடிவேலர்பேரிற் றுதிகவி.
மதுரைஜில்லா, கூத்தலூர்,
ரா. ம. வேங்கடாசலச் செட்டியாரவர்கள் குமாரரும்
ஸ்ரீ-ல-ஸ்ரீ-அ. வன்றொண்டச் செட்டியா
ரவர்கள் மாணுக்கருளொருவருமாகிய
இராமநாதச் செட்டியாரவர்கள்,
இயற்றியது.
இஃது.
பினங்கில்வசிக்கின்ற,
நாட்டுக்கோட்டை நகரத்தாரால்,
பினங்கு,
"பினங் அன்ட் ஸ்டெரெயிட்ஸ் பிரஸ்,"
அச்சியந்திரசாலையிற் பதிப்பிக்கப்பட்டது.
விஜய-வருஷம் மார்கழி-மீ
1894.

Title: தண்ணீர்மலை வடிவேலர்பேரிற் றுதிகவி (*Thanneermalai Vadivelarperil Thuthikavi*; Poems Sung in Praise of Lord Muruga at Thanneermalai Temple)

Author: இராமநாதச் செட்டியார் (Iramanatha Chettiar)

Year published: 1894

Publisher: Nattukottai Nagarathar (Penang)

Printer: Penang & Straits Press

Language: Tamil

Type: Book; 16 pages

Call no.: RRARE 894.81114 RAM

Accession no.: B18835668A

One of the oldest Tamil works in the National Library's Rare Materials Collection is a set of poems titled *Thanneermalai Vadivelarperil Thuthikavi* (தண்ணீர்மலை வடிவேலர்பேரிற் றுதிகவி), which translates as "Poems Sung in Praise of Lord Muruga at Thanneermalai Temple". Printed in Penang in 1894, this 16-page book by Iramanatha Chettiar (இராமநாதச் செட்டியார்) contains 60 devotional poems grouped into six sections.

The poems were written in praise of the patron deity of the Nattukottai Chettiar community – Lord Muruga, the Hindu God of War[1] who is also associated with joy, youth, beauty, fertility and love. The word "*Vadivelar*" (வடிவேலர்) in the title is one of the many names associated with Lord Muruga.

"*Thanneermalai*" is the Tamil word for "waterfall". This is most likely a reference to the Nattukottai Chettiar Thandayuthapani Temple in Penang located on Waterfall Road, Georgetown.[2] The temple was consecrated in 1857[3] and it is one of the largest Hindu

Information about the author, Iramanatha Chettiar, the name of his father and teacher as well as details about the printer and publisher are stated on the title page.

Kavadi decoration featuring image of Lord Muruga used during the Thaipusam Festival. *Ronni Pinsler Collection, courtesy of National Archives of Singapore.*

temples in Penang.[4] It was and continues to be a focal point in the state for Hindu festivals such as Thaipusam.

As was common with Tamil works printed in the late 19th and early 20th centuries, the title, name of the author, the author's ancestry and mentor are stated on the title page of this book. These details reveal that Iramanatha Chettiar was the son of Venkatachala Chettiar from Koothalur, Madurai district in Tamil Nadu.[5] The poet's mentor was Vandrondar Chettiar, an eminent Tamil scholar and philanthropist whose real name was Narayana Chettiar.[6] Not much else is known about the poet.

It is typical for volumes of Tamil poetry of the time to feature an introductory verse, usually written by someone who knows the poet, paying tribute to the latter. Following that tradition, this book begins with an introductory poem written by Kandamanikam Meiyappa Chettiar praising Iramanatha Chettiar. There is no indication as to how both men are related to each other.

In 19th-century Malaya, the predominant themes addressed in poetic works included religion, devotion and ethics.[7] *Thanneermalai Vadivelarperil Thuthikavi* is part of this tradition.

The 60 poems in this volume are divided equally into six sections. The first section consists of verses known as *santhakkavi* (சந்தக்கவி). In these poems, the poet praises Lord Muruga as a saviour who helps the soul attain eternal bliss. The second section comprises poems known as *aasiriyavirutham* (ஆசிரியவிருத்தம்), where the poet thanks Lord Muruga for protecting the community in Penang. The third section is made up of *oonjal* (ஊஞ்சல்), which the poet penned to extol Lord Muruga's valour.

The fourth section exemplifies a form of verse known as *aruseeradi aasiriyavirutham* (அறுசீரடி ஆசிரியவிருத்தம்), which are four-line verses similar to quatrains. They are also similar to, but shorter than, *aasiriyavirutham*. The verses featured here exhort devotees to worship Lord Muruga at Nattukottai Chettiar Thandayuthapani Temple to wash away their sins. The fifth section – a variation of *aruseeradi aasiriyavirutham* – contains verses capturing the poet's plea to Lord Muruga for help to maintain restraint and overcome temptation. The final section is made up of *venba* (வெண்பா), four-line verses that focus on the significance of Thaipusam and offer guidance on how to worship Lord Muruga during the auspicious months of the Tamil calendar.

It is not surprising that this volume of poetry was written in praise of Lord Muruga as the poet was part of the Nattukottai Chettiar community. This community – generally known as Chettiars, or Nagarathar (townsfolk)[8] – traditionally worships and venerates Lord Muruga.

The Chettiars came from Tamil Nadu, India and established their business firms in Penang around 1828[9] and they built temples where they settled so that they could worship Lord Muruga.[10] The temple mentioned in this volume of poetry, the Nattukottai Chettiar Thandayuthapani Temple,[11] is one such place of worship.[12]

Iramanatha Chettiar's poetry bears testimony to how the literary and religious lives of the Chettiars in Malaya were intertwined. In addition, the poems, together with various temples and religious festivals, demonstrate how the Chettiars were able to retain their beliefs and practices in a new land. ♦ **Sundari Balasubramaniam and Makeswary Periasamy**

Notes

1 Klostermaier, K.K. (1994). *A survey of Hinduism: second edition* (p. 298). New York: State University of New York Press. (Not available in NLB holdings); Parpola, A. (2015). *The roots of Hinduism: The early Aryans and the Indus Civilization* (p. 285). New York: Oxford University Press. (Not available in NLB holdings)

2 Another temple in Penang, Arulmigu Balathandayuthapani Temple, was also popularly referred to as Waterfall Temple. This temple is also called மேல் கோயில் (*mel-kovil*, or "temple at the top of the hill"). However, it is unlikely that Iramanatha Chettiar was alluding to it in the title of his book as Arulmigu Balathandayuthapani Temple was not built by the Chettiars.

3 Nattukottai Nagarathar Heritage Society (2018). *Penang Thaipusam - a journey of faith: a pioneering effort of the Penang Nattukottai Chettiars since 1857* (p. 19). Penang: Nattukottai Nagarathar Heritage Society. (Call no.: RSEA 294.53609595 PEN)

4 Nattukottai Chettiar Temple – Penang. Retrieved from MalaysiaHere website.

5 இராமநாதச் செட்டியார். (1894). தண்ணீரமலை வடிவேலற்பேரிற் றுதிகவி, பக்கம் 1. தண்ணீரமலை வடிவேலற்பேரிற் றுதிகவி, பக்கம்: பினாங் அண்ட் ஸ்டெரெயிட்ஸ் பிரஸ்,. (Microfilm no.: NL28657)

6 வன்றொண்டர். *Project Madurai, Digital Archive of Tamil Literature*. Retrieved from Project Madurai website.

7 (2011). ஜொகூர் மாநிலத் தமிழர் சங்கம் சிங்கப்பூர் தமிழ் அமைப்புகள் ஏற்பாட்டில் மலேசியா சிங்கப்பூர் தமிழ் இலக்கிய உறவுப்பாலமாநாடு 2011 (p. 74). (Call no.: RSING 894.81109 MAL)

8 Muthiah, S. [et al]. (2000). *The Chettiar heritage* (front flap). Chennai: The Chettiar Heritage. (Call no.: R 954.089 CHE-[SRN])

9 முத்துப்பழநியப்ப செட்டியார், பெ. நா. மு. (1938). மலாயாவின் தோற்றம் [*Happy Malaya*]. (p. 99). Penang: Mercantile Press. B17740725K

10 Belle, C. V. (2017). *Thaipusam in Malaysia : a Hindu festival in the Tamil diaspora* (pp. 91–93). Singapore: ISEAS-Yusof Ishak Institute. (Call no: RSEA 294.53609595 BEL); Nattukottai Nagarathar Heritage Society (2018). *Penang Thaipusam- a journey of faith: a pioneering effort of the Penang Nattukottai Chettiars since 1857* (p. 19). Penang: Nattukottai Nagarathar Heritage Society. (Call no.: RSEA 294.53609595 PEN); Collins, E. F. (1997). *Pierced by Murugan's Lance: ritual, power and moral redemption among Malaysian Hindus* (p. 47). Dekalb: Northern Illinois University Press. (Call no.: RSEA 294.536095951 COL)

11 "Thandayuthapani" is another of Lord Muraga's names. Another name for Nattukottai Chettiar Thandayuthapani Temple is Arulmigu Sri Thandayuthapani Temple. See Nattukottai Chettiar Temple – Penang. Retrieved from MalaysiaHere website.

12 It is also known as கீழ் கோயில் – *keal-kovil* (temple at the bottom of the hill), with its premises on Jalan Kebun Bunga (Waterfall Road) in Georgetown, Penang. Nattukotai Nagarathar Heritage Society (2018). *Penang Thaipusam- a journey of faith: a pioneering effort of the Penang Nattukottai Chettiars since 1857* (pp. (i), 6, 17–19). Penang: Nattukotai Nagarathar Heritage Society. (Call no.: RSEA 294.53609595 PEN); அருள்மிகு தண்டாயுதபாணி ஆலயம், மலேசியா. Retrieved from Dinamalar website.

SNAPSHOTS OF EARLY SARAWAK

Punan men of the Tinjar River. Hose described the Punan as "the shyest and most reserved" of the groups he met in Sarawak.[3]

Title: *Sarawak*
Authors: Charles Hose (1863–1929), and Robert Walter Campbell Shelford (1872–1912)
Year published: c. 1900
Type: Photo album; 170 photographs
Call no.: RRARE 959.54 HOS
Accession no.: B31659063K

In 1884, Charles Hose (1863–1929), a young man from Hertfordshire, England, arrived in Borneo to work for the Sarawak government as an administrator, and eventually rose to become Resident of a district. This career led him to spend 23 years working in the remote interior of Sarawak. It brought him in close contact with the land and people of Sarawak, which fostered in him an interest in the geography and ethnology of the area.

One of the many works to emerge from his experience is a 47-page album of 170 black-and-white photographs in platinum print[1] that he compiled around 1900 with Robert Shelford (1872–1912), who was then curator of the Sarawak Museum. Although the album was not produced en masse, copies of it were distributed to museums and libraries around the world.[2]

Titled *Sarawak*, the album is a valuable record of the different groups of people living in Sarawak at a time when their way of life was relatively unaffected by Western influences. Such images would have been difficult to obtain if not for Hose's and Shelford's familiarity with the land

and people of Sarawak, as well as Hose's position of authority among the locals. One of the photographs features Tama Bulan, the *Penghulu* (the leading chief of a district) of the Kenyah people, who provided invaluable help to Hose in administering law and order in the Baram district.

The album begins with a signed photograph of Rajah Charles Brooke[4] followed by snapshots of scenes in and around Kuching, the capital of Sarawak, including views of the Astana (the Rajah's palace) and public buildings.[5] Most of the images capture the natural landscape and the people living around the Baram, Rejang (Rajang) and Tinjar rivers in the interior of Sarawak. Rivers are one of the recurring subjects in the album, likely because these form a large part of Sarawak's natural landscape and are crucial in studying population movements.[6] Most locals lived along rivers and relied on them for water, transportation and also agriculture.

Specific subjects depicted include gorges, waterfalls, and men navigating their boats through treacherous rapids. There are also individuals from different groups such as the Sea Dayak (or Iban), Kayan, Kenyah, Murut, Punan and Kelabit[7] and photos of their dwellings, ornamental items and musical instruments.[8] Daily activities such as rice planting and rice husking, spinning thread and weaving to make cotton cloth, making darts and blowpipes for hunting, and gathering natural products such as gutta percha were also captured, as were rituals such as tribal warfare and peace-making traditions.[9] A few grim photographs are related to the practice of head-hunting, including photographs of the decapitated heads of fallen enemies.

Hose prided himself on the photographs of the Punan as this group was not well known then. Hose was one of the earliest Europeans to have contact with them and he considered them to be "the shyest and most reserved" of all these groups living in Sarawak.[10]

Charles Hose

Charles Hose started his career in the Sarawak civil service as a cadet in the Baram district in northern Sarawak in 1884. He later rose through the ranks to become Resident of the district in 1891, a post he held till 1904. His work involved administering law and order on behalf of the Rajah, which often required him to undertake journeys to remote parts of the district.

As a result, he encountered many different ethnic groups living in the inner region of Sarawak. Apart from administrative duties, he dedicated himself to scientific study and "distinguished himself as a geographer, anthropologist and collector of natural history specimens."[11] From 1904–1907, Hose was Resident of the Third Division and Member of the Supreme Council; he was also member of the Council Negri (the Legislative Assembly in Sarawak) from 1894 to 1907. After more than 20 years in the Sarawak civil service, Hose retired in 1907. He returned to England, devoting his time to research and writing about his days in Sarawak. A prolific writer, Hose wrote many books, papers and journal articles. These include *The Pagan Tribes of Borneo* (1912), which was co-published with William McDougall, and *Natural Man: A Record from Borneo* (1926). Both are considered significant works on the ethnology of Borneo. In 1919, Hose was appointed member of the Sarawak State Advisory Council in England. He passed away in London in 1929.[12]

Charles Hose, Resident of the Baram district from 1891–1904. *Image reproduced from Hose, C. (1926). The natural man: a record from Borneo. London: Macmillan and Co.*

[Clockwise from top left] Sacrificial poles outside a Kenyah village. After a battle, victorious Kenyah warriors would head home with the heads of their enemies. The next day, a tall pole would be erected near the altar of the war god, and from its tip, the head of an enemy would be suspended with a long cord. Several shorter poles would be erected in front of the altar-post and pieces of the dead enemies' flesh were then fastened on each pole with skewers. These were used as offerings to omen birds such as hawks; Tama Bulan, the *Penghulu* (the leading chief of a district) of the Kenyah, provided invaluable help to Hose in administering law and order in the Baram district; A posed photograph depicting Kenyah warriors.

Robert Shelford

Robert Shelford, curator of Sarawak Museum from 1897 to 1905. *Image reproduced from Shelford, R. W. C. (1916). A naturalist in Borneo. London: T. F. Unwin.*

Born in Singapore, Robert Shelford studied at King's College, London, and Cambridge University, where he obtained a degree in natural science.[13] In 1897, he was appointed curator at the Sarawak Museum, which had been established by the Rajah in 1888. Although research on insects was his focus, Shelford was a naturalist with varied interests. He collaborated with Charles Hose to compile photographs of the people and landscapes in Sarawak, as well as to publish several articles about the natural history and anthropology of Sarawak.

After his term at the Sarawak Museum ended, he left Borneo to become an assistant curator at Oxford University in 1905. He died in Margate, England, 1912 and his book, *A Naturalist in Borneo*, was published posthumously in 1916.

Each photograph in the album is labelled with a caption which identifies or describes the subject though there are instances of "inaccuracy and ambiguity".[14]

In the late 19th and early 20th centuries, photography was seen as a useful instrument in ethnographic documentation. It was thought that photographs were exact copies of reality, devoid of subjective interpretation, and thus deemed to convey greater veracity compared to other types of scientific evidence.[15] Apart from the fact that some images were posed shots, we also know that subjectivity is inherent in photography because the choice of subject and the way it is framed are themselves subjective decisions made by the photographer.

Despite its flaws, this album is an interesting artefact for modern readers. It offers glimpses of Sarawak from more than a century ago and allows us to see how indigenous communities were perceived by Western colonial administrators then.

♦ **Ong Eng Chuan**

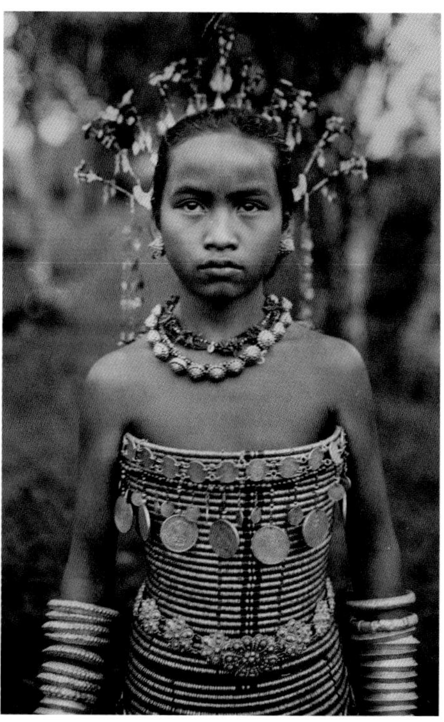

Two photographs of the Iban people. The Iban trace their origins to the Kapuas Lake area in Kalimantan. Infamous as Borneo's head-hunters, they were known to use human heads as trophies or symbols of courageous achievement.[16]

Notes

1 A platinum print is made with paper containing light sensitive iron salts and a platinum compound, instead of the conventional silver salts. Introduced in the 1870s, the platinum printing process was a popular technique, but became less so when the price of platinum soared during World War I. See National Portrait Gallery. *Platinum print, Palladium print.* Retrieved from National Portrait Gallery website; Stulik, D.C., & Kaplan, A. (2013). *The atlas of analytical signatures of photographic processes: platinotype* (pp. 5–6, 9). Retrieved from The Getty Conservation Institute website.

2 Durrans, B. (1994). Introduction. In Charles Hose, *Fifty years of romance and research in Borneo* (p. xvii). Kuala Lumpur; New York: Oxford University Press. (Call no.: RSEA 959.8022092 HOS)

3 Hose, C. (1994). *Fifty years of romance and research in Borneo* (pp. 71–73). Kuala Lumpur; New York: Oxford University Press. (Call no.: RSEA 959.8022092 HOS)

4 From 1841 to 1946, Sarawak was ruled by a dynasty of so-called "White Rajahs". James Brooke (1803–68) was the first White Rajah of Sarawak and Charles Brooke (1829-1917) was his nephew and successor.

5 The Astana is a palace built by Charles Brooke in 1870 as a wedding gift for his wife Margaret Alice Lili de Windt.

6 Hose, C. & McDougall, W. (1912). *The pagan tribes of Borneo: a description of their physical, moral and intellectual condition with some discussion of their ethnic relations, Vol. 1,* (p. 2). London: Macmillan. (Call no.: 572.9911 HOS-[RFL])

7 Hose wrote that although the different people of Borneo had often been indiscriminately grouped together as Dayak, they could be clearly distinguished from one another by differences in customs, as well as physical and psychological traits. Hose & McDougall,1912, p. 30.

8 The musical instruments include drums, guitars, zithers, fiddles and harps, as well as brass gongs, which some groups used in various ceremonies, for signalling and as a form of currency. Hose & McDougall,1912, p. 60.

9 Gutta percha would be processed and moulded into slabs and exported to places such as Singapore where it fetched a high price. Hose & McDougall,1912, pp. 150–151.

10 Hose, 1994, pp. 71–73.

11 Hose, 1994, p. 265.

12 Saturday, August 24, 1907. (1907, August 29). *The Singapore Free Press and Mercantile Advertiser (Weekly)*, p. 6; Death of Dr. Chas Hose. (1929, December 10). *The Straits Times*, p. 8.

13 For a biography of Robert Shelford, see Edward B. Poulton's introduction in Shelford, R. W. C. (1917). *A naturalist in Borneo.* London: T. F. Unwin. (Call no.: RCLOS 574.95952 SHE -[RFL]); Late Mr. R. Shelford. (1912, July 23). *The Singapore Free Press and Mercantile Advertiser*, p. 7. Retrieved from NewspaperSG.

14 For example, a young man in one of the photographs is labelled "Rejak, a Malay"; however, the same man appears in other photographs taken by Hose and is described as "a Klemantan" and "a Klemantan chief". See Durrans, B. 1994, p. xviii.

15 Chiarelli, C. & Guntarik, O. (2013). Borneo through the lens: A.C. Haddon's Photographic Collections, Sarawak 1898–99. *Sojourn: Journal of Social Issues in Southeast Asia, 28*(3), 441. Retrieved from JSTOR.

16 Hood Salleh. (Ed.) (1998 –). *The encyclopedia of Malaysia (Vol. 12).* (p. 92). Singapore: Archipelago Press. (Call no.: RSEA 959.5003 ENC)

Raffles in His Own Words

Stamford Raffles, who was Lieutenant-General of Bencoolen (Bengkulu) in southwestern Sumatra at the time the letter was written. *Courtesy of the National Museum of Singapore, National Heritage Board.*

Title: *Autograph letter from Sir Thomas Stamford Raffles to his cousin, Reverend Dr Thomas Raffles, with salutation "My dear cousin"*
Author: Sir Thomas Stamford Raffles (1781–1826)
Date: 14 October 1819
Language: English
Type: Manuscript; 28 pages on 14 leaves
Call no.: RRARE 959.5703 RAF-[JSB]
Accession no.: B29029416K

Stamford Raffles was a prolific letter writer throughout his life, and many of his letters have survived as invaluable primary source material. While most relate to his public career and professional pursuits, some are personal in nature, giving insights into his character and private life. A 28-page letter dated 14 October 1819, which is addressed to his cousin, the Reverend Dr Thomas Raffles, stands out as the only known attempt by Raffles to write an autobiographical account.

It was onboard the brig *Favourite* during a voyage from Bencoolen (now Bengkulu in southwestern Sumatra, Indonesia) to Calcutta that Raffles wrote this letter, after reading a derogatory description of himself in a book.[1] The author claimed that Raffles had obtained his posting in the East "in an inferior capacity" through the favour of William Ramsay, Secretary of the East India Company (EIC), who was connected with Raffles' first wife, Olivia.[2] Raffles believed

At Sea 14th October 1819

My dear Cousin

I have just perused a very incorrect & unpleasant account of my progress in life published in the Supplement to the Biographical Dictionary of Living Authors &c – a Work printed for Henry Colburn Public Library Conduit St. Hanover Square London – This Work from its nature must be in general circulation and the mention it makes of one who is no more as well as the general tendency of the article altogether is as disagreeable to my feelings as discreditable to my Character – My first Wife was in no manner connected with Mr Ramsay, they never saw each other, neither could my advancement in life possibly be accelerated by that marriage – It gave me no new Connections – no wealth, but on the contrary a load of debt, which I had to clear off – it increased my difficulties & thus increased my

Revd Thomas Raffles. energies

little one – or little ones – as it may be – that they have an Uncle who does not forget them – Affectionately Yrs

TSRaffles

[Left] The only known autobiographical account penned by Sir Stamford Raffles appears in a letter dated 14 October 1819, which he wrote to his cousin, the Reverend Dr Thomas Raffles. **[Bottom left]** Detail from the final page of Raffles' letter.
[Facing page] Dr Thomas Raffles (1788–1863) **(right)** was very close to Raffles. *Image reproduced from Bastin, J. S. (2019). Sir Stamford Raffles and some of his friends and contemporaries. Singapore: World Scientific.*
(Far right) Robert Rollo Gillespie (1766–1814), Commander of the Forces in Java when Raffles was the Lieutenant-Governor. He harboured resentment against Raffles for being passed over for the position of Lieutenant-Governor. *Image reproduced from Thorn, W. (1816). A Memoir of Major General Sir RR Gillespie. London: T. Egerton.*

that the insinuation originated from someone associated with his rival, Major-General Robert Rollo Gillespie, who was Commander of the Forces in Java during the time when Raffles was Lieutenant-Governor there.

In writing to his cousin, Raffles launched into a lengthy rebuttal that turned into a "sketch of his public life", in which he highlighted his major accomplishments thus far. In response to the claim that he owed his posting to Penang to Olivia's relationship with Ramsay, Raffles averred that the two had never met and that the appointment had been made before his marriage. In the letter, he traced his career progression from its humble beginnings in order to show that his success had been due to his own efforts and accomplishments, as well as the favour of those who recognised them in him. "Successful as my career may be considered to have been", Raffles emphasised in the letter, "my advancement has been entirely owing to my own personal exertions and to what I have always called my good fortune – family, friends, and connections have done nothing for me".

Due to family hardship, Raffles had withdrawn from school at the age of 14 and worked as a clerk for the EIC.[3] There, he developed a friendship with William Ramsay's son, William Brown Ramsay. The EIC Secretary recognised Raffles' potential and, when the opportunity arose, recommended him for the post of Assistant-Secretary of the new Presidency government at Prince of Wales Island (Penang).[4] Raffles welcomed the posting as it provided financial relief for his family and was an opportunity to realise his ambitions.

While in Penang, Raffles' performance caught the attention of Lord Minto, then Governor-General of Bengal. Raffles later convinced Lord Minto to conquer Java, in the face of strong opposition from others. In August 1811, the British began its rule of Java for the next five years, with Raffles appointed as Lieutenant-Governor.

The half-decade in Java proved to be a trying time for Raffles. Major-General Gillespie harboured deep resentment against him for being passed over for the position of Lieutenant-Governor.[5] When Gillespie was transferred to India in 1813, he made charges of maladministration and corruption against Raffles; these eventually led to the latter's removal from Java in 1816.[6]

Olivia was often ill and died at Buitenzorg (Bogor in West Java, Indonesia) in November 1814, leaving Raffles devastated and in poor health.[7] Some of these afflictions are alluded to in the letter.

Raffles' time in England between 1816 and 1817 was a turning point: he was exonerated of all the charges made by Gillespie, got remarried to Sophia Hull, published *The History of Java* and was knighted by the Prince Regent (who later became King George IV).[8] When this letter was written in October 1819, Raffles had taken up office as Lieutenant-General of Bencoolen. He also

wrote proudly of having founded a British settlement in Singapore, which "ensured the navigation and command of the Straits of Malacca" and secured the British against the Dutch monopoly of trade in the region.

Political exploits aside, Raffles waxed lyrical about his academic endeavours, tracing his passion for knowledge to his younger days, when he would light a candle to study at night. In the midst of his career as a statesman, Raffles maintained his scholarly pursuits – those cited in the letter include publishing a paper on the 'Maritime Laws of the Malays', reviving the Literary Society of Batavia, and assisting the prominent naturalist Dr Thomas Horsfield in his research. Ultimately, *The History of Java* established Raffles as a scholar.

Raffles also highlighted some of his charitable and religious efforts, including the establishment of the Benevolent Society at Batavia to abolish slavery and serving as the president of the Bible Society.[9] When he wrote the letter, Raffles had embarked on a mission to establish educational institutions in the lands he governed, seeing this as the most important means for "the improvement of [man's] condition".[10]

Raffles' First Wife: Olivia Mariamne Devenish (1771–1814)

Miniature portrait of Olivia Mariamne Devenish by Andrew Plimer, London, 1805. *Image reproduced from Bastin, J. S. (2016). The Family of Sir Stamford Raffles. Singapore: National Library Board, Singapore and Marshall Cavendish Editions.*

The illegitimate daughter of an unknown Circassian woman and Irishman George (or Godfrey) Devenish, Olivia was brought up in Ireland and went to India when she was 21. On the voyage, she had a relationship with the ship captain, John Hamilton Dempster, and became pregnant. She gave birth to a daughter, Harriet, who was brought up by Dempster. Olivia later married Jacob Cassivelaun Fancourt, an Assistant Surgeon of the East India Company (EIC) in Madras in 1793, who died in 1800. In 1804, she successfully petitioned the EIC in London for a widow's pension. Around the same time, she met 23-year-old Raffles, who was then a clerk with the Company[11] and 10 years her junior. The following year, Raffles was appointed Assistant-Secretary at Penang. He married Olivia in London in 1805, and shortly after, both of them left for Penang.[12]

Raffles ended his letter with a request that his cousin set the record straight with the publisher on his behalf. It is not known whether this was done, but Raffles would have felt vindicated to know that in 1897, this letter was fully transcribed and published.[13] More than a century later, in 2015, the National Library acquired the letter from Dr John Bastin, the leading scholar and author of numerous books on Raffles, along with more than 5,000 books and manuscripts in his personal collection. ♦ **Chung Sang Hong**

Notes

1 Upcott, W. (1816). *A biographical dictionary of the living authors of Great Britain and Ireland: Comprising literary memoirs and anecdotes of their lives, and a chronological register of their publications, with the number of editions printed; including notices of some foreign writers whose works have been occasionally published in England* (p. 445). London: Henry Colburn. (Call no.: RRARE 928.2 BIO JSB)

2 The entry states in full: "Raffles, T. S. Esq. lieutenant governor of Batavia, to which situation he was appointed by Lord Minto on the conquest of the island of Java, in 1812. Mr. Raffles went out to India in an inferior capacity through the interest of Mr Ramsay's secretary to the company; and in consequence of his marrying a lady connected with that gentleman. Mrs. Raffles died at Batavia, Nov. 26, 1814. Her husband, who is now on his return to Europe, has printed, A Statistical account of the Island of Java, 4to. 1815."

3 Bastin, J. (2019). *Sir Stamford Raffles and some of his friends and contemporaries: a memoir of the founder of Singapore* (pp. 6–8). Singapore: World Scientific Publishing Co. Pte. Ltd. (Call no.: RSING 959.5703092 BAS-[HIS])

4 Bastin, 2019, pp. 9–10.

5 Bastin, J. (2012). *The founding of Singapore 1819: Based on the private letters of Sir Stamford Raffles to the Governor-General and Commander-in-Chief in India, the Marquess of Hastings, preserved in the Bute Collection at Mount Stuart, Isle of Bute, Scotland* (p. 5). Singapore: National Library. (Call no.: RSING 959.5703 BAS-[HIS])

6 Bastin, 2012, pp. 6–7.

7 Bastin, J. (2016). *The Family of Sir Stamford Raffles* (p. 108). Singapore: National Library Board & Marshall Cavendish Editions. (Call no.: RSING 959.57030922 BAS-[HIS])

8 Bastin, 2012, p. 7.

9 This refers to Java Auxiliary Bible Society. Jordaan, R. The British Interregnum in Java (1811–1816): an experiment in supranational fraternal governance (p. 470). In L. Prager, M. Prager, & G. Sprenger (Eds.). (2016). *Parts and wholes: essays on social morphology, cosmology, and exchange in honour of J.D.M. Platenkamp.* Zurich: LIT Verlag. (Not in NLB holdings)

10 He wrote: "But it is to man, and the state in which he is found, that my attention is at this moment directed, and among other measures for the improvement of his condition, the most important and, perhaps, the most certain of eventual success, has been the establishment of schools on the Lancastrian plan." The Lancastrian plan refers to a teaching method practised in the 19th century. It involves having older or better students teach the younger or weaker ones.

11 Bastin, 2016, pp. 57–59, 71–72.

12 Bastin, J. (2002). *Olivia Mariamne Raffles* (p. 11). Singapore: Landmark Books. (Call no.: RSING 959.5703092 BAS-[HIS])

13 Boulger, D. (1897). *Life of Sir Stamford Raffles* (pp. 21–32). London: Horace Marshall & Son. (Call no.: RCLOS 959.8022 BOU-[JSB])

A LITERARY PIONEER'S AWAKENING

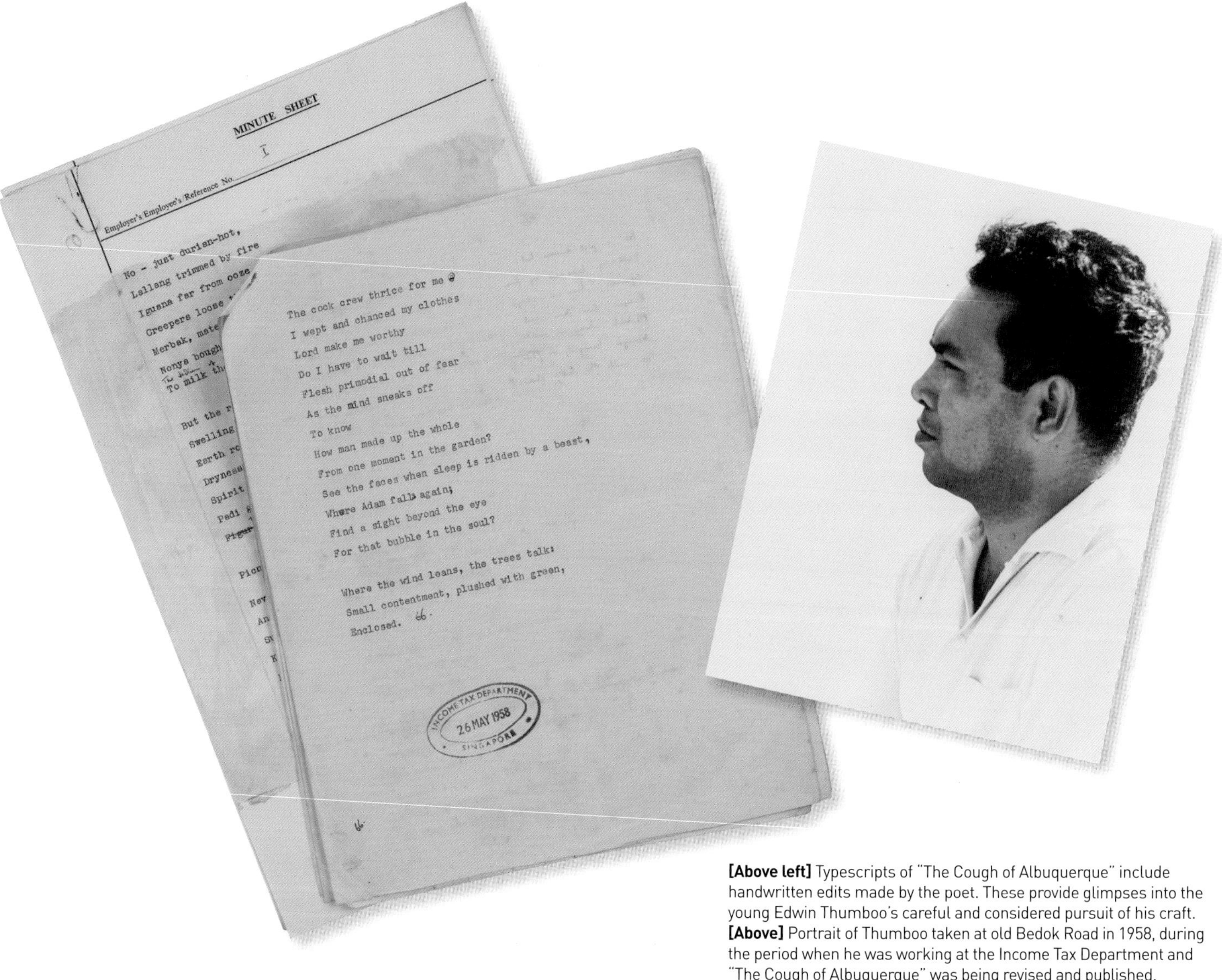

[Above left] Typescripts of "The Cough of Albuquerque" include handwritten edits made by the poet. These provide glimpses into the young Edwin Thumboo's careful and considered pursuit of his craft. **[Above]** Portrait of Thumboo taken at old Bedok Road in 1958, during the period when he was working at the Income Tax Department and "The Cough of Albuquerque" was being revised and published.

Title: *The Cough of Albuquerque*
Author: Edwin Thumboo
Date: mid-1950s
Language: English
Type: Manuscript; 15 sets
Call no.: RCLOS 378.12095957 THU -[ET]
Accession no.: B20056083B
Donated by: Edwin Thumboo

Sensuous. Earthy. Feverish. These are descriptions that might come to mind as one pores over "The Cough of Albuquerque" – a daring opus that anticipated the rise of local pioneer poet Edwin Nadason Thumboo (1933–). The five-part poem was first published in full in *Write* (1958), an independent student publication of the University of Malaya in Singapore.[1]

In 2006, 15 sets of sepia-toned authorial drafts of "The Cough of Albuquerque" were donated to the National Library along with a comprehensive collection of the poet's other manuscripts, photographs and books. The manuscripts and typescripts of this work bear testimony to the challenges of writing a long poem.

"The Cough of Albuquerque" is Thumboo's attempt at accomplishing for Malayan culture what poet William Butler Yeats did for Ireland.[2] He hoped to forge an artistic identity by establishing a personal mytholo-

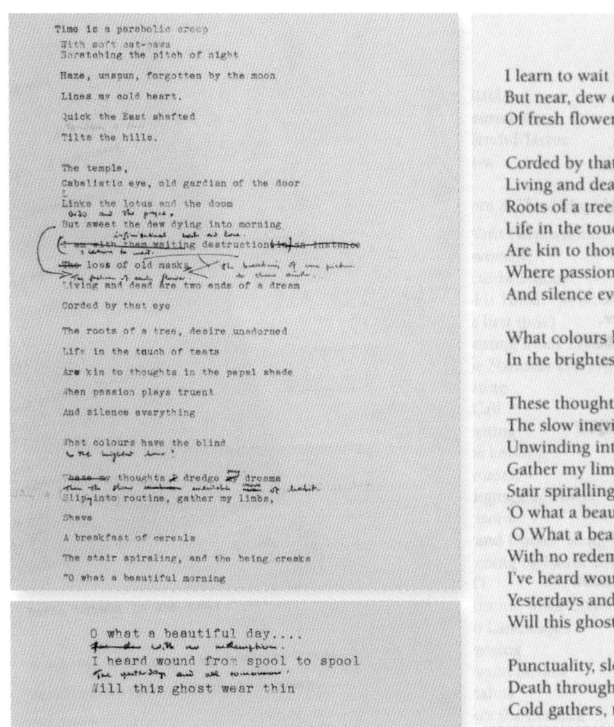

Time is a parabolic creep
With soft cat-paws
Scratching the pitch of night

Haze, unspun, forgotten by the moon

Lines my cold heart.

Quick the East shafted

Tilts the hills.

The temple,
Cabalistic eye, old gardian of the door

Links the lotus and the doom

But sweet the dew dying into morning

I am with them waiting destruction in an instance

The loss of old masks

Living and dead are two ends of a dream

Corded by that eye

The roots of a tree, desire unadorned

Life in the touch of teats

Are kin to thoughts in the pepal shade

When passion plays truent

And silence everything

What colours have the blind

These my thoughts dredge my dreams

Slip into routine, gather my limbs,

Shave

A breakfast of cereals

The stair spiraling, and the being creaks

"O what a beautiful morning

O what a beautiful day....

I heard wound from spool to spool

Will this ghost wear thin

Responsibility and Commitment

I learn to wait the loss of old masks:
But near, dew dying into morning
Of fresh flowers.

Corded by that eye
Living and dead are two ends of a dream;
Roots of a tree, desire unadorned,
Life in the touch of teats,
Are kin to thoughts in the pepal shade
Where passion has played truant
And silence everything.

What colours have the blind
In the brightest hour?

These thoughts dredge:
The slow inevitable move of habit
Unwinding into routine
Gather my limbs, shave, breakfast of cereal
Stair spiralling a web
'O what a beautiful morning
O What a beautiful day . . .'
With no redemption.
I've heard wound from spool to spool
Yesterdays and all tomorrow:
Will this ghost wear thin

Punctuality, slow destruction from abacus,
Death through skill:
Cold gathers, rends the trembling veil.

On the left are drafts of "The Cough of Albuquerque", with revisions marked in blue. On the right is a portion of the published poem.

gy and geography through his oeuvre.[3]

Written in the mid-1950s, in a postwar Singapore where anti-colonial sentiments were intensifying, "The Cough of Albuquerque" inevitably took on a similar flavour. Thumboo's titular character refers to Alfonso de Albuquerque, the Portuguese commander who captured Melaka in 1511. The poem also takes inspiration from the death-in-life imagery invoked by the aged protagonist in T.S. Eliot's poem "Gerontion", who muses on his past and anticipates his doomed future.[4]

Thumboo's reference to Alburquerque's "cough" alludes to the lost vitality of the protagonist in Eliot's poem,[5] and is a wry comment on the atrophied influence of colonial powers. In one of Thumboo's three-page drafts, Albuquerque's despondence is evoked through the lines: "But sweet the dew dying into morning / I am with them waiting destruction in an instance." In the published poem, this sense of decline is captured in the lines "I learn to wait the loss of old masks: / But near, dew dying into morning / of fresh flowers".[6] Albuquerque's lethargy is emphasised through heartrending lines that are further refined in the published poem. For instance, "Slipping into routine" (as seen in Thumboo's draft), becomes a more evocative "Unwinding into routine" in the published piece. Some lines from his draft were eventually published as they were, for instance, "I've heard wound from spool to spool /... / Will this ghost wear thin".

Additionally, the waning of the British empire is reflected in Thumboo's portrayal of Albuquerque's travels through Malaya.[7]

Unlike the majesty possessed by the mythical traveller Ulysses in what would become one of Thumboo's best-known poems, "Ulysses by the Merlion", his Albuquerque is merely a "ghost" taking a ""hike" through the Malayan landscape in search of "a new beginning". Albuquerque's journey does not end well, as the image of drought and infertility – a rice field (*"sawah"*) without its source of water ("missed the stream") – suggests.

In the published poem, Thumboo's description of Albuquerque's "hike" reveals the protagonist's intimate, dream-like experience of a landscape featuring local folklore and Western mythology. It also, however, turns the reader's gaze towards scenes of poverty and decay that exist alongside a thriving marketplace. "Sores by the river / Maggots merry-go-round; / Constipated lives crutching by noon" appear in a bustling city where "Across, tuakow / Stuffed with pilferings of copra / Wholesale retail rice, spreads sail. / Godowns, large spawning toads, incur our sight".[8] The jarring juxtaposition of the destitute ("Hands pure shrivel") with the wealthy traders ("Flashy and fat [...] / The tycoon who lives by doing his partners in") paints a stark picture of inequalities. Such social commentary was to be a recurrent theme in Thumboo's future works.

A glimpse of Thumboo's youth helps shed light on the cauldron of emotions and instincts in "The Cough of Albuquerque". Thumboo spent his childhood in the foothills of Mandai,[9] which inspired much of the lush imagery observed in the poem.

During his undergraduate years, Thumboo was involved in *Fajar*, the magazine published by the left-wing University Socialist Club. An anti-colonial editorial titled "Aggression in Asia", which was published in *Fajar* in May 1954, resulted in the arrest of its nine-member editorial team, including Thumboo. Initially charged with sedition, the students were later acquitted. Thumboo wrote "The Cough of Albuquerque" around the time of the *Fajar* trial, a tumultuous period of his life. He then spent the next few years reworking and refining the poem.

While the gossamer-thin typing paper on which this poem was lovingly crafted may have grown fragile over the years, interest in this poem, as well as Thumboo's other early works, has ripened with the fullness of time, as evidenced by the number of academics and poetry enthusiasts who study the poet today. ♦ **Michelle Heng**

Notes

1 Thumboo, E. (October, 1958). "The Cough of Albuquerque" in *Write* (pp. 6–7). Singapore: University of Malaya.

2 National Library Board. (2011). *Book Abstract: The Cough of Albuquerque*. Retrieved from National Online Repository of the Arts (NORA) website.

3 Edwin Thumboo. In P. Nazareth (Ed.). (2008). *Interlogue: Studies in Singapore literature: Edwin Thumboo, Creating a nation through poetry* (Vol. 7). (p. 199). Singapore: Ethos Books. (Call no.: RSING 809.895957 INT)

4 J.B. Vickery (1973). Gerontion. In *Critics on T.S. Eliot* (p. 26). London: Allen and Unwin (Call no. R 821.91 ELIS)

5 "The goat may be a real one in some field above Gerontion's house [...] But the goat might also be the landlord, some other tenant, or the speaker himself (an old "goat" who has lost his passion) in a different room at night." Diane Stockmar Bonds (1982). The house of mirrors: Language in Eliot's "Gerontion". p. 46. *College Literature, Vol. 9 No. 1* (Winter, 1982). Retrieved from JSTOR. For the full poem, see T.S. Eliot (1951). "Gerontion". In *Collected Poems 1909 – 1935* (p. 37). London: Faber & Faber Limited (Call no. RDET 821.912 ELI)

6 "The Cough of Albuquerque". In Leong, L.G. (Ed.). (1997). *Responsibility and Commitment: The Poetry of Edwin Thumboo* (p. 94), Singapore: Centre for Advanced Studies; Singapore University Press. (Call no.: RSING S821.09 EE)

7 Two locations specified in the poem are Kepong (a town in northern Kuala Lumpur), and Ophir (presumably Mount Ophir, the tallest peak in Johor).

8 "Tuakow", also known as a lighter, refers to a flat-bottomed boat used to carry freight and passengers. "Copra" refers to dried coconut kernels. For the full, published poem, see Thumboo, E. (October, 1958). "The Cough of Albuquerque". In *Write* (pp 6-7). Singapore: University of Malaya.

9 Heng. M., Gwee L.S. (Eds.) (2012) Biography. In *Edwin Thumboo – Time-travelling: A Select, Annotated Bibliography* (p. 32). Singapore: National Library Board. (Call no.: RSING S821 EDW)

Two Early Studies of the Malay Language

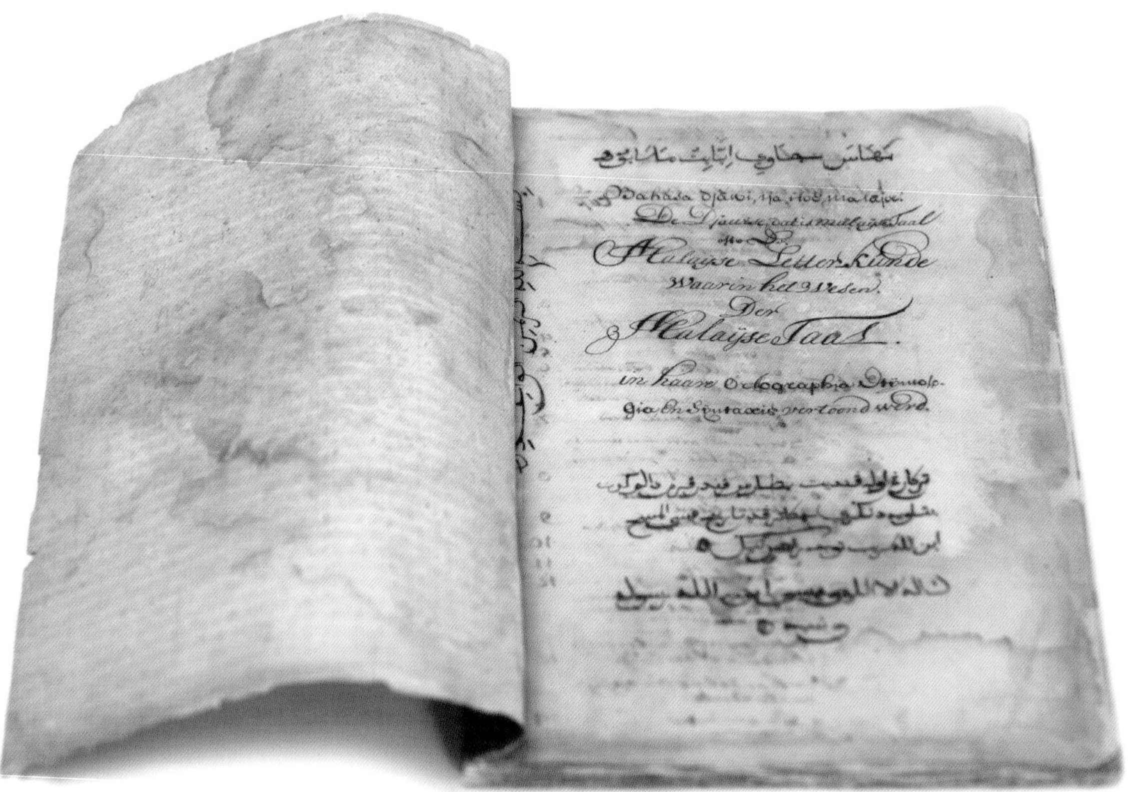

Title page of Pieter van der Vorm's *Malay Grammar* (1703).

Title: *Bahasa djawi ija itoe Malajoe. De Djawise dat is Malayse taal ofte de Malayse letterkunde waarin het wesen. Der Malayse taal in haare orthographia etymologia, en syntaxis vertoond werd* (Jawi language, i.e. Malay language or Literature in which the essence of the Malay language is shown in its orthography, etymology and syntax)
Author: Pieter van der Vorm
Date: 1703
Language: Dutch and Malay
Type: Manuscript; 62 pages
Call no.: RRARE 499.221 VOR
Accession no.: B32426430B

Title: *Dutch-Malay Lexicon*
Date: 1790
Language: Dutch and Malay
Type: Manuscript; 134 pages
Call no.: RRARE 439.31399221 DUT
Accession no.: B31660071B

In the last decades of the 17th century, the church authorities linked to the Dutch East India Company, better known by its Dutch abbreviation VOC, became increasingly alarmed about the erosion of morals among its traders, sailors, soldiers and their local spouses and offspring who were living in Batavia (now Jakarta).

This community did not have access to basic education and had adopted pidginised forms of Portuguese and Malay as their mother tongue. In such an environment, the Christian faith of these people was also at risk as they were likely to adopt religious customs that differed from the Dutch Protestant faith.

To counter this and to propagate Protestanism in this region, the Dutch authorities decided to translate the Bible into a Malay that was devoid of any colloquialisms or words with Portuguese, and therefore by extension Catholic, origins.

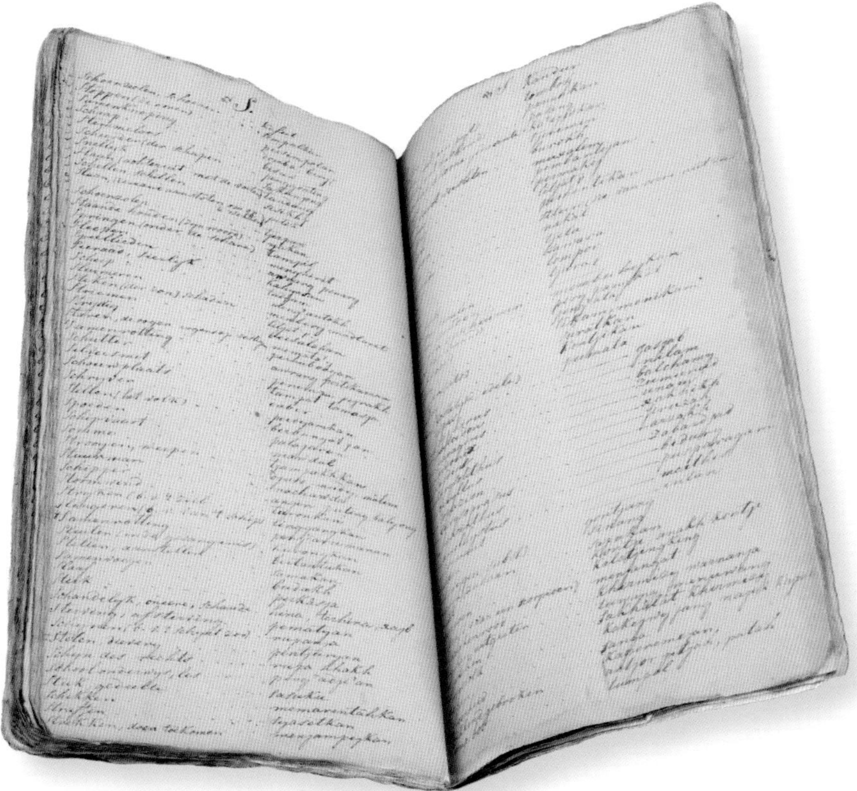

(Above left) A page from the *Dutch-Malay Lexicon*. **(Above)** François Valentijn, who assisted Leydekker in the translation of the Bible, was a minister, naturalist and writer who devoted much of his life in serving the Dutch VOC, with a significant tenure in the East Indies from 1685 to 1714. *Courtesy of the National Museum of Singapore, National Heritage Board.*

Although proponents such as Reverend François Valentijn encouraged the use of a colloquial form of Malay that would be more easily understood,[1] the VOC Directors in the Netherlands demanded that the "degenerated" version of Malay be restored to its old purity.[2] The VOC held the view that only this "pure" form of the language could become the basis of the translated Bible.

The translation effort was led by Reverend Melchior Leydekker and after his death in 1701, continued by the Reverend Pieter van der Vorm. The Dutch-translated New Testament in "pure" Malay was finally published in 1731, and both the Old and New Testaments were published together in 1733.

Over the 30-year period it took to translate this Bible, a number of linguistic studies were also produced. The two studies in manuscript form found in the National Library's collection were most probably carried out by members of the team that also worked on the Bible translation.

The first manuscript is Pieter van der Vorm's *Malay Grammar* of 1703: *Bahasa djawi ija itoe Malajoe. De Djawise dat is Malayse taal ofte de Malayse letterkunde waarin het wesen. Der Malayse taal in haare orthographia etymologia, en syntaxis vertoond werd.* Translated, it means: "Jawi language, i.e. Malay language or Literature in which the essence of the Malay language is shown in its orthography, etymology and syntax".

Van der Vorm's *Grammar* is elaborate and thorough, and illustrates the materials available and used by these scholars when they researched Malay literature to find the words and phrases that were most faithful to their original intent and meaning.

This work was one of the sources used by theologian and linguist George Henric Werndly (sometimes spelt as Georg Heinrich Werndly or Werndlij) to produce his acclaimed *Maleische Spraakkunst* (*Malay Grammar*), published in 1736.[3] In fact, according to the introduction to Werndly's book, he initially wanted to edit and augment van der Vorm's work but later decided to revise it more substantially in accordance with the latest Dutch grammar.[4]

The other manuscript is an anonymous Dutch-Malay lexicon that is about 130 pages long. This lexicon is likely to have been written by the same group of Biblical scholars who were known to have produced such vocabulary lists at the time but which were never published.[5]

This manuscript dictionary provides interesting data that may be useful for long-overdue research on the etymological and historical sources of the Malay language. In the manuscript's wordlist, for instance, we find old forms of written Malay such as *suratkan*, meaning "to write", instead of the more modern *tulis*, and *kasut* for "shoe", instead of the Portuguese-derived *sepatu*. Other words such as *harij mawlid* for "birthday", *majnun* for "possessed by the devil", and *pang'aji'an* for "lesson at school" suggest a preference for Arabic-derived terminologies above Malay forms.

♦ **Jan van der Putten**

Notes

1 Maier, H. M. J. (1993). From heteroglossia to polyglossia: The creation of Malay and Dutch in the Indies. *Indonesia, 56* (October 1993), 37–65, p. 45. Retrieved from Cornell University Library eCommons website.

2 Hoffman, J. (1979). A foreign investment: Indies Malay to 1901. *Indonesia, 27* (April 1979), 65–92, p. 69. Retrieved from Cornell University Library eCommons website.

3 Werndly, G. H. (1736). *Maleische spraakkunst, uit de eige schriften der Maleiers opgemaakt. Met eene voorreden, behelzende eene inleiding tot dit werk en een dubbeld.* Amsterdam: R. & G. Wetstein. (Call no.: RRARE 499.23 WER)

4 Mahdi, W. (2018). The first standard grammar of Malay. George Werndly's 1736 *Maleische Spraakkunst. Wacana, 19* (2), 257–290, p. 262. Retrieved from Wacana website.

5 Notably, Reverend Leydekker has been cited as a compiler of such a lexicon. See Kemp, P. H. van der (1914). Uit Den Tijd Van C. P. J. Elout's Toewijding aan de Maleische Taal. Een bijdrage tot de geschiedenis van de beoefening der Indologische wetenschappen. *Bijdragen tot de Taal-, Land- en Volkenkunde, 69* (1), 141–218, pp. 185–186. In the 19th century, these manuscripts were supposed to be used as sources for a new standardised Malay-Dutch dictionary, but this did not materialise.

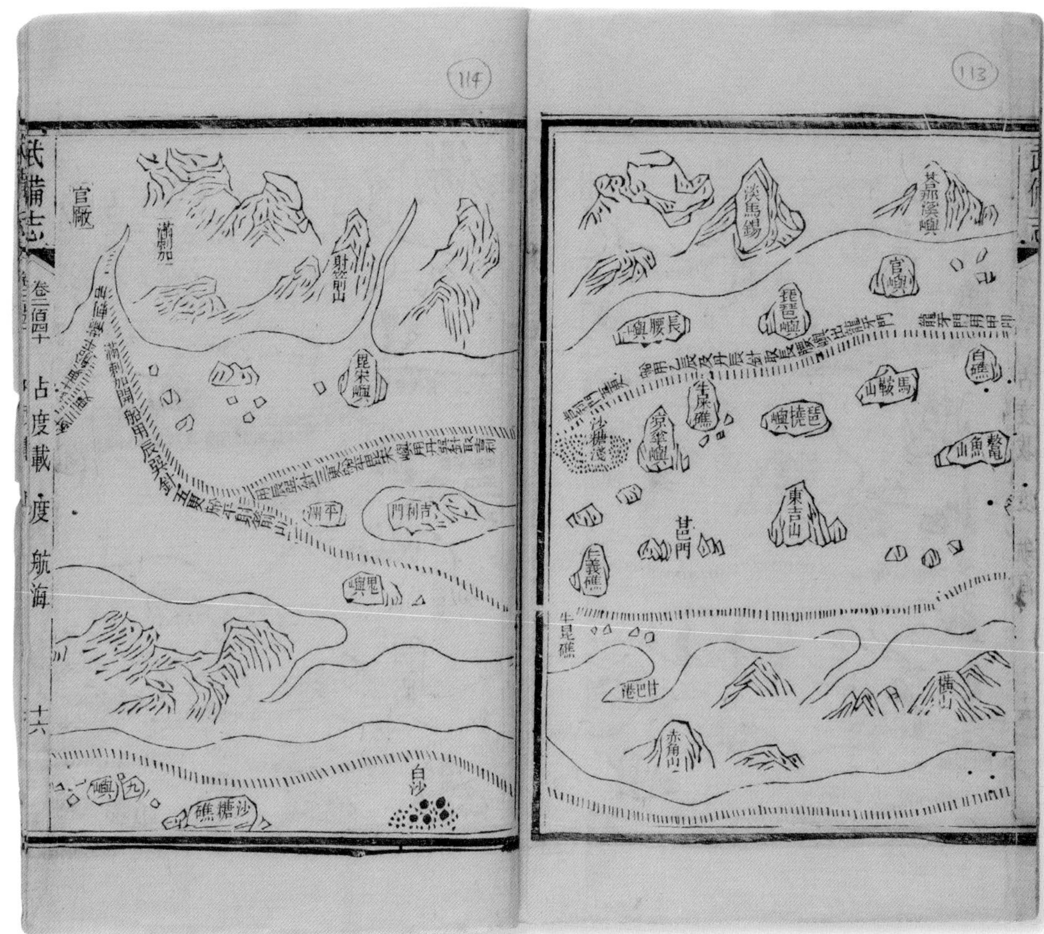

Admiral Zheng He's Navigation Map

Title: Mao Kun Map (茅坤图), from *Wu Bei Zhi*《武备志》, Chapter 240
Compiler: Mao Yuanyi (茅元仪, 1594–1640)
Year published: Late 19th century
Language: Chinese
Type: Map
Call no.: RRARE 355.00951 WBZ
Accession no.: B26078782G
Donated by: Singapore Federation of Chinese Clan Associations

The Mao Kun Map (茅坤图) is the collective name for a set of navigational maps that are based on the 15th-century expeditions of the Indian Ocean by renowned Ming dynasty explorer Admiral Zheng He (郑和, 1371–1433 or 1435).

Also known as Zheng He's Navigation Map (郑和航海图) or the Wu Bei Zhi Chart, the map is believed to have been drawn between 1425 and 1430, although scholars have offered differing views of its exact date of origin.[1] The term Mao Kun Map, as coined by the Dutch sinologist Jan Julius Lodewijk Duyvendak (1889–1954), is the most commonly used name today for this set of Chinese navigational maps.

The Mao Kun Map was first published in the late-Ming publication *Wu Bei Zhi*《武备志》.[2] It was compiled in 1621 by Mao Yuanyi (茅元仪, 1594–1640), who served as a strategist in the Ming court, and published in 1628. Mao's grandfather, Mao Kun (茅坤, 1512–1601), owned a large and distinguished personal library, and it is believed that this map was part of his collection. Given that three generations of the Mao family had served in the Ming dynasty's imperial service – either in a military or naval capacity – it is not surprising that the map ended up in their possession.

Originally drawn as a scroll measuring 20.5 cm by 560 cm (in the manner of traditional Chinese paintings), which today no longer exists, the Mao Kun Map was recast into 40 pages – essentially an atlas format – for publication in the 240-chapter *Wu Bei Zhi*. The map is featured in the final chapter of *Wu Bei Zhi*, in the "Geographical Surveys" section, which discusses astronomical observations and geographical surveys for military operations. After more than 250 years of obscurity, the Mao Kun Map was made known to the rest of the world around 1885–86 in a journal article written by George Phillips (1836–96).[3]

The National Library's copy of the Mao Kun Map in the "Geographical Surveys" chapter is from a late 19th-century edition of *Wu Bei Zhi*. It is among one of six known editions of *Wu Bei Zhi* published over the centuries. All six editions are still extant and held in various private and public collections around the world, but it is not known how many copies there are of each.

The navigational map is to be read from right to left in the tradition of classical Chinese writing and painting. The voyage begins at the Treasure Ship factory near the Ming capital city of Nanjing and follows a southerly course along the coast of China for 19 pages until it reaches Chiêm Thành in Vietnam. It then continues to various places in Southeast Asia over the next 12 pages, before reaching Martaban in Myanmar. The last nine pages depict the routes to Ceylon (Sri Lanka), India, Arabia and the east coast of Africa. The furthest point reached on the map is Malindi in Kenya.

The Mao Kun Map was conceived and drawn as a strip map, with the sailing route taking centre stage and the geographical features rendered in a linear fashion along the sailing route. As such, both the orientation and scale vary from one segment to the next on the map, leading to a "distortion" of space as we generally understand it.

To further compound the difficulty of interpreting the map, upon reaching the Southeast Asian archipelago, the journeys no longer progress in a linear route. From this point onwards, the map has to be read as two distinct parts: the upper half of each page depicting one journey, and the lower half presenting a separate and unrelated journey. Both narratives continue onto the subsequent pages – but at different travel speeds. In order to understand the map better, the two halves have to be interpreted separately from the other.

While land masses and islands are depicted in plan view (i.e. bird's eye view), the major cities and mountains are portrayed in elevation view (i.e. like cardboard stand-ups). The sailing routes are shown as dashed lines, while important places like settlements and landmarks are labelled. Altogether, some 500 place names appear on the map, with the most prominent place names – such as countries, provinces and prefectures, and official installations like forts or depots – boxed up.

The Mao Kun Map uses two navigational techniques. The first is the Chinese 24-point compass, with 15 degrees for each compass point or "needle" (or compass needle) employed throughout the map. The second is the "star altitude" technique (过洋牵星术), which navigators used only to cross the Indian Ocean. This technique made use of the known altitude of selected stars and compared them with markings on a reference board. If the altitude of a selected star matched a certain pre-marked altitude line on the reference board, the exact position and location of the ship could be determined.

In order to achieve this feat, the people living in places along the coasts of the Indian Ocean would have been called upon to assist with this type of navigation. Four pages of "star altitudes" are appended at the end of the Mao Kun Map.

Of interest is the fact that the name Temasek (淡马锡) appears at the top centre of page 27 while Melaka (满剌加) appears at the top left of page 28. Other familiar places on page 27 as identified by scholar J.V.G. Mills include Pulau Sakijang Pelepah[4] (琵琶屿), Pulau Tembakul[5] (官屿/龟屿岛), Pulau Satumu[6] (长腰屿) and Pedra Branca[7] (白礁).

The sailing directions radiating from Melaka depict the homeward journey from Melaka to China across the South China Sea. The route passes through Karimun (吉利门) and to the South China Sea via Longyamen (龙牙门), or Dragon's Teeth Gate, which was a significant navigational landmark in those days. Longyamen as indicated on the map refers to the main Strait of Singapore or the Singapore Straits.

The Mao Kun Map is of great significance to Singapore as it is the only known cartographic work that mentions "Temasek" – the name that was used in ancient documents to indicate the site of modern Singapore. Other place names on the map have helped to narrow the location of Temasek to an area consistent with where Singapore is found today. There is, however, uncertainty over what exactly Temasek means on the map – does it refer to the island itself or to a larger region encompassing the island?

What is certain is that the Mao Kun Map is testimony that the Singapore Straits was used as a sailing route between the Indian Ocean and China in the 15th century, pointing to the importance of Singapore's location in the regional trade network during this period. ♦ **Mok Ly Yng**

Notes

1 徐玉虎. (2005). 郑和下西洋航海图考. In《郑和下西洋研究文选》(p. 530). Beijing: China Ocean Press. (Call no.: R q951.06092 ZHX); 巩珍 & 向达. (2012). 《西洋番国志 郑和航海图 两种海道针经》. Beijing: Zhonghua. (RSEA 959 GZ); 马欢 & 万明. (2005). 《明钞本瀛涯胜览校注》. Beijing: China Ocean Press (Not available in NLB holdings); Ma Huan. (1997). *Ying Yai Sheng Lan (The overall survey of the ocean shores)*. C-C. Feng (Ed.), translation with introduction, notes and appendices by J.V.G. Mills. Bangkok: White Lotus Press. (Call no.: R 915.04 MA -[TRA])

2 Translated by J.V.G. Mills as Records of Military Preparations.

3 Phillips, G. (1885–1886). The seaports of India and Ceylon described by Chinese voyages of the 15th century. *Journal of the North China Branch of the Royal Asiatic Society* XX: 209–226; XXI: 30–42. Retrieved from JSTOR.

4 Pulau Sakijang Pelepah is also known as Lazarus Island.

5 Pulau Tembakul is also known as Kusu Island.

6 Pulau Satumu is where Raffles Lighthouse is located.

7 Pedra Branca is where Horsburgh Lighthouse is located.

[Facing page] The Mao Kun map is believed to be based on the naval expeditions of the early 15th-century Ming admiral, Zheng He, who made several voyages from China to Southeast Asia and across the Indian Ocean. The pages shown here depict the return route between Melaka and China through the Straits of Singapore. The name Danmaxi (淡马锡), is marked on a hill on the recto (right) page. Pedra Branca (白礁) appears on the same page, whereas Melaka (满剌加) is labelled at the top left of the left page.

[Above] Overlay of six pages from the Mao Kun Map over a map of the Malay Peninsula. *Image overlay provided by Mok Ly Yng.*

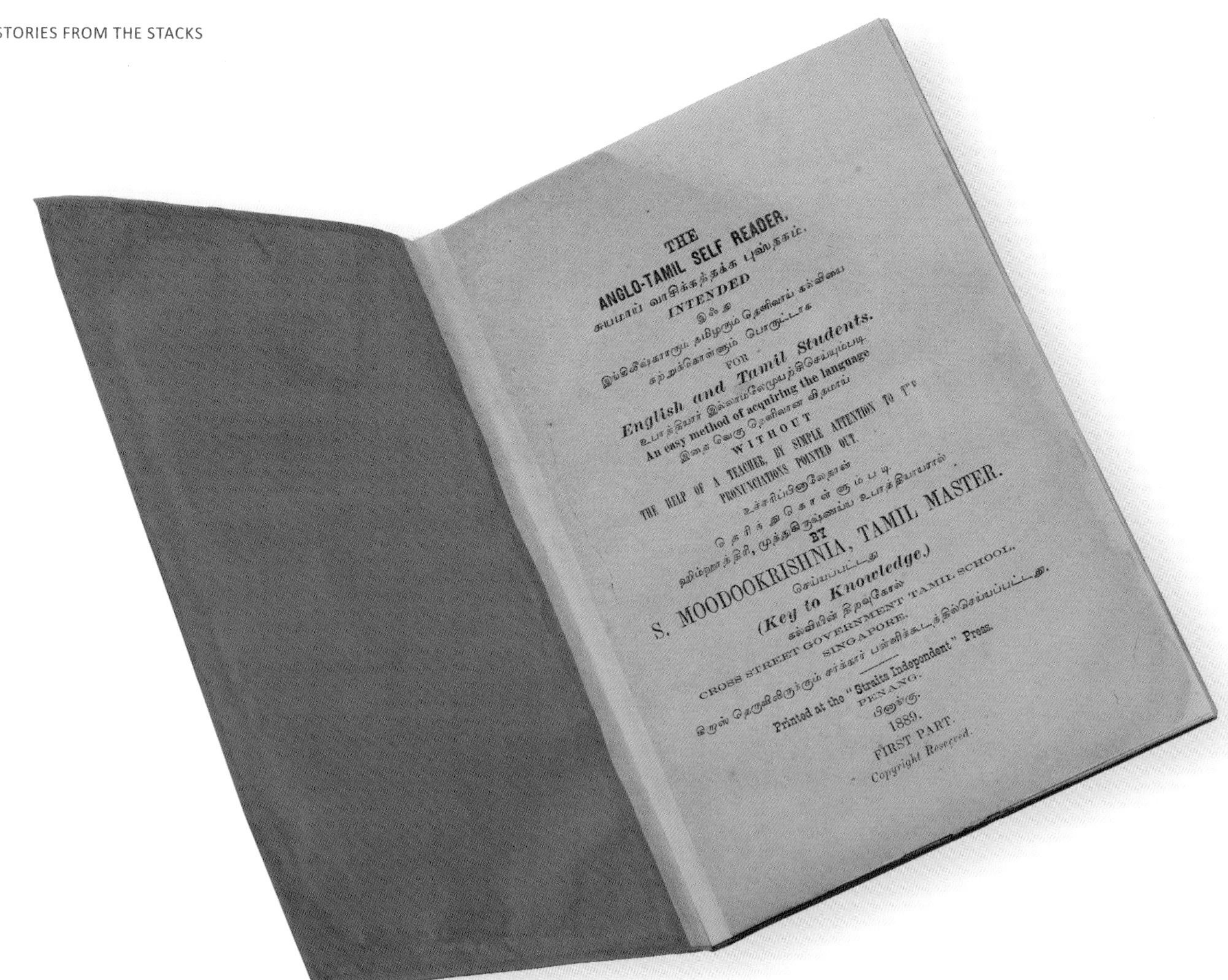
THE
ANGLO-TAMIL SELF READER,
INTENDED
FOR
English and Tamil Students.
An easy method of acquiring the language
WITHOUT
THE HELP OF A TEACHER, BY SIMPLE ATTENTION TO THE
PRONUNCIATIONS POINTED OUT.
BY
S. MOODOOKRISHNIA, TAMIL MASTER.
(Key to Knowledge.)
CROSS STREET GOVERNMENT TAMIL SCHOOL,
SINGAPORE.
Printed at the "Straits Independent" Press.
PENANG.
1889.
FIRST PART.
Copyright Reserved.

A Tamil-English Bilingual Book

Title: *Anglo-Tamil Self Reader: Intended for English and Tamil Students*
Author: S. Moodookrishnia
Year published: 1889
Publisher: Straits Independent Press (Penang)
Language: English and Tamil
Type: Book; 17 pages
Call no.: RRARE 428.3494811 MOO
Accession no.: B01477912I

The early Tamil educational materials used in the Straits Settlements colonies of Singapore, Melaka and Penang consisted primarily of dictionaries and readers on language and grammar. Prior to World War II, Tamil schools in Singapore largely used textbooks that were imported from South India.

Among the first Tamil educational materials that were produced and printed in this region was the *Tamil First Book of Lessons*, written by K.T. Mariathas Pillai and printed in 1887 for the use of pupils in Our Lady of Lourdes Anglo-Tamil School in Singapore.

Nonetheless, one of the oldest Tamil textbooks in the National Library's collection – S. Moodookrishnia's 17-page *Anglo-Tamil Self Reader*, which was published in 1889 – is unique for two reasons.

First, the book was written by a Tamil teacher in Singapore and printed at the Straits Independent Press in Penang. Second, unlike most Tamil textbooks of this period, *Anglo-Tamil Self Reader* was a bilingual book written in Tamil and English, and likely served as a useful learning aid for Tamil students who could learn English independently without the assistance of a teacher. Although the subtitle of the *Anglo-Tamil Self Reader* states that the book was "intended for English and Tamil Students", it is probable that most users of this book were Tamil speakers who wanted to learn English, or to improve their rudimentary skills in the language.

A report published in the *Straits Times Weekly Issue* in August 1889 praised the book as "extremely useful" for Tamils living in the Straits Settlements, while adding at the same time that "Englishmen learning Tamil" would also find the book beneficial.[1]

The *Anglo-Tamil Self Reader* was used by students in the "Government Tamil School, Cross Street" in Singapore, where Moodookrishnia taught.[2] He may have been the school's only Tamil master at the time.[3] Unfortunately, that is all we know about him.

The Tamil school was likely a branch of the Cross Street Government School, of which we know more of: the latter was one of the government all-boys' schools that existed in Singapore during the 19th century.[4] In its early days, classes were conducted by Eurasian and Tamil masters (as teachers were referred to then), with students paying school fees of 15 cents a month. European teachers were subsequently hired, and the monthly school fee was raised to a dollar. The school provided education up to the Fourth Standard, conducting lessons on the basic pronunciation and writing of the English alphabet and numbers in the different vernacular mediums.[5] At a prize-giving ceremony in 1897, the Headmaster of the school, Mr Hellier, praised the teaching of the English language in the school and acknowledged that the students' knowledge of the English language "would give them access to books, and admit of their becoming acquainted with Western ideas."[6]

Moodookrishnia's well-structured reader was said to have been prepared based on "original and simple ideas".[7] It contains sections that illustrate the basic usage of language, vocabulary and grammar. For instance, the first section of the book instructs Tamil-speaking students about the formation and pronunciation of English words using the Tamil language. It also teaches English-speaking students about the formation and pronunciation of Tamil vowels and consonants using the English language. Another section lists Tamil syllables with their English equivalent and vice versa.[8]

The reader illustrates English words written in the cursive script, and includes a brief section on numbers, showing how Roman numerals are expressed in Arabic numerals and Tamil. Simple three-letter English words alongside their Tamil translations are listed too. Written exercises are provided as well, enabling English and Tamil students to apply what they had learnt by constructing simple sentences in English and Tamil.

Given that English was a foreign language that most of the population would have struggled with in 19th-century Singapore, the colonial authorities established schools that facilitated the teaching of English through the vernacular medium. The Government Tamil School, Cross Street was one such institution. To support the growing demand for Tamil interpreters and English-speaking Indian clerks to work in Singapore's flourishing port, two Anglo-Tamil schools were established by the colonial government, in 1873 and 1876 respectively, to teach English through the Tamil medium. Although the schools initially served as "branch English schools" to the Raffles Institution, the Education Department gradually dropped Tamil as a medium of instruction and converted them into preparatory English schools due to increasingly poor enrolment.[9] ♦ **Liviniyah P.**

Notes

1 Local and general. (1889, August 7). *Straits Times Weekly Issue*, p. 2. Retrieved from NewspaperSG.
2 Local and general. (1889, August 7). *Straits Times Weekly Issue*, p. 2. Retrieved from NewspaperSG.
3 Upper Cross Street Government School. (1887, November 14). *Straits Times Weekly Issue*, p. 5. Retrieved from NewspaperSG.
4 Upper Cross Street Government School. (1887, November 14). *Straits Times Weekly Issue*, p. 5. Retrieved from NewspaperSG.
5 The Education Report for 1888. (1889, May 23). *Straits Times Weekly Issue*, p. 6; Upper Cross Street Government School. (1887, November 14). *Straits Times Weekly Issue*, p. 5. Retrieved from NewspaperSG.
6 The government schools. (1897, April 6). *The Singapore Free Press and Mercantile Advertiser (Weekly)*, p. 3. Retrieved from NewspaperSG.
7 Local and general. (1889, August 7). *Straits Times Weekly Issue*, p. 2. Retrieved from NewspaperSG.
8 Moodookrishnia, S. (1889). *The Anglo-Tamil self reader: Intended for English and Tamil students.* Penang: Straits Independent Press. (Call no.: RRARE 428.3494811 MOO)
9 Koh, T., et al. (Eds.). (2006). *Singapore: The Encyclopedia* (p. 533). Singapore: Editions Didier Millet in association with the National Heritage Board. (Call no.: RSING 959.57003 SIN -[HIS])

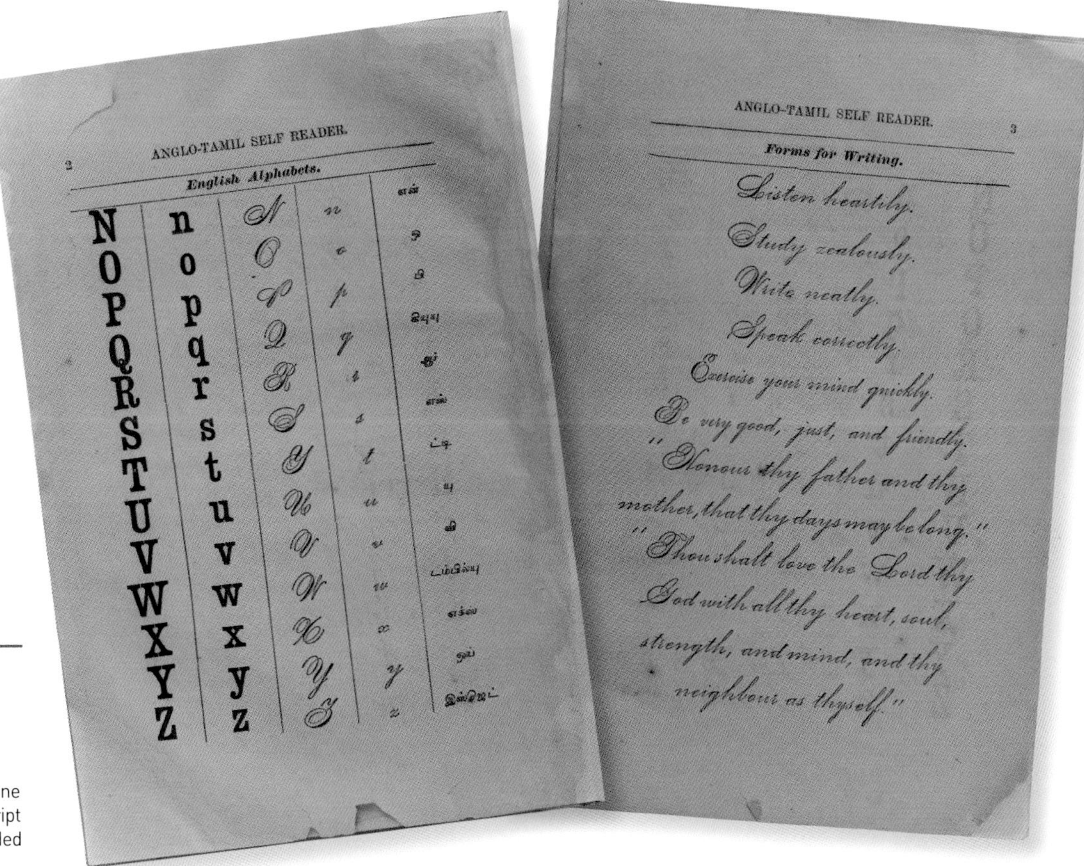
2 ANGLO-TAMIL SELF READER.

English Alphabets.

N n
O o
P p
Q q
R r
S s
T t
U u
V v
W w
X x
Y y
Z z

ANGLO-TAMIL SELF READER. 3

Forms for Writing.

Listen heartily.
Study zealously.
Write neatly.
Speak correctly.
Exercise your mind quickly.
Be very good, just, and friendly.
"Honour thy father and thy mother, that thy days may be long."
"Thou shalt love the Lord thy God with all thy heart, soul, strength, and mind, and thy neighbour as thyself."

[Facing page] Title page of S. Moodookrishnia's *Anglo-Tamil Self Reader*.
[Right] Well-organised lists of English and Tamil alphabets, as well as short exercises such as one for practising cursive English script shown on the far right, are provided in the *Anglo-Tamil Self Reader*.

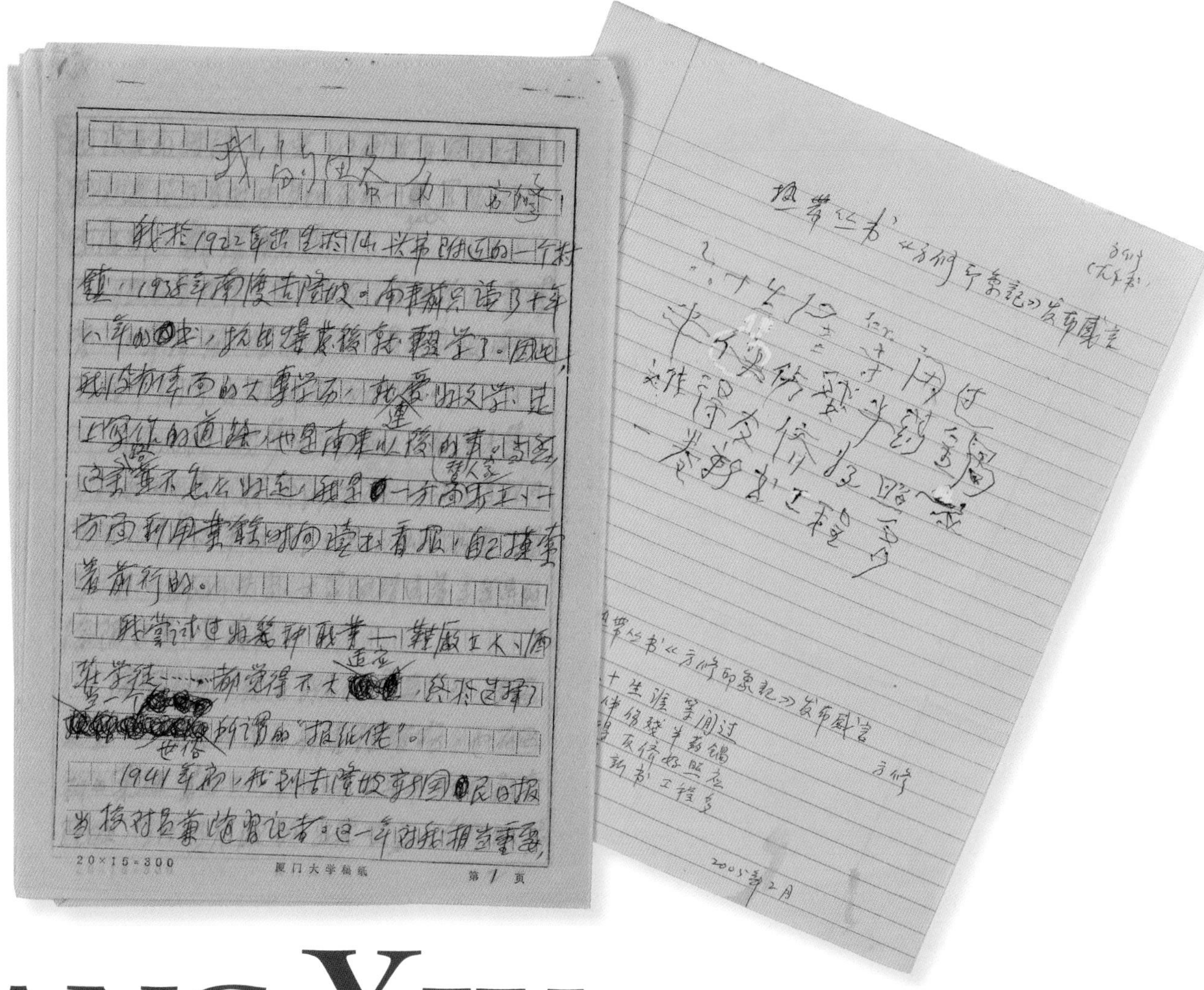

FANG XIU A WRITER'S DEDICATION

Title: 方修作品集 (Works by Fang Xiu)
Author: 方修 (Fang Xiu)
Creation years: 1992–2007
Language: Chinese
Type: Manuscript; 410 pages
Call no.: RRARE Chinese C810.08 FX
Accession no.: B20557684D
Donated by: Tan Suan Poh

(Above left) Fang Xiu's account of his life from his childhood until his retirement in 1978 is captured in this six-page handwritten manuscript titled "我的略历" ("My Life in Brief").
(Above right) Manuscripts dated after 2003 reflect Fang Xiu's attempts to continue writing despite injuries sustained from a fall that affected his right hand. His uneven handwriting in the poem titled "热带丛书《方修印象记》发布感言" ("Words on the Launch of *Impressions of Fang Xiu*"), which he had composed in February 2005 for a book launch, attests to his persistence. The same four lines in a clearer script appear beneath his, likely transcribed by an assistant. The poem was eventually published in a literary magazine and an anthology of his poems titled《重楼诗补》(More Poems from the High Floors).

A revered pioneer of Chinese literature in Singapore, the poet, researcher, editor and writer Goh Tze Kwong (吴之光) – better known by one of his pseudonyms, Fang Xiu (方修) – once said that he was constantly bothered by the thought of having unfinished tasks and hoped that he would be able to finish what he had set out to do.[1] Fang Xiu's dedication to his literary and academic pursuits is evident in a set of manuscripts donated to the National Library in 2008.

Comprising 410 pages of work written or edited by Fang Xiu when he was in his 70s and 80s, the manuscripts include drafts of his poems and non-fiction prose (散文), essays on the history of Chinese literature in Singapore and Malaya, as well as prefaces and postfaces – most of which have been published. Two documents in particular shed light on Fang Xiu's reflections on some of the major turning points in his life and how these had a bearing on his creative development.

The first is a six-page autobiographical manuscript titled "我的略历" ("My Life in Brief"), which might not have been published in its entirety. Drafted by Fang Xiu in April 1992 and rewritten in June 2000, it offers a succinct summary of his life, his childhood as well as his career as a journalist, writer and researcher.[2]

The manuscript begins with a short description of his early life and education, when Fang Xiu received several years of education in China before moving to Malaya in 1938. He added that he did not have a university degree, and only started to write and appreciate Chinese literature upon his arrival in Malaya. Fang Xiu also acknowledged that it had not been easy for him to pursue literary interests and research as he had to use his spare time outside of work to read and improve himself.[3]

In the same manuscript, Fang Xiu highlighted that working for the newspaper *Sin Kok Min Jit Poh* (新国民日报) in Kuala Lumpur in 1941 was an important period in his life. He was able to spend more time reading and started sending his works for publication. He also met several writers – such as Li Yunlang (李蕴郎), who were based in Kuala Lumpur or nearby cities. He recalled his time in Singapore joining the 文化青年训练班 (Cultured Youth Training Squad) before the Japanese Occupation, participating in activities run by the reading club 求知社 (Society for Seeking Knowledge) and meeting other fellow writers after the war.

Although Fang Xiu taught at various primary schools in Johor, the Riau Islands and Singapore from the end of 1946 to 1951,[4] he wrote that his interests did not lie in teaching, hence he joined *Sin Chew Jit Poh* (星洲日报) in Singapore in 1951. The almost three decades spent working for the press was a relatively stable period in his life which enabled him to indulge in his passion for research and writing.

The manuscript ends with Fang Xiu's humble confession that a majority of his publications could have been better written. He did, however, identify examples of what he thought were good attempts, such as his books on the history of Chinese literature in Singapore and Malaya, and his compilations on Chinese literary works in Malaya.

In 2003, at the age of 81, Fang Xiu had a fall which affected his mobility and the use of his right hand.[5] He had difficulty writing after this. A draft of his poem titled "热带丛书《方修印象记》发布感言" ("Words on the Launch of *Impressions of Fang Xiu*") attests to this. Dated February 2005, the four-line verse reads:

六十生涯等闲过
半伴伤残半药锅
难得友侪好照应
一卷新书工程多

(Clockwise from top left) Fang Xiu with his colleagues from *Sin Chew Jit Poh* in 1968. Fang Xiu worked for the newspaper from 1951 until his retirement in 1978; Fang Xiu autographing books at the launch on 24 June 2000 of his two-volume compilation on Chinese novels published in post-war Singapore; Photo of Fang Xiu (second from right) taken on 24 June 2000 at the launch.

Fang Xiu: A Literary Giant

Born Goh Tze Kwong (吴之光; 1922–2010) in Chao'an, Guangdong province in China, Fang Xiu (方修) has written non-fiction prose, poems, literary criticism and scholarly works. In his lifetime, he penned and edited more than 100 publications, including his seminal study on the development of Chinese modern literature in Malaya.[6]

In 1938, at age 16, Fang Xiu moved to Malaya with his mother. He worked in a factory then for a trading business. His career in the press began in 1941 when he was employed as a proofreader and later a trainee journalist at the *Sin Kok Min Jit Poh* (新国民日报) newspaper in Kuala Lumpur.

When the Japanese army invaded Malaya in December 1941, Fang Xiu fled to Singapore with his colleagues from *Sin Kok Min Jit Poh*. Shortly after, he joined 文化青年训练班 (Cultured Youth Training Squad) to make a living and contribute to anti-Japanese efforts during the war. The squad disbanded shortly before the fall of Singapore in February 1942, and Fang Xiu returned to Kuala Lumpur in around June or July that year when railway services resumed.

A photo of Fang Xiu taken in his study room.

When World War II ended, Fang Xiu worked for two newspapers – first with *Min Sheng Pau* (民声报) then with *Chung Wah Evening Post* (中华晚报). He returned to Singapore when the latter closed down in mid-1946.

Fang Xiu then worked as a primary school teacher in Johor, the Riau Islands and Singapore for a number of years, before joining *Sin Chew Jit Poh* (星洲日报) in early 1951. Later that year, he became the editor of the magazine, *Sin Chew Weekly* (星洲周刊).

The 1950s also marked the time when Fang Xiu began researching and compiling materials on Chinese literature in Malaya. Key publications he published include the reference work 《马华新文学大系》(A Comprehensive Anthology of Modern Chinese Literature in Malaya), which was first printed from 1970 to 1972 and covered literary works published between 1919 and 1942.[7] He also published its companion, 《马华新文学大系：战后》(A Comprehensive Anthology of Modern Chinese Literature in Malaya: Postwar), which featured works published from 1945 to 1969.

While working as a full-time editor at *Sin Chew Jit Poh*, Fang Xiu was appointed an adjunct lecturer in the Chinese department at the University of Singapore, a position he held from 1966 to 1978. He taught modern Chinese literature in Malaya, Singapore and China.

Upon his retirement from *Sin Chew Jit Poh* in 1978, Fang Xiu continued to be active in the literary scene in Singapore. He became chief editor of the bimonthly literary magazine, *Native Soil* (乡土), in 1980. Subsequently in 1997, he founded the Tropical Literature & Art Club, a Chinese literary group where he served as a consultant for many years.

In recognition of Fang Xiu's contributions to the literary arts in Singapore, the Confucius Institute at Nanyang Technological University presented him with the inaugural Nanyang Chinese Literature Award in 2008.[9] Fang Xiu donated the prize money of S$40,000 to establish a literary award, which was eventually named after him as a tribute.[10]

The first two lines reveal Fang Xiu's frustration as it was a struggle for him to write, and he felt that the past 60 years of his creative life had come to nought. The last two lines, however, express his gratitude to friends who had worked hard to produce a book about him titled《方修印象集》(Impressions of Fang Xiu). Although the poem was composed specially for the book launch, it was subsequently published in a literary magazine and an anthology of his poetry titled《重楼诗补》 (More Poems from the High Floors).

Undeterred by his handicap, a determined Fang Xiu continued to write by learning to write with his left hand. He also made audio recordings of what he intended to write, and had these transcribed and edited by his close friend, Tan Suan Poh (陈川波), who was also a writer.[8] Oftentimes, an assistant added contextual details such as the date, or rewrote the poems in a more legible script.[11]

Fang Xiu passed away in Singapore on 4 March 2010. His collection of manuscripts not only sheds light on the development of Chinese literature in Singapore and Malaya, but also reflects his lifelong dedication to research and writing. ♦ **Goh Yu Mei**

Notes

1 In Fang Xiu's words, "我一直觉得东西没做完，事情还没完满，心里很不满意，一直希望能把还没做完的工作补充完."张曦娜 [Zhang, X. N.]. (2005, January 13). 方修心愿：把还没做完的补充完. [Fang Xiu's wish: To complete the incomplete.]. 联合早报, p. 37. Retrieved from NewspaperSG.

2 In comparison, Fang Xiu had published a more detailed interview of his life in the book《文学・报刊・生活》(*Literature, Newspapers, Life*) in 1988. Transcribed and compiled by Lin Zhen (林臻) from Fang Xiu's recording of his literary activities, involvement in newspaper publishing and other activities, the book includes details such as Fang Xiu's ties to other writers and descriptions of activities he was involved in – such details were not mentioned in the six-page manuscript.

3 His original lines read "因此，我没有体面的大专学历，就连爱好文学，走上写作的道路，也是南来以后的事。当然，这条路并不怎么好走，我是一方面替人家打工、一方面利用业余的时间读书看报，自己摸索着前行的。"

4 Except for a brief period in the latter half of 1949 when he was involved in the setting up of two tabloids. In 1950, while holding a teaching position, he edited two magazines published by a friend.

5 Zhang, 2005, January 13.

6 方修获奖评述 南洋理工大学孔子学院基金 南洋华文文学奖 2008. (2009). In《方修选集》（上册）(p. xiii). 新加坡：八方文化创作室. (Call no.: RSING Chinese C810.08 FX); 方修生平简介 [Brief biography of Fang Xiu]. (2010). In 热带文学俱乐部编 [Tropical Literature & Art Club (Ed.)]. 《纪念方修》(not paginated). 新加坡：热带文学俱乐部. (Call no.: RSING Chinese C810.092 JNF)

7 方修获奖评述 南洋理工大学孔子学院基金 南洋华文文学奖 2008. (2009). In《方修选集》（上册）(p. xiii). 新加坡：八方文化创作室. (Call no.: RSING Chinese C810.08 FX)

8 Tan Suan Poh wrote under the pen name Chang He (长河). 张曦娜 [Zhang, X. N.]. (2008, March 7). 国家图书馆 热带文学艺术俱乐部 青年书局 文学盛会 向文学史家方修敬礼 [National Library, Tropical Literature & Art Club and Youth Book Company jointly present a literary extravaganza and pay tribute to Fang Xiu, a historian of Chinese literature in Singapore]. 联合早报, p. 32. Retrieved from NewspaperSG.

9 方修获奖评述 南洋理工大学孔子学院基金 南洋华文文学奖 2008. (2009). In《方修选集》（上册）(pp. xiii–xiv). 新加坡：八方文化创作室. (Call no.: RSING Chinese C810.08 FX)

10 关于方修文学奖缘起 [On the establishment of the Fang Xiu Literary Award]. (2015). In《首届方修文学奖 2008 – 2010 获奖作品集 文学评论卷》[Collection of winning entries for inaugural Fang Xiu Literary Award: Literary criticism]. (p. viii). 新加坡：八方文化创作室. (Call no.: RSING Chinese C810.08 SJF); Suryadinata, L. (Ed.). (2012). *Southeast Asian personalities of Chinese descent: A biographical dictionary* (p. 262). Singapore: Institute of Southeast Asian Studies. (Call no.: RSING 959.004951 SOU)

11 长河 [Chang He]. (2010). 记方老最后八年著述与未了心愿. [On Fang Xiu's works writing in the last eight years of his life and his unfulfilled wishes]. In 热带文学俱乐部编 [Tropical Literature & Art Club (Ed.)].《纪念方修》(p. 65). 新加坡：热带文学俱乐部. (Call no.: RSING Chinese C810.092 JNF)

Papers from the Past

The Lee Kip Lee and Lee Kip Lin Archives

Title: Messrs Lee Kip Lee and Lee Kip Lin Family Archives
Year: c. 1890s–1980s
Type: Ephemera
Call no.: RRARE 338.092 LEE
Accession nos.: B32410073I; B32409648C; B32409652I; B32409591K; B32410074J; B32409653J; B32409652I
Donated by: Messrs Lee Kip Lee and Lee Kip Lin Family Archives

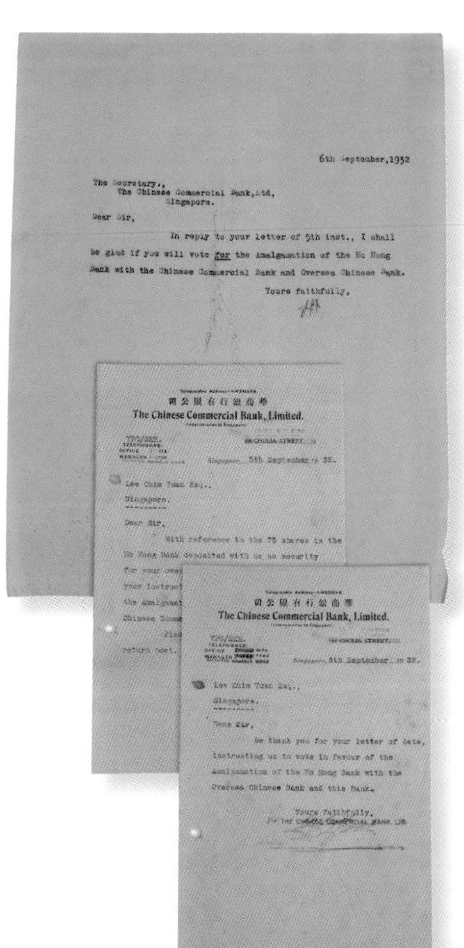

6th September,1932

The Secretary.,
The Chinese Commercial Bank,Ltd,
Singapore.

Dear Sir,

In reply to your letter of 5th inst., I shall be glad if you will vote <u>for</u> the Amalgamation of the Ho Hong Bank with the Chinese Commercial Bank and Oversea Chinese Bank.

Yours faithfully,

華商銀行有限公司
The Chinese Commercial Bank, Limited.

Singapore, 5th September 19 32.

Lee Chim Tuan Esq.,
Singapore.

Dear Sir,

With reference to the 75 shares in the Ho Hong Bank deposited with us as security ...

華商銀行有限公司
The Chinese Commercial Bank, Limited.

TPG/SKH.

Singapore, 5th September 19 32.

Lee Chim Tuan Esq.,
Singapore.

Dear Sir,

We thank you for your letter of date, instructing us to vote in favour of the Amalgamation of the Ho Hong Bank with the Oversea Chinese Bank and this Bank.

Yours faithfully,
For THE CHINESE COMMERCIAL BANK LTD

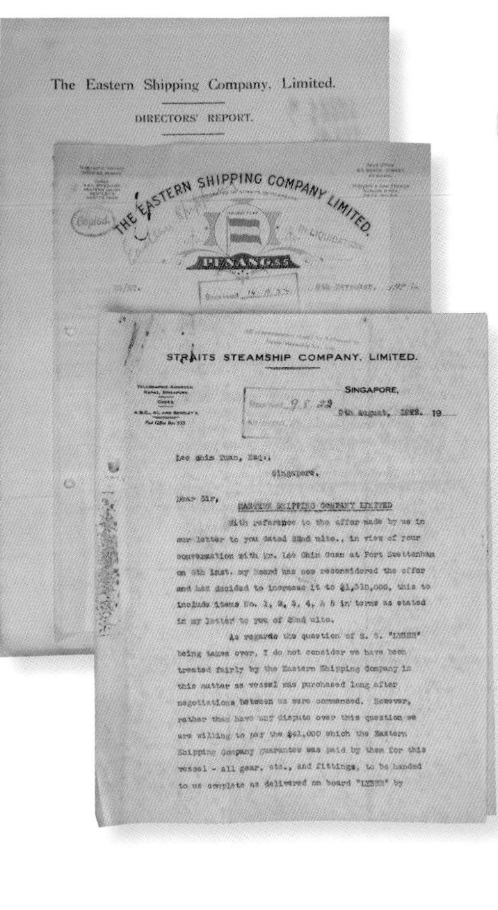

The Eastern Shipping Company, Limited.

DIRECTORS' REPORT.

THE EASTERN SHIPPING COMPANY LIMITED
PENANG S.S.

STRAITS STEAMSHIP COMPANY, LIMITED.

SINGAPORE,
9th August, 1922. 19

Lee Chim Tuan, Esq.,
Singapore.

Dear Sir,

<u>EASTERN SHIPPING COMPANY LIMITED</u>

With reference to the offer made by us in our letter to you dated 22nd ulto., in view of your conversation with Mr. Lee Chin Guan at Port Swettenham on 6th inst. my Board has now reconsidered the offer and has decided to increase it to $1,310,000, this to include items No. 1, 2, 3, 4, & 5 in terms as stated in my letter to you of 22nd ulto.

As regards the question of S. S. "LESER" being taken over, I do not consider we have been treated fairly by the Eastern Shipping Company in this matter as vessel was purchased long after negotiations between us were commenced. However, rather than have any dispute over this question we are willing to pay the $41,000 which the Eastern Shipping Company guarantee was paid by them for this vessel - all gear, etc., and fittings, to be handed to us complete as delivered on board "LESER" by

Correspondence pertaining to key corporate deals involving Lee Chim Tuan. **[Above left]** Three letters dated 5 and 6 September 1932 attest to a critical juncture in the history of banking in Singapore: the amalgamation of the three Hokkien banks – Chinese Commercial Bank, Ho Hong Bank and Oversea-Chinese Bank – to form the Oversea-Chinese Banking Corporation in 1932. **[Above right]** Letters regarding the acquisition of Eastern Steamship Company by the Straits Steamship Company in 1922.

Comprising over 6,000 business and personal papers belonging to a prominent Peranakan family in Singapore, the Lee Kip Lee and Lee Kip Lin Family Archives offers invaluable insights into the economic, social and cultural worlds the Lee family inhabited between the 1890s and 1980s. Among the collection are letters, company reports, meeting minutes, business and household ledgers, remittance slips, receipts, invitation cards and postcards that bear testimony to the family's extensive business and social networks.

The Lee family hail from a distinguished Peranakan family whose roots in the region stretch back to 1776. In 2016, the family of two Lee brothers, Lee Kip Lee and Lee Kip Lin, donated the collection to the National Library. Kip Lee (1922–2018), a successful businessman who ran a stevedoring company, had served as president of the Peranakan Association from 1996 to 2010. His younger brother, Kip Lin (1925–2011), was an architect, professor and author. The family sank their roots in Singapore in the 19th century when their grandfather, Lee Keng Kiat (1851–1917), moved here from Melaka. Keng Kiat, who was in the shipping business, had nine children. His fifth son was Lee Chim Huk (1889–1958), Kip Lee and Kip Lin's father.

Among his siblings, Chim Huk was closest to his elder brother, Lee Chim Tuan (1880–1955). Their brotherly bonds were so tight that they pooled their financial resources into a common kitty, which they called the "Tuan-Huk" accounts.[1] Both of them worked in the trading firm Lee Cheng Yan & Co., which was owned by their father's cousin Lee Choon Guan (1868–1924). Chim Tuan, the general manager of the company, was widely known as Choon Guan's "right-hand man". Most of the documents in the collection belong to Lee Chim Tuan and Lee Chim Huk, as well as extended family members such as Lee Choon Guan.

Choon Guan was an astute businessman. He owned Lee Cheng Yan & Co. in addition to being a director of the Straits Steamship Company (SSC).[2] In its early years, the SSC focused its operations on the western coast of the Malay Peninsula and mainly transported tin ore. Noteworthy correspondence regarding the SSC's acquisition of Penang-based Eastern Shipping Company in 1922 is one of the highlights of the collection. Sensing a business opportunity as the Eastern Shipping Company was struggling to maintain its fleet, the SSC negotiated a takeover. A letter dated 9 August 1922 documents the SSC's agreement to increase its offer price to $1.3 million, thus sealing the deal. Chim Tuan, who negotiated the transaction, was paid a handsome commission for his effort.

Another highlight is Chim Tuan's papers pertaining to an important milestone in Singapore's banking history – the formation of Oversea-Chinese Banking Corporation (OCBC) in 1932. OCBC was established through the amalgamation of three major banks belonging to the Hokkien clan in Singapore: Chinese Commercial Bank, Ho Hong Bank and Oversea Chinese Bank.[3] In a short note addressed to the secretary of the Chinese Commercial Bank on 6 September 1932, Chim Tuan, who owned some shares in this bank, said that he was voting in favour of the merger. The amalgamation scheme was eventually passed by the shareholders of all three banks.[4]

Choon Guan passed away in 1924 before OCBC was formed, but his contribution to its birth deserves mention. He had a hand in two of the three banks that became the OCBC: in 1912, Choon Guan co-founded the Chinese Commercial Bank together with the Straits Chinese luminary Dr Lim Boon Keng and a few other Chinese merchants, and in 1917, he was one of the founding directors of Ho Hong Bank.

DINNER
IN HONOUR OF
HIS EXCELLENCY
SIR LAURENCE NUNNS GUILLEMARD K.C.B.
AND
LADY GUILLEMARD
GIVEN
BY THE
CHINESE COMMUNITY
AT THE
GARDEN CLUB.
SINGAPORE 18TH MARCH 1920.

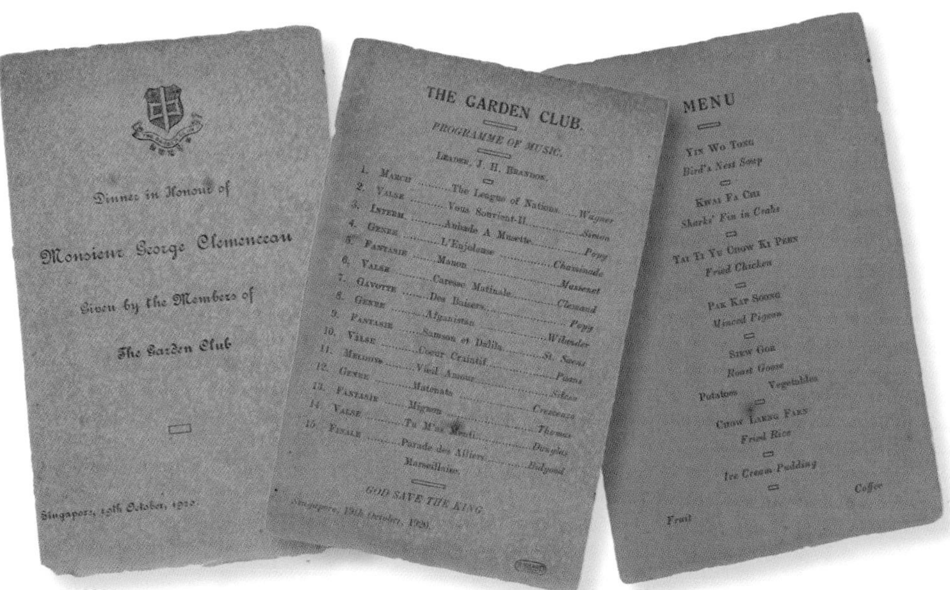

Dinner in Honour of
Monsieur George Clemenceau
Given by the Members of
The Garden Club

Singapore, 19th October, 1920.

THE GARDEN CLUB.
PROGRAMME OF MUSIC.
Leader, J. H. Brandon.

1. March ....The League of Nations ....Wagner
2. Valse ....Vous Souvient-Il ....Simon
3. Interm. ....Aubade A Musette ....Popy
4. Genre ....L'Enjoleuse ....Chaminade
5. Fantasie ....Manon ....Massenet
6. Valse ....Caresse Matinale ....Clemand
7. Gavotte ....Des Baisers ....Popy
8. Genre ....Afganistan ....Wilander
9. Fantasie ....Samson et Dalila ....St. Saens
10. Valse ....Coeur Craintif ....Pians
11. Melodie ....Vieil Amour ....Siléso
12. Genre ....Matenata ....Crescenzo
13. Fantasie ....Mignon ....Thomas
14. Valse ....Tu M'as Menti ....Douglas
15. Finale ....Parade des Alliers ....Bidgood
Marseillaise.

GOD SAVE THE KING

Singapore, 19th October, 1920.

MENU

Yin Wo Tong
Bird's Nest Soup

Kwai Fa Chi
Sharks' Fin in Crabs

Tai Ti Yu Chow Ki Peen
Fried Chicken

Pak Kap Soong
Minced Pigeon

Siew Gor
Roast Goose
Potatoes Vegetables

Chow Leang Fang
Fried Rice

Ice Cream Pudding

Coffee

Fruit

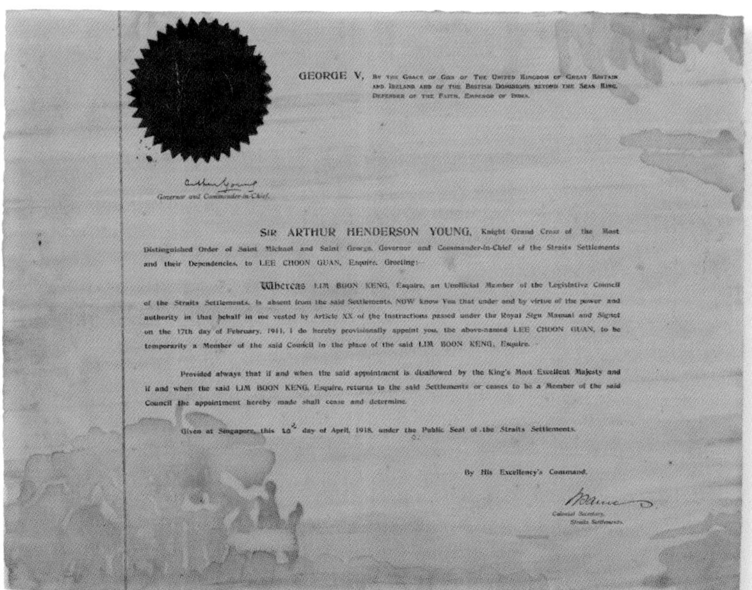

GEORGE V, By the Grace of God of The United Kingdom of Great Britain and Ireland and of the British Dominions beyond the Seas King, Defender of the Faith, Emperor of India.

Arthur Young
Governor and Commander-in-Chief.

SIR ARTHUR HENDERSON YOUNG, Knight Grand Cross of the Most Distinguished Order of Saint Michael and Saint George, Governor and Commander-in-Chief of the Straits Settlements and their Dependencies, to LEE CHOON GUAN, Esquire, Greeting:—

Whereas LIM BOON KENG, Esquire, an Unofficial Member of the Legislative Council of the Straits Settlements, is absent from the said Settlements, NOW know You that under and by virtue of the power and authority in that behalf in me vested by Article XX of the Instructions passed under the Royal Sign Manual and Signet on the 17th day of February, 1911, I do hereby provisionally appoint you, the above-named LEE CHOON GUAN, to be temporarily a Member of the said Council in the place of the said LIM BOON KENG, Esquire.

Provided always that if and when the said appointment is disallowed by the King's Most Excellent Majesty and if and when the said LIM BOON KENG, Esquire, returns to the said Settlements or ceases to be a Member of the said Council the appointment hereby made shall cease and determine.

Given at Singapore, this 20th day of April, 1918, under the Public Seal of the Straits Settlements.

By His Excellency's Command.

Colonial Secretary,
Straits Settlements.

[Clockwise from top left] The extent of Lee Choon Guan's social capital and his varied contributions to the public service are illustrated in documents such as: an invitation to a dinner party on 18 March 1920, which was organised by the Chinese community for the newly appointed Governor of the Straits Settlements Laurence Nunns Guillemard; another invitation to a dinner held on 19 October 1920 in honour of Georges Clemenceau, then Prime Minister of France; and a certificate from Sir Arthur Henderson Young appointing Choon Guan an unofficial member of the Legislative Council of the Straits Settlements on 20 April 1918.

Numerous letters and invitation cards in the collection bear testimony to Choon Guan's life as an illustrious businessman and philanthropist who enjoyed ties with prominent Straits Chinese merchants, Europeans and Malay royalty. A letter written in Jawi dated 2 Rajab 1330 (17 June 1912) for

[Top] Mr and Mrs Lee Choon Guan (she is dressed in a *qun-ao* [裙袄] and standing next to her husband in a Western-style suit) in a photograph taken in the 1920s. Lee Chim Tuan, who was the trusted aide of Lee Choon Guan (his father's cousin and a director of the Straits Steamship Company) is standing at the extreme left wearing a hat. *Courtesy of Peter Lee.*
[Above] Lee Chim Huk, father of Lee Kip Lee and Lee Kip Lin, striking a pose with his brother Lee Chim Tuan (standing) and a niece, in the vicinity of Amoy Street, where they grew up, c. 1900. *Courtesy of Peter Lee.*

instance, tells us that the Sultan of Kelantan Muhammad IV informed Choon Guan of his impending visit to Singapore and asked for a meeting.[5] The sultan arrived in Singapore on 8 July 1912 for a 20-day visit. Choon Guan maintained such good relations with the sultan that when the latter visited Singapore again in 1914, he was hosted at Magenta Cottage, Choon Guan's villa at the corner of Killiney and River Valley roads.[6]

Certificates and letters in the collection highlight Choon Guan's active participation in public service, such as his appointment to the Committee of Food Control during World War I, and his role in Tan Tock Seng Hospital's Committee of Management.[7] The colonial government had such high regard for Choon Guan that he was also invited to serve in official bodies. A certificate from Sir Arthur Henderson Young indicates that Choon Guan was made an unofficial member of the Legislative Council of the Straits Settlements on 20 April 1918. Choon Guan was appointed as an acting member to fill the position temporarily vacated by Dr Lim Boon Keng. Choon Guan became an unofficial member of the Legislative Council again in 1922, a role he served until 1924.[8]

The Lee Kip Lee and Lee Kip Lin Family Archives is a treasure trove for research on the Chinese Peranakan community and early 20th-century Singapore. Not only does it shed light on the Lee family's businesses and social networks, other aspects of the collection – too varied in scope and subject matter to examine within the confines of this essay – provide insights into important periods in Singapore's history, such as the conditions and deprivation they experienced during World War II. Additionally, the glimpses it offers on important Chinese leaders in Singapore and Malaya, such as Tan Cheng Lock, make the collection all the more valuable as a historical resource.

♦ **Ong Eng Chuan**

Notes

1 Death. (1955, May 3). *Singapore Standard*, p. 13; Durai, J. (2011, July 15). Architect Lee Kip Lin dies. *The Straits Times*. Retrieved from NewspaperSG; Lee, K. L. (1999). *Amber sands: A boyhood memoir*. (p. x). Singapore: Federal Publications. (Call no.: RSING 920.71 LEE); Lim, M. (1998, October–December). Lee Kip Lee – 76 golden years. *The Peranakan*, 4–5. Retrieved from The Peranakan Association website; National Heritage Board. (2013). *Tiong Bahru Heritage* Trail. Retrieved from National Heritage Board website; New man at the helm: Lee Kip Lee elected as new President. (1996, June). *The Peranakan*, 1–2. Retrieved from The Peranakan Association website; Old Singapore resident dies. (1958, April 15). *Singapore Standard*. Retrieved from NewspaperSG; Tan, T. (2019, January 5). Peranakan Association's ex-chief Lee Kip Lee dies at 96. *The Straits Times*. Retrieved from Factiva.

2 Choon Guan's father, Lee Cheng Yan (1841–1911), was a Malacca-born businessman who started Lee Cheng Yan & Co. in 1858, and served as a director of the Straits Steamship Company. When he passed away, Choon Guan took over and expanded the family business. Death of Mr. Lee Choon Guan. (1924, August 28). *The Straits Times*, p. 9. Retrieved from NewspaperSG; Dossett, J. W. (1918). *Who's who in Malaya*, 1918. (pp. x, 76). Singapore: Printed for Dossett & Co. by Methodist Pub. House. (Microfilm no.: NL5829); Wright, A., & Cartwright, H. A. (Eds.). (1908). *Twentieth century impressions of British Malaya: Its history, people, commerce, industries, and resources* (pp. 633, 636). London: Lloyd's Greater Britain Publishing Company, Limited. (Call no.: RCLOS 959.51033 TWE)

3 Yong, C. F. (1992). *Chinese leadership and power in colonial Singapore* (p. 71). Singapore: Times Academic Press. (Call no.: RSING 959.5702 YON)

4 Chinese Commercial Bank. (1932, September 15). *The Straits Times*, p. 9. Retrieved from NewspaperSG.

5 The letter had been translated in English for Lee. See Asian Civilisations Museum. (2015). *Great Peranakans: Fifty remarkable lives* (p. 131). Singapore: Asian Civilisations Museum. (Call no.: RSING 305.895105957 GRE)

6 The Sultan of Kelantan. (1914, April 28). *Malaya Tribune*. Retrieved from NewspaperSG.

7 Annual report of Tan Tock Seng's Hospital, for the year 1913. (1914, April 11). *Malaya Tribune*, p. 4. Retrieved from NewspaperSG.

8 Death of Mr. Lee Choon Guan. (1924, August 28). *The Straits Times*, p. 9. Retrieved from NewspaperSG.

A FOOTBALL RULEBOOK IN JAWI

Title: *Inilah Risalat Peraturan Bola Sepak yang Dinamai oleh Inggeris Football* (A Book of Football Rules)
Author: Mahmud ibn Almarhum Sayyid Abdul Kadir al-Hindi (translator)
Year published: 1895
Publisher: Lembaga Keadilan (Committee) Persekutuan Dar al-Adab
Language: Malay (Jawi script)
Type: Booklet, 16 pages with a fold-out plan of a football field

[Top] At the bottom of the cover page of *Risalat Peraturan Bola Sepak*, it is indicated that the booklet is registered under chapter five of the Book Register Ordinance 1886.

Although it is not clear exactly when the football-loving British introduced the game to Malaya, it became so popular among Malay youths here that a guide to the sport was published by the Ethical Committee of the Dar al-Adab Association[1] in 1895. Printed by the American Mission Press in Singapore, *Inilah Risalat Peraturan Bola Sepak yang Dinamai oleh Inggeris Football* (henceforth referred to as *Risalat Peraturan Bola Sepak*) covers the rules of the game over 17 topics (or *bab*) in Jawi – the Arabic script adapted for writing the Malay language.

The title, author, publisher and printer of the booklet are stated on the front cover. Inside the 16-page booklet is a fold-out plan of a football field with the positions of the players indicated in Jawi. Below the diagram of the field, Jawi references to player positions are accompanied by their English equivalents.

With the exception of the fold-out plan and a glossary of terms where the corresponding English explanations such as "offside" and "free kick" appear next to the Jawi phrases, everything else in *Risalat Peraturan Bola Sepak* is written in Jawi script.

It is not known which English source (or sources) the writer, Mahmud ibn Almarhum Sayyid Abdul Kadir al-Hindi, used as a reference to produce this book of football rules. In the foreword, Mahmud writes that arguments and disputes on the playing field became commonplace as more Malays took to the game. Seeing the need to explain the basic rules of football to new enthusiasts, the Dar al-Adab Association commissioned him to write the book.

Although Mahmud was well versed in Malay linguistics – between 1881 and 1918, he was involved as the author or translator of 16 Malay works, including a Malay dictionary (*Kamus Mahmudiyyah*) – he admitted in the foreword that the task of translating football rules from English to Malay was challenging.

To make the text clearer for his readers, he used basic English terms that the Malay players were already familiar with, such as "goal", "corner" and "free kick". Even so, Mahmud was dissatisfied with his attempt, and in his foreword, expressed hopes of producing a more detailed book on football rules in future. However, to date, no other football-related book authored by Mahmud has ever been found.

Another key person involved in the publication of *Risalat Peraturan Bola Sepak* was Haji Muhammad Siraj bin Haji Salih. He was an accomplished copyist-editor, a prolific printer and the biggest bookseller of Muslim publications in Singapore in the late 19th century. As the Honorary Secretary of Dar al-Adab, Haji Muhammad Siraj was instrumental in engaging the services of the American Mission Press to print Mahmud's work.[2] Copies of the booklet were sold at Haji Muhammad Siraj's shop at 43 Sultan Road.[3] When he passed away in 1909, *The Straits Times* described him as "one of the best known of the Malays of Singapore".[4]

Dar al-Adab, the publisher of *Risalat Peraturan Bola Sepak*, was one of the earliest Malay/Muslim recreation clubs in Singapore. The club was established in 1893 and had its own grounds in Jalan Besar, where it held sports events that were well-attended by locals and Europeans.[5] Dar al-Adab likely had a vested interest in commissioning the book of football rules as it was the organiser of the annual football competition, the Darul Adab Cup. Several recreation clubs and local football teams competed for this trophy.[6]

Interestingly, the British regarded football as a tool to civilise the ignorant "natives" living in its colonies.[7] A 1894 report in *The Singapore Free Press and Mercantile Advertiser* noted in rather grandiose terms:

> "All these native races have readily taken to various forms of athletic sport, and the sight of men of every race, colour and creed assembled together on the cricket or football field, afford striking evidence of the good results attending British protection, whilst the mere assembly for a common purpose by teaching men of different races to know and respect one another exercises a by no means unimportant influence on their general civilisation".[8]

It is debatable whether football had any civilising effect on the "men of different races" in Singapore. What is more certain is that *Risalat Peraturan Bola Sepak* was helpful in teaching Malay youths the basic rules of the game.[9] More than a century after its publication, the sport remains hugely popular, not just among Malays in Singapore, but among all communities. ♦ **Mazelan Anuar**

Notes

1 Also spelled "Daral Adab" and "Darul Adab".
2 Proudfoot, I. (1993). *Early Malay printed books: A provisional account of materials published in the Singapore-Malaysia area up to 1920, noting holdings in major public collections* (p. 41). Kuala Lumpur: Academy of Malay Studies and the Library, University of Malaya. (Call no.: RSING 015.5957 PRO-[LIB])
3 Proudfoot, I. A Nineteenth-century Malay bookseller's catalogue (pp. 6, 8). *Kekal Abadi, 6*(4), December 1987. Retrieved from Malay Concordance Project website.
4 Social and Personal. (1909, October 29). *The Straits Times*, p. 6. Retrieved from NewspaperSG.
5 Darul Adab Athletic Sports. (1900, June 21). *The Singapore Free Press and Mercantile Advertiser*, p. 9. Retrieved from NewspaperSG.
6 The Darul Adab Cup. (1900, October 8). *The Straits Times*, p. 15. Retrieved from NewspaperSG.
7 Cho, Y. & Little, C. (Ed.). (2015). *Football in Asia: History, culture and business* (p. 19). Abingdon, Oxon: Routledge. (Call no.: RSEA 796.334095 FOO)
8 Selangor in 1894. (1895, July 15). *The Singapore Free Press and Mercantile Advertiser* (p. 3). Retrieved from NewspaperSG.
9 Cho & Little, 2015, p. 19.

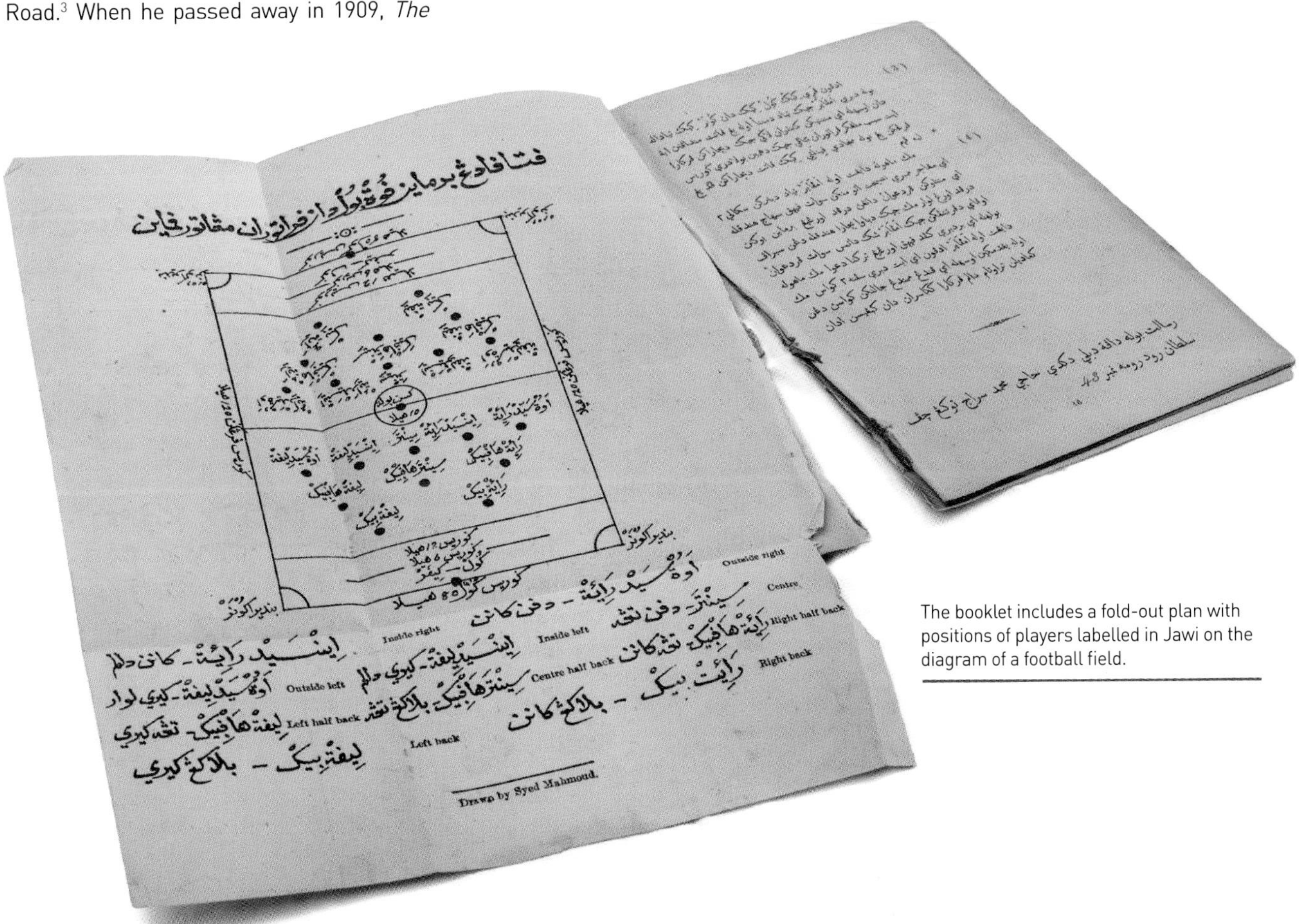

The booklet includes a fold-out plan with positions of players labelled in Jawi on the diagram of a football field.

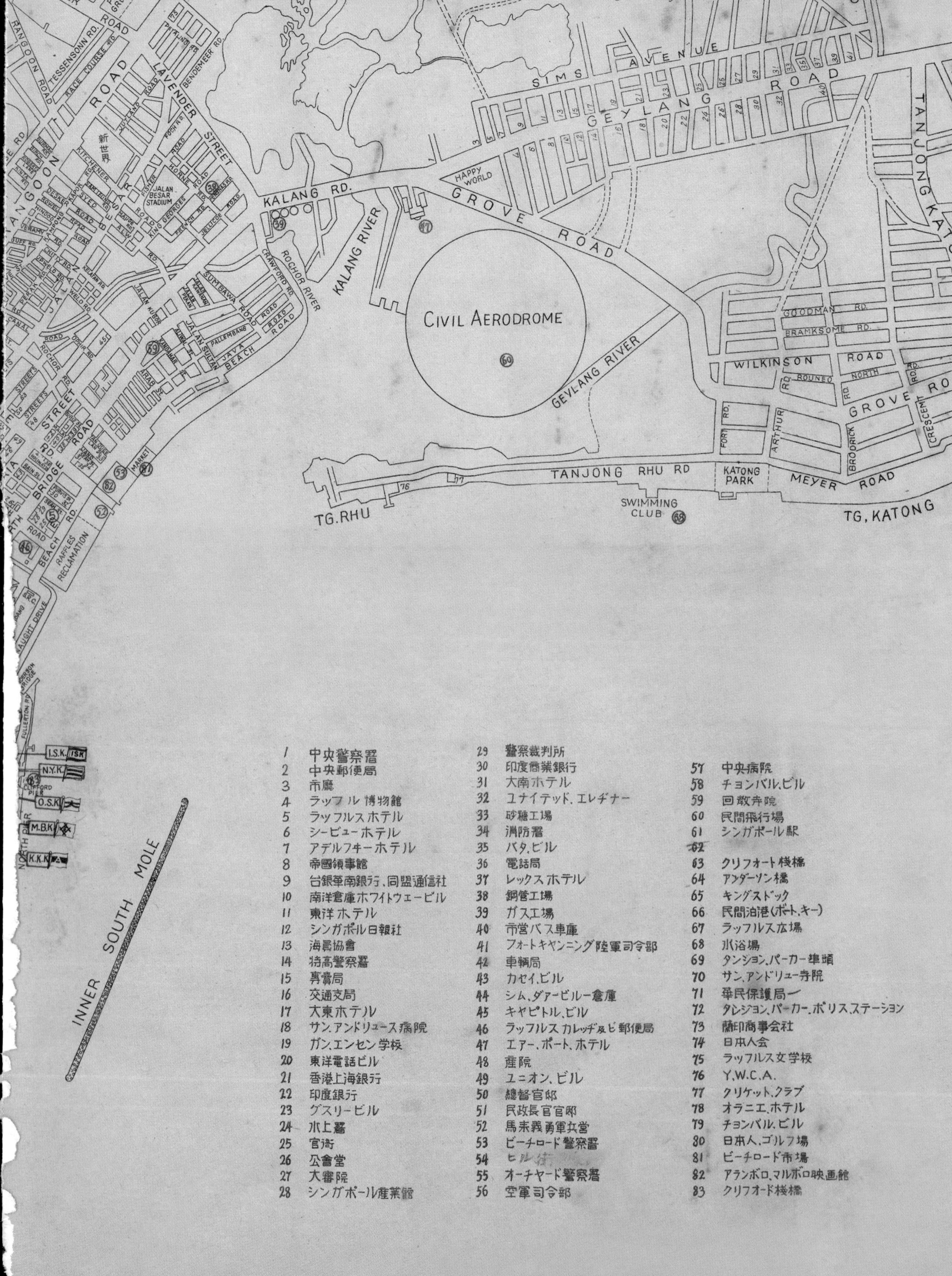

SIMS AVENUE
GEYLANG ROAD
TANJONG KATONG ROAD
HAIG ROAD
KALANG RD.
GROVE ROAD
HAPPY WORLD
KALANG RIVER
CIVIL AERODROME
GEYLANG RIVER
ROCHOR RIVER
CRAWFORD RD.
JALAN BESAR STADIUM
LAVENDER STREET
BENDEMEER RD.
RANGOON ROAD
TESSENSONN RD.
RACE COURSE RD.
KITCHENER
KING GEORGES
JELLICOE ROAD
SUMBAWA ROAD
JALAN SULTAN
JAVA
BEACH ROAD
MARKET
RAFFLES RECLAMATION
BRIDGE RD.
NORTH BRIDGE ROAD
FULLERTON RD.
CLIFFORD PIER
I.S.K.
N.Y.K.
O.S.K.
M.B.K.
K.K.K.
INNER SOUTH MOLE
GOODMAN RD.
BRAMKSOME RD.
WILKINSON ROAD
NORTH
GROVE ROAD
FORT RD.
ARTHUR RD.
BRODRICK RD.
CRESCENT
TANJONG RHU RD
KATONG PARK
MEYER ROAD
SWIMMING CLUB
TG. RHU
TG. KATONG
1 中央警察署
2 中央郵便局
3 市廳
4 ラッフル 博物館
5 ラッフルスホテル
6 シービューホテル
7 アデルフキーホテル
8 帝國領事館
9 台銀華南銀行、同盟通信社
10 南洋倉庫ホワイトウェービル
11 東洋ホテル
12 シンガポル日報社
13 海員協會
14 特高警察署
15 專賣局
16 交通支局
17 大東ホテル
18 サン.アンドリュース病院
19 ガン、エンセン学校
20 東洋電話ビル
21 香港上海銀行
22 印度銀行
23 グスリービル
24 水上署
25 官衙
26 公會堂
27 大審院
28 シンガポール産業館
29 警察裁判所
30 印度商業銀行
31 大南ホテル
32 ユナイテッド.エレチナー
33 砂糖工場
34 消防署
35 バタ.ビル
36 電話局
37 レックスホテル
38 鋼管工場
39 ガス工場
40 市営バス車庫
41 フォートキャンニング陸軍司令部
42 車輛局
43 カセイ.ビル
44 シム、ダアービルー倉庫
45 キャピトル、ビル
46 ラッフルスカレッヂ及ビ郵便局
47 エアー、ポート、ホテル
48 產院
49 ユニオン、ビル
50 總督官邸
51 民政長官官邸
52 馬來義勇軍兵営
53 ビーチロード警察署
54 ヒル街
55 オーチヤード警察署
56 空軍司令部
57 中央病院
58 チョンバル、ビル
59 回教寺院
60 民間飛行場
61 シンガポール駅
62
63 クリフォート棧橋
64 アンダーソン橋
65 キングスドック
66 民間泊港(ボート、キー)
67 ラッフルス広場
68 水浴場
69 タンジョン、パーカー埠頭
70 サン、アンドリュー寺院
71 華民保護局
72 タレジョン、パーカー、ポリスステーション
73 蘭印商事会社
74 日本人会
75 ラッフルス女学校
76 Y.W.C.A.
77 クリケット.クラブ
78 オラニエ、ホテル
79 チョンバル、ビル
80 日本人、ゴルフ場
81 ビーチロード市場
82 アランボロ、マルボロ映画館
83 クリフオード棧橋

HOLLAND ROAD
NAPIER ROAD
TANGLIN ROAD
ORCHARD ROAD
DALVEY ROAD
BALMORAL ROAD
NASSIM ROAD
CLUNY RD.
GARDEN ROAD
TYERSALL RD.
GALLOP RD.
RIDOUT RD.
STEVENS ROAD
ORANGE GROVE RD.
ANDERSON ROAD
GOODWOOD HILL
SCOTT RD.
BUKIT TIMAH ROAD
NEWTON ROAD
KENG LEE RD.
KAMPONG JAVA RD.
FARRER PARK
RACE COURSE
MONKS HILL
GOVT. HOUSE DOMAIN
EMILY HILL
CAIRN HILL ROAD
EMERALD HILL RD.
CAVANAGH ROAD
CLEMENCEAU AVENUE
MACKENZIE RD.
SELEGIE ROAD
GRANGE ROAD
ROCHALIE DRIVE
CHATS WORTH ROAD
BISHOPGATE
NATHAN RD.
LEONIE HILL
KILLINEY RD.
OXLEY RISE
TANK ROAD
STAMFORD
FORT CANNING
日本人ゴルフ場
JERVOIS ROAD
TANGLIN RD.
RIVER VALLEY ROAD
ZION RD.
大世界
KIM SENG RD.
MOHAMED SULTAN RD.
ALEXANDRA ROAD
DELTA RD.
HAVELOCK ROAD
ROBERTSON QUAY
BOON TIONG RD.
BAHRU ROAD
HENDERSON ROAD
SENG POH RD.
OUTRAM ROAD
PEARLS HILL
H.M. PRISON
NEW BRIDGE ROAD
SOUTH BRIDGE ROAD
HILL STREET
SINGAPORE RIVER
CROSS STREET
ROBINSON ROAD
TELOK AYER
GENERAL HOSPITAL
HOSPITAL ROAD
NEIL ROAD
KAMPONG BAHRU ROAD
EVERTON PARK
CANTONMENT RD.
TANJONG PAGAR ROAD
ANSON ROAD
PRINCE EDWARD RD.
RAILWAY YARD
RAEBURN PARK
SINGAPORE STATION
MT. FABER FLAGSTAFF
KEPPEL ROAD
EMPIRE DOCK
MAIN ENTRANCE ROAD
YACHT CLUB
MAIN WHARF
SEAWARD LIMIT
EAST LAGOON
EAST WHARF
TELOK BLANGAH ROAD
WEST WHARF
KEPPEL HARBOUR
CATTLE WHARF
TELEGRAPH WHARF
OIL WHARF
P. & O. WHARF
SECTION 10

PRELUDE TO WAR
JAPANESE RECONNAISSANCE MAPS

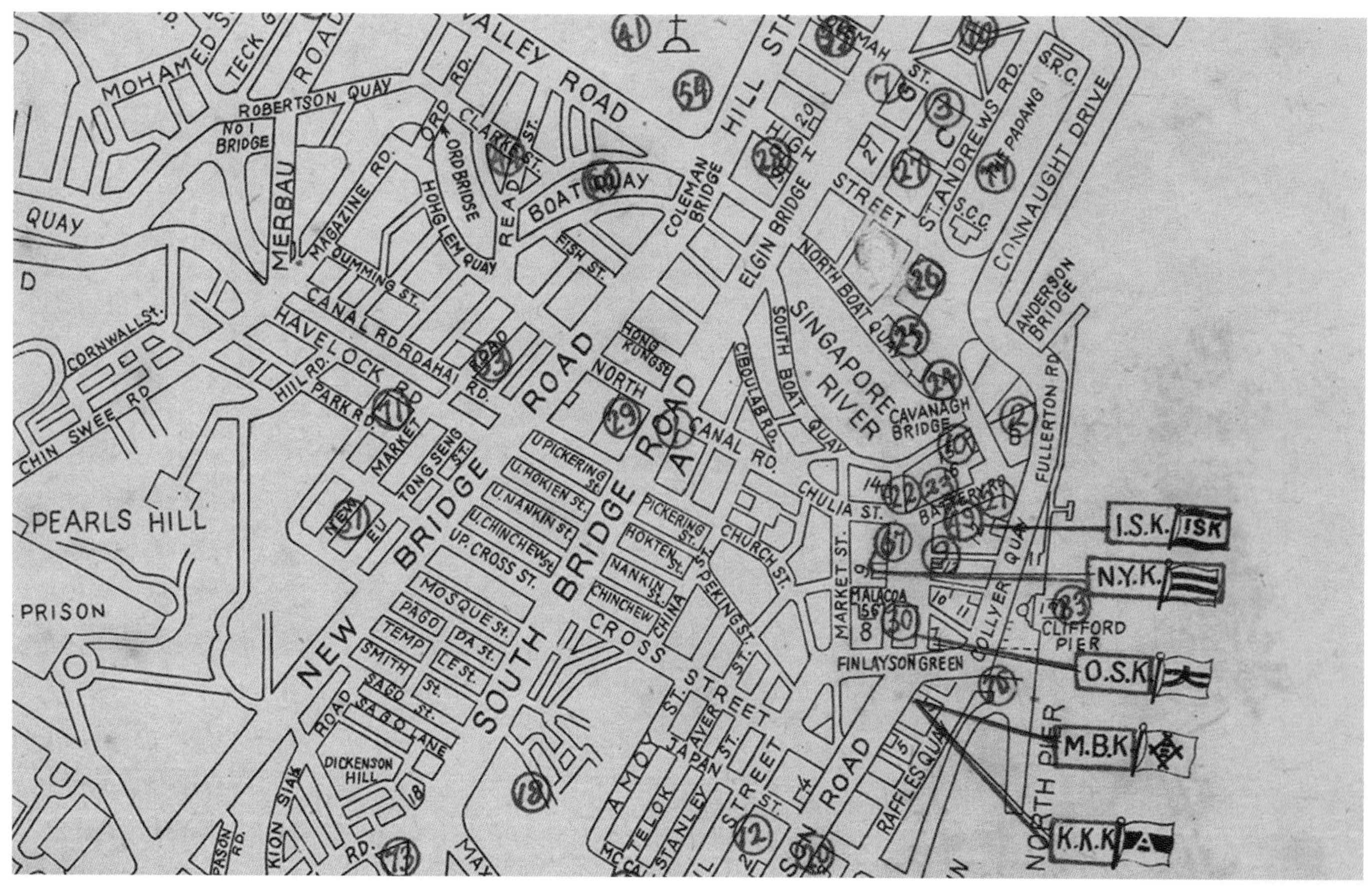

Detail from the undated *Shingapōru shigai chizu*, on which key government buildings and public infrastructure such as St Andrew's Hospital (No. 18) and the Law Courts (No. 29) were marked.

Title: 新嘉坡市街地図 *[Shingapōru shigai chizu]*
Language: Japanese and English
Type: Map and booklet
Call no.: RRARE 912.5957 SHI -[LSB]
Accession nos.: B29245121D (map); B29255626D (booklet)
Donated by: Lim Shao Bin

The Japanese military gathered vital information about Singapore even before its aircraft dropped the first bombs on the city centre on 8 December 1941. A map, likely produced by covert Japanese agents in Singapore in the months before the island fell, may have been instrumental in helping the Japanese military's requisition of key buildings in the city in the days following the British surrender.

The map, titled 新嘉坡市街地図 [*Shingapōru shigai chizu*], and its accompanying booklet, identify 83 key government and commercial buildings, such as municipal

A booklet accompanying *Shingapōru shigai chizu* contained images of strategic locations in Singapore. One such example **[top]** identified Ocean Building, Union Building and the General Post Office in Japanese. Another **[above]** was a skewed image of the Sime Darby godown at Boat Quay which might have been taken during a covert operation.

[Right] Japanese soldiers at Syonan Station (previously Singapore Railway Station), which is marked as Landmark No. 61 on the map. *Image reproduced from 大東亞戰爭 [Dai Tōa sensō] (1942), 38(11), p. 11. Tokyo: The Asahi Shimbun Publishing Co.*

offices and banks, public facilities, hotels, places of interest and Japanese-owned businesses. However, of these, No. 62 is unnamed, Clifford Pier appears twice, and two separate locations are marked as Tiong Bahru Buildings. The strategic importance of the landmarks – as the seat of British administration, and centres of business and social life in Singapore – suggests that the map was intended for use during a military takeover of the city.

Although it is unclear if this map was ever used, some of the buildings identified on it were seized for military use during the Japanese Occupation. These include the Central Police Station (No. 1), General Post Office (No. 2), Municipal Offices (No. 3), Adelphi Hotel (No. 7), Toyo Hotel (No. 11), British Army Command Centre at Fort Canning (No. 41), Raffles College (No. 46), Government House (No. 50), Singapore Volunteer Corps Headquarters (No. 52), Singapore Railway Station (No. 61), Tanjong Pagar Police Station (No. 72) and the Singapore Cricket Club (No. 77), among others.[1]

The undated map is likely based on a similar 1939 Singapore street map bearing the same title, which was published by the Singapore Japanese Club and printed by The Dai-Nippon Printing Co. Ltd. in Japan.[2] Other clues suggest that the map was likely printed between 1940 and 1941: for instance the Bata Building, identified as Landmark No. 35 on the map, was only opened in June 1940, two years after the land was acquired to build the department store.[3] Bata Shoe Company may have been a target of interest as it collected and repaired used shoes which were then sent to air raid victims in England in support of the Malaya Patriotic Fund during World War II.[4]

Photographic illustrations of 50 of the 83 landmarks were included in a booklet accompanying the map. Five unnumbered views of Singapore harbour and business

No.	Place Names in Japanese as Numbered and Printed on Map	Landmark	Featured in Booklet
1	中央警察署	Central Police Station	
2	中央郵便局	General Post Office	√ (2 pictures)
3	市廳	Municipal Offices	√
4	ラッフル博物館	Raffles Museum	√
5	ラッフルスホテル	Raffles Hotel	√
6	シービューホテル	Seaview Hotel	√ (2 pictures)
7	アデルフィーホテル	Adelphi Hotel	√
8	帝國領事館	Japanese Consulate	
9	台銀華南銀行．同盟通信社	Bank of Taiwan; The China and Southern Bank; Domei News Agency	√
10	南洋倉庫ホワイトウェービル	Nanyo Soko (The South Seas Warehouse Company); Whiteaway Laidlaw & Co. Building	√ (2 pictures)
11	東洋ホテル	Toyo Hotel	√
12	シンガポール日報社	The Straits Times Office	
13	海員協會	The Sailors' Institute	√
14	特高警察署	Special Branch Police Headquarters	√
15	專賣局	Custom House	
16	交通支局	Traffic Police Office	
17	大東ホテル	Daito Hotel	
18	サン．アンドリュース病院	St Andrew's Hospital	
19	ガン、エンセン学校	Gan Eng Seng School	
20	東洋電話ビル	Eastern Extension Telegraph Co. Building	√
21	香港上海銀行	Hong Kong & Shanghai Bank	√ (2 pictures)
22	印度銀行	Chartered Bank of India	
23	グスリービル	Guthrie & Co.	
24	水上署	Marine Police Station	√
25	官衛	Government Offices (Empress Place)	√
26	公會堂	Town Hall (Victoria Memorial Hall)	√
27	大審院	Supreme Court	√
28	シンガポール産業館	Japanese Commercial Museum	
29	警察裁判所	Law Courts	√
30	印度商業銀行	Mercantile Bank of India	
31	大南ホテル	Great Southern Hotel	
32	ユナイテッド．エレヂナー	United Engineers' Ltd.	
33	砂糖工場	Sugar Factory	
34	消防署	Central Fire Station	
35	バタビル	Bata Building	
36	電話局	Oriental Telephone and Electric Company	
37	レックスホテル	Rex Hotel	√
38	鋼管工場	Steel Pipe Factory	
39	ガス工場	Kallang Gas Works	
40	市営バス車庫	Municipal Bus Depot	
41	フォートキヤンイング陸軍司令部	Fort Canning Army Command Centre	
42	車輛局	Registry of Vehicles	
43	カセイ．ビル	Cathay Building	
44	シム．ダアービルー倉庫	Sime Darby & Co. warehouse	√
45	キャピトル．ビル	Capitol Building	√
46	ラッフルスカレッジ及郵便局	Raffles College and Post Office	√ (2 pictures)
47	エアー．ポート．ホテル	Airport Hotel	√ (2 pictures)
48	産院	Maternity Hospital	
49	ユニオン．ビル	Union Building	√
50	總督官邸	Government House	√
51	民政長官官邸	Colonial Secretary's Residence	
52	馬来義勇軍兵営	Singapore Volunteer Corps Headquarters	
53	ビーチロード警察署	Beach Road Police Station	√
54	ヒル街警察署	Hill Street Police Station	
55	オーチャード警察署	Orchard Road Police Station	
56	空軍司令部	Air Force Headquarters	
57	中央病院	General Hospital	√
58	チョンバル．ビル	Tiong Bahru buildings (Tiong Bahru also appears on the legend as No. 79, though at another location.)	
59	回教寺院	Sultan Mosque	√ (2 pictures)
60	民間飛行場	Civil airport (Kallang Airport)	√
61	シンガポール駅	Singapore Railway Station	√
62	-	-	
63	クリフォート桟橋	Clifford Pier	√
64	アンダーソン橋	Anderson Bridge	√
65	キングスドック	King's Dock	√
66	民間泊港（ボート．キー）	Boat Quay	√
67	ラッフルス広場	Raffles Place	√ (2 pictures)
68	水浴場	Singapore Swimming Club	√
69	タンジョン．パーカー準頭	Tanjong Pagar Wharf	√
70	サン．アンドリュー寺院	St Andrew's Cathedral	√ (2 pictures)
71	華民保護局	Chinese Protectorate Building	√
72	タンジョン．パーカー．ポリス．ステーション	Tanjong Pagar Police Station	
73	蘭印商事会社	Netherlands Trading Society	√
74	日本人会	The Japanese Club	√
75	ラッフルス女学校	Raffles Girls' School	√
76	Y. W. C. A.	Y. W. C. A.	√
77	クリケット．クラブ	Singapore Cricket Club	√
78	オラニエ．ホテル	Oranje Hotel	√
79	チョンバル．ビル	Tiong Bahru buildings (Tiong Bahru also appears on the legend as No. 58, though at another location.)	√
80	日本人．ゴルフ場	Japanese Golf Club	√
81	ビーチロード市場	Beach Road Market (Clyde Terrace Market)	√
82	アランボロ．マルボロ映画館	Alhambra and Marlborough Theatres	√
83	クリフオード桟橋	Clifford Pier	√

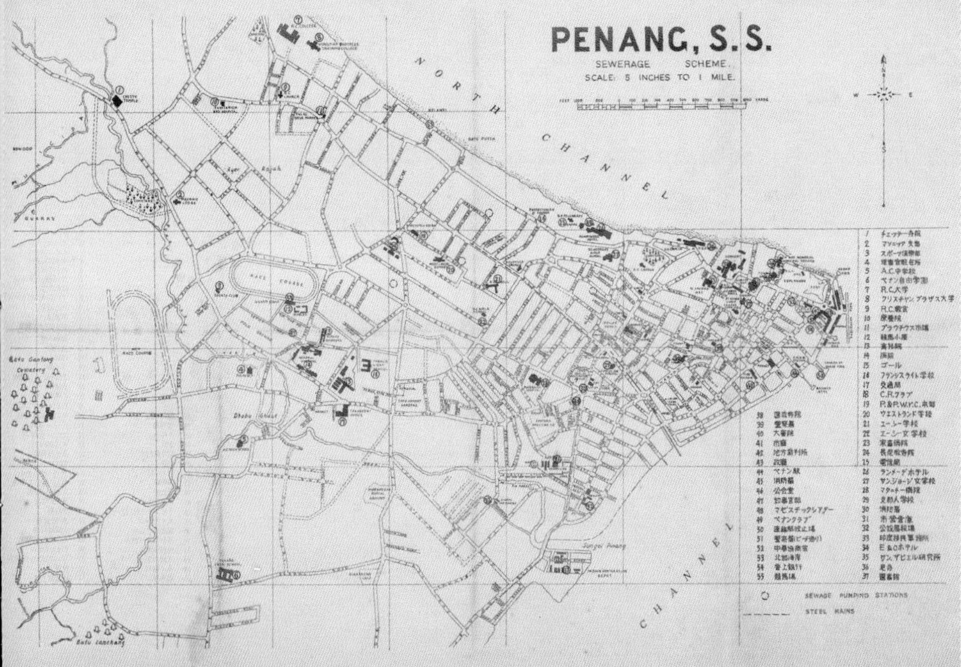

[Facing page] The undated *Shingapōru shigai chizu* in full.
[Above] One of the 23 reconaissance maps of Southeast Asia in the Lim Shao Bin collection.

thoroughfares such as Robinson Road and Battery Road are also shown in the booklet, with key buildings marked out in Japanese. While some images, such as Nos. 4, 7 and 13, were likely copied from commercial postcards or books, others – Nos. 11, 44 and 46, for instance – appear to be based on images taken as part of Japanese surveillance efforts.

The unfinished quality of the booklet and map suggests that production was carried out in haste. Although British authorities had begun monitoring Japanese activities in Singapore and Johor as early as 1917,[5] Japan set in motion its plans to invade Southeast Asia only from 1940 onwards.[6] This also coincides with the rise of Japanese espionage activities in Singapore. In his memoir, Shinozaki Mamoru, a press attaché at the Japanese Consulate-General in Singapore, recounted that Japanese military agents came here in September 1940 to survey the defence capabilities of Singapore and Malaya.[7] In neighbouring Dutch East Indies (present-day Indonesia), authorities traced the start of Japanese clandestine activities to the late 1930s.[8]

The presence of 22 other reconnaissance maps and booklets in the Lim Shao Bin collection is also proof that information gathering had been carried out by Japanese intelligence in various cities and towns in Malaya, Borneo, the Dutch East Indies and the Philippines prior to World War II. These maps were adapted from existing maps published by British, Dutch and American authorities. Although many of these maps, like the Singapore map, had been produced in haste, the numbers printed on the booklets suggest that the collection of data and photographs involved a systematic and comprehensive process.

♦ **Gracie Lee**

Reconnaissance Maps in the Lim Shao Bin Collection

Region	Title	Booklet Number
American Philippines	Proposed development plan of the city of Cebu and vicinity (Sept 1936)	3
	Manila	6
	Iloilo	8
British Malaya and British North Borneo	Ipoh	1
	Malacca	2
	Penang	3
	Singapore	5
	Taiping	7
	Kuching	16
Dutch East Indies	Amboina	1
	Belawan	6
	Buitenzorg	7
	Plattegrond van Batavia	9
	Kaart van de Wandelwegen om het Hotel San Garoet te Ngamplang	14
	Jesselton	15
	Palembang	21
	Probolinggo	22
	Haven van Pekalongan	23
	Pasoeroean	24
	Sibolga	28
	Sabang	29
	Tijlatjap	33
	Semarang en Omstreken	35

Notes

1 Shinozaki, M. (1975, reprinted 2011). *Syonan: My story: The Japanese occupation of Singapore* (pp. 40–41, 43–44, 48, 57, 59, 71–72, 77, 84, 139, 169). Singapore: Marshall Cavendish Editions. (Call No.: RSING 959.57023 SH); 大東亞戰爭 [*Dai Tōa sensō*]. (1942, March 11). Tokyo: The Asahi Shimbun, pp. 6, 11. (Call No.: RRARE 940.5425 DDYZZ)

2 The street map was originally published as an attachment to a guidebook to Singapore, 赤道を行く：新嘉坡案内 [*Sekido ō yuku: Shingapōru annai*] by the Singapore Japanese Club in 1939. The map consists of two printed sides. A street map of Singapore appears on one side, while a map of Malaya and Singapore island dated 1938 appears on the other side.

3 Big new Singapore store. (1938, July 24). *The Sunday Times*, p. 1; Bata's new premises. (1940, June 26). *Malaya Tribune*, p. 4. Retrieved from NewspaperSG.

4 New scheme for sending shoes to air raid victims at home. (1941, April 19). *Morning Tribune*, p. 4. Retrieved from NewspaperSG.

5 Ong, C. C. (2011). *Operation Matador: World War II: Britain's attempt to foil the Japanese invasion of Malaya and Singapore* (pp. 4, 27). Singapore: Marshall Cavendish Editions. (Call No.: RSING 940.542595 ONG)

6 Tsuji, M., Howe, H. V. (Ed.), Lake, M. E. (Trans.) (First published in Japanese 1952; 1997) *Japan's greatest victory, Britain's worst defeat* (pp. 1–57). Staplehurst, Kent: Spellmount. (Call No.: RSING 940.5425 TSU -[WAR]); Nakano, S. (2019). *Japan's colonial moment in Southeast Asia, 1942–1945: The occupiers' experience* (pp. 26–55). Abingdon, Oxon: New York: Routledge. (Call No.: RSEA 327.520590904 NAK)

7 Shinozaki, M. (1973). *My wartime experiences in Singapore* (pp. 3–7). Singapore: Institute of Southeast Asian Studies. (Call No.: RSING 959.57023 SHI)

8 *Ten years of Japanese burrowing in the Netherlands East Indies: Official report of the Netherlands East Indies Government on Japanese subversive activities in the archipelago during the last decade.* (1942). New York: Netherlands Information Bureau. (Call No.: RSEA 327.12 NET)

A Tamil Newspaper From Ceylon

Title: உதயதாரகை (*Utayatarakai;* Morning Star)

Year published: 1847

Publisher: American Mission Press (Manipay, Ceylon)

Language: Tamil and English

Type: Newspaper (24 issues)

Call no.: RRARE 070.1 UTA-[JK]

Accession no.: B29241047G (14 Jan, 1847, [v.] VII, no. 1)

Donated by: John Koh

Utayatarakai (உதயதாரகை), which is also known as "Morning Star" in English, was first published in 1841 as a fortnightly bilingual Tamil/English newspaper by the American Mission Press in Manipay, a town in the Jaffna District of Ceylon (Sri Lanka) , an area with a predominantly Tamil community.

The newspaper was founded and edited by Henry Martin and Seth Payson. These two young Tamil Protestant missionaries working for the American Mission in Jaffna had converted to Christianity and adopted Anglicised names. *Utayatarakai* was circulated and read in several parts of Ceylon as well as Tamil Nadu in South India.

In 1856, the newspaper began publishing exclusively in Tamil as a weekly – making it one of the earliest known Tamil newspapers in the world. Although *Utayatarakai* is not the earliest work printed by Christian missionaries in Ceylon,[1] it is nonetheless important as it offers a glimpse into the history of Tamil newspaper publishing in the 19th century.

A selection of issues of *Utayatarakai* printed in 1847.

A wide range of topics, such as religion, science, literature, agriculture, government and education, was covered in *Utayatarakai*. The newspaper also offered readers condensed articles on important world news.[2] Martin was in charge of the English section, whereas Payson edited the Tamil articles. Of the 24 bilingual issues, the earliest issue in the National Library's collection is Volume 8, Number 1, 14 January 1847, while the latest is Volume 8, Number 24, 23 December 1847.

Each copy of *Utayatarakai* was printed on a sheet measuring 48 cm by 34 cm and folded in half vertically to make four pages. On the first page of each issue, it states that the paper was "Published on the 2nd and 4th Thursday of every month at two shillings a year and payable in advance". Indicated too is a list of agents whom readers could purchase subscriptions from. Besides Jaffna, there were 11 other Sri Lankan cities with agents, as well as an agent based in Madras (Chennai), India.

Subscribers who had their copies mailed to them, as well as those based in India, paid four shillings a year. It is possible that some of these copies found their way into Singapore as the colony hosted sizable numbers of Tamil-speaking migrants from Jaffna in Ceylon and Tamil Nadu in South India.

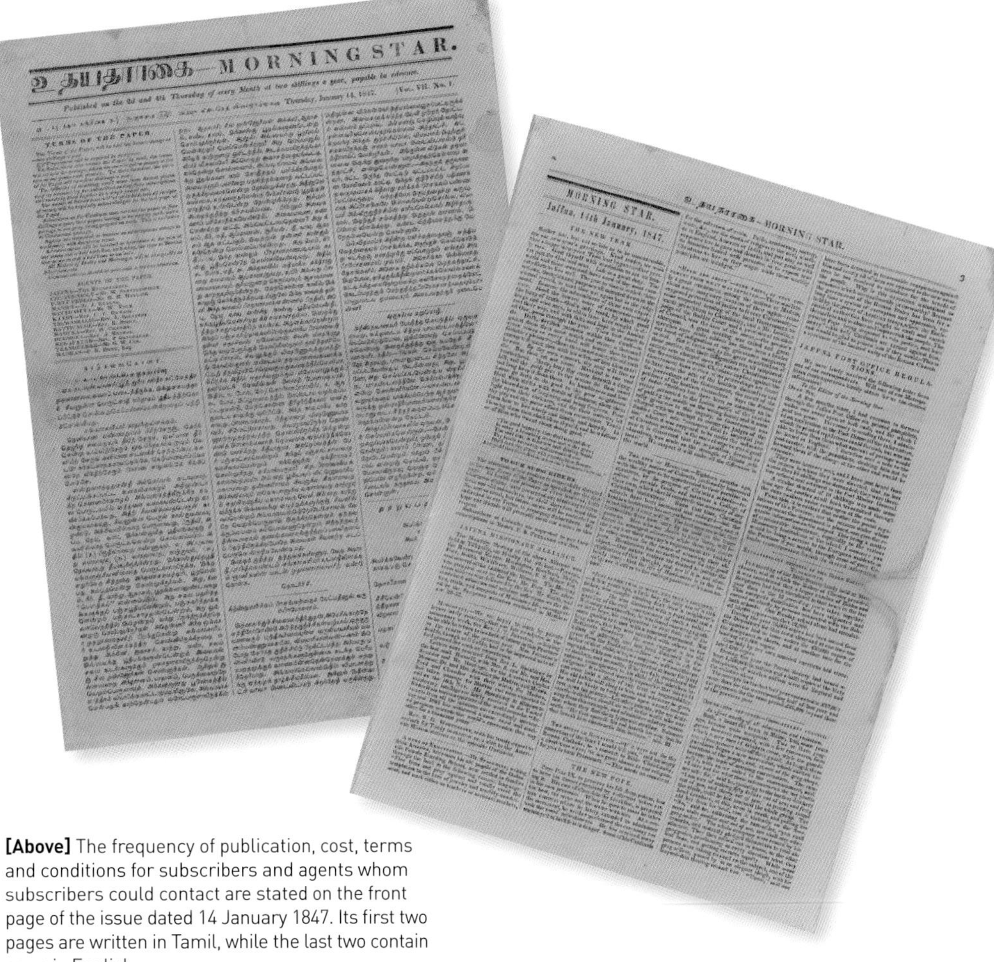
MORNING STAR.

[Above] The frequency of publication, cost, terms and conditions for subscribers and agents whom subscribers could contact are stated on the front page of the issue dated 14 January 1847. Its first two pages are written in Tamil, while the last two contain news in English.

At the bottom of the last page of each issue of *Utayatarakai* is a colophon which states that the paper was "printed and published at the American Mission Press at Jaffna by Eastman Strong Minor". The press was set up in 1834 by Minor, a newly arrived missionary and printer from Connecticut, United States.[3] The press produced many religious tracts in English and Tamil and distributed these free of charge. In addition, it also printed Tamil publications on science and medicine, the only missionary press in Ceylon to undertake such a task.[4]

The American Mission was originally established in 1816 in Jaffna when five missionaries from the American Board of Commissioners for Foreign Missions of Connecticut, United States, arrived in the city on 23 September 1816. The mission was formed at Batticotta (Vaddukkodai) within the ruins of a Dutch church. Known as the Batticotta Seminary, its main objective was to spread Christianity among the locals and provide education by teaching them English and Tamil language and literature.[5]

In articles on Christianity published in the *Utayatarakai*, the editors Martin and Payson challenged Roman Catholicism, and particularly the Hindu tradition of Shaivism, urging that their religious texts be debated and questioned in public. The two missionaries were also intent on educating Ceylonese Tamils about European culture and religion – which they believed to be superior – and also expose what they felt was the moral decadence of Tamil culture and religion.

Due to the lack of secular newspapers at that time, *Utayatarakai's* readership included Tamil Christians and non-Christians. In fact, the latter made up more than a third of its readers.[6] In 1855, the newspaper was sold to two Jaffna Tamil Christians who went by the names "Messrs Ripley and Strong".[7] A year later, there was a change of ownership again and the press was renamed "The Strong and Asbury Press" (this was when the newspaper became a weekly and was published exclusively in Tamil). Although it is not known when exactly *Utayatarakai* ceased publication, between 1841 and 1856, some 3.5 million copies of the newspaper were printed.[8]

Although the early print media in Ceylon began as a tool for spreading Christianity, the influence of the mission press contributed to the growth of the country's publishing industry. It also renewed interest in local languages and literature among the people.[9] In Jaffna, the appearance of articles in *Utayatarakai* that denounced Shaivism also heightened religious consciousness among the country's Hindu literati, motivating them to establish their own Tamil-language publications in order to promote Tamil culture and religion.[10] ♦ **Makeswary Periasamy**

Notes

1 The first printing press was brought to Colombo, Ceylon, in 1736 during the Dutch colonial period, and actual printing from the press began in 1737. The American missionaries arrived in Jaffna in 1816 and set up their own press in 1834. Church missionaries were the first to produce works in the vernacular languages in Ceylon to propagate Christianity among the locals. These Christian tracts were sent to educational institutions and churches. Maheshwaran, R. (2007). Bibliometric phenomenon of Tamil publications in Sri Lanka in 2005. (p. 9). In *Journal of the University Librarians*, Vol. 11. Retrieved from Journal of the University Librarians Association of Sri Lanka website; Wickramasinghe, N. (2006). *Sri Lanka in the modern age: a history of contested identities* (pp. 77, 79). Honolulu: University of Hawai'i Press. (Call no.: R 954.93 WIC)

2 Kularatne, T. (2006). *History of printing and publishing in Ceylon*, 1736–1912 (p. 205). Dehiwala: The Author. (Call no.: R 686.2095493 KUL)

3 Kularatne, 2006, pp. 133–135, 140.

4 Kularatne, 2006, pp. 133–135, 140.

5 Kularatne, 2006, pp. 130–131.

6 Kularatne, 2006, pp. 205.

7 Kularatne, 2006, p. 136.

8 Kularatne, 2006, p. 205.

9 Kularatne, 2006, p. 205.

10 Wickramasinghe, 2006, p. 79.

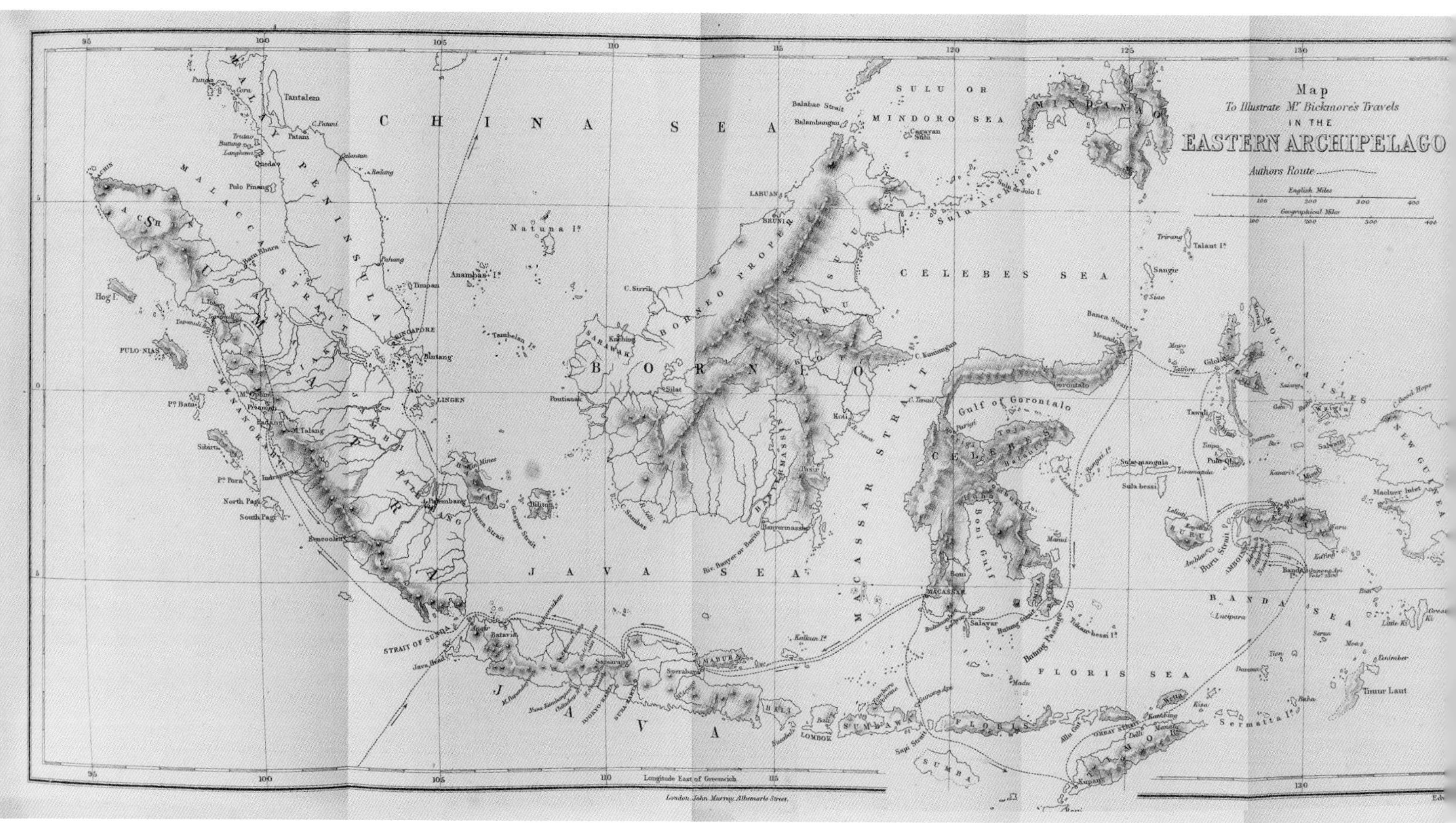

AN AMERICAN IN THE MALAY ARCHIPELAGO

Title: *Travels in the East Indian Archipelago*
Author: Albert Smith Bickmore
Year published: 1868
Publisher: John Murray (London)
Language: English
Type: Monograph; 555 pages
Call no.: RRARE 915.980422 BIC-[JSB]
Accession no.: B29032913G

[Top] A fold-out map of the Malay Archipelago was included in Albert Smith Bickmore's *Travels in the East Indian Archipelago* (1868). The map marks Bickmore's route to the Spice Islands and Singapore, where he stopped by in May 1866.

Travel narratives are among the most important genres of publications in the field of natural history and ethnography in the 18th and 19th centuries. As they contain eyewitness accounts of life in different parts of the world, these narratives provide fascinating glimpses of the ever-changing natural and social worlds.

The National Library's Rare Materials Collection contains numerous travelogues, including some that date back to the 16th century. In the words of the scholar and historian John Bastin, a work that had "enjoyed much critical acclaim at the time of its publication" was *Travels in the East Indian Archipelago* (1868).[1]

Written by Albert Smith Bickmore (1839–1914) – an American Civil War veteran, a trained naturalist and principal founder of the American Museum of Natural History in New York City – this voluminous 555-page tome documents Bickmore's expedition to the Dutch East Indies (present-day Indonesia) from April 1865 to May 1866.[2] The places he had visited include Java, Bali, Lombok, Sulawesi, the Moluccas, East Timor and

[Clockwise from left] Cover of one of the copies of Bickmore's book available at the National Library. In the book's preface, he expressed that he aimed to present an accurate narrative "even at any sacrifice of elegance"; Supplementary illustrations in the book include drawings of Bickmore's fight with a python; a Dayak man; and Bickmore saving himself from an almost fatal slip on Gunong Api.

much of Sumatra. These were depicted in two maps included in the book – one featuring the entire Malay Archipelago and the other the island of Sumatra.

Bickmore's trip to the former Dutch colony began in Batavia (present-day Jakarta), and was undertaken with the initial aim of collecting shells from the island of Ambon that were discussed in Georg Eberhard Rumphius' *Amboinsche Rariteitkamer* (1705).[3] However, after the colonial Dutch government granted Bickmore access to the rest of the Dutch East Indies, he expanded his research to cover other subjects, ranging from the flora and fauna of the places he visited to the ethnological characteristics of the different indigenous people he encountered.

Bickmore's accounts in his travelogue were compiled based on what he had meticulously recorded in his journal, which was said to have been "kept day by day with scrupulous care", as well as information drawn from the works of well-known naturalists, including Stamford Raffles, John Crawfurd and Thomas Horsfield.[4]

Sketches and illustrations in the book help readers visualise what Bickmore saw and experienced during his travels. For instance, a drawing of the Pinang palm, or betel-nut palm, supplemented his description of how the local people of Ceram (or Seram) Island enjoyed chewing betel nut.[5] Similarly, the sketch of a Dayak man was included with Bickmore's account of his first encounter with this indigenous community. Bickmore also wrote that he had learnt about headhunting rituals, with "mute[d] astonishment".[6]

The illustrations also depict his personal experiences, most notably how he managed to save himself from being "dashed to pieces" by grasping onto a fern after slipping on the slopes of Gunong Api (or Banda Api). Another sketch showed Bickmore onboard a ship, battling an enormous python with an axe after the "monster" had escaped from its enclosure.[7]

After completing his expedition of the Dutch East Indies, Bickmore made a stopover in Singapore in May 1866, where he was warmly welcomed by the American community. He was also introduced to then Governor of the Straits Settlements Orfeur Cavenagh, who not only received him "in the most polite manner", but also helped him prepare for the next leg of his journey to East Asia by writing introductory letters to the Governor of Hong Kong and the admiral commanding the British fleet in the seas of China and Japan.[8]

Bickmore returned to the United States in 1867, where he began making plans for his travelogue to be published. This materialised in December 1868 when *Travels in the East Indian Archipelago* was published in London by John Murray. In 1869, an American edition was released in New York by D. Appleton and Company. In the same year, J.E.A. Martin's German translation of the work, titled *Reisen im Ostindischen Archipel in den Jahren 1865 and 1866*, was released in Jena, Germany. This was followed by a two-volume Dutch edition in 1873. Published in Schiedam as *Reizen in den Oost-Indischen Archipel*, it contained additional notes by J.J. Hollander. In 1991, the American edition was reprinted by Oxford University Press in Singapore with an introduction by John Bastin. ♦ **Lim Tin Seng**

Notes

1 Bastin, J. (1991). Introduction. In Bickmore, A. S. *Travels in the East Indian Archipelago* (p. vii). Singapore: Oxford University Press. (Call no.: RSING 959.8 BIC)
2 Bastin, 1991, pp. v–viii.
3 Bickmore, A. S. (1868). *Travels in the East Indian Archipelago* (pp. 13–14). London: John Murray. (Call no.: RRARE 915.980422 BIC-[JSB])
4 Bastin, 1991, p. vii.
5 Bickmore, 1868, pp. 180–182.
6 Bickmore, 1868, pp. 200–207.
7 Bickmore, 1868, pp. 228–235, 538–542.
8 Bickmore, 1868, pp. 536–537.

Diaries of a Chinese Historian

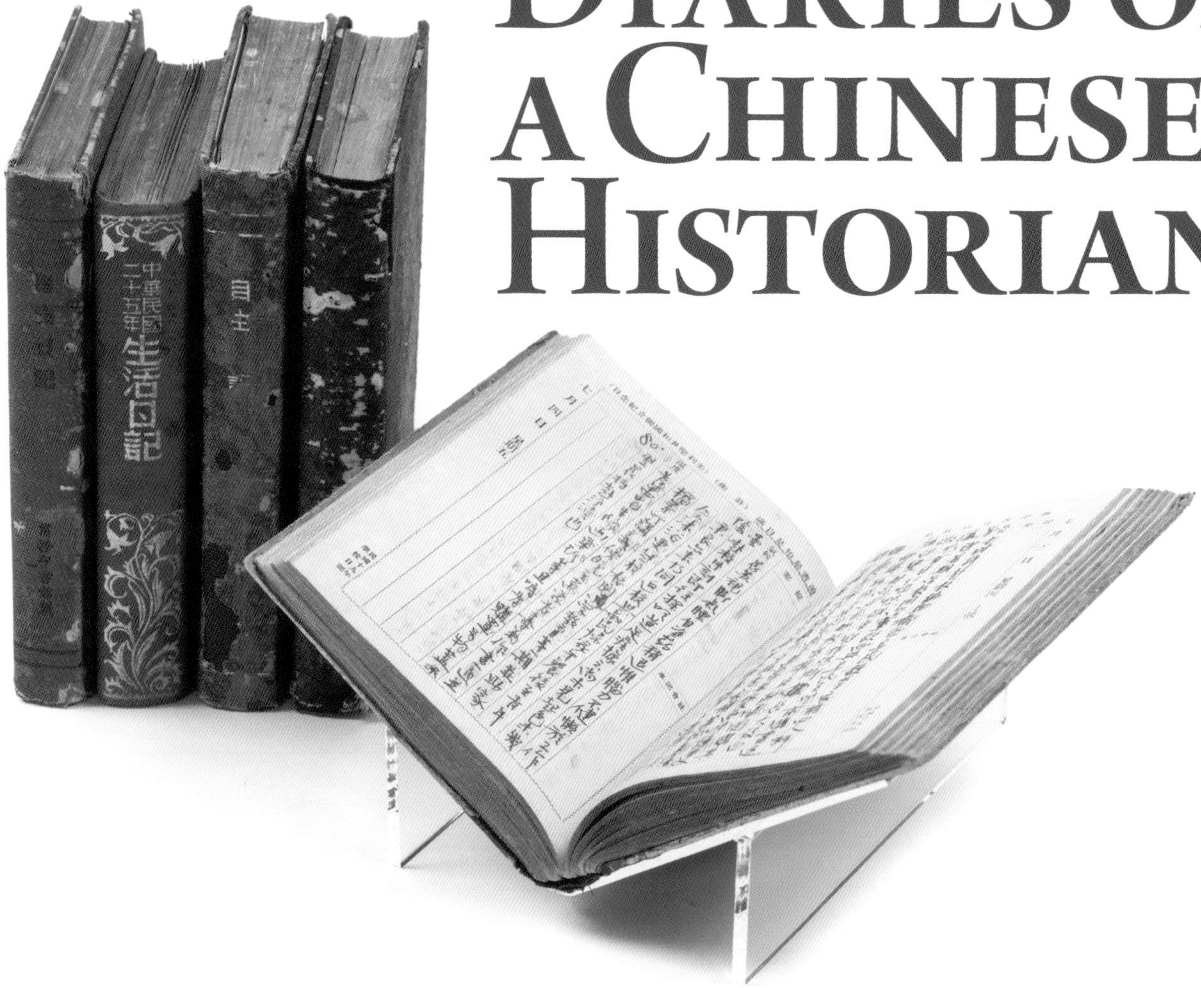

Title: 许云樵教授日记册 (Professor Hsu Yun Tsiao's Diaries)
Author: 许云樵 (Hsu Yun Tsiao)
Date: 1930–42
Language: Chinese
Type: Diary (5 volumes)
Call no.: RRARE C818.8 XYQ-[HYT]
Accession nos.: B27705373A (v. 1); B27705372K (v. 2); B27705374B (v. 3); B27705375C (v. 4); B27705376D (v. 5)
Donated by: Singapore Federation of Chinese Clan Associations

[Above] Five surviving diaries of Hsu Yun Tsiao's, written from 1930 to 24 February 1942. These cover his emigration from China to Singapore and the period up to the early days of the Japanese Occupation.
[Below] This photograph of Professor Hsu in his late fifties was taken in 1963. *Image reproduced from 许云樵 [Hsu, Y.T.]. 新加坡宗乡会馆联合总会许云樵馆藏：许云樵教授个人及家庭生活照 (照片).*

Five hardbound diaries of Professor Hsu Yun Tsiao (1905–1981),[1] written more than 70 years ago, are part of the Hsu Yun Tsiao Collection donated by the Singapore Federation of Chinese Clan Associations to the National Library in 2014. These are a valuable companion to correspondence from scholars, friends and family members, for they bring one closer to Hsu's life and personal beliefs.

In a letter dated 1968, Hsu, who was in Singapore then, urged his sixth son, Yuan'er [园儿], who was living in Thailand, to "write your journal, and please write legibly ... so that you [can] keep it as a memento".[2] Hsu himself was a journaler; as such, the diaries he wrote between 1930 and 1942 are a valuable keepsake of memories of his early years in Southeast Asia.

Widely known as an eminent Chinese scholar in Nanyang studies and for his in-depth knowledge of Southeast Asian history, Hsu was one of the founders of a group dedicated to the study of Southeast Asia – the South Seas Society – in 1940.[3] He was also chief editor of its *Journal of the South Seas Society* [南洋学报] from 1940 to 1958. A prolific writer who was later appointed an associate professor in the Department of

History and Geography at Nanyang University from 1957 to 1961, Hsu produced numerous research works and papers over the course of his long academic career.[4]

Hsu left his hometown in Suzhou, China, in 1930, at the age of 26[5] to seek greener pastures in Nanyang (or the South Seas, as Southeast Asia was known then to the Chinese). The first volume in his diaries recounts Hsu's life in Suzhou in the months before he left home and after his arrival in Singapore. These entries reveal interesting glimpses of the travel arrangements that a typical Chinese migrant might undertake on his or her journey to Nanyang in the 1930s, at a time when the entry of adult Chinese male immigrants into Malaya and Singapore was restricted under Malaya's Immigration Restriction Ordinance.[6]

In the first volume, Hsu also documented his initial thoughts of seeking employment in Nanyang through a friend's recommendation, the tedious process of completing his immigration papers, and his long days at sea before finally arriving in Singapore on 3 December 1930.

Eventually, Hsu found work as a teacher, first in Johor Bahru in 1931, and then the following year in Singapore. In 1933, he moved to Patani in southern Thailand to teach in a Chinese school.[7] A Chinese phrase, "萍踪", which refers to "the tracks of a wanderer", is written on the first page of the second volume of Hsu's diary dated 1933. This phrase aptly captures Hsu's thoughts on his peripatetic existence, constantly moving from one country to another in search of work.

Little did he expect that his stint in Thailand would be a life-changing one. Not only did Hsu meet Jingxiang [景香], the person who would become his wife, but he also completed his research on the region and published his work 《北大年史》 (History of Patani) in 1946. This became one of Hsu's key works on Southeast Asian history.[8]

Collectively, the second, third and fourth volumes (dated 1933, 1936 and 1937, respectively) of Hsu's diaries trace his teaching career in Patani and subsequently Bangkok, where he lived from 1933 to 1937.[9] These also shed light on the Chinese communities in Thailand during the 1930s, with Hsu sharing his thoughts and experiences as a teacher during a time when Chinese schools in Thailand were curtailed as a result of the government's assimilation policy.[10]

The fifth volume of Hsu's diaries contains an intriguing series of accounts of wartime Singapore and the beginning of the Japanese Occupation. One such account describes a mass screening conducted by the Japanese military police at the Oriental Theatre in Chinatown to ferret out anti-Japanese individuals for execution. Although Hsu's diary entry is dated 22 January 1942,[12] the exercise he describes matches the horrific events that took place during Operation Sook Ching – the Japanese military exercise carried out from 21 February to 4 March 1942 to eliminate people suspected of anti-Japanese activities.[13]

Although there are no entries covering 1931–32 and 1934–35, and Hsu wrote sporadically in his last volume (1938 to February 1942), his diaries provide an invaluable first-hand account of pre-war Singapore and the early days of the Japanese Occupation, as witnessed and experienced by a young historian in the making. ♦ **Seow Peck Ngiam**

[Top right] The unsettledness Hsu felt from having travelled to different places for work is captured in the phrase 萍踪 (meaning "the tracks of a wanderer"), which he wrote on the first page of the second volume of his journal dated 1933. The Thai word written on the same page generally refers to a personal diary.

[Below] Volumes 1 and 3 from the manuscript of Hsu's《北大年史》(History of Patani). The first draft was completed in 1940, but part of it was destroyed while the rest was badly damaged by silverfish as Hsu hid the manuscript in between ceiling boards during the Japanese Occupation.[11] He reworked the seven-part manuscript and eventually published it in 1946.

Notes

1 Chinese scholar dies of heart attack. (1981, November 18). *The Straits Times*, p. 10. Retrieved from NewspaperSG.
2 廖文辉 [Liao, W.] & 曾维龙 [Zeng, W.] (2007).《许云樵来往书信集》[The correspondence of Hsu Yun-Tsiao] (pp. 13, 18). 马来西亚: 新纪元学院马来西亚族群研究中心. (Call no.: Chinese RSEA C816 XYQ)
3 廖文辉 [Liao, W.]. (2014).《许云樵评传》[A Biography of Hsu Yun-Tsiao] (p. ix). 新加坡: 八方文化创作室. (Call no.: Chinese RSING 959.007202 LWH)
4 Liao, 2014, p. ix.
5 Liao, 2014, p. viii.
6 National Library Board. (2016, January). Immigration restriction ordinance. Retrieved from HistorySG website.
7 Liao, 2014, p. 11.
8 Liao, 2014, pp. 11, 13; Hsu Yun-Tsiao. In Suryadinata, L. (Ed.). (2012). *Southeast Asian personalities of Chinese descent: A biographical dictionary* (pp. 358–361). Singapore: Institute of Southeast Asian Studies, p. 359. (Call no.: RSING 959.004951 SOU)
9 Liao, 2014, p. 11.
10 Tan, C. (2013). *Routledge handbook of the Chinese diaspora* (p. 452). London; New York: Routledge. (Call no.: English RSEA 305.8951 ROU)
11 许云樵 [Xu, Y.]. (1979).《希夷室诗文集》[Poems and Essays from the room of Xiyi] (pp. 30–31). 新加坡: 东南亚研究所. (Call no.: RCLOS C810.08 XYQ -[HYT])
12 Could the dates written in these diary entries have been an error as Sook Ching took place from 21 February to 4 March 1942?
13 Tan, S., et al. (2009). *Syonan years, 1942-1945: Living beneath the rising sun* (pp. 8, 15, 18). Singapore: National Archives of Singapore. (Call no.: RING 940.530745957 TAN-[WAR]). Singapore fell to the Japanese on 15 February 1942. However, in Hsu's diary, there are entries dated 19 January and 24 January which describe activities similar to what happened during the Japanese Occupation of Singapore. Even though it is not clear why Hsu wrote "January" instead of "February", his descriptions remain significant.

Sachtler & Co.'s Images of Early Singapore

Title: *Views and Types of Singapore, 1863*
Publisher: Sachtler & Co.
Type: Photo album; 40 photographs
Call no.: RRARE 959.5703 SAC-[LKL]
Accession no.: B20019369H
Donated by: Lee Kip Lin

Forty prints in an album titled *Views and Types of Singapore, 1863* make up the oldest photographic material in the National Library's collection. The album is attributed to Sachtler & Co., one of the first commercial photography studios in Singapore. As the title suggests, the album features picturesque scenes ("views") of the settlement, as well as portraits of its racially diverse inhabitants (representing ethnographic "types"). Given that photographs from this period are very difficult to come by, the collection is a precious record of the landscape and cosmopolitan population of early Singapore.

It is hard to pinpoint the exact date of Sachtler & Co.'s founding; it was first listed in the 1864 edition of the *Straits Calendar and Directory*, and was likely set up the year before.[1] The studio would have used the collodion[2] wet-plate process, the most popular photographic method between the mid-1850s and 1880s.[3] The process of creating a wet-plate negative involved considerable preparation, skill and speed. Once the image was taken, the photographer had to work quickly to coat, expose and develop the glass plate while the light-sensitive chemical on its surface was still damp (hence the description "wet-plate").[4]

This meant that a photographer who worked away from the studio had to carry all the equipment and materials necessary to set up a portable darkroom on location. While vantage points such as Fort Canning Hill and Mount Faber offered unparalleled views of Singapore town and surroundings, the photographer capturing the scene would have had to lug his camera, tripod, tent, plates, chemicals and other paraphernalia along. Imagine his dismay if sudden changes in the weather disrupted his efforts.[5]

Portraiture, landscape and architectural views were common, as the album amply demonstrates. Leafing through its pages, one recognises historical landmarks that still stand in the Civic District today. One of them is Dalhousie Obelisk, named after the Marquis of Dalhousie and Governor-General of India, James Andrew Broun-Ramsay, to commemorate his visit to Singapore in February 1850.[6] More significantly, the photograph shows the original site of the monument near the pier close to the mouth of the Singapore River where the Marquis had landed (part of the pier is shown in the foreground). The obelisk was reportedly in a deteriorated state by 1863, and the scaffolding around the structure suggests that the photograph was taken during its repainting and repair.[7]

The album also features 14 studio portraits of individuals representing different ethnicities in Singapore. There is unfortunately no further information on their identities.

It is likely that the general population could not afford the luxury of having their portraits taken. Hence it is possible that the subjects were hired. Upon closer inspection of the portraits, one would notice that posing stands were often used to help sitters hold still for the picture, and that umbrellas were popular props.

Although cumbersome, the wet-plate technique was inexpensive and, once mastered, could churn out detailed images of a consistent quality.[8] Moreover, an unlimited number of positive prints could be produced from a single negative, thus setting the stage for the rise of commercial photography.[9] These prints were typically printed on albumen paper, which used the albumen found in egg whites to bind the photographic chemicals to paper.[10] *Views and Types of Singapore, 1863* was no exception.

The identity of Sachtler & Co.'s original proprietor remains a mystery. By July 1864, the business had been taken over by August Sachtler in partnership with a Kristen Feilberg. Sachtler was a telegrapher by profession, but his exposure to photography during an assignment to Japan in 1860 led to a career switch.[11]

Located on High Street near the Court House, Sachtler & Co. offered photography services "at any hour during the day", a wide variety of the latest frames and albums imported from England, as well as a ready selection of Singapore views for purchase.[12]

In 1865, Sachtler & Feilberg (a partnership between Hermann Sachtler, presumably a brother of August, and Feilberg), opened in Penang.[13] Feilberg went on to start his own practice in 1867, and Hermann Sachtler returned to Singapore by 1869.[14] That year, it was reported that Hermann Sachtler met with a bad accident while taking photographs from the roof of the Church of the Good Shepherd. While adjusting his camera, he lost his footing and fell, fracturing his skull and arm, but miraculously survived the ordeal.[15]

Subsequently, the business shifted to Battery Road in 1871 before returning to High Street in 1874, reopening as Sachtler's Photographic Rooms at No. 88, opposite the Hotel d'Europe.[16] By then, the firm was supplying an extensive range of photographs taken around the region, including "views and types of Borneo, Java, Sumatra, Saigon, Siam, Burmah, and Straits Settlements".[17] Sachtler & Co. ceased business shortly after. In June 1874, its stock of negatives and equipment were acquired by Carter & Co.[18]

Having been the leading studio in Singapore for over a decade, Sachtler & Co.'s closure left a gap that another firm, the prolific G.R. Lambert & Co., rose to fill, and in fact surpass. With the advent of mass travel in the late 19th century, G.R. Lambert & Co. successfully capitalised on the demand for souvenir albums and picture postcards. By then, technological advances in photography had expanded the range of subjects. More street scenes, fast-moving human figures and traffic could now be featured, thereby enriching the photographic record of early Singapore.[19] ♦ **Janice Loo**

[Facing page] Landscape shots were the stock-in-trade of Sachtler & Co. and other photographic studios in the 19th century. The hills of Singapore, such as Fort Canning Hill, offered good vantage points for panoramic shots of Singapore town and its surroundings. Pulau Saigon (a small island in the Singapore River), for instance, can be seen in the middle of this shot taken from Fort Canning Hill. As Pulau Saigon has been reclaimed to join the mainland, such photographs also reveal how much the landscape has transformed since then.
[Left] The album also features portraits representing the racial diversity of the population. The umbrella, as shown in this shot, appears to be a common prop. Posing stands were also used to help sitters hold still.
[Below] Photographic technology of the time captured moving objects and human figures as a blur. The photographer would have had to obtain the cooperation of the human subjects to compose this street scene featuring pedestrians of different ethnicities and a horse-drawn carriage (or gharry) at a standstill.

Notes

1 *The royal almanac & directory for the year 1864* (p. 91). Singapore: Straits Times Press. Retrieved from BookSG; Falconer, J. (1987). *A vision of the past: A history of early photography in Singapore and Malaya: The photographs of G.R. Lambert & Co., 1880–1910* (pp. 21, 24). Singapore: Times Editions. (Call no.: RSING 779.99597 FAL)
2 Collodion was made by dissolving gun cotton in ether and alcohol, and then adding potassium iodide. The resultant viscous mixture was then applied evenly to a glass plate. The plate was subsequently immersed into a bath of silver nitrate to produce light-sensitive silver iodide.
3 Balmer, J. (1993). Introduction. In Thomson, J, *The Straits of Malacca, Siam and Indo-China: Travels and adventures of a nineteeth-century photographer.* Singapore: Oxford University Press, p. xix. (Call no.: RSEA 915.9 THO-[TRA])
4 Balmer, 1993, pp. xix–xx; Hirsch, R. (2000). *Seizing the light: A history of photography* (p. 72). Boston: McGraw-Hill. (Call no.: RART q770.9 HIR)
5 Balmer, 1993, pp. xx–xxiii.
6 The Dalhousie Obelisk. (1971, September 17). *New Nation*, p. 9. Retrieved from NewspaperSG.
7 Municipal Committee. (1866, October 4). *The Singapore Free Press and Mercantile Advertiser*, p. 2; Municipal Committee. (1866, October 25). *The Singapore Free Press and Mercantile Advertiser*, p. 3. Retrieved from NewspaperSG.
8 Hirsch, 2000, p. 72.
9 Falconer, 1987, pp. 16–17.
10 Reilly, J.M. (1980). *The albumen & salted paper book* (p. 12). New York: Light Impressions. Retrieved from *Albumen Photographs: History, Science and Preservation* website.
11 Dobson, S. (2009, May). The Prussian expedition to Japan and its photographic activity in Nagasaki in 1861. *Old photography study, 3*, pp. 28-29. Retrieved from Nagasaki University's Academic Output SITE (NAOSITE) website.
12 Notice. (1864, October 22). *The Straits Times*, p. 5. Retrieved from NewspaperSG.
13 *The Straits calendar and directory (including Sarawak and Labuan) for the year 1865* (p. 14). Singapore: The Commercial Press. (Call no.: RRARE 382.09595 STR); *The Straits calendar and directory (including Sarawak and Labuan) for the year 1867* (p. 14). Singapore: The Commercial Press. (Call no.: RRARE 382.09595 STR)
14 Falconer, 1987, p. 24; *The Straits calendar and directory (including Sarawak and Labuan) for the year 1868* (p. 13). Singapore: The Commercial Press. (Call no.: RRARE 382.09595 STR)
15 Serious accident. (1869, March 2). *Straits Overland Journal*, p. 7. Retrieved from NewspaperSG.
16 *The Straits calendar and directory (including Sarawak and Labuan) for the year 1872* (p. 51). Singapore: The Commercial Press; *The Straits calendar and directory (including Sarawak and Labuan) for the year 1873* (p. 55). Singapore: The Commercial Press.
17 Notice. (1874, June 6). *The Straits Times*, p. 4. Retrieved from NewspaperSG.
18 Falconer, 1987, p. 25.
19 Falconer, 1987, p. 27; Toh, 2009, p. 30.

THE FIRST HYDROGRAPHIC SURVEY OF SINGAPORE

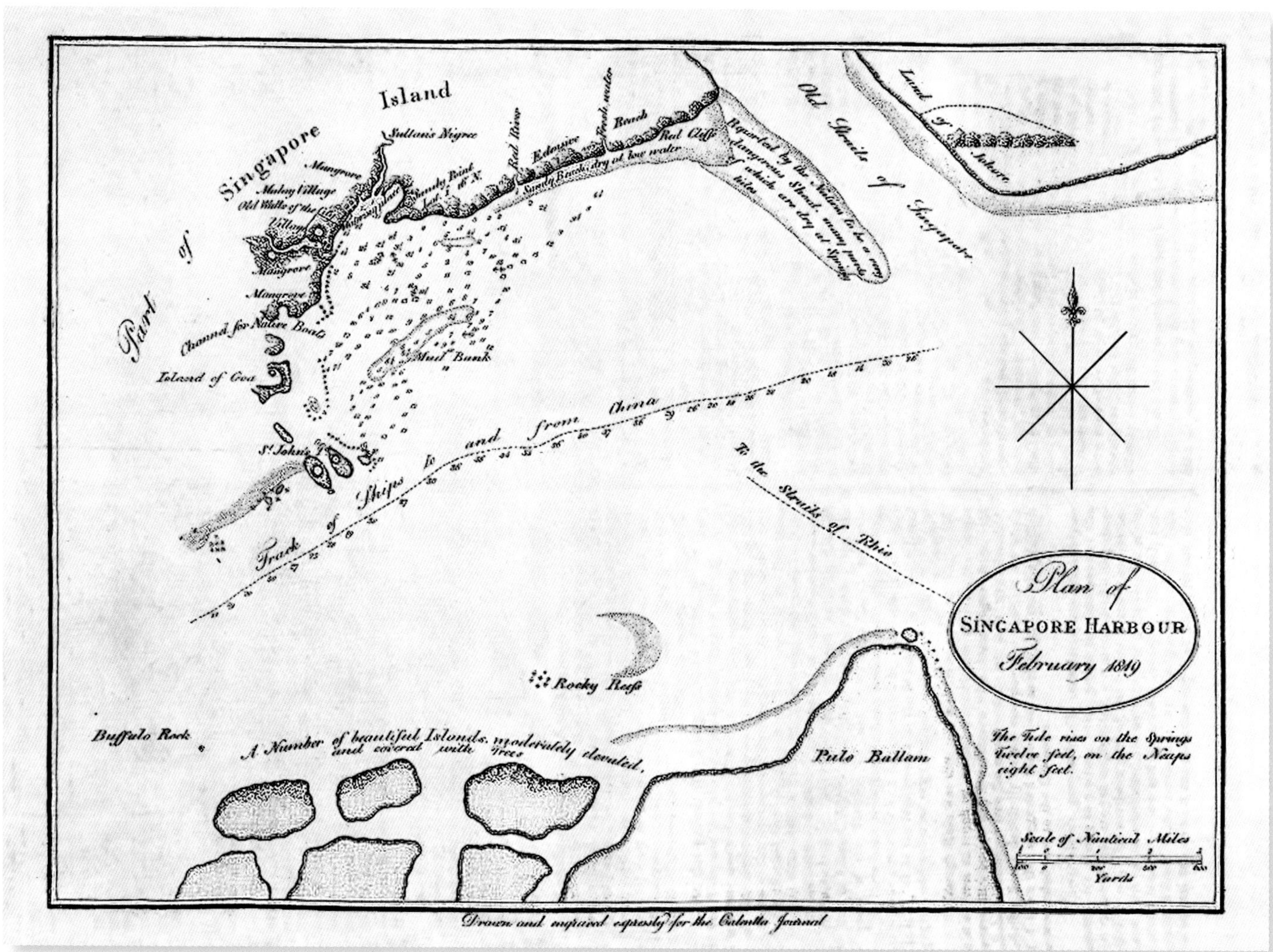

Title: *Plan of Singapore Harbour*
Creator: Daniel Ross
Year published: 1819
Publisher: Union Press
Language: English
Type: Map; 22 cm x 28.1 cm
Call no.: RRARE 954 CAL
Accession no.: B34443936C

This first map of Singapore's harbour was borne out of a cartographic survey conducted in 1819 by Captain Daniel Ross, a hydrographer with the British East India Company's (EIC) Bombay Marine, the India-based naval fleet set up to protect British trading routes in the Far East.

Ross' survey of the waters near Singapore Harbour was timely as it served to confirm Stamford Raffles' own theory that the island was indeed blessed with a good harbour and a prime location. This became a key factor in Raffles' decision to establish a British trading post in Singapore.

As it happened, Ross was already conducting a survey in the Straits of Melaka when Raffles embarked on a mission in January 1819 to set up a trading post for the

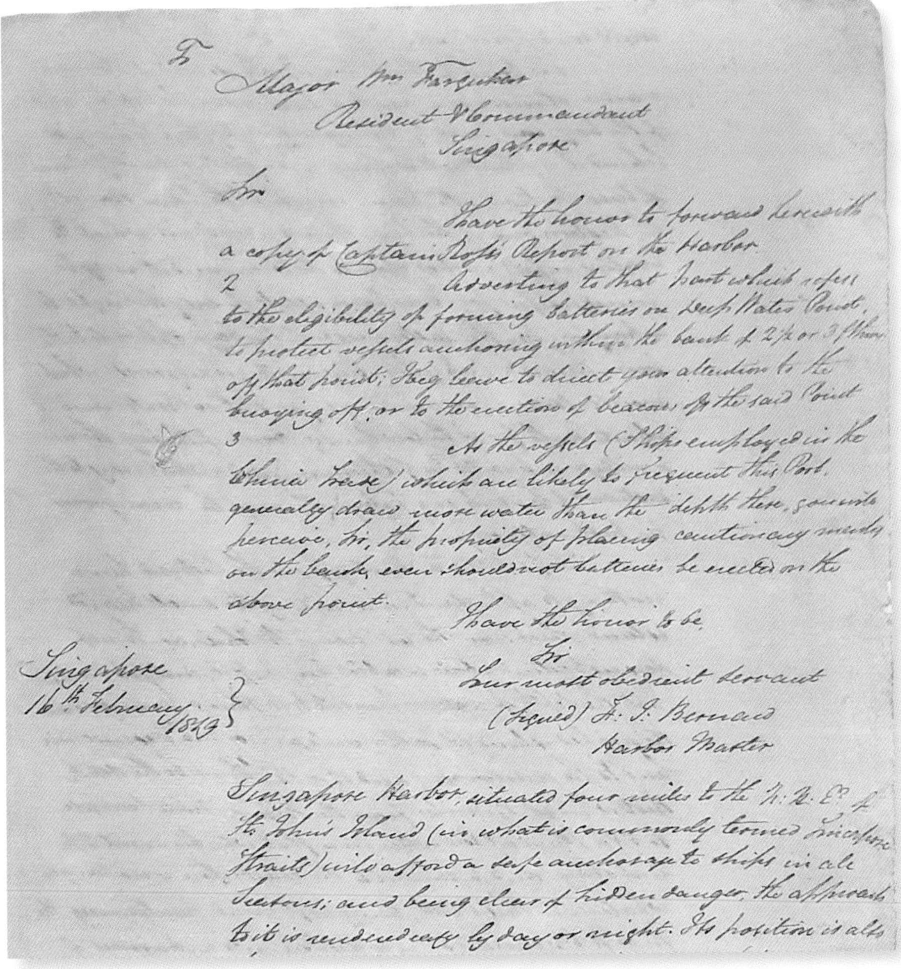

To
Major Wm Farquhar
Resident & Commandant
Singapore

Sir
I have the honor to forward herewith a copy of Captain Ross's Report on the Harbor.

2 Adverting to that part which refers to the eligibility of forming batteries on Deep Water Point, to protect vessels anchoring within the bank of 2½ or 3 fathoms off that point; I beg leave to direct your attention to the buoying off, or to the erection of beacons off the said Point.

3 As the vessels (Ships employed in the China trade) which are likely to frequent this Port, generally draw more water than the depth there, you will perceive, Sir, the propriety of placing cautionary marks on the bank, even should not batteries be erected on the above point.

I have the honor to be
Sir
Your most obedient servant
(Signed) F. J. Bernard
Harbor Master

Singapore
16th February 1819

Singapore Harbor, situated four miles to the N.N.E. of St. Johns Island (in what is commonly termed Singapore Straits) will afford a safe anchorage to ships in all seasons; and being clear of hidden danger, the approach to it is rendered easy by day or night. Its position is also

[Facing page] Plan of Singapore Harbour, as published in the *Calcutta Journal* on 1 May 1819.
[Above] Detail from scribal copy of Captain Daniel Ross' Report on Singapore Harbour. Copy made on 16 February 1819. *Courtesy of National Archives of Singapore.*

EIC that could protect Britain's China trade and command the sea traffic traversing the southern end of the Malay Peninsula. Ross was subsequently appointed as the mission's lead marine surveyor and tasked with assessing the Karimun Islands in present-day Indonesia. Finding the location unsuitable, Ross suggested surveying a more promising site that he had recently spotted, located just at the mouth of the Singapore River.[1]

Serendipitously, Ross' suggestion corresponded with Raffles' own views on Singapore's strategic location.[2] When Raffles and William Farquhar landed on the island, they negotiated with the Temenggung to grant the EIC the right to establish a British trading post. Meanwhile, Ross began a survey of the mouth of the Singapore River and the surrounding coastline.

Despite being officially secret, Ross' map was printed in the *Calcutta Journal* on 1 May 1819, about three months after the agreement to allow the British to set up a trading post was signed. Ross' report had earlier been published in the 6 April edition of the same journal. According to historian John Bastin, it was likely that Raffles engineered this leak to the Indian newspaper in order to drum up public support for his plans.[3]

In his report, Ross predicted Singapore's ability to command the trade passing through the southern entrance of the Straits of Melaka:

> Singapore harbour, situated… in what is commonly called the Singapore Straits, will afford a safe anchorage to ships in all seasons and being clear of hidden danger, the approach to it is rendered easy by day or night. Its position is also favourable for commanding the navigation of the Straits… and it may be expected from its proximity to the Malayan Islands and China Seas, that in a short time numerous vessels will resort to it for commercial purposes.[4]

Ross' use of rigorous trigonometric techniques as well as astronomical and sound observations allowed him to calculate distances and depths with great precision. This is why his survey of Singapore was such a cartographic feat: it was the first to provide detailed measurements of the island's southeastern shoreline as well as the depth of the harbour. Historian Clements Markham, who studied Ross' work, described the painstaking process:

> [Ross] measured bases on shore by running a ten-foot cord stretched tight between the extreme points, and kept in position by stakes, the direction being verified by a telescope. When work on shore was impracticable, recourse was had to measurement by sound. The vessels were anchored when the weather was calm, and the time was taken between the flash and report of a gun, on the assumption that sound travels 1,140 feet per second.[5]

Ross measured the depth of the harbour in fathoms (1 fathom being 1.83 metres in depth). Prior to this chart, there were only estimates of Singapore's topography, many of which were later proven to be unreliable. Ross' chart was also the first to use "Singapore" as the island's name, in place of other variants such as "Sincapore" and "Singapoora". However, a complete survey of the outline of the island, conducted by Captain James Franklin, would only be completed and published a decade later, in 1828.

Before mapping Singapore, Ross was already known for his meticulous survey of the coast of China, specifically the coastline of Guangdong province and the Bohai Sea – an achievement that led to his election as a Fellow of the prestigious Royal Society in 1822. The following year, Ross was posted to India, where he became the EIC's chief marine surveyor. Even today, Ross is remembered as the "father of the Indian surveys" for his contributions to the field.[6]

♦ **Kevin Khoo**

Notes

1 Bastin, J.S. (2014). *Raffles and Hastings: Private exchanges behind the founding of Singapore* (pp. 45–46). Singapore: National Library Board & Marshall Cavendish Editions. (Call no.: RSING 959.5703 BAS-[HIS])
2 Bastin, 2014, p. 34.
3 Bastin, J.S. (2012). Historical sketch of the settlement of Singapore (pp. 112–114). In Nicholas Tarling (Ed.), *Studying Singapore's past: C.M. Turnbull and the history of modern Singapore*. Singapore: NUS Press. (Call no.: RSING 959.570072 STU)
4 See transcript of Ross' report in Bastin (2012), pp. 121–122.
5 Markham, C.R. (1878). *A memoir on the Indian surveys* (2nd ed.) (p. 11). London: W.H. Allen & Company. (Not in NLB holdings)
6 Markham, 1878, pp. 8–11.

KA PERUMAL
MUSINGS BY A TAMIL POET

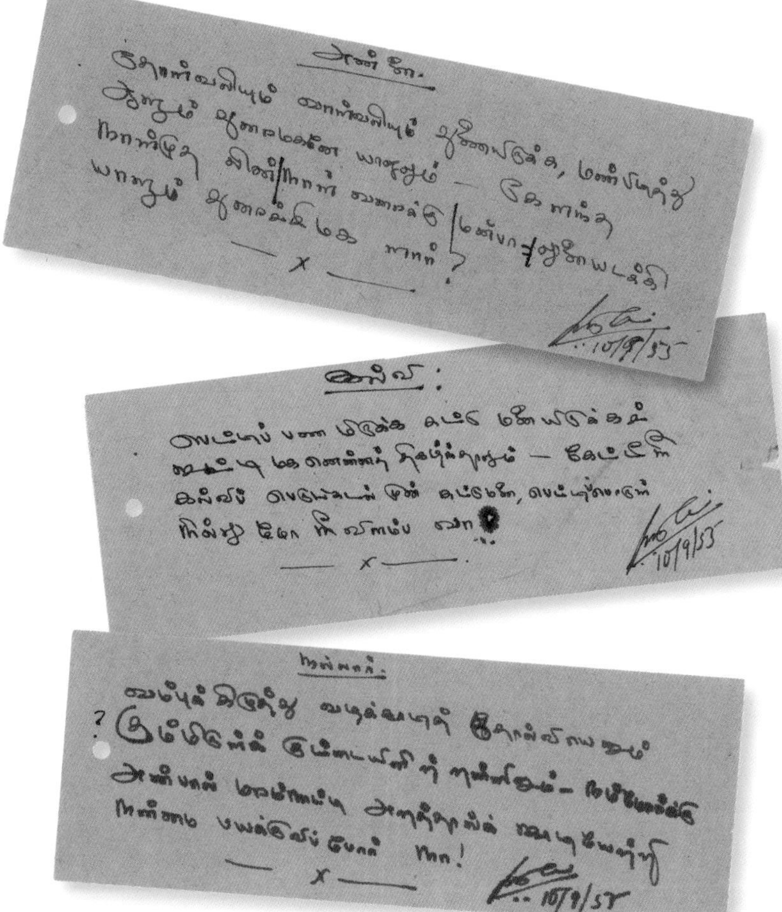

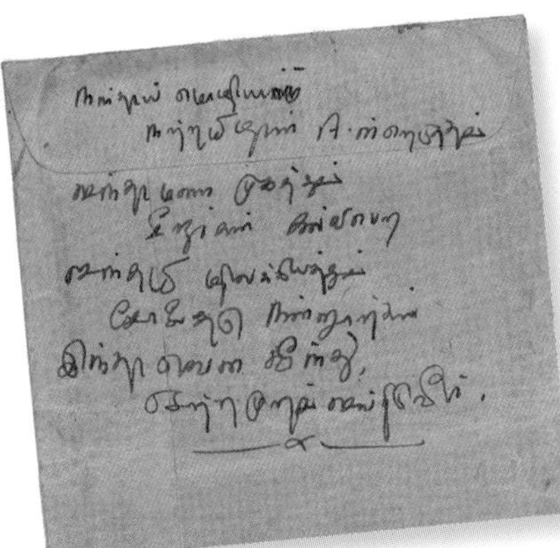

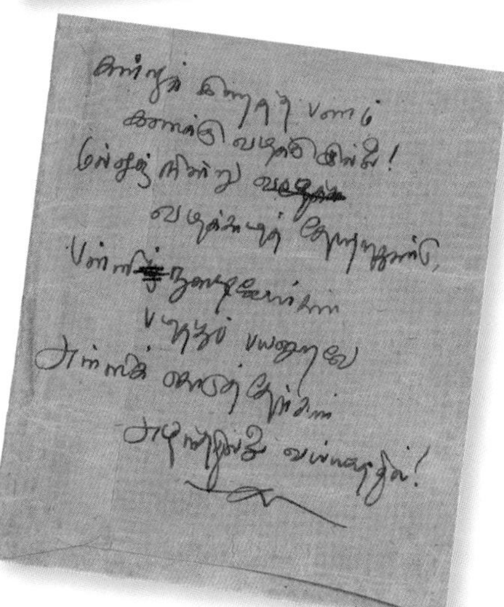

Title: கா பெருமாளின் படைப்புகள் (*Ka Perumalin Pataippukal*; The Works of Ka Perumal)
Author: கா பெருமாள் (Ka Perumal)
Year created: 1955
Language: Tamil
Type: Manuscript
Call no.: RCLOS 894.8116 PER
Accession nos.: B29227436B; B29227438D; B29227437C; B29227428C; B29227434K; B29227439E; B29227435A; B29227440H
Donated by: Family of the late Kavithaivel Ka Perumal

There are only eight short poems in this set of manuscripts, each comprising four lines and written in 1955 on scraps of paper, including two on the back of an envelope. These items, catalogued by the library as *Ka Perumalin Pataippukal* (கா பெருமாளின் படைப்புகள்), are an important part of a collection of handwritten poems and personal letters donated by the family of the late Kavithaivel Ka Perumal to the National Library, Singapore.

Ka Perumal, one of Singapore's most important Tamil literary pioneers, adopted the classical Tamil poetic form known as *venba* (வெண்பா) when he wrote these eight poems. The form typically consists of two or four lines. Perumal was particularly adept at writing *venba* poems. One of his poetry anthologies, *சிங்கப்பூர் பாடல்கள்* (Singapore Songs), is the best example of his prodigious talent.

Initially, religious poems were the main focus of Indian writers who migrated to Malaya in the 1950s. However, poets like Perumal, Na Palanivelu and Singai Mukilan moved away from spiritual matters and

The One Who Excels in Poetry

Ka Perumal (1923–1979) was a self-taught writer whose works included plays, poetry, novels and short stories. Born into an impoverished family in Namakkal in Tamil Nadu, India in 1923, he received only primary school education before arriving in Malaya in 1938 when he was 15 years old. He first worked at the Boh Tea Estate in Cameron Highlands, Pahang,[1] where he was so moved by the plight of Indian plantation workers that he wrote stories about their lives. These first appeared in the Malayan newspaper *Sangamani*, then were later published as a novel, *Thuyarap-paathai*, in 1978.[2]

Under the tutelage of Ulaga Uzhiyanaar, a well-known Tamil scholar and teacher, Perumal became adept in crafting poems, plays, fiction and novels, and wrote for various newspapers. He was well-versed in *villupattu* – a form of musical story-telling performed with a bow-shaped musical instrument. He also acted in plays and was an exponent of *silambattam*, a form of martial arts.[3]

Perumal joined Radio Malaya in 1959, and in 1963, he began working at Radio Singapore where he wrote plays, articles, poems, and other works for various programmes. Many of the patriotic songs he wrote were broadcast over radio. Pandit Ramalingam set these to music and in 1979, they were compiled and published as *சிங்கப்பூர் பாடல்கள* (Singapore Songs).[7]

One of the highlights of Perumal's career was when he presented his research article entitled *"Malainaattu Uzhaippor Ilakkiyam"* (Literature of Estate Labourers) at the second World Tamil Conference in Chennai in 1968.

Perumal passed away in 1979, leaving behind his wife and two sons. The Malaysian Tamil literary world came together and praised his contributions to the Tamil language by publishing a book in his honour. Writers and friends wrote articles commending his life and his literary works, praising him as "Kavithaivel", meaning "one who excels in poetry".[8]

Ka Perumal, one of Singapore's most important Tamil literary pioneers.

[Facing page, anti-clockwise from top left] Shown here are five of the eight unpublished poems included in Ka Perumal's manuscripts. *"Annai"* (அன்னை; "Mother") celebrates the greatness of mothers; *"Kalvi"* (கல்வி; "Education") emphasises that it is more important to be well-educated than to be immensely wealthy; *"Nallaar"* (நல்லார்; "Righteous People") highlights that the righteous remain compassionate even in the face of humiliation; as well as two untitled poems which encourage people to support educational causes.

began writing about human values and social issues.[4] They criticised the Indian caste system and addressed issues such as enslavement, alcoholism and the abuse of women in their work.[5] Around the same time, newspapers began focusing public attention on the political issues and social reforms taking place in India, Singapore and Malaya.[6]

Read against this context, the eight poems – which address universal themes relating to education and the Tamil language, ideals of motherhood, and the importance of righteousness and moral behaviour – are valuable records of Perumal's concerns about society and offer a window into his mind.

Two of these eight poems deal with the subject of motherhood. In *"Annai"* (அன்னை; "Mother"), Perumal praises women and their roles as mothers, drawing attention to the pain of pregnancy and childbirth, and the sacrifices they make for their families. In *"Pennin Perumai"* (பெண்ணின் பெருமை; "Women's Pride"), he condemns the ill treatment of women.

Education is the subject of two poems, both of which share the same title *"Kalvi"* (கல்வி; "Education"). One poem expresses the idea that material wealth is far less important compared to knowledge, while in the second poem, he says that only the ignorant think that they can defeat a wise man in an argument.

Two poems in this collection – *"Nallaar"* (நல்லார்; "Righteous People") and *"Theeyor"* (தீயோர்; "Evil People") – illustrate Perumal's firm belief in the importance of sound moral values. In the former, the poet says that righteous people will show their love and compassion even in the face of defeat and public humiliation. In the latter poem, he warns that venomous snakes that dwell among anthills are less dangerous than mean-spirited people disguised as good souls.

Perumal was a man of great conviction: in 1955, when a friend who had set up a library for Tamil students in a school in Pahang asked him to write a poem to encourage people to donate Tamil books, he contributed two poems. Both untitled pieces are part of the collection too. The first poem solicits donations of books to the library so that children will grow up with the proper foundation in the Tamil language. In the second, the poet notes that indulging in liquor and other vices have wrecked people's lives but no one has ever suffered from supporting education. ♦ **Sundari Balasubramaniam**

Notes

1 செங்கோட்டையா நல்லையா. (1993). பல்கலை வல்லுனர் கா. பெருமாள். in *கவிதைவேள் கா. பெருமாள்* (பக். 25-27). பாஹாங், மலேசியா: திருக்குறள் மன்றம். (Call no: RSING 894.8114 PER)

2 பெருமாள் கா. (1978). துயரப் பாதை, பக் 11. சென்னை: தமிழ்ப் புத்தகாலயம். (Call no: RSING S894.811371 PER)

3 பெருமாள் கா. (1978). *அன்பு எனும் தத்துவம் இஸ்லாம், பக்.* III. Madras: Simma Enterprises & Printers. (Call no: RSING 894.8111 PER); Varadpande, M.L. (1987). *History of Indian theatre, Vol. 2* (p. 125). New Delhi: Abhinav Publications. (Call no.: RART q792.0954 VAR)

4 நா. ஆண்டியப்பன். (2010). சிங்கப்பூர்த் தமிழ் இலக்கிய வரலாறு ஒரு பார்வை. In கார்த்திகேயன் ஆ., உதயசூரியன் சா. (Ed.), சிங்கப்பூர் மலேசியத் தமிழ் இலக்கியம் (பக். 40–44). தஞ்சாவூர்: தமிழ்ப் பல்கலைக்கழகம். (Call no.: RSING 894.81109 SIN)

5 செங்கோட்டையா நல்லையா. (1993). பல்கலை வல்லுனர் கா. பெருமாள். In *கவிதைவேள் கா. பெருமாள்* (பக். 25–27). பாஹாங், மலேசியா : திருக்குறள் மன்றம். (Call no: RSING 894.8114 PER)

6 Arasaratnam, S. (1967). Social reform and reformist pressure groups among the Indians of Malaya and Singapore 1930–1955. *Journal of the Malaysian Branch of the Royal Asiatic Society, 40*(2(212)), p. 64. Retrieved from JSTOR.

7 பெருமாள் கா. (1979). *சிங்கப்பூர் பாடல்கள், பக்* 2. சென்னை: பாரி நிலையம். (Call no: RSING 784.7195957 PER)

8 திருக்குறள் மன்றம். (1993). *கவிதைவேள் கா. பெருமாள்.* பாஹாங், மலேசியா: திருக்குறள் மன்றம். (Call no: RSING 894.8114 PER)

The Secret World of Magic in Colonial Singapore

Covers of six issues of the Malayan Magic Circle's official magazine *The Magic Fan*, which were designed by their resident illustrator L.A. Duckworth.

Title: *The Magic Fan*
Year published: 1938–39
Publisher: Malayan Magic Circle (Singapore)
Language: English
Type: Periodical (6 volumes)
Call no.: RRARE 793.8 MF
Accession nos.: B32431649J (Vol. 1, No. 1, Jul 1938); B32431650B (Vol. 1, No. 2, Nov 1938); B32431651C (Vol. 1, No. 3, Jan 1939); B32431652D (Vol. 1, No. 4, Apr 1939); B32431653E (Vol. 2, No. 1, Jul 1939); B32431654F (Vol. 2, No. 2, Oct 1939)

The Magic Fan was the official magazine of the Malayan Magic Circle. One of the club's objectives was "to publish a periodical or other literature relating to magic and the work of the club and to encourage and assist every effort which would tend to foster and uphold the art of magic and to found a reference library relating to magic and its kindred subjects".[1] To this end, the first issue of *The Magic Fan* was published in July 1938. Among the nine known extant issues,[2] the National Library holds the first issue, as well as five others, in its collection.

Entertainment magic, as pioneered by the French illusionist Jean Eugène Robert-Houdin, reached the zenith of its popularity betweeen the late 1880s and the 1930s. During this golden age, performance magic flourished in theatres and vaudeville circuits across Europe, North America and its settler colonies.[3] The maturation of theatrical magic as a performance art saw the proliferation of fraternal organisations where magicians could share their trade secrets and promote the art form.

In Singapore, the Malayan Magic Circle was founded in 1935 as "a club where those interested in the art could meet, practise and discuss magic and kindred subjects".[4] As the first magic society in Singapore, it played a pivotal role in the early development of stage magic in Singapore. At its height, the club had more than 100 members, most of whom were Europeans. There were also prominent non-European members, including Tengku Ahmad of Johor, Syed Ibrahim bin Omar Alsagoff, Aw Boon Par, Joseph Aaron Elias, Lee Kong Chian and Navroji Rustomji Mistri.

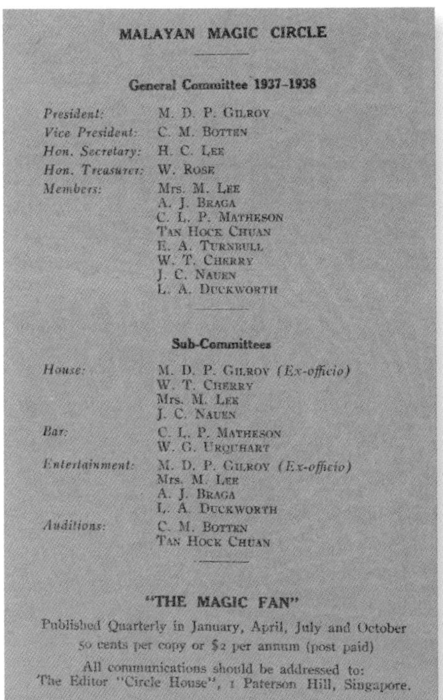

MALAYAN MAGIC CIRCLE

General Committee 1937–1938

President:	M. D. P. Gilroy
Vice President:	C. M. Botten
Hon. Secretary:	H. C. Lee
Hon. Treasurer:	W. Rose
Members:	Mrs. M. Lee A. J. Braga C. L. P. Matheson Tan Hock Chuan E. A. Turnbull W. T. Cherry J. C. Nauen L. A. Duckworth

Sub-Committees

House:	M. D. P. Gilroy (*Ex-officio*) W. T. Cherry Mrs. M. Lee J. C. Nauen
Bar:	C. L. P. Matheson W. G. Urquhart
Entertainment:	M. D. P. Gilroy (*Ex-officio*) Mrs. M. Lee A. J. Braga L. A. Duckworth
Auditions:	C. M. Botten Tan Hock Chuan

"THE MAGIC FAN"

Published Quarterly in January, April, July and October
50 cents per copy or $2 per annum (post paid)

All communications should be addressed to:
The Editor "Circle House", 1 Paterson Hill, Singapore.

MAGIC FOR ALL
by
Ten Hock Chuan

The Dissolving Ball - A large red glass ball is shown and passed for examination. It is then dropped into a clear tumbler. An open tube is then put over the tumbler. Water is poured into the tumbler through the top of the tube. When the tube is lifted, the ball is no longer to be seen. The water is also red, having apparently dissolved the solid glass sphere.

Tumbler 'A' — Fake 'B' — Celluloid tube with thread sewn across the bottom.

Method - A la the "Demon Tumbler", you require a celluloid fake to fit the tumbler. This fake is only a tube with one end prepared by having thread sewn over it as shown in the diagram 'B'. At the beginning of the trick, the fake is in the tumbler 'A'. Being of clear celluloid, it does not reveal itself. The glass ball will strike the bottom of the real tumbler when dropped into it. To vanish the ball you have only to lift the fake with the tube which is over the glass. The red liquid is nothing but our old friend, the 'Wine and Water' effect.

The fake containing the ball may be dropped into a well and the red liquid drunk if you use the phenolphthalein method.

[Clockwise from far left] List of committee members published in Vol. 1, No. 1. In the same issue, Tan Hock Chuan, who wrote a regular column, "Magic for All" for the magazine, explained a magic trick called "The Dissolving Ball"; A photographic illustration of a scene from *Subtleties*, a production staged by the society in June 1937,[8] appeared in Vol. 1, No. 4.

The society was known for its charitable performances and grand, slick productions which left audiences spellbound. It was most active in the late 1930s, and relocated its headquarters four times – in 1936, 1937, and twice in 1939.[5] Under the editorship of W.T. (Bill) Cherry, and later J.S. Davidson, the society released one issue of *The Magic Fan* every quarter as planned until the outbreak of World War II in Southeast Asia. This was a laudable feat considering the many activities it was involved in, such as staging large-scale productions in Singapore and Malaya, conducting instructional classes and organising social events.

The Magic Fan was a modest publication consisting of a coloured cover and around 26 pages of mimeographed[6] sheets. The cover design was created by the society's resident illustrator L.A. Duckworth. Each cover features a fan of playing cards (alluded to in the magazine's title), an illustration of the Sphinx, the club badge and what appears to be the club's competition trophy (called the President's Cup) in the background. *The Magic Fan* was a privately circulated magazine available only to club members and foreign affiliates. Members could purchase an annual subscription for 2 Straits dollars or a copy for 50 cents initially. The magazine was also distributed to publishers of magic-related magazines and magic organisations overseas in exchange for their publications.

Issues of *The Magic Fan* feature news about the Malayan Magic Circle and its activities, reviews of its productions as well as news about magic-related groups overseas. The magazine also contains articles on magic effects and performance, poetry, illustrations, a section on jokes, personal notices of its members and letters to the editor.

Many entries were contributed by members of the club, although some were reproduced from other foreign publications. Of note is "Magic for All", a regular column on magic effects. It was penned by Tan Hock Chuan who was renowned for his many magic trick inventions. Tan was the winner of the Sphinx Award in 1937. This award was conferred on amateur magicians who had submitted the best magical act of the year to *The Sphinx*, a leading American magazine about the magical arts.

Fascinating articles and stories on magic traditions practised in Singapore and Malaya were also featured in *The Magic Fan*. In keeping with the discourse of modernity and scientific rationality characteristic of mainstream Western-style performance magic, writers and members generally expressed their scepticism regarding practices relating to the supernatural. Not only did they disavow associations with the occult, they also articulated a code of ethics that positioned performance magic as a knowing deception between the performer and the audience.[7]

Unfortunately, the Malayan Magic Circle's activities came to a halt with the outbreak of World War II in Southeast Asia. The society lost many of its magic props when the clubhouse was seized and used as a holding place for prisoners-of-war by the Japanese army. Though attempts were made to revive the society after the war, it gradually petered out. The death of its founding president M.D.P. Gilroy in 1952 sounded the death knell. The void it left was filled by new local magician groups, such as the Singapore chapter of the International Brotherhood of Magicians (also known as Ring 115).[9]

As the official mouthpiece of the Malayan Magic Circle, *The Magic Fan* is a valuable primary source that provides insights into the practice of magic, the club's history and its role in the development of entertainment magic in colonial Singapore. In addition, the magazine also serves as a record of its many social contributions, including performances in aid of charitable causes such as the Children's Aid Society and the St. Andrew's Mission Hospital.[10] Lastly, the magazine documents the networks that were forged between the community of magicians in Singapore and those in the United States, Britain, India, Australia and New Zealand. ♦ **Gracie Lee**

Notes

1 C.L.P.M. (1938, July). The Malayan Magic Circle. *The Magic Fan*, 1 (2), unpaged. (Call no.: RRARE 793.8 MF)

2 Lawsons. (2011). *Lot 1858*. Retrieved from Lawsons Auctioneers & Valuers website; State Library of New South Wales. (n.d.) *Catalogue: Record on Magic fan*. Retrieved from State Library of New South Wales catalogue website; UC Berkeley Libraries. (n.d.). *OskiCat: Record on Magic fan*. Retrieved from UC Berkeley Libraries catalogue website.

3 Magic (In entertainment). *The Columbia Encyclopedia*. 6th edition. Retrieved from Encyclopedia.com website.

4 C.L.P.M., July 1938, unpaged.

5 Magic Circle's big sum for charity. (1937, October 25). *The Straits Times*, p. 13; Magic Circle entertains. (1938, February 5). *Morning Tribune*, p. 21; Magic Circle. (1939, July 26). *The Straits Times*, p. 14; Retrieved from NewspaperSG.

6 Mimeographed sheets were printed by forcing ink through a stencil onto paper. A single stencil could be used to make many copies.

7 Stibbe, A. (2005, Fall/Winter). ABRACADABRA, ALAKAZAM: Colonialism and the discourse of entertainment magic. *Soundings: An interdisciplinary journal*. Retrieved from JSTOR database; Goto-Jones, C. S. (2016). Modern magic in history and theory. In *Conjuring Asia: Magic, orientalism, and the making of the modern world*. (2016). Cambridge; New York: Cambridge University Press. (Call no. R 133.43095 GOT)

8 Magic Circle to give another show. (1937, June 21). *The Straits Times*, p. 13. Retrieved from NewspaperSG.

9 Chew, Y. K. (1981, January 10). Making magical moments. *The Straits Times*, p. 5; Doyen of S'pore magic. (1982, June 8). *The Straits Times*, Section 2, pp. 1, 8. Collection of the walking encyclopaedia. (1982, June 8). *The Straits Times*, p. 8. Retrieved from NewspaperSG; *The Magic Fan*. (1938-1939). Singapore: (Malayan Magic Circle). (Call no.: RRARE 793.8 MF)

10 Magic Circle show. *The Singapore Free Press and Mercantile Advertiser*, p. 7; Magic Circle's big sum for charity. (1937, October 25). *The Straits Times*, p. 13. Retrieved from NewspaperSG.

PHOTO ALBUMS OF A PLAGUE FIGHTER

Title: Wu Lien-teh Collection
(i) *Plague and Medical Scenes: Manchuria and China, 1911, 1921 up to 1936*
(ii) *Chronological Record of Anti-plague Work in Manchuria and China, 1910–1937*

Date: 1910–37

Type: Photo album; 422 photographs

Call no.: RCLOS 610.92 WU-[WLD]

Accession nos.: B20062869K; B20062870C

Donated by: Family of Dr Wu Lien-teh

[Anti-clockwise from top right] A row of eight display boards at Mukden Siaho Yuan, where the first International Plague Conference was held in April 1911; A new laboratory was built in 1921 at the Manchurian Plague Prevention Service established by Dr Wu Lien-teh in 1912; The epidemiologist Dr Robert Pollitzer (bending over the microscope) and Dr Wu running a laboratory investigation during the second pneumonic plague in Manchuria in 1920. When the plague ended, both doctors collaborated to publish their findings.

Captioned "Examining the dead found in streets" **[above]** and "Plague patient thrown out of house 1921" **[left]**, these two photographs reveal the ravages of the second pneumonic plague in Manchuria.

Thanks to his pioneering work in eradicating the first (1910–11) and the second (1920–21) pneumonic plagues in Manchuria,[1] Penang-born doctor Wu Lien-teh (1879–1960) became the first Chinese doctor nominated for the Nobel Prize in Medicine in 1935. The principles and measures he applied and implemented as chief medical officer of an anti-plague organisation in Harbin, China, continued to be studied in the 21st century as part of efforts to stem the spread of infectious diseases such as SARS (Severe Acute Respiratory Syndrome), Ebola, and most recently, COVID-19.[2]

Two albums of 422 photographs provide valuable documentation of Wu's efforts. His eldest daughter, Dr Betty Wu Yu-Lin, donated the albums – titled *Plague and Medical Scenes: Manchuria and China, 1911, 1921 up to 1936* and *Chronological Record of Anti-plague Work in Manchuria and China, 1910–1937* – on behalf of the family of Dr Wu Lien-teh to the National Library in 2010.[3] The snapshots were very likely taken and captioned by Wu himself, but it is not known who had taken those featuring him. Among others, the photographs of laboratories, isolation and protective measures, patrolling squads and medical staff at work bear testimony to a massive operation hampered by unsanitary conditions, fear, poorly equipped medical facilities as well as a lack of trained healthcare workers.[4]

Wu's photographs capture the dire conditions in Manchuria that sparked waves of infection during the first pneumonic plague in 1910. The death toll, which averaged an astounding 180 a day, and frozen grounds in Harbin's harsh winter made it impossible to bury the dead. Corpses were thus left in the open. In a bid to stem infections, Wu petitioned for imperial sanction for the mass cremation of corpses – an act considered sacrilegious in a country where ancestor worship and the care of ancestral tombs were a mark of filial piety.[5] However, imperial sanction was granted. Hence on 31 January 1911,

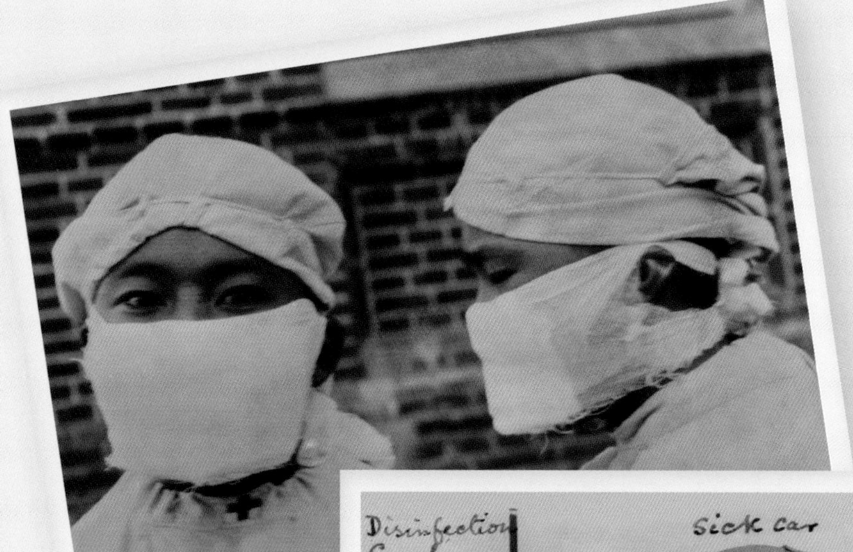

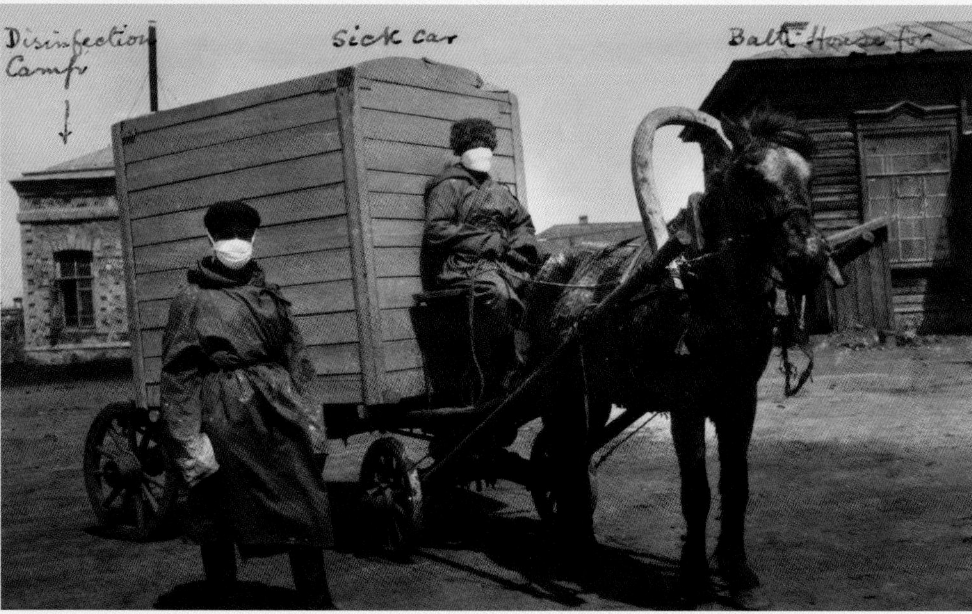

[Left] Demonstrating the correct way of wearing cotton gauze masks, c. 1920–c. 1921; **[Below]** This photograph features a "sick car" – a horse-drawn wagon driven by a medical worker wearing a face mask – which was used to transport the infected during the second pneumonic plague. The building on the left in the background is a disinfection camp, while that on the right is a bathhouse where people who had come into contact with the sick were disinfected.

22 bonfires were lit to cremate some 2,000 corpses in Harbin over three days. Other cities followed suit with mass cremation, and soon, mortality rates dropped. The plague was finally contained in April 1911.[6]

Wu thus came to be known as "the plague fighter". He went on to organise the first International Plague Conference in Mukden (now Shenyang) in April 1911 – the first international scientific conference held in China. In 1912, he established the Manchurian Plague Prevention Service in Harbin. Initially tasked to contain the epidemic, the service assumed larger public health functions in China.[7] The network of medical facilities that Wu built and the medical personnel he had trained prepared China for the second pneumonic outbreak which struck Manchuria in 1920.

Typed captions on some photographs in the albums reveal the onslaught of the second pneumonic plague.[8] These also document the containment strategies that Wu had implemented during both plagues despite initial resistance from the public, for instance the proper wearing of cotton gauze masks by patients and medical staff,[9] and other disinfection measures. When the plague ended in 1921, some 9,300 lives had been lost. This was a significant reduction compared with the estimated 60,000 deaths in the first outbreak.

Between 1910 and the 1930s, Wu modernised China's medical system, and established 20 hospitals and medical institutions in the country. Unfortunately, much of this infrastructure was destroyed or damaged during the Japanese Occupation of Manchuria in 1931 and the Second Sino-Japanese War (1937–45).

To escape from the war, Wu and his family left China for Malaya in 1937.[10] He set up a clinic in Ipoh but Malaya was invaded by the Japanese army in December 1941. When the war ended in 1945, Wu continued working as a general practitioner in Ipoh where he was known as the doctor who gave free consultations and treatments to the poor. Although Wu had spent much time away from his birthland, he felt drawn to contribute to the people of Malaya. One of the things he did was to collect donations to start the Perak Library in Ipoh.[11] In 1960, Wu retired to Penang where he passed away on 21 January that year, at the age of 81.

In addition to the two albums which capture Wu's efforts as a plague fighter, the Wu Lien-teh Collection also includes his publications, works about him and more photographs relating to his personal and professional life. The collection, which comprises more than 900 items, is a rich repository offering precious insights into Wu's life and the times he lived in. ♦ **Lee Meiyu**

Wu Lien-teh: The Plague Fighter

A Malayan who made a name for himself internationally as a doctor, Wu Lien-teh (伍连德; also known as Gnoh Lean Tuck or Ng Leen Tuck), was born to a Straits Chinese family in Penang in 1879. He was educated at the Penang Free School where he excelled in his studies. In 1896, Wu was awarded the prestigious Queen's Scholarship. He enrolled at Cambridge University – the first medical student of Chinese descent to do so. He then undertook postgraduate research in medical institutes in Europe before returning to Malaya in 1903, where he became involved in various social reforms.[12]

In 1906, Wu established the Anti-Opium Association in Penang, a group which aimed to discourage opium smoking by, for instance, distributing free medicine to help addicts quit. He also organised the first Anti-Opium Conference of the Straits Settlements, which was held in Ipoh in 1907.[13] In addition, from 1903 to 1907, Wu served as one of the editors (along with Lim Boon Keng and Song Ong Siang) of *The Straits Chinese Magazine: A Quarterly Journal of Oriental and Occidental Culture*, the first English-language magazine entirely edited and published by Malayans.[14]

Wu left for China in 1908 to take up the post of vice-director of the Imperial Medical College in Tientsin (Tianjin).[15] He was appointed to investigate an epidemic that had broken out in Manchuria in late 1910. Wu arrived in Harbin, Northern Manchuria, on 20 December 1910 to begin work. He continued contributing to China's public health in various capacities. He headed the Manchurian Plague Prevention Service established in 1912, and was director of the National Quarantine Service headquartered in Shanghai from 1930 to 1937.[16] By the time Wu returned to Malaya in 1937, he had spent close to 30 years improving China's healthcare system.

Dr Wu Lien-teh, chief medical officer of the anti-plague organisation in Harbin, in his office during the first pneumonic plague in Manchuria, c. 1910s.

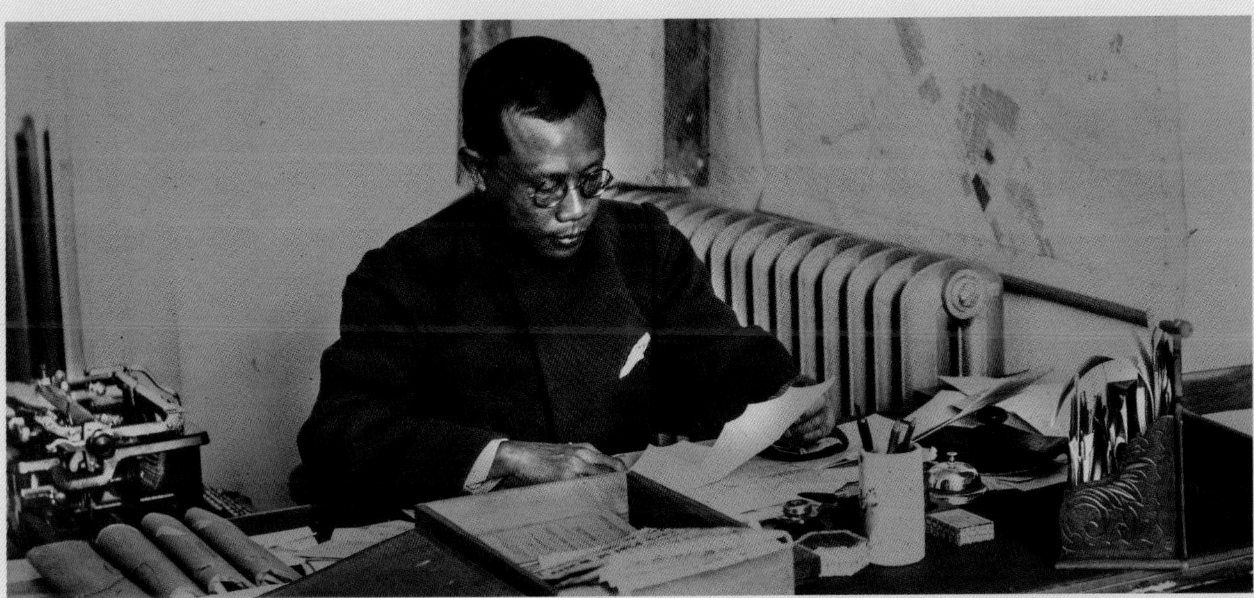

Notes

1 Both plagues were associated with the practice of hunting marmots, a rodent priced for its fur and commonly found in Mongolia and Manchuria. Hunters who came into contact with diseased marmots were the first to fall sick, and later spread the disease to other people through contact with their sputum (coughed up saliva and mucous). The plague spread widely and rapidly as infected humans travelled along the railway network built across the vast region. Both plagues claimed almost 70,000 lives. Also see Wu, L.-T. (2014). *Plague fighter: The autobiography of a modern Chinese physician* (pp. 33, 113). Penang, Malaysia: Areca Books. (Call no.: RSEA 610.92 WU)

2 Ma, Z.L., & Li, Y.L. (March 2016). Dr. Wu Lien Teh, plague fighter and father of the Chinese public health system. *Protein & Cell, 7*(3), 157. Retrieved from National Center for Biotechnology Information, U.S. National Library of Medicine website; Liu, H., et al. (2015, April). Controlling Ebola: What we can learn from China's 1911 battle against the pneumonic plague in Manchuria. *International Journal of Infectious Diseases*, Vol. 33, 222–236; Kool, J.L. (2005, April). Risk of person-to-person transmission of pneumonic plague. *Clinical Infectious Diseases, 40*(8), 1166–1172. Retrieved from Oxford University Press website; Liu, L.W. (2020, July 18). He fought the plague in China and inspired descendants to be doctors like him – the legacy of Wu Lien-teh. *South China Morning Post.* Retrieved from South China Morning Post website.

3 Digitised versions are available on PictureSG (eresources.nlb.gov.sg/pictures/).

4 Wu, 2014, pp. 5–38.

5 Wu, 2014, pp. 26, 28–29.

6 Wu, 2014, pp. 29–31.

7 Liew, L.K. (2009). Re(claiming) sovereignty: The Manchuria Plague Prevention Services (1912–31). In I. Borowy (Ed.), *Uneasy encounters: The politics of medicine and health in China, 1900–1937.* (pp. 125–148). Frankfurt: Peter Lang. (Call no.: RU 362.10951 UNE)

8 Wu, 2014, pp. 21, 26–28.

9 Wu, L.-T. (1923, May). The second pneumonic plague epidemic in Manchuria, 1920–21. *The Journal of Hygiene, 21*(3), 262–288, p. 277. Retrieved from JSTOR.

10 Wu, 2014, pp. 39, 43, 109–110, 113, 450–469; Wu Y.-L. (2016). *Memories of Dr. Wu Lien-teh: Plague fighter* (pp. 113, 131–132). Penang, Malaysia: Areca Books. (Call no.: RSEA 610.92 WU)

11 Wu, 2016, pp. 132–153.

12 Wu, 2014, pp. 149, 196; Wu, 2016, p. 27.

13 Penang Anti-Opium Association. (1906, November 14). *Eastern Daily Mail and Straits Morning Advertiser*, p. 1; Penang Anti-Opium Association. (1907, February 5). *The Singapore Free Press and Mercantile Advertiser*, p. 5. Retrieved from NewspaperSG.

14 Literary works and social commentaries written by the Straits Chinese community were published in the magazine. Wu, 2014, p. 221; and Chong, A. *Wu Lien-Teh – Plague fighter extraordinaire* (p. 96). Retrieved from The Old Frees' Association (Singapore) website.

15 Wu, 2014, pp. 242–270.

16 Wu, 2016, pp. 32, 100.

MASURI S.N.
A POET WITH A SOCIAL CONSCIENCE

Masuri's folder, titled *Puisi puisi 2005: Insya Allah*, contains his manuscripts of some 30 poems. Included in it are two drafts of Masuri's "Addenda", one with the date 3/10/2004 written on it, while "7:30am" (but no date) is written on the other.

Title: *Puisi puisi 2005: Insya Allah* (Poems (2005): God Willing)
Author: Masuri S.N. (1927–2005)
Date: 2005
Type: Manuscript; typescript
Call no: RCLOS 899.28108 MAS
Accession no: B20110143A
Donated by: The family of Masuri Salikun

In reality, the death of a poet does not mean that his poems will follow him to the grave. In fact, his poems which are of high literary merit will continue to flourish and influence future generations. Eventually, they will become part of life.[1]

Translated from Malay, this quote by Masuri S.N. (1927–2005) aptly describes his lasting legacy as an important and prolific poet known for his mastery of *sajak*, a modern form of Malay poetry. Masuri, whose full name is Masuri bin Salikun, also used the pen name Martina. He was a founding member of Angkatan Sasterawan '50 (Asas '50), a leading Malay literary organisation in Singapore. During his lifetime, Masuri wrote more than 1,000 poems and earned numerous awards, including the Southeast Asia Write Award in 1980, the Tun Seri Lanang Award in 1995, and the Meritorious Service Medal in 2000.

Among Masuri's collection of handwritten manuscripts, typescripts, plays, essays and other materials donated by his family to the National Library in 2011 is a paper file titled *Puisi puisi 2005: Insya Allah.* In it are manuscripts of about 30 handwritten poems, most of which have not been published and were written possibly during the last two years of his life.

Portrait of Masuri S.N. *Courtesy of Majlis Bahasa Melayu Singapura.*

One particular poem titled "Addenda" deserves highlighting. It is a 16-line *sajak* that warns about the perils of materialism. Many of Masuri's works revolve around the human condition and the importance of striving for a meaningful existence. The date "3/10/2004" was written on one page of the manuscript, while "7.30am" was written on another. Based on observations of the other manuscripts in this file, it appears to be Masuri's practice to consider a poem complete only after he had typed it out and signed it. As such, handwritten versions of poems were for him drafts until they were typed out on paper. The title of the poem, "Addenda", which refers to additional material added at the end of a book or a publication,[2] suggests that Masuri still wanted to add to his oeuvre even in his late 70s.

This poem is made all the more significant because following Masuri's passing on 6 December 2005, a typewritten sheet with the title "Addenda" and the first four words – "*Berkali-kali kami diberitahu*" (Many a time we've been told) – was found in his typewriter. A photograph of the incomplete, typewritten sheet was subsequently published in *Berita Harian* on 10 December 2005.[3] Razif Bahari's translation of the poem[4] reads:

Addenda

Many a time we've been told
But still we refuse to know,
Hundreds of advice and umpteenth
sermons later
Yet we still refuse to hear.

We are in a maelstrom of mayhem
Man is in a mad grab for things
And producing all kinds of lunacy
Snapping up things
They are obsessed with.

We go all out
To be in debt and employ our
utmost ingenuity
To acquire things
And void them of meaning,
While we let our souls languish
In the heart of the city.

As academic Azhar Ibrahim points out, the first line of "Addenda" also reminds us how Masuri returns to the same universal social themes in many of his poems.[5] These themes include extolling the importance of discovering one's humanity or humaneness, and encouraging one to engage with others for the betterment of society. Some of these concerns are echoed in "Addenda". For instance, the poet cautions humans against being too materialistic or being overly obsessed about worldly pursuits "that [are] void of meaning" as they risk losing their humanity ("let our souls languish / In the heart of the city").

Another highlight of Masuri's unpublished manuscripts is a draft of "Panorama Seni" ("Arts Panorama"), dated 19 August 2005. In "Panorama Seni", he expresses his reservations about the development of Singapore's arts and culture scene in a globalised society, and calls for more creativity and bolder visions, rather than merely "polishing" outdated traditions. This version, clearly marked as a draft, is interesting because there are numerous amendments and notes on it. A numbered list appears on the first page of the manuscript – it could be an outline of the changing landscape explored in the poem, that is, from a fishermen's coast (*Pantai Nelayan*), to a village (*kampung*), city (*Bandar*), cosmopolitan city (*Kota Kosmopolitan*), and global city (*Kota Global*).

A copy of this poem was also donated to the National Library by the influential Malay playwright Almahdi Al-Haj Ibrahim (better known as Nadiputra).[6] Accompanying it was a note that "Panorama Seni" was used as a prologue for *Me Dia*, a play written and directed by Nadiputra. *Me Dia* was staged in January 2006, about two months after Masuri's death.

All in all, this collection of manuscripts attests to the painstaking effort Masuri took to draft his poems and highlights his determination to continue writing for as long as he was able to. One can only hope that his dedication and energy, as captured in the phrase, "*Selagi hayat dikandung badan*" (As long as I live),[7] which incidentally is also the title of an anthology he published in 1970, will continue to inspire future generations.

♦ **Juffri Supa'at**

Notes

1 The original quote reads "*Pada hakikatnya, matinya seorang penyair yang penting bukanlah mesti berkubur semua puisinya. Malah puisi-puisi yang bernilai akan terus hidup maju mengubah selera generasi yang akan datang. Dan puisi-puisinya itu makin meresap ke dalam kehidupan, sambil 'menyapa' penyair-penyair yang hasil puisinya memuaskan kehendak umat manusia yang berhak.*" Karyawan Persuratan Singapura. (2004). *SEKATA. Jurnal Pembinaan Bahasa dan Persuratan. Majlis Bahasa Melayu Singapura.* (Call No: RCLOS 499.28 S [MSN])

2 Cambridge Dictionary. *Addendum.* Retrieved from Cambridge Dictionary website.

3 Ini mesin taip yang kugunakan. (2005, December 10). *Berita Harian.* (p. 1). Retrieved from NewspaperSG.

4 Sa'eda Buang. (Ed.). (2012). *Ode to Masuri S.N.* (p. 65). Singapore: National Arts Council; Maths Paper Press. (Call No: RSING 899.282 MAS)

5 Pitchay Gani Aziz & Azhar Ibrahim Alwee (2015). *Di Sebalik Tabir Masuri S.N. Biografi dan Karya Pilihan yang Belum Tersiar* (pp. 133–138). Singapore: National Library Board & Bizmedia Publishing. (Call No: RSING 899.2809 MOH)

6 Masuri S. N. (2005). *Panorama Seni.* (Donated by Nadiputra). (Call No: RCLOS 899.282.MAS)

7 Masuri S. N. (1970). *Sa-lagi hayat di-kandong badan.* Singapura: Pustaka Nasional. (Call No: RSING 899.2305 MAS)

SHAME OF SURRENDER
JAPANESE POWs IN SINGAPORE

火焰樹

九号

Title: 火焰樹 (*Kaenju;* The Flame Tree)
Editors: 森力男; 柴崎初太
Date: June 1946–June 1947
Publisher: The Cultural Division of the Woodland Work Unit (ウッドランド作業隊文化部)
Language: Japanese
Type: Periodical; Bound copy of issues 2 to 12 (11 issues, 548 pages in total)
Call no.: RRARE 895.685 K
Accession no.: B29234663B

Personal accounts written by World War II Japanese prisoners-of-war (POWs) who served in the Imperial Japanese Army are unusual. This has largely to do with the wartime Japanese ethos which upheld that being captured alive by the enemy was the ultimate disgrace for a soldier, and that committing suicide to avoid imprisonment was a far more honourable outcome.

This idea was further reinforced by the *Senjinkun* (戦陣訓 or Japanese Army Field Service Code) issued to the Japanese public in January 1941 by General Hideki Tojo, who became Prime Minister 10 months later. The *Senjinkun*, which was issued by an imperial edict, declared that it was impermissible for Japanese soldiers to become prisoners-of-war.[1] Indoctrinated by this official imprimatur, Japanese troops were known to fight until their last breath even in potentially doomed situations: to be captured would bring shame not only to themselves, but to their families too.[2]

Few Japanese soldiers who survived incarceration during the war have dared to put pen to paper or openly talk about the matter and relive what traditional Japanese society considers a shameful episode of the country's history. Many Japanese POWs have taken decades to come to terms with their role in the war.[3] Given this context, the bound copy of *Kaenju*, which translates into "Flame Tree" in English, is an important document. It contains 11 issues of *Kaenju*, the magazine that was produced by

Illustration on cover page of one issue from *Kaenju*.

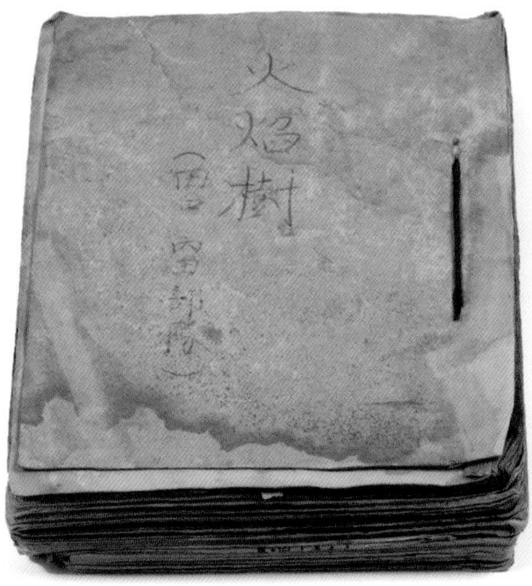

[Left] The bound copy of issues 2–12 of *Kaenju*; The logo of the "Cultural Division of the Woodland Work Unit". **[Below]** Japanese prisoners-of-war (POWs) working in the field – reading literary works written by their fellow inmates in their mother tongue would have been welcome relaxation after a day of hard work. *RAFSA Collection, courtesy of National Archives of Singapore.*

Japanese soldiers who were incarcerated in the Woodlands POW camp in Singapore and circulated among them. *Kaenju* is an important wartime record because it provides insight into how some Japanese POWs felt in the period immediately after their country was defeated in World War II.

The magazine was edited, published and circulated by the "Cultural Division of the Woodland Work Unit",[4] a group of Japanese POWs who occupied a small corner of the camp. Materials published in *Kaenju* included novels, play scripts, poems, prose, critical essays, research articles, as well as music scores and lyrics. While these were mimeographed on relatively coarse paper, the front cover of each issue was hand-drawn.

It is likely that limited copies of each issue were produced, with each well-thumbed copy passed from one inmate to another after one had finished reading it. Based on the dates of issues 2 to 12 in a bound copy,[5] it seems that the magazine was published monthly between June 1946 and June 1947.

In a few issues, the shortage of paper was mentioned in the afterword. This may explain why there are more pages in some issues than others: one issue, for instance, contains as few as 28 pages, while another has 112 pages. The shortage of paper was likely another reason why recycled paper was frequently used as the cover of *Kaenju*, with large maps and charts cut into smaller pieces for this purpose and illustrated by hand on the blank side.

Notwithstanding the paper shortage, the editor's remarks in the foreword to issue 2 suggest that his fellow inmates rendered their support enthusiastically by submitting their creative works for publication. In the afterword of issue 6, the editor notes that the Cultural Division had presented the "Flame Award" to 20 individuals who had been faithfully contributing to *Kaenju* ever since its first issue was published.

Leafing through issues of the publication, we get a sense of the conflicted emotions experienced by the Japanese prisoners. For instance, in the foreword of issue 2, the editor describes how their prospects were bleak, but at the same time cautions that since the soldiers had joined the military to show their loyalty, they should not openly criticise policies made by Japan's top officials.

In the afterword of issue 12, the editor ends on a more upbeat note, thanking his fellow inmates for their support and affirming that *Kaenju* was "a manifestation of their heartfelt strength". In response to the news that the POW camp would be relocated, the editor notes that the publishing of *Kaenju* might cease, and hopes that the prisoners would be repatriated as soon as possible to their homeland.

This reference is especially poignant as returning home alive from a POW camp was a delicate matter. As becoming a wartime prisoner would bring disgrace to a soldier's family,[6] Japanese authorities tended not to report such captures,[7] and would instead dispatch an official death notification to the family, informing them that the soldier had died a "glorious death" while battling the enemy, and that the "deceased" would be enshrined to commemorate his "heroic act".[8] It is thus remarkable that the editor of *Kaenju* openly expresses a yearning to return home.

The National Library's Rare Materials Collection contains numerous accounts penned by POWs from the Allied forces of their experiences after the fall of Singapore in February 1942 and during the Japanese Occupation. *Kaenju* is unique as it provides a glimpse of the Japanese POWs after they surrendered in September 1945. ♦ **Jessie Yak**

Notes

1 A sternly phrased reminder was stated in the *Senjinkun* under the heading "Regard for Reputation": "Those who know shame are weak. Always think of [preserving] the honour of your community and be a credit to yourself and your family. Redouble your efforts and respond to their expectations. Never live to experience shame as a prisoner. By dying you will avoid leaving behind the crime of a stain on your honour." Also see Straus, U.A. (2003). *The anguish of surrender: Japanese POWs of World War II* (pp. 38–39). Seattle: University of Washington Press. (Call no.: R 940.54727309 STR-[WAR])

2 Straus, 2003, pp. 50–51.

3 Straus, 2003, p. xii.

4 The English transliteration of a logo printed on the back cover of *Kaenju*, and the name of the publisher in Japanese (ウッドランド作業隊文化部), is "The Cultural Division of the Woodland Work Unit". It is, however, likely that the "s" sound was left out in the Japanese name, and that "Woodland" refers to "Woodlands".

5 The NLB only holds issues 2–12 (published between June 1946 and June 1947) in a bound copy, and a single copy of issue 4 (published in August 1947), because the collection was acquired as such. The whereabouts of issue 1 is not known.

6 Towle, P., Kosuge, M., & Kibata, Y. (Eds.). (2000). *Japanese prisoners of war* (p. 59). London: Hambledon and London. (Call no.: RSING 940.5472 JAP-[WAR])

7 Moore, B., Fedorowich, K. (Eds.). (1996). *Prisoners of war and their captors in World War II* (p. 265). Oxford: BERG. (Call no.: RSING 940.5472 PRI-[WAR])

8 Straus, 2003, pp. 234–235.

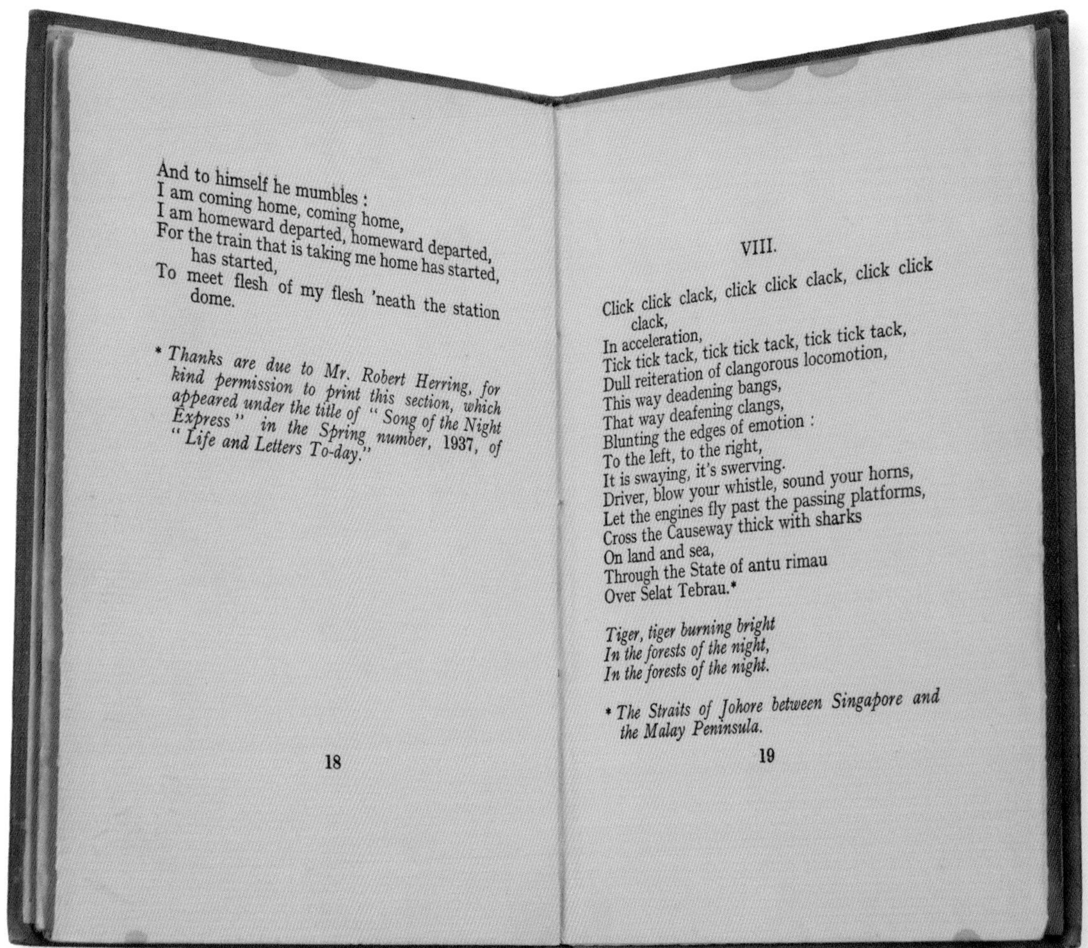

And to himself he mumbles :
I am coming home, coming home,
I am homeward departed, homeward departed,
For the train that is taking me home has started,
has started,
To meet flesh of my flesh 'neath the station
dome.

* *Thanks are due to Mr. Robert Herring, for kind permission to print this section, which appeared under the title of "Song of the Night Express" in the Spring number, 1937, of "Life and Letters To-day."*

18

VIII.

Click click clack, click click clack, click click
clack,
In acceleration,
Tick tick tack, tick tick tack, tick tick tack,
Dull reiteration of clangorous locomotion,
This way deadening bangs,
That way deafening clangs,
Blunting the edges of emotion :
To the left, to the right,
It is swaying, it's swerving.
Driver, blow your whistle, sound your horns,
Let the engines fly past the passing platforms,
Cross the Causeway thick with sharks
On land and sea,
Through the State of antu rimau
Over Selat Tebrau.*

Tiger, tiger burning bright
In the forests of the night,
In the forests of the night.

* *The Straits of Johore between Singapore and the Malay Peninsula.*

19

A Mysterious Poet
A Tragic Ending

Title: *F.M.S.R.: a poem*
Author: Francis P. Ng (pen name); Teo Poh Leng (actual name)
Year published: 1937
Publisher: Arthur H. Stockwell (London)
Language: English
Type: Book; 24 pages
Call nos.: RRARE 821.9 PNG-[RFL]; RRARE 821.9 PNG
Accession nos.: B03012471G; B02991729F

[Top] The footnote on page 18 of *F.M.S.R: a poem* was one of the clues used by Dr Eriko Ogihara-Schuck to uncover the mystery of the poet behind the pseudonym of Francis P. Ng. On page 19, Section VIII of *F.M.S.R.* opens with onomatopoeia that evokes the sound of a train moving across the Causeway.

In 1937, a 24-page long poem titled *F.M.S.R.* and published in London attempted to capture life in British Malaya during the Great Depression. The 10-part poem was attributed to Francis P. Ng and bore the influence of, among others, T.S. Eliot. Today, the poem is regarded as "the first notable work of English poetry produced by a Singaporean writer".[1]

F.M.S.R. consists of vignettes of the tropical and social landscape as observed on a train journey from Singapore to Kuala Lumpur. The train service was operated by the Federated Malay States Railways (FMSR), hence the title. A 1938 advertisement in the *Morning Tribune* newspaper in Singapore described *F.M.S.R.* as an "interesting book of poems" in which "local allusions and place names" are used. The book retailed for $1.50 locally.[2]

In the poem, British Malaya of the 1930s is portrayed as an emporium for "millionaires from the New World with nothing else to do". Specific references to Singapore abound, such as "the Ponggol Zoo... to meet living tigers, snakes and armadilloes / Or Raffles Museum to stare at stupid animals".[3] Reference is also made to the three entertainment parks (Beauty World, Gay World and New World), where "Night the undertaker mutters: / Dancing in the three Worlds, / Jazzing in their cabarets / Whirling in a drunken pace, / With a drunken grace."[4]

In his preface, the poet briefly explained that he chose "varying metres so as to express the varying rhythms of the railways".[5] By drawing attention to the unique

[Above] A poster by FMSR in the 1930s, promoting its services to explore Malaya by train. *Courtesy of the National Museum of Singapore, National Heritage Board.*
[Left] An example of an "S" class express engine that ran on the FMSR network. *Lee Kip Lin Collection, courtesy of National Archives of Singapore.*

poetic structure, coupled with the use of onomatopoeia to describe the sights and sounds of the journey, Teo creates distinctive "sensory experiences" for readers.[6]

According to the preface, the poem was composed between 1932 and 1934, and completed in 1935, with one part of the poem first appearing in the 1937 spring issue of the British literary journal, *Life and Letters To-day*.[7]

F.M.S.R. was published by Arthur H. Stockwell of London but only a few surviving copies of the work exist.[8] Extant copies of the original publication are currently available in five libraries around the world, with two copies residing in the National Library, Singapore. Both came into the library's collection in 1938 through its predecessor, the Raffles Library.

For a long time, little was known about the poet. No other poems attributed to Francis P. Ng were known and no biographical details of him were available. However, in 2013, a Japanese professor teaching American Studies at a German university became interested in the poet, thanks in part to the fact that his work displayed the influence of Eliot's *The Waste Land*. Determined to know more, Dr Eriko Ogihara-Schuck began a two-and-half year search for the man who had written *F.M.S.R.*

Through dogged detective work, she discovered that Francis P. Ng was actually the pen name of primary school teacher Teo Poh Leng. Teo was born in 1912 and had studied at St Joseph's Institution and Raffles College. His education in English-medium schools may have exposed him to Western literature and influenced his poetic sensibilities. This could explain why his poem, *F.M.S.R.*, alludes to the works of English poets such as W. B. Yeats' "The Wanderings of Oisin" (1889) and William Blake's "The Tyger" (1794).[9]

In 2015, Ogihara-Schuck contributed an essay to the National Library's journal, *BiblioAsia*, about her search for the poet Francis P. Ng and her discovery of his real name Teo Poh Leng. At that point though, she had only the barest details of his life. However, her piece led to a story in *The Straits Times* and thanks to the resulting publicity, Teo Poh Leng's niece, Anne Teo, came forward. Anne Teo is the daughter of Teo Kah Leng, the older brother of Poh Leng. Teo Kah Leng wrote poetry as well and had penned a poem entitled "I Found A Bone". The poem is about the deaths of the narrator's brothers – Peter and Paul – and the moment the narrator encounters Paul's arm bone half-buried in the sand on Punggol Beach. Anne Teo confirmed that her uncles Teo Kee Leng and Teo Poh Leng (whose Christian names were Peter and Paul respectively), had been killed during the Sook Ching massacre in 1942, in the days following the fall of Singapore.[10]

Ethos Books, a publisher in Singapore, re-published *F.M.S.R.* in late 2015 in the book *Finding Francis: A Poetic Adventure*, which included three shorter poems by Teo Poh Leng, as well as articles examining his work and life.[11] In 2016, Ethos Books published *I Found a Bone and Other Poems*, a collection of poetry by the elder brother, Teo Kah Leng. ♦ **Nadia Arianna Bte Ramli**

Notes

1 Ogihara-Schuck, E. (2015). Introduction (pp. 8–9). In E. Ogihara-Schuck & A. Teo. (Eds.), *Finding Francis: A poetic adventure*. Singapore: Ethos Books. (Call no.: RSING S821 NG)
2 Advertisement. (1938, January 22). *Morning Tribune*, p. 15. Retrieved from NewspaperSG.
3 Ng, F. P. (1937). *F.M.S.R.: A poem*. (p. 8). London: Arthur H. Stockwell. (Call no.: RRARE 821.9 PNG-[RFL])
4 Ng, 1937, p. 13.
5 Ng, 1937, p. 6.
6 Ogihara-Schuck, 2015, pp. 20, 22.
7 Ng, 1937, p. 18; Ogihara-Schuck, E. (2015, Jan–Mar). On the trail of Francis P. Ng: author of F.M.S.R. *BiblioAsia, 10*(4), 39. (Call no.: RSING 027.495957 SNBBA-[LIB])
8 Nanda, A. (2015, February 22). Do you know Teo Poh Leng? *The Straits Times*. Retrieved from Factiva.
9 Ng, 1937, pp. 12, 19.
10 Ogihara-Schuck, 2015, pp. 10, 20.
11 Heng, M. (2017, Jan–Mar). Ties that bind: The story of two brother poets. In *BiblioAsia, 12*(4), 38–41. (Call no.: RSING 027.495957 SNBBA-[LIB]); Ogihara-Schuck, 2015, *BiblioAsia* pp. 38–45; Nanda, A. (2015, February 22). Do you know Teo Poh Leng? *The Straits Times*. Retrieved from Factiva.

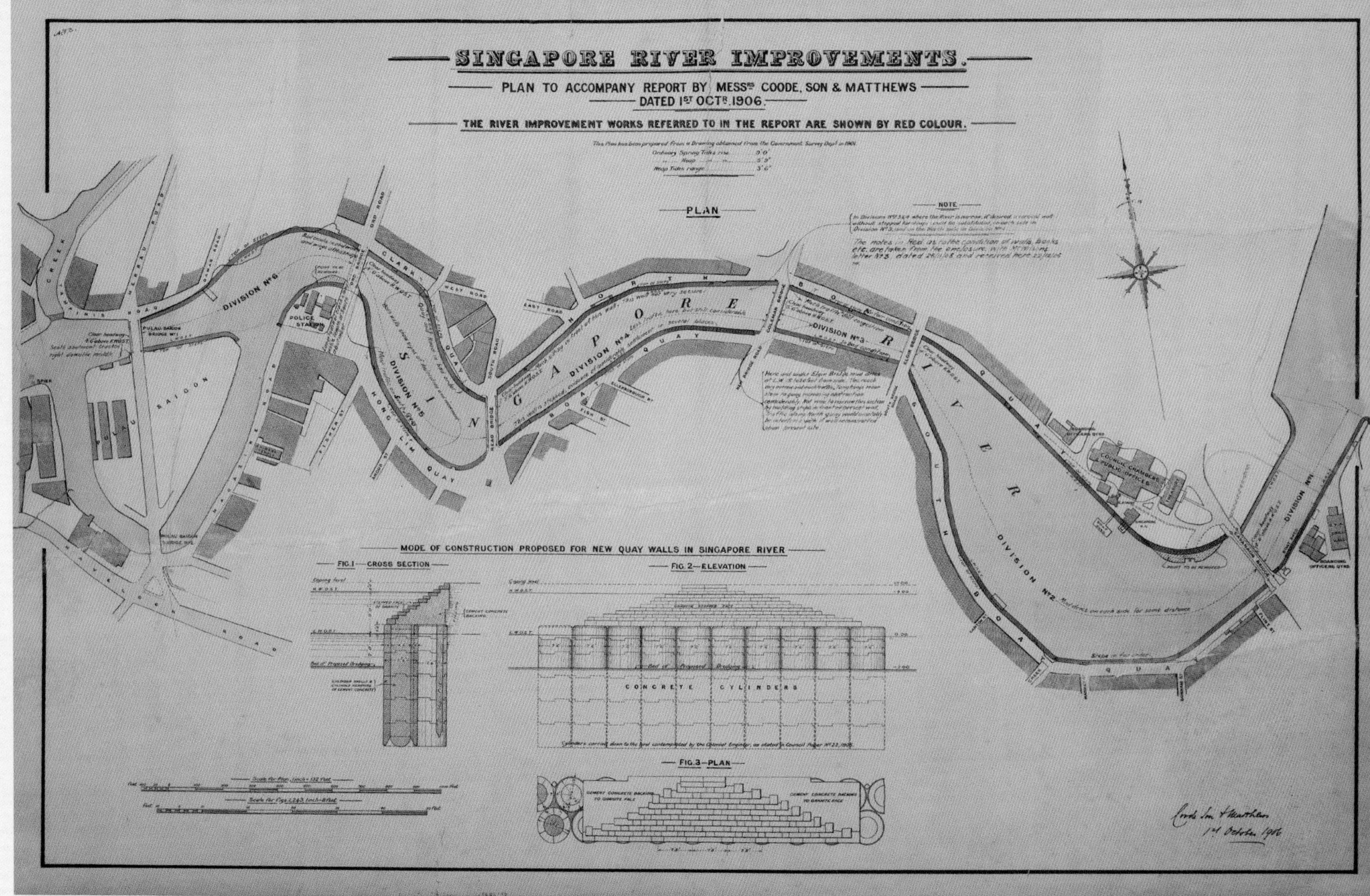

A Plan to Revive the Singapore River

Title: *Singapore River improvements: plan to accompany report by Messrs. Coode, Son & Matthews dated 1st. Octr. 1906*
Year published: 1906
Publisher: Coode, Son & Matthews
Type: Map; 57.5 cm x 94 cm
Call no.: RRARE 627.12095957 COO
Accession no.: B29240179A

By the dawn of the 20th century, the Singapore River was being strained to its limits. Thanks to Singapore's success as a free port, the river was busy with riverine traffic as vessels – particularly small coastal ships and various other craft – sailed along its length transporting goods to and from the many warehouses along its banks. The river became congested, polluted and constantly silted up.[1] The last, in particular, af-

fected the ability of boats to use the river, and thus impacted commerce. The colonial government realised that something had to be done.

The plan "Singapore River Improvements" is dated 1 October 1906 and accompanied a report by Consulting Engineers Messrs. Coode, Son & Matthews on improving the Singapore River. Measuring some 57.5 cm by 94 cm, the plan was prepared from a drawing obtained from the Government Survey Department.

In the plan, the river is divided into six sections. Division No. 1 covers the river from its mouth to Cavenagh Bridge; Division No. 2 from Cavenagh Bridge to Elgin Bridge; Division No. 3 from Elgin Bridge to Coleman Bridge; Division No. 4 from Coleman Bridge to Read Bridge; Division No. 5 from Read Bridge to Ord Bridge; and Division No. 6 from Ord Bridge to Pulau Saigon Bridge No. 1.

The red lines indicated on both banks of the river represented new quay walls proposed by the engineers. The new walls totalled 10,965 feet (3.3 km) in length.

There are also handwritten notes in red that record the condition of the existing walls along the river bank at various points. In Division No. 3, the walls of the south bank near the Elgin Bridge were "in bad condition." In Division No. 4, the wall at North Boat Quay was described as "not very secure" with "much silting in front of this wall", while the wall on the opposite bank had "evidence of considerable settlement in several places". The walls along both Clark Quay and Hong Lim Quay in Division No. 5 were said to "show signs of dislocation and movement".

Silting in the river was a concern because it made navigation harder in the already narrow and shallow waterway. In the early days, the silt was cleared by hand.[2] However, the authorities eventually began to use a dredge to clear the silt and deepen the river.

In the last quarter of the 19th century, the problem of silting and overcrowding became worse as the population around the river rose in tandem with increased trade activities. In 1898, a River Commission was established to look into the contaminated and congested state of the river. The Commission recommended a slew of measures, including two major works – the construction of a boat harbour in the river or at the sea near the river mouth, and the raising of all the bridges. These measures, however, were not implemented as there was no agreement on how the works could be funded.[3]

[Facing page] *Singapore river improvements: plan to accompany report by Messrs. Coode, Son & Matthews.* The Consulting Engineer's signature and date of 1st October 1906 can be seen at the bottom right corner of the plan. Central to the plan was the reconstruction of revetment walls, so that these would not collapse when regular dredging was carried out in the river to remove accumulated deposits and to deepen it.
[Above] The Singapore river in the 1800s, jam-packed with boats which were used to ferry cargo between the ships and the godowns.

In 1969, then Prime Minister Lee Kuan Yew called upon the authorities to clean up the Singapore River. An aerial view of the Singapore River after the successful completion of the clean-up programme in 1987 is shown above.

In 1905, in response to the increasingly pressing need to improve conditions in the river, the Colonial Engineer, Alexander Murray, submitted three proposals to the government. All three options required the reconstruction of the quay walls, which were in poor condition, so that they would be able to withstand regular dredging without collapsing.

The Governor of the Straits Settlements, Sir John Anderson, submitted the proposals to a special committee for deliberation, and later to the Consulting Engineers Messrs. Coode, Son & Matthews for assessment.[4] Messrs. Coode, Son & Matthews was a highly reputable engineering firm founded by Sir John Coode, with William Matthews – an eminent English dock and harbour engineer – as a partner. The company had done projects for the harbour and dock authorities as well as private enterprise in various British colonies.[5]

The report by Coode, Son & Matthews reviewed Murray's designs and recommended an alternative construction method for the new quay walls as depicted in figures 1, 2 and 3 in the plan. This method, in brief, consisted of a series of concrete cylinders sunk in two rows to form the wall of the river bank. Each cylinder would be 7 feet 6 inches (2.3 m) in external diameter. Stepped landings would be built over the cylinders, using them as the foundation. The design called for a concrete landing with a granite face for the steps that would stand up to rough daily use.

The estimated cost of this proposal was $4,686,214, comparable to Murray's cheapest option which involved the use of ferro-concrete for remaking the quay walls on the banks.[6]

However, none of these recommendations were eventually implemented because the colonial government lacked the financial resources. A subsequent improvement plan in the 1950s was similarly set aside mainly for the same reason.[7]

The limitations of the Singapore River provided an incentive to develop docks in New Harbour, now known as Keppel Harbour. Because of deeper waters there, those docks had the advantage of being able to service larger ships. Eventually, the docks and wharves at Tanjong Pagar began to eclipse the facilities at the Singapore River.

Tanjong Pagar's importance received a further boost when container shipping emerged in the early 1970s and trading activities began shifting to the Telok Ayer Basin. These facilities, which were operated by the Port Authority of Singapore (PSA), could accommodate large ocean-going freighters.

A large number of ships from China continued using the Singapore River but in the mid-1970s, the PSA succeeded in moving them over to its wharves.[8] This brought an end to the river's role as a port.

It was around this time when the Singapore government began the project to clean up the Singapore River. In 1969, then Prime Minister Lee Kuan Yew called on the Public Works Department and the Public Utilities Board to curb pollution of the waterways.[9] The effort picked up speed in 1977. Ten years and millions of dollars later, the river was finally free of congestion and pollution.[10] ♦ **Joanna Tan**

Notes

1 Dobbs, S. (2003). *The Singapore River: A social history, 1819–2002* (pp. 10–11). Singapore: Singapore University Press. (Call no.: RSING 959.57 DOB-[HIS])
2 Dobbs, 2003, pp. 53–54.
3 Dobbs, 2003, pp. 12–13.
4 River improvements: exhaustive report by the consulting engineers. (1906, November 24). *The Straits Times*, p. 9. Retrieved from NewspaperSG.
5 Future harbour improvements and the man. (1901, February 21). *The Singapore Free Press and Mercantile Advertiser (Weekly)*, p. 6. Retrieved from NewspaperSG.
6 River improvements: exhaustive report by the consulting engineers. (1906, November 24). *The Straits Times*, p. 9. Retrieved from NewspaperSG.
7 Dobbs, 2003, pp. 13–14.
8 Dobbs, 2003, pp. 15–16.
9 Joshi, Y. K., Tortajada, C., & Biswas, A. K. (2012, November). Cleaning of the Singapore River and Kallang Basin in Singapore: Human and environmental dimensions. *Ambio, 41*(7), 777–781. Retrieved from National Center for Biotechnology Information, U.S. National Library of Medicine website.
10 Choo, F. (2014, July 5). 5 interesting facts about the Singapore River clean-up. *The Straits Times*. Retrieved from *The Straits Times* website.

Master Poet Khoo Seok Wan's Critiques

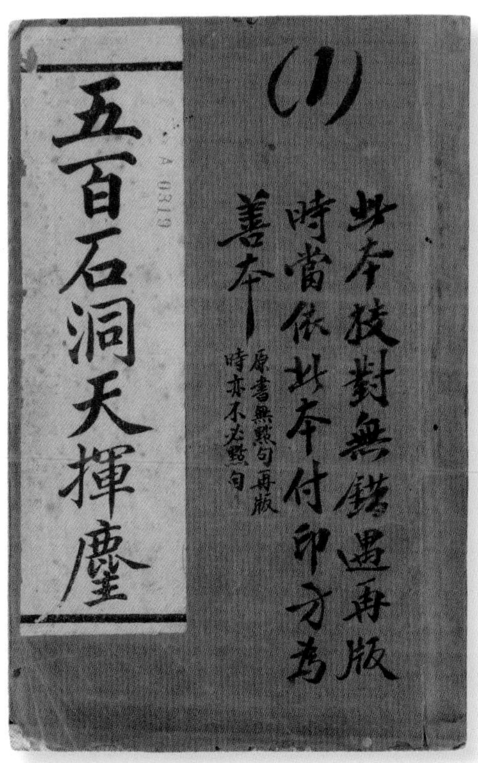

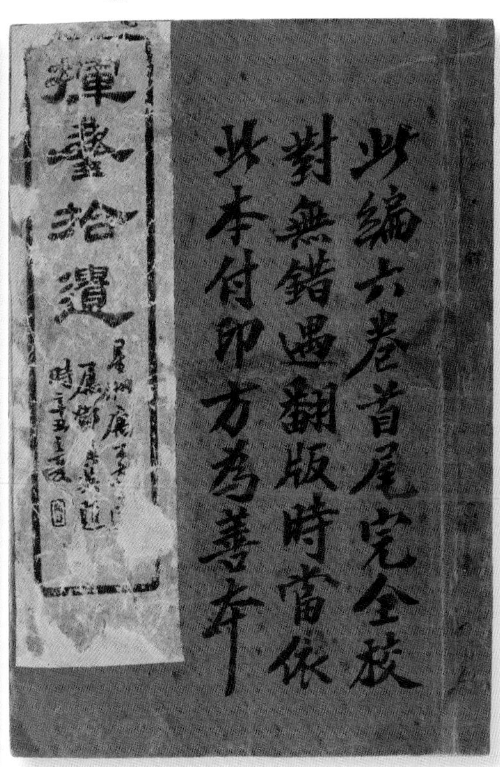

On the covers of 《五百石洞天挥麈》 (Chatters in Khoo's Fascinating Study) and 《挥麈拾遗》 (Addendum to Chatters in Khoo's Fascinating Study), Khoo Seok Wan expressed his intention to have his edits in both copies reflected in a second edition should that be published.

Title: (i) 《五百石洞天挥麈》 (Chatters in Khoo's Fascinating Study); (ii) 《挥麈拾遗》 (Addendum to Chatters in Khoo's Fascinating Study)

Author: Khoo Seok Wan (邱菽园; Qiu Shuyuan) (1874– 1941)

Year published: (i) 1900; (ii) 1901

Publisher: (i) Fuwen zhai (富文斋)(Guangzhou); (ii) not stated

Language: Chinese

Type: (i) Six bound volumes with two issues each (issues 1 to 12); (ii) Single bound volume of six issues

Call no.: RRARE C811.07004 QSY

Accession nos.: (i) B32426244E, B32426243D, B32426242C, B32426241B, B32426240A, B32426239I; (ii) B32426245F

The renowned literary pioneer Khoo Seok Wan (邱菽园; 1874–1941) was a prolific poet believed to have composed over 1,000 poems in his lifetime.[1] His extraordinary achievements in poetry earned him the title of "Master Poet of the South" (南侨诗宗) from his fans and followers.[2] A scholar and active community leader, Khoo was also known for his fervent advocacy of Chinese culture and education in early Singapore.

Two of Khoo's published works that illustrate his commitment to writing literary and social critiques are 《五百石洞天挥麈》 (1900) and 《挥麈拾遗》 (1901). Both collections of essays belong to the *shihua* (诗话) genre, which focuses on analysing poetry as well as the poets' approach in composing poems and anecdotes.[3] They reflect Khoo's opinions on Chinese poets and poetry, literary activities, social practices and Singapore. Significantly, the National Library's copies bear Khoo's handwritten amendments and addenda. He planned to publish a second edition of both books, but passed away before this could materialise.

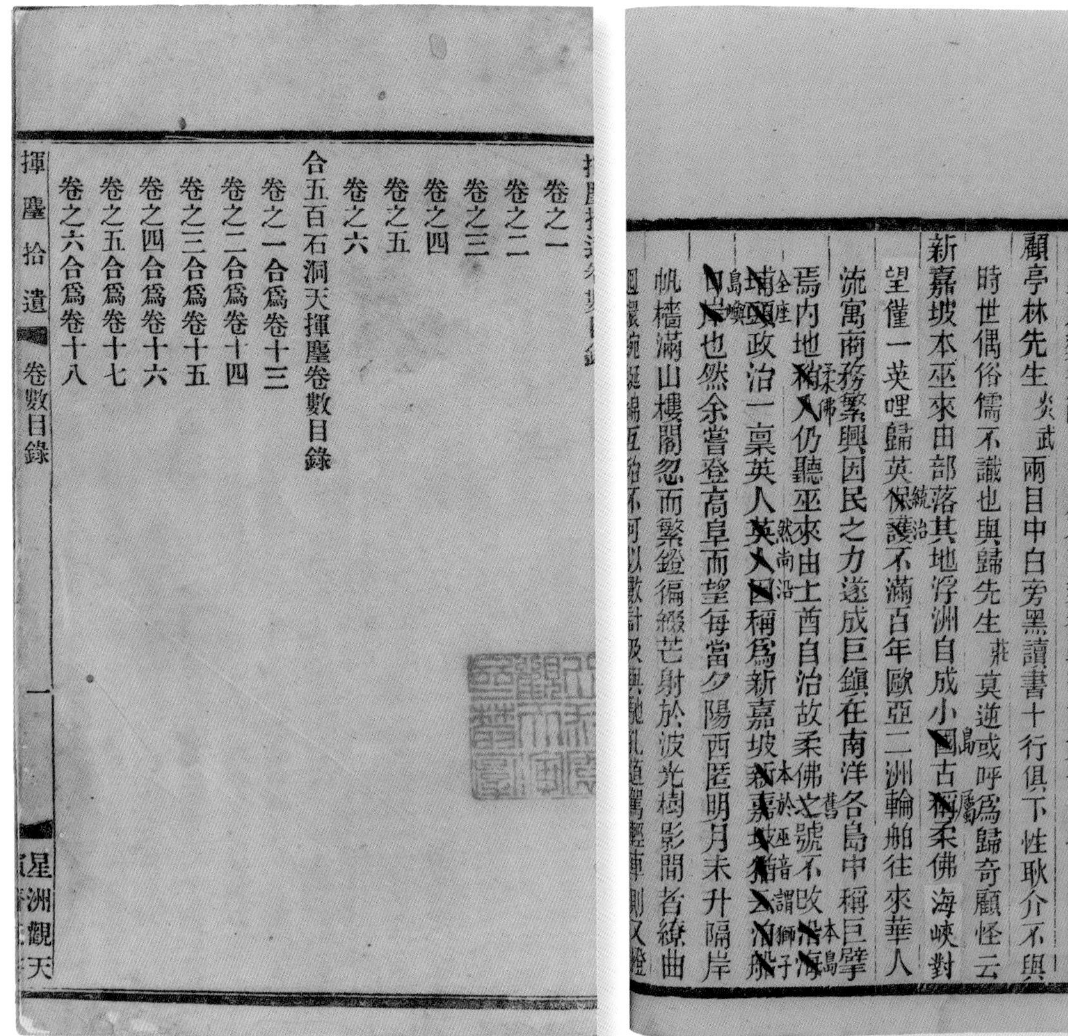

揮麈拾遺卷數目錄

卷之一
卷之二
卷之三
卷之四
卷之五
卷之六

合五百石洞天揮麈卷數目錄
卷之一合爲卷十三
卷之二合爲卷十四
卷之三合爲卷十五
卷之四合爲卷十六
卷之五合爲卷十七
卷之六合爲卷十八

揮麈拾遺 卷數目錄 一 星洲觀天

原曠野自唐以後爲文之一大變然而文章之美惡不與焉
其所變者辭而已所不可變者雖千古如一日也
顧亭林先生炎武兩目中白旁黑讀書十行俱下性耿介不與
時世偶俗儒不識也與歸先生莊莫逆或呼爲歸奇顧怪云
新嘉坡本巫來由部落其地浮洲自成小國古稱柔佛海峽對
望僅一英哩歸英保護不滿百年歐亞二洲輪舶往來華人
流寓商務繁興因民之力遂成巨鎮在南洋各島中稱巨擘
帆檣滿山樓閣忽而繁鐙徧綴芒射於波光樹影間者繚曲

[Above left] The contents page of《揮麈拾遺》(Addendum to Chatters in Khoo's Fascinating Study) on which Khoo explained that it could be regarded as issues 13 to 18 of《五百石洞天揮麈》(Chatters in Khoo's Fascinating Study).
[Above right] It is not known when Khoo revised the text. An interesting edit on page 24 in issue 1 of《五百石洞天揮麈》shows that he hoped to say that the name "新嘉坡" (Singapore) originated from the Malay word for "Island of lions".

Born in the county of Haicheng, Fujian province, China, in 1874, Khoo left for Singapore with his mother when he was eight. They joined his father, who had migrated before his birth and built a successful rice business in the colony. In Singapore, Khoo was schooled in the traditional way as practised in China, and was home tutored in Chinese classics. He was especially talented in literature, and became a learned scholar of poetry and prose at a tender age.

At the age of 15, Khoo headed to Haicheng to prepare for the imperial examination. He began to gain attention for his literary talent after composing the poem titled "On the Jade Flute" (玉笛诗). Having passed the district and provincial examinations in 1894, he attained the level of *juren* (举人), qualifying for the central government imperial examination held in Beijing in 1895.[4] However, he failed in this attempt. Thereafter, he spent more time composing poems and travelling in China. In 1896, Khoo returned to Singapore upon receiving news that his father was ill.[5] Unfortunately, his father passed away that year.

Subsequent years saw Khoo's growth as a writer, publisher and community leader in Singapore. His strong political views about China, for instance, led him to establish the Chinese newspaper *Thien Nan Shin Pao* (天南新报) in 1898 to support Kang Youwei's reformist ideas in China.[6] To advocate education for girls, Khoo co-founded the Singapore Chinese Girls' School in 1899 along with prominent contemporaries such as medical doctor Lim Boon Keng and lawyer Song Ong Siang.

Between 1898 and 1899, Khoo penned the essays compiled in the 12 issues of《五百石洞天挥麈》, whereas he took just two months in 1901 to write the essays in the six issues of《挥麈拾遗》.[7] On the contents page of the latter publication, Khoo wrote that the six issues could be regarded as issues 13 to 18 of《五百石洞天挥麈》.

The title《五百石洞天挥麈》means "Chatters in Khoo's Fascinating Study". It highlights Khoo's extraordinary collection of carved seals (also known as "stones", or "石" in Chinese) and, as the phrase "洞天" suggests, describes his study room as a fascinating place.[8] "五百", which means "500", refers to the number of seals Khoo had in his collection at the time.[9] The phrase

An acclaimed poet, Khoo Seok Wan's poems address themes such as politics in China, life in Singapore, Western culture and news, Buddhism, his relationships as well as his personal experiences.[10] *Lee Brothers Studio Collection, courtesy of National Archives of Singapore.*

"挥麈" is a synonym for "chatting" in traditional Chinese.[11] In the past, the phrase was used to describe how scholars of the Wei (386–534/535 BCE) and Jin dynasties (265–420 BCE) wielded ("挥") a fan, or *hossu* (a fly whisk which had tassels made from animal hair at its end) known as *zhuwei* (麈尾), to emphasise their views during casual discussions.[12] Hence, the title《挥麈拾遗 》literally means that the book is an addendum to《五百石洞天挥麈》, as "拾遗" means "to retrieve what has been left behind".[13]

Khoo had extensive knowledge about poets from different eras in the history of China, and his critique of their works make up a substantial portion of these two publications. In the ninth issue of《五百石洞天挥麈》for instance, he assessed and praised the 四言乐府 poems[14] composed by the Eastern Han (25–220 BCE) warlord and poet, Cao Mengde (曹孟德; also known as Cao Cao 曹操), for being so well-written that Cao was deemed to have surpassed all his contemporaries, even his own sons who were acclaimed poets themselves.[15]

Other essays in《五百石洞天挥麈》reveal Khoo's thoughts on gatherings attended by him and his friends,[16] such as newspaperman and poet Yih Chih Yun (叶季允).[17] The literary club *li ze she* (丽泽社; Society of Mutual Learning)[18] founded by Khoo in 1896 is frequently mentioned too. Although *li ze she* was formed so that fellow poetry-lovers could gather and appreciate each other's works, its activities came to include lessons on preparing for the imperial examinations.[19]

Khoo offered his views on social practices as well. On page 31 in issue 12 of《五百石洞天挥麈》, he expressed strong disdain for the practice of foot-binding. His words "余尝箸三害质言一卷问世以鸦片时文缠足平列" reveal that he considered foot-binding one of the three evils of late Qing society, the other two being opium-smoking and writing essays in a prescribed style for the civil examinations in China.[20] Although some scholars have noted that Khoo believed in *shi jiao* (诗教), which means to criticise society and social practices using euphemisms in his writings,[21] this appears to be one occasion when Khoo was partial, harsh and direct in his critique.

Of Khoo's handwritten amendments, page 24 in issue 1 of《五百石洞天挥麈》shows that he hoped to add a mention that the name "新嘉坡" (Singapore) originated from the Malay word for "Island of Lions".[22] On its facing page, his revision indicated that the population of the Chinese in Singapore should be "廿三万" (230,000) instead of "廿余万" (over 200,000). It is not known when Khoo jotted down changes such as these. However, his note on the cover of each bound volume tells us that he hoped to publish a second edition. Translated, it reads: "This copy has been proofread and is error-free; should there be a second edition, this should be used as the final version for printing."

While Khoo enjoyed much literary success, he was less capable of managing his wealth and was declared bankrupt when he was 34. He supported his family by working as a secretary and newspaper editor, but spent his final years in poverty and illness. Khoo died[23] at the age of 67 without achieving his goal of publishing the second edition of the two works he had laboured over.

Nonetheless, Khoo's neutrality and impartiality have been lauded by present-day scholars, who praised his skill and competency in critiquing poems as well as his ability to present unique opinions and arguments while encompassing the views of other critics.[24] ♦ **Jessie Yak**

Notes

1 Lee, G. K. (李元瑾). (2001).《东西文化的撞击与新华知识分子的三种回应：邱菽园、林文庆、宋旺相的比较研究》(p. 200). Singapore: Department of Chinese Studies, National University of Singapore and Global Publishing Co. Inc. (Call no.: RSING 305.552095957 LYJ)

2 Qiu, X. M. (邱新民). (1993).《邱菽园生平》(p. 17). Singapore: Seng Yew Book Store. (Call no.: RSING 920.05957 QXM)

3 诗话: 中国古代评论诗歌、诗人、诗派，记录诗人议论、事迹的著作. 在线新华字典 [Xinhua Dictionary Online]. (2019). 诗话. Retrieved from 在线新华字典 [Xinhua Dictionary Online] website.

4 Lee, 2001, pp. 33–36

5 Lee, 2001, pp. 33–36; Yak, J., Bryant, S., & Ho, Y. K. (2013). *A life in poems: selected works of Khoo Seok Wan* (pp. 6-7). Singapore: National Library Board. (Call no.: RSING 895.11 Qiu)

6 When the Hundred Days' Reform Movement (11 June–22 September 1898) led by Kang Youwei was launched in China in June 1898, Khoo donated generously using his inheritance. Although the movement failed in September, Khoo invited Kang to Singapore and also paid for his expenses here. However, a disagreement later strained their relationship. In a notice published in *Thien Nan Shin Pao* on 22 October 1901, Khoo announced his dissociation from the reformists. In 1905, *Thien Nan Shin Pao* ceased publication. See Yak, 2013, p. 7; Chen, M.H. (1967). *The early Chinese newspapers of Singapore 1881–1912* (p. 66). Singapore: University of Malaya Press. (Call no.: RSING 079.5702 CHE)

7 Tam, Y. H. (谭勇辉). (2015). *南洋华人诗坛发展史的重要奠基石—邱菽园和他的 "诗话三部曲"* (p. 2). Retrieved from 马来西亚汉学研究会 [Persatuan Sinologi Malaysia] website.

8 洞天: 道教指神仙居住的地方，现在多用来指引人入胜的境地。在线新华字典 [Xinhua Dictionary Online]. (2019). 洞天. Retrieved from 在线新华字典 [Xinhua Dictionary Online] website.

9 Qiu, 1993, pp. 50–53.

10 Yak, 2013, pp. 6-7.

11 挥麈: 晋代人们清谈时，常挥麈以为谈助，后称谈论为 "挥麈"。汉典. [Han Dictionary Online]. (2019). 挥麈. Retrieved from 汉典 [Han Dictionary Online] website.

12 麈尾: 以犀角为柄的麈尾。魏晋名士清谈常持麈尾。在线新华字典 [Xinhua Dictionary Online]. (2019). 麈尾. Retrieved from 在线新华字典 [Xinhua Dictionary Online] website.

13 补录缺漏。在线新华字典 [Xinhua Dictionary Online]. (2019). 拾遗. Retrieved from 在线新华字典 [Xinhua Dictionary Online] website.

14 A form of traditional Chinese poetry which has four characters in each line.

15 邱菽园 [Khoo, S.W.]. (1900).《五百石洞天挥麈》(卷九，页三十五). 广州 [Guangzhou]: 富文斋 [Fuwen zhai]. (Call no.: RRARE C811.07004 QSY)

16 邱, 1900, 卷九，页十三.

17 National Library Board. (2020). *Yeh Chih Yun* 叶季允. Retrieved from Resource Guides website.

18 邱, 1900, 卷十一，页二十三.

19 邱, 1900, 卷十一，页二十三.

20 时文 refers to 八股文 (literally "eight-legged essay"), a kind of essay written by candidates as part of the imperial examinations during the Ming and Qing dynasties in China. 时文 was deemed an overly-restrictive form as test-takers had to conform to its format, and could not write in more innovative or creative ways.

21 Keok, L. H. (郭联福), & Fan, P. W. (潘碧华). (2017). Eclecticism and convergence: On the inheritance and transformation of Yuan Mei's poetics of disposition by forebear of Nanyang poetry Khoo Seok Wan (pp. 3– 4). *Journal of Chinese Literature and Culture, 5*(2), 1–8. Retrieved from University of Malaya's eJournal website.

22 The name Singapore comes from the Malay word "Singapura", which is believed to have been derived from the Sanskrit word "Sinhapura" which means "lion city".

23 National Library Board. (2010). *Khoo Seok Wan* 邱菽园 written by Jane Wee. Retrieved from Singapore Infopedia website.

24 Keok & Fan, 2017, p. 7.

A Book of Tamil Names

Title: *List of Tamil Proper Names*
Author: Alfred Vanhouse Brown
Year published: 1904
Publisher: Government Printing Office (Kuala Lumpur)
Language: Tamil/English
Type: Book; 48 pages
Call no.: RRARE 929.4 BRO
Accession No.: B16331012F

NAMES OF CASTES.

ÁSARI — UDAIYÁN

Ásari	ஆசாரி
Chetti	செட்டி
Dévan	தேவன்
Kallan	கள்ளன்
Kandian	கண்டியன்
Kavundan	கவுண்டன்
Kónán	கோனான்
Muthali	முதலி
Múppan	மூப்பன்
Nádán	நாடான்
Náykkan—Nayidu	நாய்க்கன், நாயிடு
Padaiyáchi	படையாச்சி
Pattan	பத்தன்
Pillai	பிள்ளை
Ráju	ராஜு
Reddi	ரெட்டி
Sérvai	சேர்வை
Tondamán	தொண்டமான்
Udaiyán	உடையான்

In governing a population that spoke and wrote a variety of languages, the British colonial administrators in Singapore and Malaya faced many challenges. The languages used in Malaya, China and India have their own writing systems, none of which were remotely similar to the Latin script familiar to the British. This would have made the identification of individuals, with their names rendered in different scripts, a problem. To overcome this, the colonial government commissioned the compilation of lists containing the romanised versions of common Asian names.

One such document used by colonial officials to transcribe Tamil names[1] is a 48-page *List of Tamil Proper Names*, published in Kuala Lumpur in 1904. Although this was neither the first nor the longest list produced by the Government Printing Office of the Federated Malay States, the personal and caste names in the book shed light on the patterns of Indian migration into British Malaya during the 19th and early 20th centuries.

The Indian subcontinent is home to numerous ethno-linguistic groups. Of these, South Indians formed the largest segment of the Indian immigrant population into British Malaya, particularly from the late 19th century onwards. The Tamils, most of whom were employed as labourers in the plantation, harbour, transportation and municipal sectors, constituted the majority of these migrants,[2] with smaller groups of Malayalees and Telugus.[3] This explains why the British saw the need to commission a book of specifically Tamil names.

Alfred Vanhouse Brown, an officer of the Federated Malay States Civil Service who was based in Kuala Lumpur, compiled the list with the assistance of A. Swaminatha Pillai, an interpreter of Indian languages from Batu Gajah, Perak.[4]

Brown was educated at the Merchant Taylor's School in London and Queen's Col-

[Facing page] A glimpse of the personal and caste names used by the Tamil community in British Malaya. The list was collated by colonial officer Alfred Vanhouse Brown and A. Swaminatha Pillai, an intrepreter of Tamil and Hindi languages from Perak. Interestingly, some caste names in the booklet, such as "Nayidu" and "Reddi", are typically associated with the Telugu community, rather than Tamils.
[Above] A Chettiar moneylender, c. 1890. Originally from South India, the Chettiars started coming to Singapore during the 19th century. *Courtesy of the National Museum of Singapore, National Heritage Board.*

lege in Oxford, graduating with a Bachelor of Arts degree in 1896. That year, he was appointed to serve the Eastern cadetships, specifically the civil service in the Federated Malay States. He undertook several positions there until 1906, when he was appointed Superintendent of Posts and Telegraphs in Selangor, Negri Sembilan and Pahang. In the same year, Brown also served as the Acting District Officer and Indian Immigration Agent in Perak.[5]

There is not much more information about Brown, Pillai or how they collated the names. According to the Note at the front of the book, Brown adhered closely to the transliteration system laid down by the Board of Revenue in Madras, Tamil Nadu.[6] He also provided a useful guide to help readers pronounce vowels in the romanised Tamil names by using corresponding vowel sounds found in English words.

Page 1 (unnumbered) to page 45 of the book contain the romanised spellings of common Tamil personal names. This list is organised in alphabetical order, alongside a column that indicates if the names belong to men ("M") or women (labelled "F"). The third column on the page contains the corresponding names written in Tamil script.

On the last page of the book is a list of 19 caste names, most of which tended to belong to those from the upper castes, including widely recognised names such as "Chetti" and "Pillai".[7] The former, for instance, refers to the Chettiar community, a Tamil trading caste of businessmen and moneylenders. The Chettiars who migrated to British Malaya consisted mainly of the Nattukottai Chettiars, a subgroup involved principally in moneylending,[8] and who became a key fixture of the business landscape in British Malaya.

Interestingly, some of the caste names in the list, such as "Nayidu" and "Reddi", are typically associated with the Telugu community, rather than the Tamils. Both names may have been used by Telugu migrants who moved from the coastal districts of Andhra Pradesh to Tamil Nadu, before migrating to British Malaya. Over time, these immigrants from various caste and linguistic groups who settled in Tamil Nadu may have adopted the language and cultural practices of the Tamils.[9]

Names provide a window into an individual's identity – whether it be gender, ethnicity, religious affiliation, nationality and even social position. For instance, Tamil names traditionally do not carry a family name. Instead, both males and females adopt their father's name in front of their personal name. Upon marriage, a Tamil woman would traditionally adopt her husband's personal name in place of her father's name.

The *List of Tamil Proper Names* is a useful historical source for anyone reseaching the migration and settlement history of Singapore's Tamil community. It also serves as an accompaniment to similar publications in the National Library that list the common names of members of the Malay and Chinese communities in the Straits Settlements.

♦ **Liviniyah P.**

Notes

1 Sandhu, K. S. (2010). *Indians in Malaya: Immigration and settlement: 1786–1957* (p. 15). Cambridge: Cambridge University Press. (Call No.: RSEA 325.25409595 SAN)
2 Sandhu, 2010, p. 286
3 Sinnappah, A. (1979). *Indians in Malaysia and Singapore* (pp. 44–45). Kuala Lumpur; New York: Oxford University Press. (Call No.: RSING 325.25409595 ARA)
4 Brown, A. V. (1904). *List of Tamil proper names* (title page). Kuala Lumpur: Government Printing Office. (Call No: RRARE 929.4 BRO)
5 The Civil Services of Ceylon, the Straits Settlements and Hong Kong were collectively referred to as the Eastern Cadetships. See Mills, L. A. (2012). *Ceylon under British rule 1795–1932* (p. 90). Routledge. (Not available in NLB holdings). For details about Alfred V. Brown, see *The Directory & Chronicle of China, Japan, Straits Settlements, Malaya, Borneo, Siam, the Philippines, Korea, Indo-China, Netherlands Indies, etc. (1906)*. (p. 1192). Cambridge: Harvard University. Retrieved from Google Books website; Wright, A., & Cartwright, H. A. (1908). *Twentieth century impressions of British Malaya: Its history, people, commerce, industries, and resources* (p. 328). London: Lloyd's Greater Britain Publishing Company, Limited. (Call No.: RRARE 959.5103 TWE)
6 Brown, 1904, "Note".
7 Britto, F. (1986). Personal names in Tamil society. *Anthropological Linguistics, 28*(3), 349–365. Retrieved from JSTOR.
8 Sinnappah, 1979, p. 36.
9 Vijaya, M., et al. (2007). A study on Telugu-speaking immigrants of Tamil Nadu, South India. *International Journal of Human Genetics*. Retrieved from Pennsylvania State University's CiteSeerX website.

A NOVEL APPROACH TO MALAYAN HISTORY

Title: *Popular History of Malaya and the Netherlands Indies*
Author: Gregory W. de Silva
Year published: 1939
Publisher: Kyle, Palmer and Company (Kuala Lumpur)
Language: English
Type: Book; 199 pages
Call no.: RRARE 959.503 DES-[JSB]
Accession no.: B29034124C

History is commonly perceived as a dull and ponderous subject. In the early 20th century, Gregory W. de Silva, a Malayan lawyer and history buff, sought to dispel this with his book *Popular History of Malaya and the Netherland Indies*.

Published in 1939, it was the "first time a complete story-history of Malaya in a digestible form" had been written.[1] The 199-page book presents readers with an account of Malaya from prehistory to the 19th century through a love story. The book featured cover illustrations by award-winning Malayan cartoonist and artist Yan Kee Leong, and retailed at $1.50.

Up until then, works of Malayan history, such as Frank Swettenham's *British Malaya* (1906) and R.O. Winstedt's *A History of Malaya* (1935), were primarily written for a scholarly and learned audience. De Silva's book was his attempt to produce a simple and readable history of Malaya for the general reader. To appeal to those who had little or no knowledge on the subject, he took the unconventional approach of presenting Malayan history in the form of a romance novel.

The book's main narrative is a fictional love story which drives and directs the retelling of Malayan history. Set in the 1930s, it follows the main protagonists William Haytor, a promising young man from Shanghai; Delysia Clearbrook, an American heiress; and her husband John Lorrimer, a British diplomat, as they head for Shanghai where John is taking up a new posting.

During the journey, William, a friend and former classmate of John's, entertains Delysia with stories from the history of Malaya. Through these storytelling sessions, readers are introduced to Malaya's past: from its prehistory, the period of Indianization of Southeast Asia, early Chinese travels to the region, the courts of the Melaka Sultanate, the arriv-

Gregory W. de Silva: Lawyer and Novelist

Gregory W. de Silva (d. 1949)[2] was a well-known lawyer in Kuala Lumpur who migrated from Ceylon (Sri Lanka) in the 1920s.[3]

De Silva was one of the few Asians writing fiction in English in Malaya and Singapore then.[4] *Popular History of Malaya and the Netherlands Indies* was his fourth book. His first book, *The Princess of Malacca* (1937), is a historical novel inspired by the Portuguese and Dutch conquests of Melaka which was later adapted for the stage. *Suleiman Goes to London* (1938) is a novel about an Asian student's experiences in London, while *Only a Taxi Dancer: A Romance of Singapore* (1939) is about a cabaret dancer who migrates to Singapore and returns to China as a nurse in the war of resistance against Japan. His last book, *Lupe: An Historical Romance of Portuguese Malacca* (1940), is a historical novel.

G. W. de Silva. *The Straits Times, 9 October 1938, p. 18. Retrieved from NewspaperSG.*

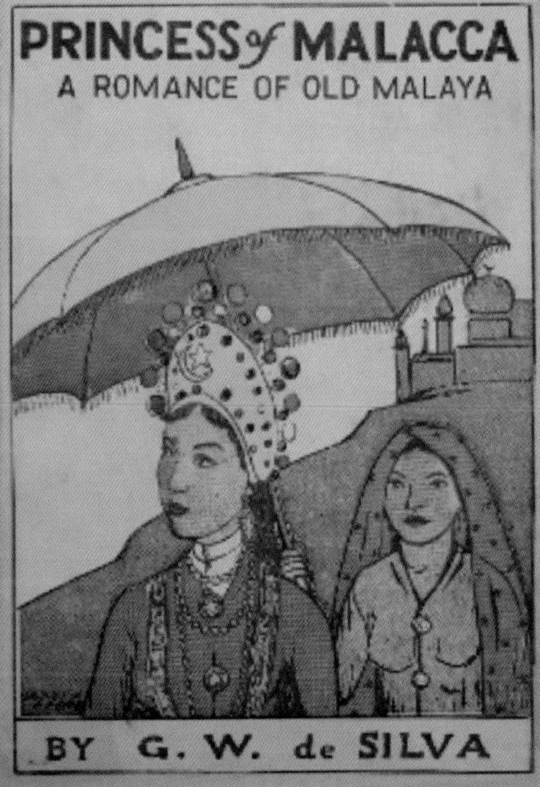

[Facing page] Cover of Gregory W. de Silva's *Popular History of Malaya and the Netherlands Indies.*
[Above right] Malayan artist Yan Kee Leong (1899–1986), whose artwork appears on the cover of *Popular History of Malaya and the Netherlands Indies*, and on at least three of de Silva's other works. Yan's political cartoons and caricatures regularly appeared in the local newspaper *The Malaya Tribune*. He also won several awards for his posters and paintings.[5] *Singapore Standard, 22 October 1952, p. 5. Retrieved from NewspaperSG.*
[Left] De Silva's first book, *The Princess of Malacca* (1937), with cover art by Yan Kee Leong. *Image reproduced from De Silva, Gregory W. (1937). The Princess of Malacca: A Historical Romance of Old Malaya. Malacca: Wah Seong Press.*

al of the Portuguese and the Dutch, the British founding of Singapore to its subsequent expansion into the Malay States. At one point in the story, Delysia invites William to tell her something about Singapore. He then shares with her the archaeological and documentary evidence of pre-colonial Singapore found on the stone inscriptions on the Karimun Island and the Singapore Stone, 14th-century Chinese records, and the Malay Annals.

As they spend time together, William develops a fondness for Delysia. The story reaches a turning point when John is killed by anti-aircraft fire while flying over Chungking during the Second Sino-Japanese War. A bereft Delysia returns to America. 18 months later, she meets William in Honolulu by chance. William confesses his feelings to Delysia and proposes. She accepts his offer of marriage and agrees to move to Malaya with him.

Though the romantic plot was primarily created as a narrative device to convey the history of Malaya in an engaging way, it reflected the historical times of its writing. De Silva's work was completed in October 1939, a month after the outbreak of World War II in Europe. The turbulent state of world affairs is hinted at one point in the story when the character John dismisses the appeal of these conversations on history, saying "Is there not enough thrills in the immediate present with Hitler, Mussolini, and the master men of China, Japan and Spain occupying the variety stage?"[6] At another point in the story, the cruise ship carrying the protagonists is intercepted by a Japanese warship.

The economic progress of 1930s Singapore is also noted in the story. When the trio disembarked in Singapore during a port-of-call, they saw a "busy, prosperous, pleasure filled town" and a "Malayan metropolis".[7] At John's request, William takes Delysia on a tour of Singapore and Johor where they visit Seletar air base, Kallang Airport, the Airport Hotel and the Sultan's Palace.

De Silva was encouraged to write this book by George L. Peet, a well-known journalist with *The Straits Times*. For research, de Silva drew on a rich body of Malayan scholarship that included the works of Richard James Wilkinson, Frank Swettenham and William George Maxwell. In his preface and dedication, de Silva thanked these scholars "who devoted their valuable leisure in order to enrich the historical literature of Malaya". He also relied on works such as the *Sejarah Melayu* (Malay Annals), the *Hikayat Merong Mahawangsa* (Kedah Annals), D.C. Boulger's *Life of Sir Stamford Raffles* and Isabella Bird's *The Golden Chersonese and the Way Thither*.

In addition to *Popular History of Malaya and the Netherlands Indies*, de Silva also wrote four other books, two of which are historical fiction set in the region. ♦ **Gracie Lee**

Notes

1 Malaya. (1939, December 24). *The Sunday Times*, p. 6. Retrieved from NewspaperSG.
2 Sudden death of K. L. lawyer. (1949, June 29). *Malaya Tribune*, p. 1. Retrieved from NewspaperSG.
3 Mainly about Malayans (1938, April 10). *The Sunday Times*, p. 18. Retrieved from NewspaperSG.
4 Patke, R. S. & Holden, P. (2010). *The Routledge concise history of Southeast Asian writing in English* (p. 46). London; New York: Routledge. (Call no.: RSING 895.9 PAT)
5 Page 14 Miscellaneous Column 1. (1932, March 2). *The Malaya Tribune*, p. 14; Mr Yan Kee Leong. (1936, August 7). *The Straits Times*, p. 16. Retrieved from NewspaperSG.
6 De Silva, G. W. (1939). *Popular History of Malaya and the Netherlands Indies* (p. 7). Kuala Lumpur: Kyle, Palmer and Company. (Call no.: RRARE 959.503 DES-[JSB])
7 De Silva, 1939, pp. 33, 154.

A Wartime Magazine

Title: *Fajar Asia* [Dawn of Asia]
Publisher: Pejabat Pembangunan Melayu Baru (Sinsei Malai Kensetsu Sha); Malai Sinbun Sya [Singapore]
Sinsei Malai Kensetsu Sha
[year]1 no. 1–15, 1943
[year]2, no. 1–2, 1944
Malai Sinbun Sya
[year]no. 1, 1944
[year]no. 2, 1944
Year published: 1943–44
Language: Malay
Type: Periodical
Call no.: RRARE Malay 959.052 FA
Accession nos.: B30160420E ([year]1 no. 1, 1943); B30160417K ([year]1, no. 12, 1943); B30160413G ([year]2, no. 1, 1944); B30160412F (Gogatsu 2604 issue (May 1944))

Fajar Asia (Dawn of Asia) is a magazine of essays and literary works in Malay that was published in Singapore during the Japanese Occupation.[1] The periodical existed from 1943 to 1944, and consisted largely of opinion pieces on topics such as education, social issues and heroism. It also published short stories and poems by writers from Malaya and Sumatra. Although the magazine only lasted for two years, it represents an important milestone in the history of Malay intellectual and literary development in the 20th century.

Fajar Asia is significant because at the time, it gave Malay writers a platform to be heard in the Malay world. The essays and literary works it published allow scholars today to see how nationalist sentiments and Malay literature and language developed during this period. Remarkably, its influence even extended to the area of modern Malay spelling.

It is believed that a total of 23 issues were produced. Of these, 19 issues (15 issues from 1943 and four from 1944) are available in the National Library's Rare Materials Collection. The National Library also has the first issue, dated 25 Ichigatsu 2603 (25 January 1943), which was helmed by Zainal Abidin Ahmad as *ketua pengarang* (chief editor). The launch issue indicated that *Fajar Asia* would be published twice a month and each issue would be sold at 25 cents per copy.[2] The magazine's tagline was *Memajukan Kebudayaan dan Kesenian* (Promoting Culture and Arts) and each issue was between 40 and 48 pages long.[3]

The first 19 issues of *Fajar Asia* were published by Pejabat Pembangunan Melayu Baru (Sinsei Malai Kensetsu Sha) – the New

[Facing page] Covers of *Fajar Asia* (Dawn of Asia), including that of its first issue on the right. On the far left is the cover of the first issue of *Fajar Asia* following its merger with *Semangat Asia* (Spirit of Asia) in 1944. Dated Gogatsu 2604 (May 1944), this issue covered Kaigun Kinenbi (Navy Day), which the Japanese army ensured was observed in Malaya on 27 May annually during the Occupation to commemorate their destruction of the Russian fleet at the Battle of Tsushima Strait in the Russo-Japanese War (1904–05). Heihachiro Togo, the admiral deemed to have led the Japanese fleet to victory in that fight, is featured on the cover too.[4]
[Right] The first article in *Fajar Asia*'s first issue; **[Far right]** A. Samad Ismail's short story "Budak2 main seldadu" (Boys playing soldiers) was published in *Fajar Asia*'s May 1944 issue. The narrative describes how Malay boys pretending to be Japanese and British soldiers engage in a play-fight, with the team representing the British defeated.

FAJAR ASIA
MAJALLAH 2 KALI SEBULAN
No. 1 | 25 Ichigatsu (Syowa 18) | Tahun 1
PERMULAAN KATA

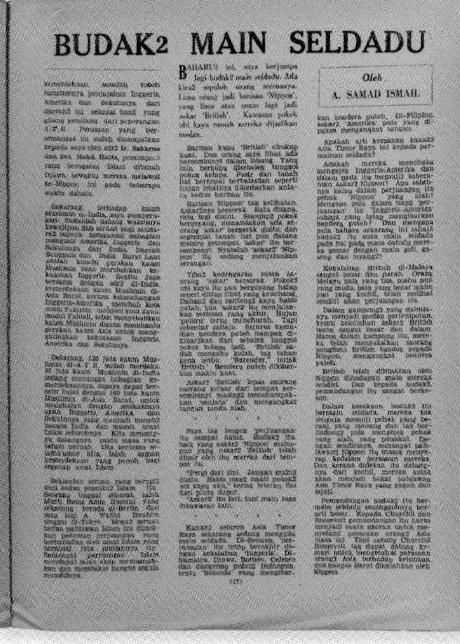
BUDAK2 MAIN SELDADU
Oleh
A. SAMAD ISMAIL

Malay Development Office – and printed at 101 Jalan Sultan on the premises of al-Ahmadiah Press.[5] In 1944, *Fajar Asia* merged with another magazine, *Semangat Asia* (Spirit of Asia), in a cost-cutting move. The new entity kept the *Fajar Asia* name while its operations were taken over by Malai Sinbun Sya, which was located at 146 Cecil Street.[6] Malai Sinbun Sya published four issues.[7]

As publications such as *Fajar Asia* were used to spread Japanese propaganda, these publications had to follow guidelines set by the Japanese army, which included praising or glorifying the Japanese army and its vision.[8] This explains the *Fajar Asia* pieces that expressed a pro-Japanese and anti-British stance that were aligned with the slogan "Asia for Asians", such as the 1943 essay "*Musnahkanlah Sifat Imperialisme*" (Destroy the Imperialism Character). This was likely to have originally been a speech by Sukarno. Billed as a great leader, he was credited as the author of the piece which pointed to how Western imperialism had wrought destruction in Asia.

Pro-Japanese propaganda notwithstanding, *Fajar Asia* provided a platform for a new generation of writers, poets and critics such as Ahmady Asmara, Bachtiar Effendi and A. Hasjmy who contributed to the development of Malay literature. These and other writers went on to reshape political ideas, as well as Malay literature and language after World War II.

The short stories that *Fajar Asia* published contain vivid portrayals of social conditions, reflections on the spirit of the age, and exhortations to love and serve the homeland. Some of the stories also dealt with social issues. In Abdul Samad Ismail's "*Budak2 main seldadu*" ("Boys playing soldiers"), published in May 1944, Ismail describes Malay boys pretending to be Japanese and British soldiers. He writes that in the boys' play-fight, the British soldiers lost to the Japanese, as had happened in real life. Ismail notes that the boys had witnessed Britain's humiliating defeat in Malaya and that this event had changed how the boys viewed Malaya's former colonial masters.

As a platform for Japanese propaganda, *Fajar Asia* did not attempt to capture the brutalities inflicted by the Japanese during the Occupation. The literary works it published are a contrast to the short stories printed after the war, which describe the Japanese occupying forces as being cruel, inhumane, and even worse than the British.[9]

On top of its contribution to Malay literature, *Fajar Asia* also played a significant role in the development of the modern Malay spelling system using the Roman alphabet. In the early 20th century, C.A. van Ophuisen and R.J. Wilkinson had separately created Romanised spelling systems for the Malay language. Van Ophuisen's system was used in Indonesian schools while Wilkinson's was used in Malaya. In 1933, the prominent traditional grammarian Za'ba (Zainal Abidin Ahmad)[10] improved on the Wilkinson spelling system and established the Ejaan Sekolah (school spelling) system, which became widely used in schools in Malaya.

Fajar Asia then developed and used a system that came to be known as Ejaan Fajar Asia (Dawn of Asia spelling). This used the Ophuisen system for vowels and the Wilkinson/Za'ba system for consonants.[11] Angkatan Sasterawan '50 (Asas '50), the leading Malay literary association in Singapore, subsequently adopted Ejaan Fajar Asia because of its ease of use and practicality.[12] There were further refinements to the Malay spelling system over succeeding decades. The Fajar Asia spelling was another important stepping stone as the Malay language made its transition from Jawi to the Roman system of writing. ♦ **Mazelan Anuar**

Notes

1 Fajar Asia (1999). In *Ensiklopedia sejarah dan kebudayaan Melayu Vol. 2* (p. 724). Kuala Lumpur: Dewan Bahasa dan Pustaka, Kementerian Pendidikan, Malaysia. (Call no. R 959.003 ENS)
2 *Fajar Asia*. (Year 1, number 1; Jan 1943). Syonan-To: Pejabat Pembangunan Melayu Baru (Sinsei Malai Kensetsu Sha). (Call no. RRARE 959.052FA)
3 *Ensiklopedia sejarah dan kebudayaan Melayu vol. 2*, pp. 724–725.
4 Admiral Togo–Japan's hero of heroes. (1933, January 4). *Singapore Daily News*, p. 6; Page 5 Miscellaneous Column 1. (1943, May 27). *Synonan Shimbun*. Retrieved from NewspaperSG.
5 The al-Ahmadiah Press had been established in 1920 by Malay nobility from the Natuna Islands, Riau. Low, C. M. G & Karthigesu, T. (2012). *Kampong Glam: A heritage trail* (pp. 18–19). Singapore: National Heritage Board. (Call no. RSING 599.2 KAM)
6 Sohaimi Abdul Aziz (2008). Re-visiting the Slogan "Asia for Asians" and the "Look East" Policy: A study of Malay short stories, p. 79. Retrieved from MyJurnal website.
7 *Ensiklopedia sejarah dan kebudayaan Melayu vol. 2*, 1999, p. 724.
8 Sohaimi Abdul Aziz, 2008, p. 79.
9 A famous example would be Murad's *Nyawa di Hujong Pedang* (Life at the Edge of the Sword), first published in 1946. NLB's collection includes the 1959, 1963, 1966, 1967 and 2011 editions.
10 Coincidentally, Zainal Abidin Ahmad (also known as Za'ba) shares the same name as the Chief Editor of *Fajar Asia*. While Za'ba was not involved in the running of *Fajar Asia*, he contributed a few articles to the magazine.
11 Misteri Ejaan 'Fajar Asia'. (2014, June 9). *Berita Harian*. Retrieved from NewspaperSG.
12 Sejarah Awal Ejaan Rumi Melayu. (1981, February 22). *Berita Harian*, p. 5. Retrieved from NewspaperSG; Asmah Haji Omar. Standard Language and the Standardization of Malay (pp. 83–84). In *Anthropological Linguistics, 13*(2) (Feb., 1971), 75–89. Retrieved from JSTOR.

SAVING SINGAPORE'S FORESTS

First page of Nathaniel Cantley's "Report on the Forests of the Straits Settlements". The full report can be found in the 1883 issue of the *Proceedings of the Legislative Council of the Straits Settlements.*

Title: *Report on the Forests of the Straits Settlements*
Author: Nathaniel Cantley
Year published: 1883
Publisher: Government Printing Office
Language: English
Type: Government publication; 70 pages
Call no.: RRARE 328.5957 SSLCPL
Accession no.: B20048240I
Donated by: Lee Kip Lin

The 1883 "Report on the Forests of the Straits Settlements" is one of the earliest and most important documents related to the greening of Singapore. Tucked in the pages of the 1883 issue of the *Proceedings of the Legislative Council of the Straits Settlements,* it introduced the idea of nature reserves to Singapore and the rest of the Straits Settlements. Commissioned by Frederick A. Weld (then Governor of the Straits Settlements), and prepared by Nathaniel Cantley, then Superintendent of the Singapore Botanic Gardens,[1] the 70-page report came at a time when the Straits Settlements was facing a serious deforestation problem.

Cantley started the report by painting a bleak picture of the state of forest lands in the Straits Settlements. He lamented that the forests had been drastically reduced over the decades because of the "reckless migratory" clearing for the growing of lucrative agricultural commodities such as gambier and pepper.[2] This "evil", as Cantley termed it, took hold mainly because the colonial government made "no sufficient attempts" to conserve the forest lands. At the same time, there were "absolutely no Forest Rules or Regulations, or Forest law of any kind" to prevent forest clearing.[3]

Cantley estimated in the report that at least half of the island of Singapore was under cultivation in 1882, and the 5,000 acres (20.2 sq km) of forests that remained were "widely distributed in isolated patches" all over the island.[4] Ranging from half an acre to 25 acres in size, these pockets of forest were surrounded by lalang-covered "wastelands" which were previously forest lands but had been cleared to make way for plantations and later abandoned.[5]

To protect forests in the Straits Settlements, Cantley called on the colonial government to start creating nature reserves using the patches of primary forest that remained and the wastelands surrounding them. These reserves would be legislated, properly mapped out and managed by a government department. To prevent

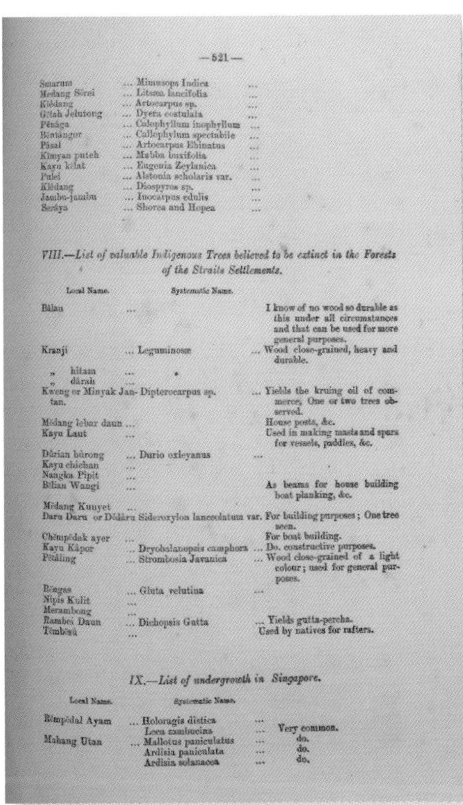

—521—

Smarum	... Mimusops Indica	...
Medang Sérei	... Litsæa lancifolia	...
Klèdang	... Artocarpus sp.	...
Gitah Jelutong	... Dyera costulata	...
Pènaga	... Calophyllum inophyllum	...
Bintangor	... Callophylum spectabile	...
Pisal	... Artocarpus Ehinatus	...
Kimyan puteh	... Mabba buxifolia	...
Kayu kèlat	... Eugenia Zeylanica	...
Pulei	... Alstonia scholaris var.	...
Klèdang	... Diospyros sp.	...
Jambu-jambu	... Inocarpus edulis	...
Serâya	... Shorea and Hopea	...

VIII.—List of valuable Indigenous Trees believed to be extinct in the Forests of the Straits Settlements.

Local Name.	Systematic Name.	
Bàlau	...	I know of no wood so durable as this under all circumstances and that can be used for more general purposes.
Kranji	... Leguminosæ	... Wood close-grained, heavy and durable.
" hitam	...	
" dàrah	...	
Kweng or Minyak Jantan.	Dipterocarpus sp.	... Yields the kruing oil of commerce, One or two trees observed.
Mèdang lebar daun	...	House posts, &c.
Kayu Laut	...	Used in making masts and spars for vessels, paddles, &c.
Dùrian bùrong	... Durio oxleyanus	...
Kayu chichan	...	
Nangka Pipit	...	
Bilian Wangi	...	As beams for house building boat planking, &c.
Mèdang Kunyet	...	
Daru Daru or Dèdàru	Sideroxylon lanceolatum var.	For building purposes; One tree seen.
Chèmpèdak ayer	...	For boat building.
Kayu Kàpor	... Dryobalanopsis camphora	... Do. constructive purposes.
Pètàling	... Strombosia Javanica	... Wood close-grained of a light colour; used for general purposes.
Bèngas	... Gluta velutina	...
Nipis Kulit	...	
Merambong	...	
Rambei Daun	... Dichopsis Gutta	... Yields gutta-percha.
Tèmbèsu	...	Used by natives for rafters.

IX.—List of undergrowth in Singapore.

Local Name.	Systematic Name.		
Rèmpèdal Ayam	... Holoragis distica	...	
	Leea sambucina	...	Very common.
Mahang Utan	... Mallotus paniculatus	...	do.
	Ardisia paniculata	...	do.
	Ardisia solanacea	...	do.

[Above] View in the Jungle, Singapore c. 1845. This view shows a recently cleared stretch of jungle, with a broad path. By the late 19th century, much of Singapore's jungles had been felled to make way for the expanding plantations and a growing migrant population. This print was originally published in Charles Ramsay Drinkwater Bethune's *Views in the Eastern Archipelago: Borneo, Sarawak, Labuan, &c. &c. &c. Courtesy of the National Museum of Singapore, National Heritage Board.*
[Left] The Kranji tree is one of the species of trees believed to have become extinct in the Straits Settlements, as listed in this page from Cantley's report.

illegal deforestation, the reserves would be patrolled by watchmen. There would also be a tree-planting programme to reforest the "wastelands".[6]

To build a case for his recommendations, Cantley warned in the report that deforestation in the Straits Settlements had "sensibly affected" the climate of the colony as rainfall was becoming less frequent and more localised. This had not only adversely affected agricultural production, but also dried up smaller streams.[7] Furthermore, the drier weather was leaving the colony more susceptible to epidemics and diseases as there was less rain to "flush the sewers and ditches, and wash away all pestilential matter".[8]

Cantley also stated that the extensive clearings were either endangering or driving native tree species to extinction. To make matters worse, many of the affected species were timber trees, thus disrupting the local timber supply. Cantley noted in the report that Singapore was using about 800,000 cubic feet of timber annually. However, due to the loss of its primary forest over the decades, the island could only meet half of this demand. It had to import the rest from Johor and the Riau Islands.[9] As such, Cantley felt that the establishment of nature reserves could help the Straits Settlements safeguard its domestic timber supply. This demonstrates that Cantley envisioned that the proposed reserves would fulfill a practical commercial function, as well as protect the climate and environment.

A year after the report was released, the first eight nature reserves in Singapore were demarcated. An accompanying map shows that these were located in Bukit Timah, Jurong, Mandai, Chan Chu Kang [sic.], Sambawang [sic.], Seletar, Changie [sic.] and an area referred to as Military, which was just north of Singapore town. The reserves made up a total of 8,000 acres (32.4 sq km) of land.[10] They were placed under the supervision of a newly minted Forest Department which was part of the Singapore Botanic Gardens.[11] Headed by Cantley, the department was also in charge of the reserves in Penang and Melaka. Established together with the reserves in Singapore, the hill forest reserves in Penang as well as the Ayer Panas, Jus, Sungei Udang and Merlimau reserves in Melaka were created to conserve the remaining primary forests there.[12]

To manage the nature reserves in Singapore, Cantley was provided with four officers, a group of forest watchmen and hundreds of labourers. Their work included marking the boundaries of the reserves, preventing illegal clearings and reforesting wastelands.[13] Some of the trees that were used for the reforestation effort in Singapore included native species such as *Bintangor* (*Calophyllum inophyllum*), Malacca ironwood (*Kumpassia malaccana*) and *Tampinis* (*Sloetia sideroxylon*), as well as imported ones like teak (*Tectona grandis*), American rain tree (*Inga saman*) and mahogany (*Swietenia mahogani*).[14]

The Forest Department was administered by the Singapore Botanic Gardens until 1895, when forestry matters were transferred to the Collector of Land Revenue at the Land Office. This was after the colonial government decided to scale back its support for the forest reserves.[15] By then, 66,191 acres (267.9 sq km) of land had been designated as Forest Reserves in the Straits Settlements, of which 12,965 acres (52.5 sq km) were in Singapore. This was an increase from the 8,000 acres (32.4 sq km) of reserves Singapore had in 1883.[16] The number of forest reserves between 1883 and 1895 also increased from eight to 14.[17]

However, under the Land Office both the number and size of the forest reserves in Singapore were reduced drastically after 1895. This is despite the enactment of the Forest Ordinance in 1909 which gazetted the reserves in the Straits Settlements.[18] This was because the government decided to open up the reserves for development projects and resource gathering activities. By the mid-1930s, the colonial government made the fateful decision to revoke all forest reserves. This prompted the Botanic Gardens to launch a campaign to save what was left of them. The Forest Ordinance of 1939 reinstated three reserves – Bukit Timah, Kranji and Pandan.[19]

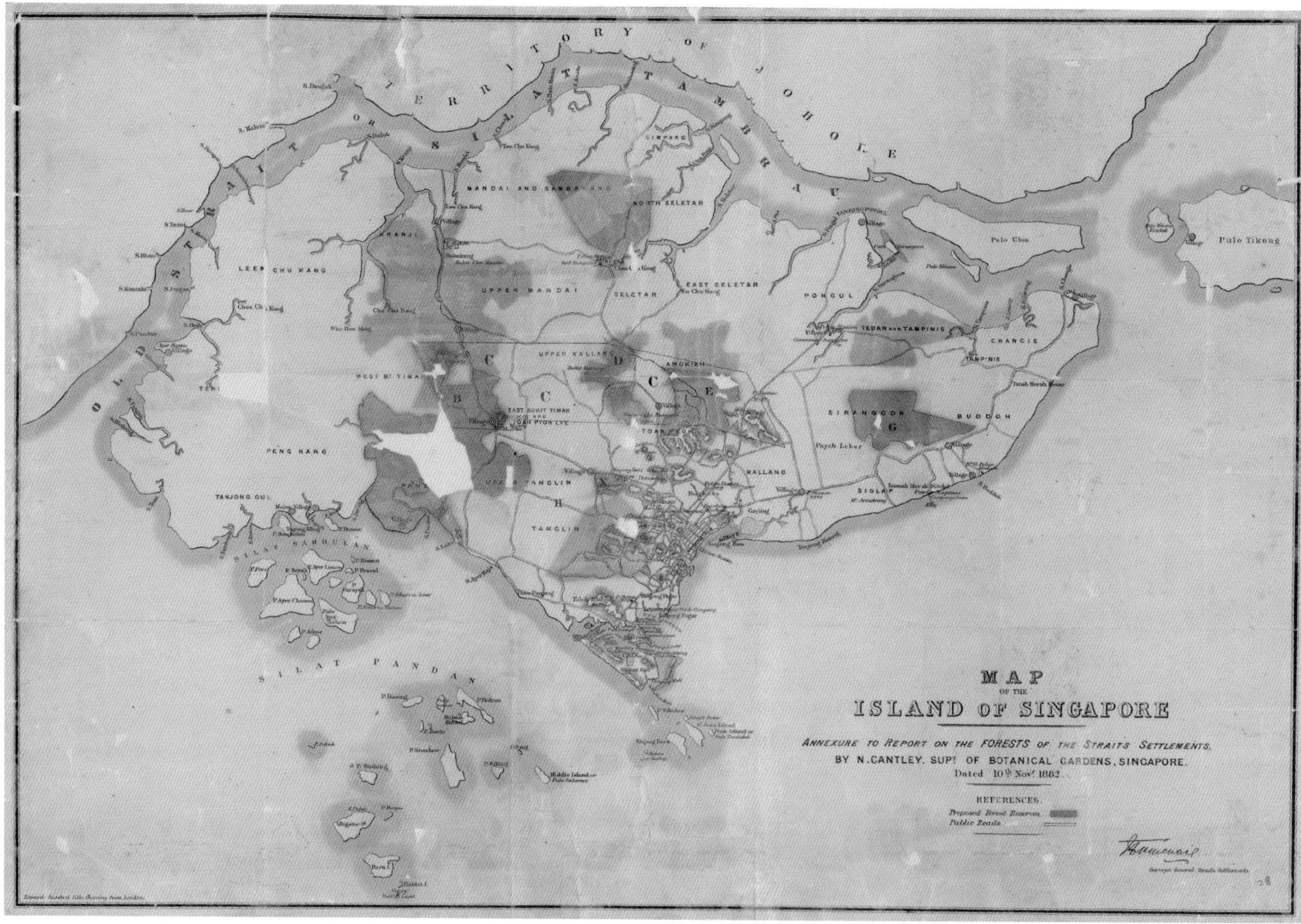

Cantley's report introduced the idea of nature reserves in the Straits Settlements. This map, which is attached to the report, shows the proposed locations of the first reserves in Singapore. *Courtesy of National Archives of Singapore.*

Control of the reserves in Singapore was officially returned to the Botanic Gardens in 1939 under the Forest Reserves Ordinance.[20] The number of reserves increased to five when the Nature Reserves Ordinance was extended in 1951 to include the protection of Labrador Cliff and the central water catchment areas.[21] Today, there are four nature reserves in Singapore: Bukit Timah, Sungei Buloh, Labrador and the Central Catchment. Covering 8,271 acres (33.5 sq km), they are protected by the Parks and Trees Act and come under the purview of the National Parks Board.[22] ♦ **Lim Tin Seng**

Notes

1 In the 19th century, the Singapore Botanic Gardens was also known as the Botanical Gardens. Much has been written about Nathaniel Cantley's contributions to the Botanical Gardens; see, for instance, *Nature contained: Environmental histories of Singapore* (2014), and *Gardens of perpetual summer: The Singapore Botanic Gardens* (2009). However, photographs of Cantley remain elusive.

2 "Migratory clearing" refers to the periodic clearing of a fresh patch of forest. Cantley, N. (1883). Report on the forests of the Straits Settlements. In *Proceedings of the Legislative Council of the Straits Settlements for the year 1883* (p. 491). Singapore: Government Printing Office. (Call no.: RRARE 328.5957 SSLCPL)

3 Cantley, 1883, p. 491.

4 Cantley, 1883, p. 499.

5 Cantley, 1883, p. 499.

6 Cantley, 1883, pp. 514–515.

7 Cantley, 1883, p. 491.

8 Cantley, 1883, pp. 491, 496.

9 Cantley, 1883, pp. 491–492, 498–499, 502–504.

10 Cantley, N. (1885). Annual report on the Forest Department, Straits Settlements, for the year 1884. In *Proceedings of the Legislative Council of the Straits Settlements for the year 1885* (pp. C229–C230). Singapore: Government Printing Office. (Call no.: RRARE 328.5957 SSLCPL)

11 Cantley, 1885, pp. C229–C230.

12 Cantley, 1885, pp. C232–C235; Cantley, 1883, pp. 511–514.

13 Cantley, 1885, pp. C229–C230.

14 Cantley, 1885, pp. C231–C232.

15 Barnard, T. (2016). *Nature's colony: Empire, nation and environment in the Singapore Botanic Gardens* (p. 75). Singapore: NUS Press. (Call no.: RSING 580.735957 BAR).

16 Hill, H.C. (1900). *Report on the present system of forest conservancy in the Straits Settlements with suggestions for future management* (p. 2). Singapore: Government Printing Office. Retrieved from Biodiversity Heritage Library website.

17 Cantley, 1885, pp. C229–C230; Ridley, H. N. (1890). *Annual report on the Botanic Gardens and Forest Department for the year 1889* (pp. 10–11). Singapore: Government Printing Office. Retrieved from Biodiversity Heritage Library website.

18 Burn-Murdoch, A.M. (1910). *Annual report on Forest Administration in the Straits Settlements for the year 1909* (p. 1). Singapore: Government Printing Office; Burn-Murdoch, A.M. (1911). *Annual report on forest administration in the Straits Settlements for the year 1910* (p. 1). Singapore: Government Printing Office. Retrieved from Biodiversity Heritage Library website.

19 Lum, S. & Sharp, I. (Eds.). (1996). *A view from the summit: The story of Bukit Timah Nature Reserve* (pp. 22–25). Singapore: Nanyang Technological University and the National University of Singapore. (Call no.: RSING 333.78095957 VIE)

20 Holttum, R.E. (1939). *Annual report of the Gardens Department, Straits Settlements, for the year 1938* (p. 3). Singapore: Government Printing Office; Holttum, R.E. (1940). *Annual report of the Gardens Department, Straits Settlements, for the year 1939* (pp. 2–3). Singapore: Government Printing Office. Retrieved from Biodiversity Heritage Library website.

21 Henderson, R. (1952). *Botanic Gardens Department annual report for 1951* (p. 6). Singapore: Government Printing Office. Retrieved from Biodiversity Heritage Library website.

22 National Parks Board. (2019). *Annual report 2018/2019* (p. 57). Retrieved from National Parks Board website; Republic of Singapore. (2006, July 31). *Parks and Trees Act (Chapter 216)*; Republic of Singapore. (2018, April 1). *National Parks Board Act (Chapter 198A)*. Retrieved from Singapore Statutes Online website.

PATRIOT AND PHILANTHROPIST
LIM KONG THING

Title: 林光挺文献集 (Lim Kong Thing Collection)
Date: 1912–99
Language: Chinese and English
Type: Correspondence, eulogies, elegies, photographs, notices, newspaper cuttings, certificates and other ephemera
Call no.: RRARE 305.89510595 LGT
Accession nos.: B20032061C (v. 1); B20032062D (v. 2); B20032063E (v. 3); B20032064F (v. 4); B20032065G (v. 5); B20032066H (v. 6)
Donated by: Lin Qiong

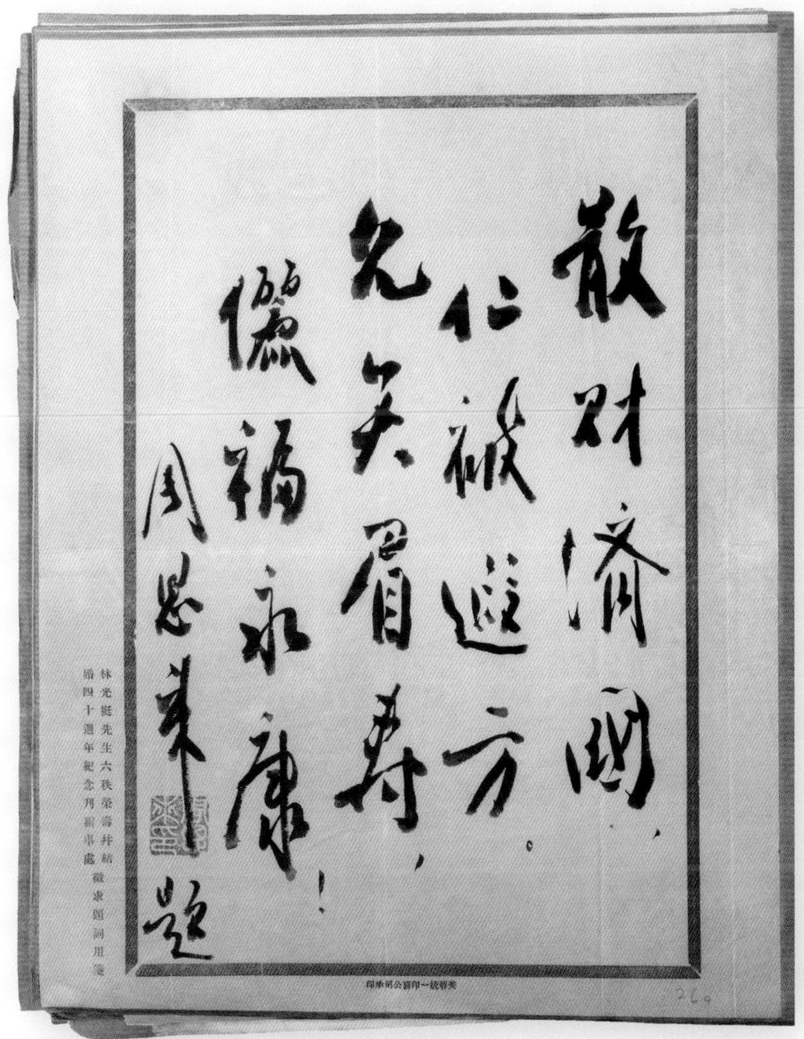

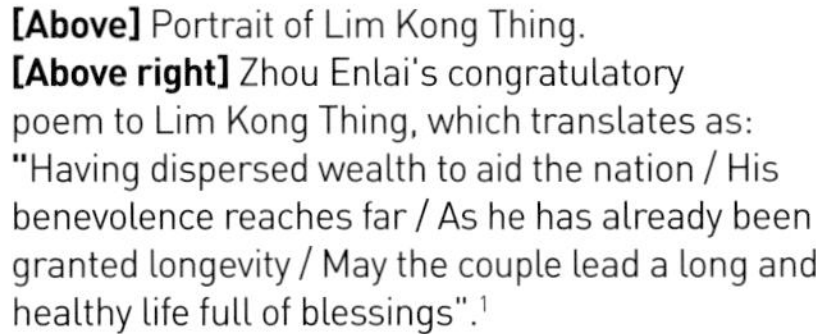
[Above] Portrait of Lim Kong Thing.
[Above right] Zhou Enlai's congratulatory poem to Lim Kong Thing, which translates as: "Having dispersed wealth to aid the nation / His benevolence reaches far / As he has already been granted longevity / May the couple lead a long and healthy life full of blessings".[1]

Such was the prominence of Malayan businessman Lim Kong Thing (林光挺; Lin Guangting) that on the occasion celebrating his 60th birthday and his 40th wedding anniversary in 1939, he received a congratulatory poem[2] penned by Zhou Enlai,[3] the future premier of the People's Republic of China.

Lim (b. 1879, Fujian, China–d. 1940, Negeri Sembilan, Federated Malay States) was born to a poor family in Xialing village in China. He came to Southeast Asia at the age of 20 and eventually settled down in Kuala Pilah in Negeri Sembilan. Described as a burly man with a square face and large

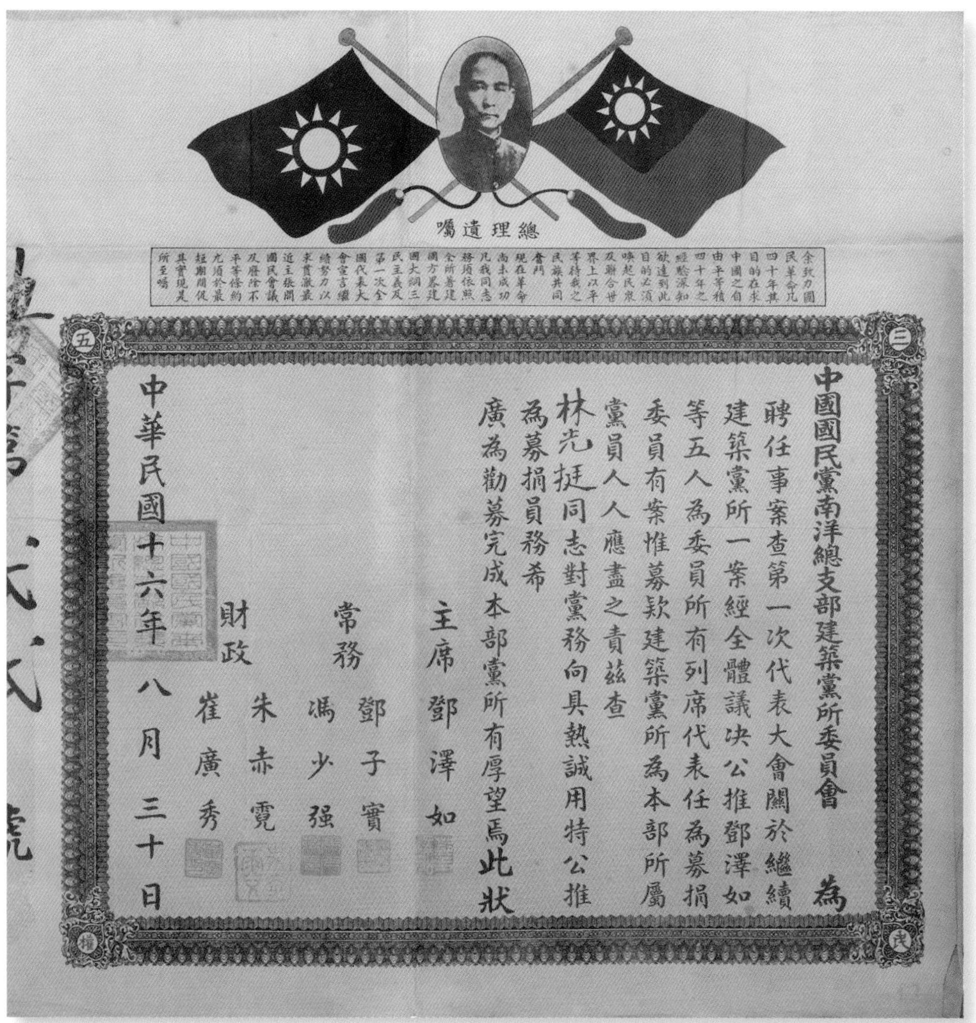

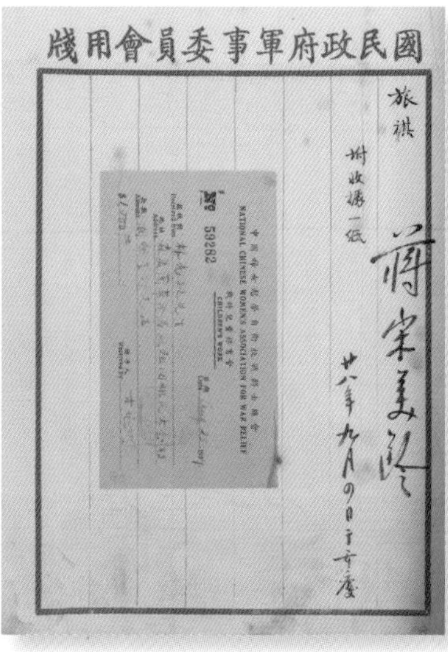

[Above] This announcement, which identifies Lim as a member of the fundraising committee, acknowledges his contributions to the Kuomintang. The party's "blue sky and white sun" flag and the "blue sky, white sun and red earth" national flag of the Republic of China are shown at the top of the document. A portrait of Dr Sun Yat Sen is shown between both flags, and his political beliefs are printed in red text beneath the portrait.

[Above right] A personal note dated 1939 and signed by Song Meiling (First Lady of the Republic of China; the wife of President Chiang Kai-shek; and Chairwoman of the National Chinese Women's Association for War Relief) accompanied the receipt acknowledging Lim's donation to the Children's Work department.

ears, Lim would go on to become a prominent community leader and a successful businessman dealing in the tin, rattan, rubber, textiles and the hotel industries. Among other things, he was the president of the Rubber Association, the Kuala Pilah Chinese Chamber of Commerce, and the China Relief Distress Committee.[4]

In 2007, six volumes of Lim's documents dated 1912–99 were donated to the National Library by Lin Qiong, Lim's youngest son and an award-winning Singapore literary pioneer. These consist of over 800 pages of notices, correspondence, manuscripts, photographs, certificates, newspaper cuttings, and elegies and eulogies about Lim.

These documents include a letter dated 14 September 1927 signed by the reigning Yamtuan Besar[5] of Negeri Sembilan, Tuanku Muhammad Shah. It states that Lim had been appointed his "attorney". As such, Lim had the right to "purchase lands and mines" and "apply for lands for buildings, mining, agricultural or other purposes" on behalf of the Yamtuan Besar. This position, colloquially referred to as *gua sha* (掛莎), was considered a great honour.[6]

Another set of documents attests to Lim's contributions. Inspired by Dr Sun Yat Sen, leader of the revolutionary movement in China, whom he had met in 1909, Lim joined the Tongmenghui (同盟会; Chinese Revolutionary Alliance), an underground resistance movement led by Dr Sun to overthrow the dynastic Qing government and to establish a republic in China. Consequently, Lim became involved in the spreading of its ideologies and fundraising to support its activities. He continued to contribute after the Tongmenghui evolved into the Kuomintang (KMT). An announcement made by the KMT Nanyang Main Branch dated 30 August 1927 notes that Lim was among the committee members appointed to raise funds for the construction of the party's building. It states that Lim was nominated because he was known for being a "passionate" contributor to the KMT.

Lim also donated generously to the establishment of schools, youth organisations, and reading clubs in Southeast Asia and China, as well as other charitable organisations and causes. In a letter dated 12 December 1932, the Consulate General of the Republic of China asked Lim, who was with the Rubber Association then, if he could encourage friends to donate to the building of a hospital. A receipt dated 23 August 1939 shows that Lim donated 1,000 yuan to the Children's Work department of the National Chinese Women's Association for War Relief to support their work in helping war orphans. The receipt was accompanied by a note signed by Mrs Chiang Kai-shek.

Because of his patriotism and philanthropic acts, when his friends made a public call for congratulatory poems or messages to celebrate Lim's 60th birthday and 40th

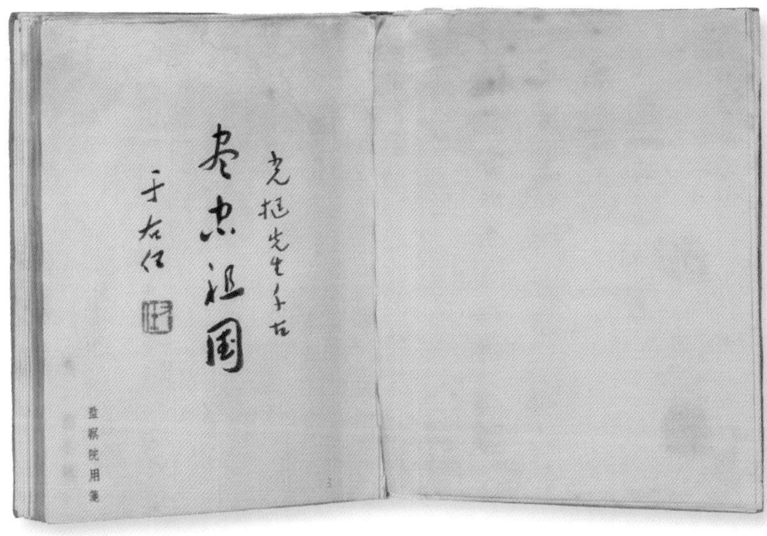

Volumes 1 **(above)** and 6 **(right)** of the six volumes of Lim Kong Thing's documents donated to the National Library. A page from Volume 6 contains the phrase 尽忠祖国, which was written by Yu Youren (a master calligrapher, poet and member of the KMT) in praise of Lim's commitment and loyalty to his motherland, China. Yu's personal seal in red ink appears next to the phrase.

wedding anniversary in 1939,[7] many well-known names responded. Besides Zhou Enlai, there were contributions from Tay Koh Yat (founder of the Tay Koh Yat Bus company, which was once the biggest Chinese bus company in Singapore), and Chen Shuren (a famous political leader and painter in China).[8] Unfortunately, Lim passed away from illness the following year at the age of 61.[9] In memory of him, numerous elegies and eulogies were written. Preserved by his family, these form part of the collection that was donated to the National Library.

The Lim Kong Thing collection is a rich source of primary material which offers insights into the socio-economic networks and the political alignments of a prominent Southeast Asian Chinese personality during the first half of the 20th century. The collection is also a valuable addition to Singapore's arts and cultural heritage, as many manuscripts were written by famous personalities of that period, such as Zhou Enlai, poet and calligrapher Yu Youren, and poet and short story writer Yu Dafu.

Many documents also offer glimpses of the anti-Japanese fundraising activities that were carried out. The discovery of these documents would have cost the lives of many donors as their names were listed.[10] Lim's son, Lin Qiong, recalled that to hide them, his family first slipped the documents into the ceiling, and subsequently buried them during the Japanese Occupation.[11]

The sixth and final volume of Lim's documents ends with a saying he had shared with his children, and which sums up his philanthropic principles:

吾之於财，为散而聚，不为守财虏而聚。
聚也以私力，散也以公义。
吾手所聚之财，决将由吾手而散之。
散吾财於社会国家，不贻财於子孙。
吾之子若孙，如其不肖也，得吾财将为罪孽之媒，
如其贤也，得吾财将减削其造诣之机。[12]

Wealth is gathered in order for us to disperse it, not for us to become a slave to it. The wealth gathered through private means will be dispersed for the cause of social righteousness. The wealth I have gathered will also be dispersed by me. I will disperse this wealth to society and country, and not leave it to my descendants. For if my descendants are unworthy people, the wealth they receive from me will become the medium for their sins, and if my descendants are virtuous people, the wealth they receive from me will reduce the chances for them to obtain a higher level of life attainments. ♦ **Lee Meiyu**

Notes

1 A translation provided by the writer of this article.
2 《林光挺文献集》 [Lim Kong Thing collection], Volume 1. Unpublished. (Call no.: RRARE 305.89510595 LGT)
3 Zhou Enlai became the PRC's first premier 10 years after penning the poem. He was remembered as a skilled and able diplomat and leader after his death. See Barnouin, B. & Yu, C. (2006). *Zhou Enlai: a political life* (p. 315). Hong Kong: The Chinese University of Hong Kong. (Call no.: R 951.05092 BAR)
4 《林光挺文献集》 [Lim Kong Thing collection], Volume 3. Unpublished. (Call no.: RRARE 305.89510595 LGT)
5 Yang di-Pertuan Besar, or "Malay Ruler".
6 《林光挺文献集》 [Lim Kong Thing collection], Volume 1. Unpublished. (Call no.: RRARE 305.89510595 LGT)
7 南侨闻人林光挺君六十诞辰徵文纪念 [Calling for submission of articles to commemorate the 60th birthday of famous Southeast Asian Overseas Chinese personality Lim Kong Thing]. (1939, May 26). 南洋商报 [*Nanyang Siang Pau*], p. 40. Retrieved from NewspaperSG.
8 《林光挺文献集》 [Lim Kong Thing collection], Volumes 1–3. Unpublished. (Call no.: RRARE 305.89510595 LGT)
9 瓜朥庇朥闻人林光挺昨晨逝世 [Kuala Pilah famous personality Lim Kong Thing passed away yesterday morning]. (1940, May 13). 南洋商报 [*Nanyang Siang Pau*], p. 28. Retrieved from NewspaperSG.
10 Lai, Y. P. (October 2008). 林光挺文献集简介 [A brief introduction to the Lim Kong Thing collection]. *BiblioAsia*, 4(3), 32–33. Retrieved from NLB's BiblioAsia website.
11 图书馆局希望公众借出珍藏品供研究 [National Library Board hopes that private collections can be loaned for research]. (2009, February 27). 联合早报 [*Lianhe Zaobao*], p. 11. Retrieved from NewspaperSG.
12 《林光挺文献集》 [Lim Kong Thing collection], Volume 6. Unpublished. (Call no.: RRARE 305.89510595 LGT)

Tanjong Pagar Dock Widens its Berth

Title: *Plan of the Docks, Wharves and Buildings of the Tanjong Pagar Dock Company*
Creators: F.W. Austen; Babajee Rajaram; John Frederick Aldophus; W.D. Bayliss
Year published: 1878
Publisher: Maclure & MacDonald (London)
Language: English
Type: Map; 73 cm x 95 cm
Call no.: RRARE 387.15095957 PLA-[KSC]
Accession no.: B29233014B
Donated by: Koh Seow Chuan

The second half of the 19th century saw rapid developments in the port of Singapore, which paved the way for the island's prosperity. Up to that time, the Singapore River had served as the settlement's main port, but as congestion at the river mouth worsened, some companies began building wharves at New Harbour (later known as Keppel Harbour), where the waters near the shore were deep. Here, larger steam vessels could berth for coaling (refuelling) as well as loading and unloading.[1] One such company which became a key player in the development of Singapore's port was Tanjong Pagar Dock Company, whose premises are shown on this coloured plan dated 2 August 1878.

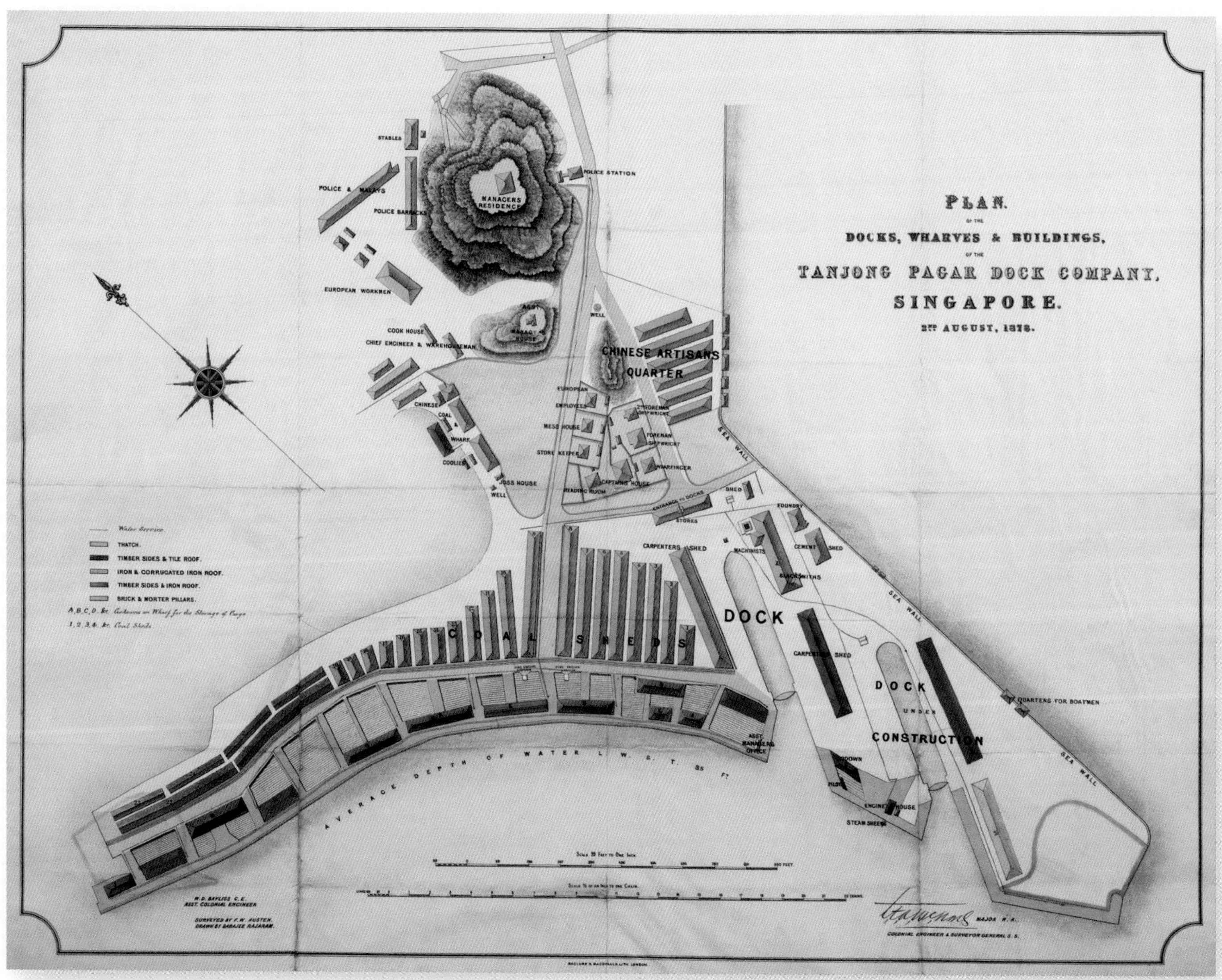

[Facing page] *Plan of the docks, wharves and buildings of the Tanjong Pagar Dock Company, 1878.* The plan bears the signature of Major J.F.A. McNair, the first Colonial Engineer and Surveyor-General of the Straits Settlements.[2]
[Above] Two vessels undergoing repairs and maintenance in Victoria Dock.

Established in 1864, Tanjong Pagar Dock Company began constructing wharves and a dry dock at the western side of Tanjong Pagar.[3] The length of the completed wharf was 750 feet (0.2 km), which allowed four vessels to berth. But as shipping continued to expand worldwide, more space had to be added to cope with demand.

By 1879, the year after this plan was drawn up, the length of the wharf had reached 3,305 feet (1 km). It was later extended to about 6,600 feet (2 km) in 1885 through the acquisition of the Borneo Company's wharves.[4] Compared to other wharves at New Harbour, the Tanjong Pagar Dock Company's had the advantage of being located nearer the town centre.[5]

Meanwhile, the dry dock had also been built to cater to the bigger steamers that were coming in for repairs and maintenance, which none of the docks at New Harbour were equipped to handle then.[6] It was officially opened on 17 October 1868 by the Governor of the Straits Settlements, Sir Harry St. George Ord, and named Victoria Dock.

With the opening of the Suez Canal in November 1869, the time it took for ships to travel between Europe and Asia was dramatically reduced. Singapore's port experienced a sharp increase in steamships arriving for repairs and coaling. Consequently, in 1879 Tanjong Pagar Dock Company opened a second – and larger – dry dock named Albert Dock, located to the east of Victoria Dock.[7] This can be seen marked on the 1878 plan as being "under construction". The availability of these facilities was instrumental in consolidating Singapore's status as a major port in the East.

Many shipping and coal companies stored their coal in sheds on Tanjong Pagar Dock Company's premises, a provision that was an important part of the company's business proposition.[8] These sheds, located north of the wharf and godowns, were originally built of wood, with attap roofs. However, a serious fire that broke out in April 1877 and took two weeks to subdue destroyed an enormous stock of coal. This disaster galvanised the company to invest more money in building sheds using more resilient materials, such as bricks, tiles, corrugated zinc and iron.[9]

Besides storage services, a coaling station required labourers who could load the coal efficiently onto the ships. In Singapore, this labour-intensive work was carried out by Chinese coolies, most of whom were migrants from southern China. Tanjong Pagar Dock Company housed the coolies in an area on its premises marked "Chinese Artisans Quarter", which was located north of the coal sheds.[10]

On the printed plan of the company's premises, some hand-drawn red lines can be seen. These represent planned water services. As the government-run water system in town often malfunctioned, the supply of water at the harbour was then operated by private companies, with boats carrying water to the ships. In 1880, Tanjong Pagar Dock Company completed its installation of a pipe network to supply water directly to the ships from their own pumps, for a fee.[11]

Through its acquisition of competitors and the 1899 merger with its main rival, the New Harbour Dock Company, Tanjong Pagar Dock Company came to control virtually the entire shipping business in Singapore. However, in the late 19th century, few improvements were made to the facilities to meet demand as the company was unwilling to invest more money in upgrading works.

Eventually, the company was acquired by the government in 1905, thus bringing an end to private ownership of the port.[12] Subsequently, the Singapore Harbour Board, which was formed in 1913, assumed control of the port facilities.[13] In 1964, the board was replaced by the Port of Singapore Authority.[14] Today, port facilities are operated by PSA Corporation and Jurong Port Pte Ltd, while the Maritime Port Authority of Singapore is responsible for regulating port and marine services and facilities.[15] ♦ **Joanna Tan**

Notes

1 Lim, R. (1993). *Tough men, bold visions: The story of Keppel* (p. 31). Singapore: Keppel Corporation. (Call no.: RSING 338.762383095957 LIM)
2 National Library Board. (2015). *Visualising space: Maps of Singapore and the region: Collections from the National Library and National Archives of Singapore* (p. 97). Singapore: National Library Board. (Call no.: RSING 911.5957 SIN)
3 Lim, 1993, p. 32.
4 Tanjong Pagar Citizens' Consultative Committee. (1989). *Tanjong Pagar: Singapore's cradle of development* (p. 55). Singapore: Tanjong Pagar Citizens' Consultative Committee. (Call no.: RSING 959.57 TAN-[HIS])
5 Bogaars, G. (1956). *The Tanjong Pagar Dock Company, 1864–1905* (p. 131). Singapore: Government Printing Office. (Call no.: RLCOS 959.51 BOG)
6 Tanjong Pagar, the story of its rise and progress. (1896, May 5). *The Singapore Free Press and Mercantile Advertiser (Weekly)*, p. 9. Retrieved from NewspaperSG.
7 Tanjong Pagar Citizens' Consultative Committee, 1989, p. 45.
8 Bogaars, 1956, p. 133.
9 Tanjong Pagar Citizens' Consultative Committee, 1989, p. 46.
10 Bogaars, 1956, p. 145.
11 Bogaars, 1956, pp. 151–152.
12 Tanjong Pagar Citizens' Consultative Committee, 1989, pp. 48–49.
13 Harbour Boards. (1913, July 1). *The Straits Times*, p. 9. Retrieved from NewspaperSG.
14 Port of Singapore Authority. (1984). *Singapore: Portrait of a port: A pictorial history of the port and harbour of Singapore 1819–1984* (pp. 14–15). Singapore: MPH Magazines. (Call no.: RSING 779.93871095957 SIN)
15 Bill for new body to regulate port industry passed. (1996, January 19). *The Straits Times*, p. 1. Retrieved from NewspaperSG.

An Early Lithograph of Singapore

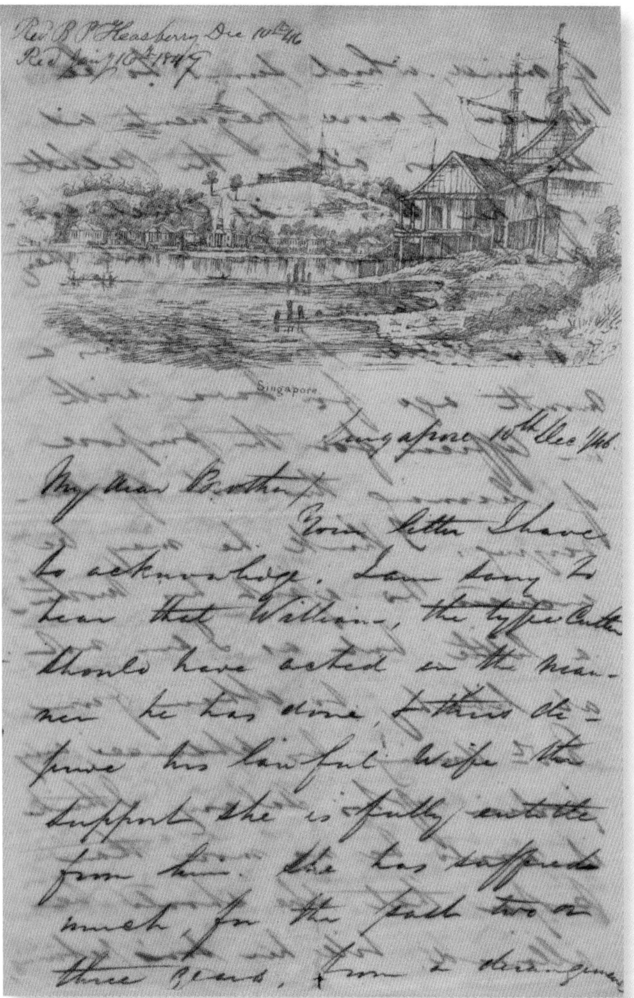

Rev B P Keasberry Dec 10th 46
Re'd January 16th 184?

Singapore 10th Dec 1846

My dear brother,

Your letter I have to acknowledge. I am sorry to hear that Williams, the type cutter should have acted in the manner he has done, and thus deprive his lawful wife the support she is fully entitled from him. She has suffered much, for the past two or three years from a derangement of mind, which seems to be severe and more frequent as she grows older, the result of her husband's cruel conduct towards her while they were together.

Her eldest son left [ ] a month ago for Java. An officer for the [ ], I think he may be [ ] his mother a little, but as I am not at liberty to obtain from Govt during his absence any portion of his salary. I think it should be no more than proper that she should be allowed [ ] her son's returns at least $3 [ ] of her husband's pay. [ ] the second son is with me & earns monthly $2 for assisting in printing. He is obliged to pay for his board & clothing out of it, & has scarcely any to spare for his mother.

Mrs Keasberry & myself will be most happy to have you take a room in our family during your stay here. Brother Thomson is at present with us, with his two daughters. He expects to leave [ ] as soon as a good opportunity offers, from Europe, on his way to America [ ], I shall not fail to deliver your letter [ ] as soon as they arrive.

You are aware, I suppose, that I am the only missionary in Singapore, which I think ought not to be so for it is [ ] that one can do justice to the people here who are yearly increasing in great number. There is talk among the Scot portion of the community here, of a Scots minister being sent to them, measure has been taken to obtain the necessary [ ] to support a minister. I hope they will proceed.

Give our [ ] regards to [ ] I have [ ] & also [ ].

Yours affectionately
Keasberry

[Left] The first page of Benjamin Keasberry's illustrated letter sheet dated 10 December 1846. **[Right]** A transcription of the letter, with brackets [ ] referring to text that is not legible.

Title: *Illustrated Letter Sheet of Early Singapore*
Author: Benjamin Peach Keasberry
Date: 10 December 1846
Publisher: Singapore, s.n.
Language: English
Type: Letter, 4 pages on one leaf
Call no.: RRARE 959.5703 ILL-[KSC]
Accession no.: B26056251E
Donated by: Koh Seow Chuan

Illustrations, drawings, paintings and prints constituted some of the most important visual records of early Singapore before the advent of photography.[1] A lithographed[2] image captioned "Singapore", which appears on the front of a four-page letter sheet dated 10 December 1846, is among the oldest surviving examples of a topographical view printed in Singapore.

The image depicts the colonial town and indigenous dwellings along the Singapore waterfront. The initials "B.P.K.", at the bottom right corner of the scene identify the artist and printer as Benjamin Peach Keasberry (1811–75), the writer of this letter.

Due to text loss and illegibility, the identities of the persons mentioned in the letter are unclear. Based on what has been transcribed, the letter was possibly addressed to a fellow missionary, and it concerns the

A drawing by Scottish artist Charles Dyce titled *Singapore from Sandy Point* (1842–47). Similarities between this and Keasberry's lithograph suggest that the latter piece was also drawn from Sandy Point (now Tanjong Rhu). *Courtesy of the National University of Singapore Museum Collection.*

dire financial situation of a single mother whose son was working for Keasberry as a printing assistant.

Keasberry was a Protestant missionary, educator, translator, artist and prodigious printer who played an instrumental role in the development of printing in Singapore, especially in the area of lithography.[3] He had learnt the art of lithographic printing during his apprenticeship with missionary and printer Walter Henry Medhurst of the London Missionary Society (LMS) in Batavia (present-day Jakarta) in the 1830s. In 1839, Keasberry relocated to Singapore as an independent missionary and later joined the LMS, where he helped grow its mission, school and printing press.

In 1840, Keasberry began experimenting with a lithographic press, which he had borrowed from the American Board of Commissioners for Foreign Missions, to print educational materials. However, defective lithographic printing stones hindered his progress. Keasberry then appealed to the LMS for new equipment and in 1842 the society transferred its printing press from Melaka to Singapore.[4] By the following year, Keasberry had made significant headway with the medium and was likely the printer behind the earliest known locally printed map.[5] Three years later, he was creating topographic scenes, such as the illustration which appears on his letter dated 10 December 1846.

While most European prints of this period favoured panoramic views of the town of Singapore as seen from the harbour or from elevated spots such as Government Hill (present-day Fort Canning Hill), Keasberry's sketch offers a less common perspective.[6] Similarities with a contemporaneous drawing by the Scottish artist Charles Dyce[7] suggest that Keasberry's illustration was drawn from Sandy Point (now Tanjong Rhu). The scene presents a striking contrast between the local dwellings in the foreground, and the European town and Government Hill in the background – reflecting the rapid growth of the British settlement and the displacement of local inhabitants from the Singapore River.

As far as can be ascertained, Keasberry created at least one other illustrated letter sheet. As shown on the next page, the other known example is an eight-page letter dated 5 December 1846, which contains two lithographed images:[8] The first, captioned "Singapore", offers a similar view of the Singapore waterfront and bears the initials "B.P.K." at the bottom right corner. The second, with the caption "Mission School, Singapore", is a sketch of the Mission School and Keasberry's residence with the initials "B.P.K." and the abbreviation "Lith." (which means "lithographed"). Based on the content of the letters, which were penned five days apart, one may surmise that the lithographs were meant to illustrate Keasberry's life and work in Singapore.

It is worth mentioning that while the waterfront scenes in the two letters seem similar, closer inspection reveals subtle differences between them, such as in the depiction of the sailing vessels in the harbour. It may be that Keasberry simply wanted to capture another view of the same scene, or that he was experimenting and refining his lithographic technique.

[Anti-clockwise from top right] Reverend Benjamin Keasberry (1811–75). *Courtesy of Prinsep Street Presbyterian Church (Singapore)*; A view of Singapore's waterfront captioned "Singapore" from Keasberry's earlier letter dated 5 December 1846. *Courtesy of Archives for the Council for World Mission, SOAS Library, University of London*; Close-up of Keasberry's print from his letter dated 10 December 1846.

Lithography suited Keasberry's artistic inclinations. Prior to its introduction in Singapore, the main printing methods available were letterpress and woodblock printing.[9] Although both techniques were well-suited to printing texts, the production of detailed illustrations, patterns and maps required highly skilled engravers and expensive equipment that the fledging settlement lacked. With lithography, such images could be produced with relative ease by using a wax crayon on a limestone plate.[10]

This illustrated letter amply demonstrates Keasberry's mastery of lithographic techniques. He is especially known for his skilful application of this method to the printing of Malay works in Jawi, tapping on the decorative potential of the technique to reproduce the natural flow of handwritten script. His quarterly periodical, *Cermin Mata Bagi Segala Orang Yang Menuntut Pengetahuan* (1858–59) (literally translated as "An Eye Glass for All Who Seek Knowledge"), with its intricately coloured frontispieces and chapter headings,[11] is regarded as one of the most beautiful Malay printed works of the 19th century and showcases Keasberry's achievements as a printer.

♦ **Gracie Lee**

Notes

1 Wong, H. S. (2010). *Singapore through 19th century prints & paintings* (p. 9). Singapore: National Museum of Singapore & Editions Didier Millet. (Call no.: RSING 769.499595703 WON)

2 Lithography was invented by the German dramatist Alois Senefelder in the 1790s as a cheaper way to publish his plays. The ease of use soon made lithography a more popular choice than other printing methods such as intaglio and relief printing. Lithography works on the principle that water and oil do not mix. The printer first writes or draws on a semi-porous flat surface of a printing stone (usually limestone) using a greasy substance such as a crayon. The surface is moistened and a layer of oil-based ink is then applied to the surface with a roller. The ink adheres to the greasy marks but is repelled by the water. The ink on the stone is then transferred onto a sheet of paper. See Teo, M., Chong, Y., & Oh, J. (1987). *Nineteenth century prints of Singapore* (p. 18). Singapore: National Museum. (Call no.: RSING 769.4995957 TEO)

3 Gallop, A. (1990). Early Malay printing: An introduction to the British Library Collections. *Journal of the Malaysian Branch of the Royal Asiatic Society, 63*(1), 98. (Call no.: RSING 959.5 JMBRAS); Proudfoot, I. (1998). Lithography at the crossroads of the East. *Journal of the Printing Historical Society*, 27, 122–127. Retrieved from the Malay Concordance Project website.

4 Teo, E. L. (2009). *Malay encounter during Benjamin Peach Keasberry's time in Singapore, 1835 to 1875* (pp. 193, 197, 215–216, 219). Singapore: Trinity Theological College (Call no.: RSING 266.02342095957 TEO); Su, C. (1996). *The printing presses of the London Missionary Society among the Chinese* (pp. 150, 175). [Unpublished dissertation]. Retrieved from the University College of London website.

5 Thomson, J. T. (1843). *Plan of the town of Singapore surveyed in the year 1843 by J. T. Thomson Govt. Surveyor.* Singapore: London Mission Press. Retrieved from National Archives of Singapore website; Mok, L. Y. (2015). Mapping Singapore 1819–2014. In *Visualising space: Maps of Singapore and the region: Collections from the National Library and National Archives of Singapore* (p. 93). Singapore: National Library Board. (Call no. RSING 911.5957 SIN)

6 Wong, 2010, pp. 34–42.

7 Lim, I. (2003). *Sketches in the Straits: Nineteenth-century watercolours and manuscript of Singapore, Malacca, Penang and Batavia by Charles Dyce* (p. 49). Singapore: NUS Museums, National University of Singapore. (Call no.: RSING 759.2911 LIM); Liu, G. (1999). *Singapore: A pictorial history, 1819–2000* (pp. 32–33). Singapore: Archipelago Press in association with the National Heritage Board. (Call no.: RSING 959.57 LIU)

8 The writer thanks Darryl Lim and Dr Annabel Teh Gallop for highlighting this other lithographed letter by Keasberry in the collection of the LMS archive, School of Oriental and African Studies, University of London. Council for World Mission (Great Britain). (1978). *The archives of the Council for World Mission: 1775–1940.* Zug, Switzerland: Inter Documentation Co. (Call no.: RCLOS 016.266 ARC -[LIB])

9 Su, 1996, pp. 151–175.

10 Eliot, S. & Rose, J. (2009). *A companion to the history of the book* (pp. 284–285). Oxford: Wiley-Blackwell. (Call no.: R 002.29 COM)

11 Mazelan Anuar. (2016, Jan–Mar). Through the eye glass. *BiblioAsia, 11(4).* Retrieved from *BiblioAsia* website.

Tales From the Account Books

The seven volumes of Hong San See Temple account books donated to the National Library in 2018.

Title: 新加坡南安会馆珍藏：凤山寺新建凤山寺帐簿 (Hong San See Temple account books)

Date: 1907–59

Language: Chinese

Type: Account books (7 volumes)

Call no.: RRARE 657.2095957 XJP

Accession nos.: B32426882B (1907, v.1); B32426885E (1907, v.2); B32426883C (1908, v. 3); B32426884D (1908, v. 4); B32426886F (1908, v. 5); B32426887G (1910–1911, v. 6); B32426888H (1945, v. 7)

Donated by: Singapore Lam Ann Association

For as long as Chinese settlers have been in Singapore, there have been Chinese temples. There are more than 1,000 Chinese temples in Singapore, some dating as far back as the early 19th century.[1]

Seven handwritten account books from one of the oldest temples in Singapore, Hong San See Temple (水廊头凤山寺),[2] also known as 凤山寺, shed light on the bookkeeping practices of Singapore's early Chinese communities. With entries dating from about 1907 to 1959, these account books were donated by the Singapore Lam Ann Association – which assumed management of Hong San See Temple in 1973 – to the National Library in 2018.

Established in 1836, Hong San See Temple served Hokkien immigrants from Nan'an (南安), or Lam Ann, a county in southern Fujian province.[3] In 1907, the colonial government acquired its original site at Tras Street for a road widening project.[4] Nan'an builder and architect Lim Loh (林路)[5] subsequently purchased a plot of land at Mohamed Sultan Road for the new temple.[6] Construction of the new temple took almost five years, from 1908 to 1913, at a cost of 56,000 Straits dollars.[7]

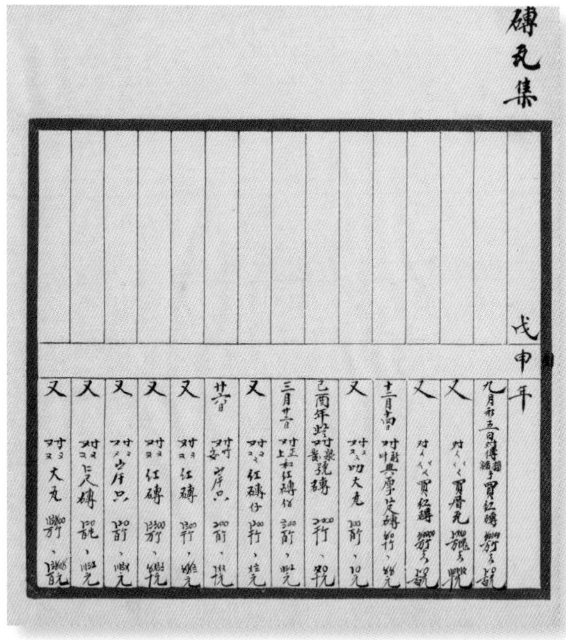

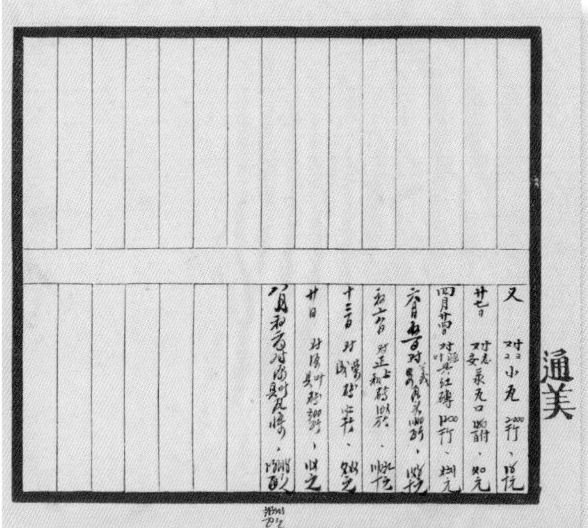

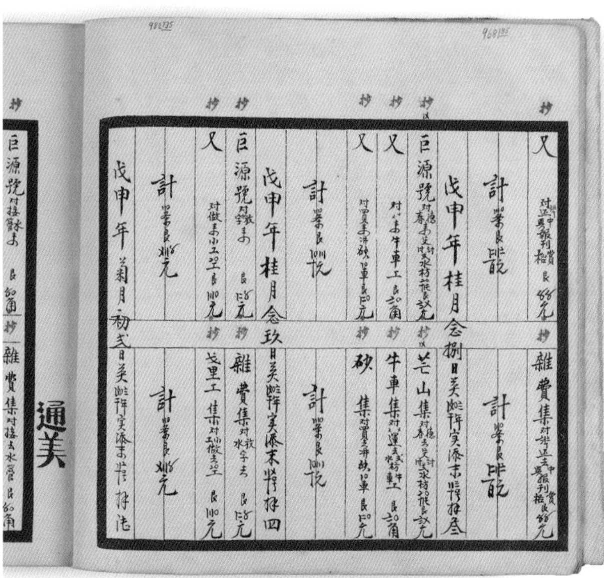

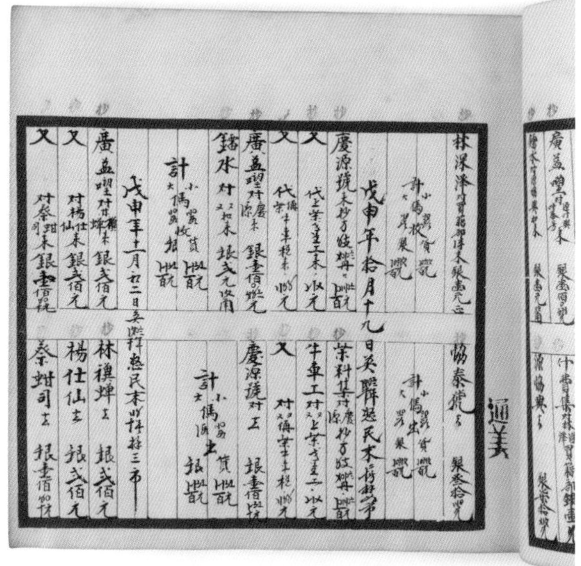

[Top] This page from one of the records indicates the amount paid for tiles and bricks. The second entry of the page (right) shows that green glazed eave tiles were bought.[8]
[Above] Shown here are two pages from different volumes. The entries from Vol. 3 on the left feature lunar months named after flowers, whereas the entries from Vol. 1 on the right present another form of writing dates. For instance, the first entry (from the right) is dated "Wu-shen (戊申) year 10th lunar month 19th day, Gregorian year 1908 November (怒民末) 12th".

Interestingly, the dates recorded in the temple's early account books reflect both Gregorian and Chinese lunar calendars as well as the Chinese era name of the reigning emperor, which can be found at the top-edge of some of the account books. For instance, there is an entry dated Wu-shen (戊申) year 11th lunar month 2nd day, for the Gregorian year 1908, November (怒民末) 25th. The same Gregorian year appears in a variant dated Wu-shen (戊申) year, month of the osmanthus (8th lunar month) and 28th day, Gregorian year 1908 September (实添末) 23rd.

Additionally, Suzhou numerals – special symbols used to represent digits for book-keeping purposes,[9] which differ from Chinese characters and Arabic numerals, are used in the account books to indicate the prices of raw materials purchased. These include sand, timber, bricks, tiles, cement and paint, and the hiring of bullock carts. Miscellaneous fees and receipts are also recorded.

During the restoration of Hong San See Temple between 2006 and 2009, these account books provided vital information that helped the Temple's Trustee's consultants and the Preservation of Monuments Board's consultants decide on the use of green glazed roof tiles.[10] This was because one of the entries in 凤山寺总簿: 大清光绪33年岁次丁未孟冬月立 (1907) reveals that green glazed eave tiles were purchased in Wu-shen (戊申) year (1908) during the construction of the temple.

The names of the craftsmen involved and costs incurred in hiring them are also captured in the books. The temple used a construction method known as rival building method (对场), whereby the building under construction is divided at the central line into two parts, either left-right two-team construction or front-back two-team construction. These two parts are completed by two teams of craftsmen working simultaneously using their own methods, techniques and designs while ensuring an integrated final form.[11] The names of the Quanzhou craftsmen[12] for instance, Wang Yaosi (汪摇司) and Yang Shixian (杨仕仙), are stated in the account books.

The temple's transactions with companies and banks, such as Kwong Yik Bank (广益银行) and a Chinese company called 瑞通號, are also documented in the account books. These provide a snapshot of the Chinese commercial firms operating in early 20th century Singapore, and offer valuable glimpses of Chinese business life during early Singapore.

Gazetted as a national monument on 10 November 1978,[13] the historic Hong San See Temple serves as an example of unique Minnan architectural heritage for the study of local Chinese architecture.

♦ **Ang Seow Leng**

[Right] This recent photo of Hong San See Temple shows it juxtaposed against modern condominiums. *Image reproduced from Dean, K., & Hue, G.T. (2017). Chinese Epigraphy in Singapore 1811—1911 (Vol. 1, p. 405). Singapore: NUS Press; Guilin City: Guangxi Normal University.*

[Bottom left] Names of craftsmen involved in the construction of the temple, such as Wang Yaosi (汪摇司) and Yang Shixian (杨仕仙), are written in the top right hand corner of this page from Vol. 5.[14]

[Bottom right] The temple's transactions with other organisations, such as Kwong Yik Bank (广益银行) and a Chinese company called 瑞通號, are recorded in the account books.[15]

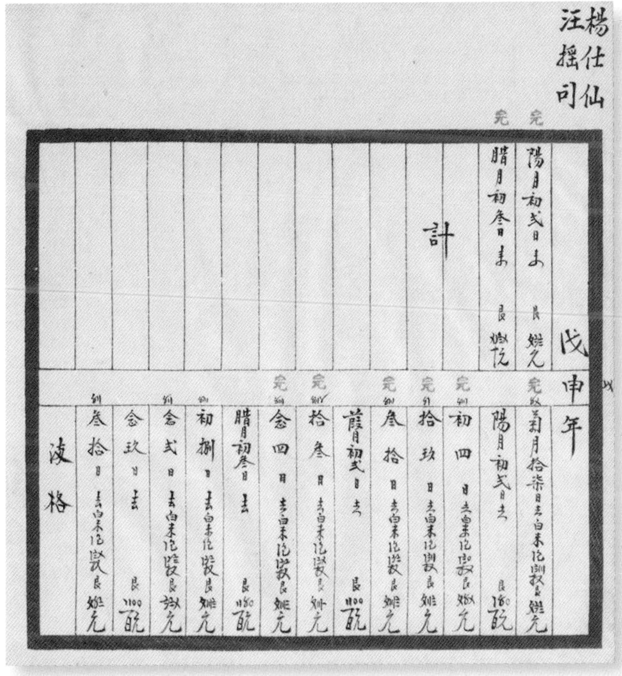

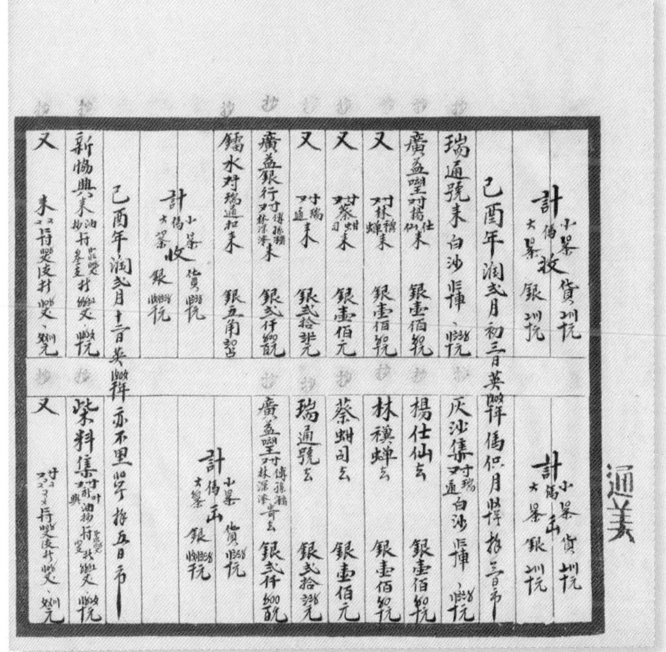

Notes

1 Zaccheus, M. (2016, November 20). Nuggets of Singapore history, from inscriptions. *The Straits Times*. Retrieved from Factiva.

2 水廊头凤山寺 (*Shui Lang Tou Feng Shan Si*) is the name given to the temple to differentiate it from other temples in Singapore that are also called Hong San See. "水廊头" refers to a well that used to exist at Mohamed Sultan Road in the early 20th century. It was the main source of water for the villagers living in the area at the time. The use of this name was believed to have started in 1905, according to an inscription found at the 水廊头大伯公庙 (*Shui Lang Tou Da Bo Gong Miao*), a Tua Pek Kong temple. See 林文川. (2003, October 5). 本地多家寺庙取名"凤山寺".《联合晚报》[*Lianhe Wanbao*], p. 6; 新加坡地名趣谈. (1991, February 10).《联合早报》[*Lianhe Zaobao*], p. 40. Retrieved from NewspaperSG.

3 Dean, K., & Hue, G. T. (2017). *Chinese epigraphy in Singapore 1819–1911* (Vol. 1, p. 434). Singapore: NUS Press; Guilin City: Guangxi Normal University. (Call no.: RSING 495.111 DEA); 陈省堂. (1893, December 16). 游凤山寺记. 星报, p. 5. Retrieved from National University of Singapore website.

4 Urban Redevelopment Authority (Singapore), 1992, vol. 1, p. 5.

5 Lim Loh, who was also known as Lim Chee Gee (林志义) and Lim Hoon Leong (林云龙), made his fortune during pre-war Singapore from rubber estates, brick and biscuit factories, and the trading and construction businesses. He was involved in the building of Goodwood Park Hotel and Victoria Memorial Hall, and also designed and built Hong San See Temple. See Tan, T. (2008, August 14). Rare gift for SAM. *The Straits Times*, p, 8. Retrieved from NewspaperSG.

6 郭志阳主编. (2006). 新加坡南安会馆80周年纪念特刊, 1926–2006 [*Singapore Lam Ann Association 80th anniversary souvenir magazine*] (p. 65). 新加坡: 新加坡南安会馆. (Call no.: RSING 369.2597 SIN); Dean & Hue, 2017, vol. 1, p. 434.

7 Dean & Hue, 2017, vol. 1, pp. 406, 434.

8 凤山寺总簿：大清光绪叁拾叁年岁次丁未孟冬月立, [Vol. 2; pp. 185-186]

9 柯木林. (2018, April 1). 南安会馆捐献凤山寺文物 老账簿会说话.《联合早报周刊》[*Lianhe Zaobao Weekly*]. Retrieved from Factiva.

10 2010 联合国亚太文化资产保存卓越奖授奖典礼特辑编委会. (2010). 新加坡凤山寺: 荣膺2010联合国亚太文化资产保存卓越奖授奖典礼 [*Singapore Hong San See Temple awarded 2010 UNESCO Asia Pacific Heritage awards for culture heritage conservation*] (p. 10). 新加坡: 新加坡南安会馆. (Call no.: Chinese RSING 203.5095957 SIN)

11 Urban Redevelopment Authority. 30 Mohamed Sultan Road: The phoenix rises again. Retrieved from Urban Redevelopment Authority website.

12 刘宏量. (2011, November 7). 从南安会馆，凤山寺开始新移民"会馆走透透". 联合早报. Retrieved from 联合早报 [*Lianhe Zaobao*] website.

13 Urban Redevelopment Authority (Singapore). (1992). *Hong San See preservation guidelines* (Vol. 1, p. 4). Singapore: Preservation of Monuments Board. (Call no.: RSING 363.69095957 HON)

14 新建凤山寺大总簿：大清光绪三十四年岁次戊申瓜月英1908年乌兀吉立[商]人工匠, [Vol. 5; p. 137]

15 凤山寺草清[簿]：大清光绪叁拾叁年岁次丁未孟冬月立, [Vol. 1; p. 34]

A Malay Translation of an Urdu Tale

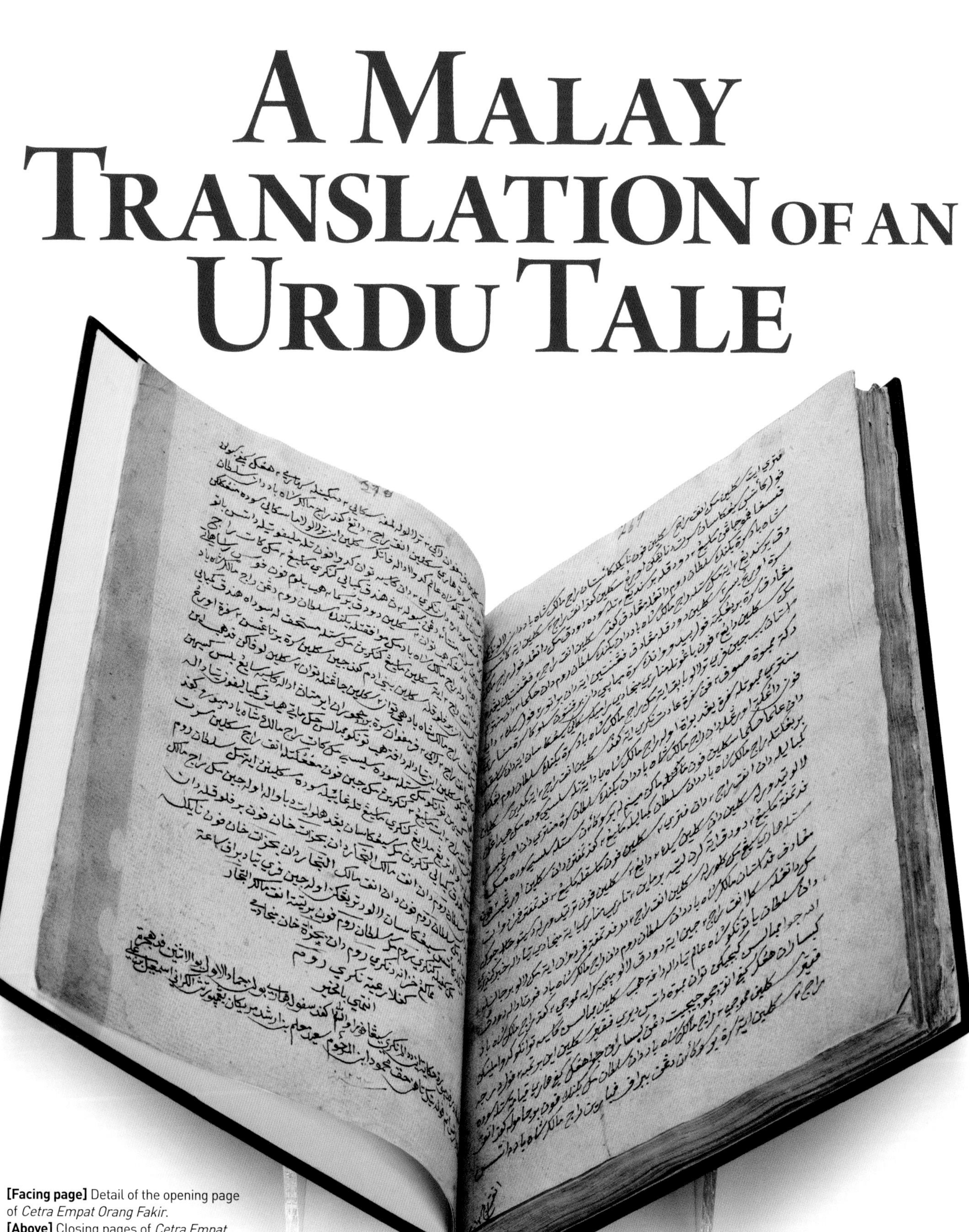

[Facing page] Detail of the opening page of *Cetra Empat Orang Fakir*.
[Above] Closing pages of *Cetra Empat Orang Fakir*.

Title: *Cetra Empat Orang Fakir* (Tale of Four Dervishes)
Copyist: Ismail b. Ali
Year created: 10 Jamadilawal 1263 AH (26 April 1847)
Language: Malay (Jawi script)
Type: Manuscript; 270 pages

1

Literary ties between Islamic India and the Malay world experienced two waves of intensive interactions in history. The first, which took place between the 14th and 17th centuries, brought literary writings in Persian from India. In the 19th century, the second wave occurred, introducing literary and theatrical works in Urdu to the Malay world. These latter works were popular in Singapore and Penang, especially among the Jawi Peranakans (local-born Muslims of mixed Indian and Malay ancestry).

Until recently, the earliest literature from the second wave were thought to date from the 1870s. However, the manuscript *Cetra Empat Orang Fakir* (Tale of Four Dervishes) held in the National Library's Rare Materials Collection, indicates that the second wave from India had, in fact, reached the Straits Settlements as early as the 1840s.

The manuscript – written in black ink, in large *naskh* script with cursive features – on good-quality, thick Italian laid paper with a ribbed surface, features the watermarks "*tre lune*" (three moon-faces) with the letters "VG" (indicating that the paper was manufactured in the early 19th century).[1] Phrases in Arabic, the words *Allah* and *Qur'an* and indicators of a new "paragraph", *sebermula* (in the beginning), *al-kisah* (the story [says]) and other such features in the manuscript are distinguished by their irregular rubrication written in red ink.

Copied by the scribe Ismail b. Ali, the manuscript is dated 10 Jamadilawal 1263 AH (26 April 1847). On the inside of the front cover is a slip of paper pasted on it and bearing the words *Bunga Anggrek di atas Pagar* (An Orchid on the Fence), possibly an alternative title of the tale. The origin and relation of this title to the manuscript, however, is puzzling, as there is no mention of orchids within the story.

The preface of the manuscript describes its translator as Mahmud b. Sayid Mu'alim b. Arsyad Marikan, a Jawi Peranakan from Melaka. Mahmud had received a copy of the Urdu version of *Cetra Empat Orang Fakir* when he visited Singapore on business. Entitled *Qissa-ye char darvesh*, this Urdu manuscript was brought to Singapore by his friend, Rahman Khan, another Jawi Peranakan, who not only provided him with the work, but also helped Mahmud, who was not proficient in written Malay, to translate it.

Mahmud either began or finished his translation on 8 Zulhijja in the year, which – extraordinarily for Malay literature – is designated by a chronogram, *bi-sargh*, meaning in Arabic "on the offshoot of the vine" and pointing to 1262 AH. The Islamic date corresponds to 27 November 1846.

According to Mahmud, he translated *Qissa-ye char darvesh* from the Persian version written by the great poet of India, Amir Khusrau Dehlavi (1253–1325). This, however, is incorrect. While the tale of four dervishes exists in both Persian and Urdu traditions, *Cetra Empat Orang Fakir* displays all of the characteristic features of the Urdu and not Persian *dastan* (or romantic tale) of the four dervishes, more precisely *Bagh-o-bahar* (Garden and Spring, 1802) by the famous Urdu writer Mir Amman.[2]

Like the Urdu and Persian versions, *Cetra Empat Orang Fakir* tells of King Azadbakht of Rum (Turkey), who overhears four dervishes recounting their stories of life and love to each other. One of them was originally the son of a rich merchant, while the other three were princes from Fars, Ajam and China respectively. Each has fallen in love with a princess and experiences various adventures in their attempts to unite with their beloved. However, the vicissitudes of fate dash their hopes and eventually bring them to the brink of suicide. At that moment, a mysterious horseman in green appears before them and sends them to King Azadbakht, who, in the end, arranges weddings for all four pairs of lovers.

Cetra Empat Orang Fakir demonstrates some curious aspects of Mahmud's translation. Narrative sections of the tale follow the Urdu original fairly closely, although rendering it sentence by sentence, rather than word by word. However, descriptive sections – such as palaces, parks, weddings and so on – have been replaced by Malay stock depictions, with only rare elements of Urdu imagery retained. ♦ **Vladimir Braginsky**

Notes

1 Iskandar, T. (1999). *Catalogue of Malay, Minangkabau, and South Sumatran manuscripts in the Netherlands* (*Vol. II*) (pp. 775–776) Leiden: Universiteit Leiden, Faculteit der Godgeleerdheid, Documentatiebureau Islam-Christendom. (Not in NLB holdings)

2 Braginsky, V. (2017). The tale of the four dervishes: the first Urdu romance translated into Malay. *Malay Literature, 30*(1), 23–60, pp. 27–34, 51–52.

An Early Architectural Perspective

Title: *The Journal of the Singapore Society of Architects*
Year published: 1923 (December)
Publisher: Singapore Society of Architects
Language: English
Type: Periodical; 45 pages
Call no.: RRARE 720.95957 JSSA
Accession no.: B02908478E

"It is a bold venture, but we wish it all success, for there is room enough in Singapore to improve public taste in building design."[1] This was a comment by *The Straits Times* in January 1924 in its review of the inaugural issue of *The Journal of the Singapore Society of Architects*.

Published by the Singapore Society of Architects, the precursor of the Singapore Institute of Architects, the monthly publication was aimed at fostering public interest in the architectural profession in Singapore. It was launched in December 1923, nine months after the society was established.[2]

The essays published in the journal over the course of its history covered many topics related to architecture and the archi-

Cover of the first issue of *The Journal of the Singapore Society of Architects*, December 1923.

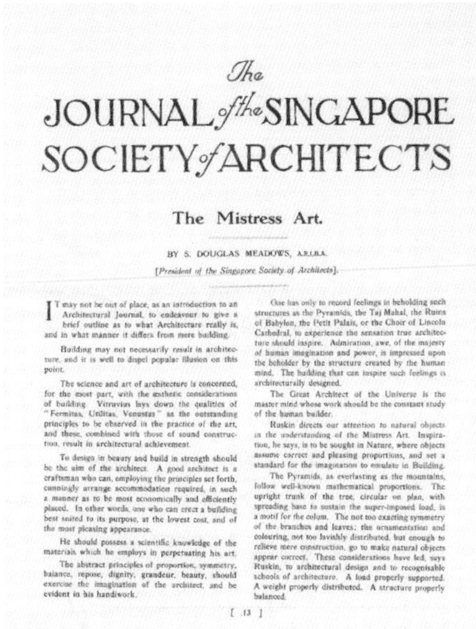

The
JOURNAL *of the* SINGAPORE SOCIETY *of* ARCHITECTS

The Mistress Art.

BY S. DOUGLAS MEADOWS, A.R.I.B.A.
[President of the Singapore Society of Architects].

IT may not be out of place, as an introduction to an Architectural Journal, to endeavour to give a brief outline as to what Architecture really is, and in what manner it differs from mere building.

Building may not necessarily result in architecture, and it is well to dispel popular illusion on this point.

The science and art of architecture is concerned, for the most part, with the esthetic considerations of building. Vitruvius lays down the qualities of "Fermitas, Utilitas, Venustas" as the outstanding principles to be observed in the practice of the art, and these, combined with those of sound construction, result in architectural achievement.

To design in beauty and build in strength should be the aim of the architect. A good architect is a craftsman who can, employing the principles set forth, cunningly arrange accommodation required, in such a manner as to be most economically and efficiently placed. In other words, one who can erect a building best suited to its purpose, at the lowest cost, and of the most pleasing appearance.

He should possess a scientific knowledge of the materials which he employs in perpetuating his art.

The abstract principles of proportion, symmetry, balance, repose, dignity, grandeur, beauty, should exercise the imagination of the architect, and be evident in his handiwork.

One has only to record feelings in beholding such structures as the Pyramids, the Taj Mahal, the Ruins of Babylon, the Petit Palais, or the Choir of Lincoln Cathedral, to experience the sensation true architecture should inspire. Admiration, awe, of the majesty of human imagination and power, is impressed upon the beholder by the structure created by the human mind. The building that can inspire such feelings is architecturally designed.

The Great Architect of the Universe is the master mind whose work should be the constant study of the human builder.

Ruskin directs our attention to natural objects in the understanding of the Mistress Art. Inspiration, he says, is to be sought in Nature, where objects assume correct and pleasing proportions, and set a standard for the imagination to emulate in Building.

The Pyramids, as everlasting as the mountains, follow well-known mathematical proportions. The upright trunk of the tree, circular on plan, with spreading base to sustain the super-imposed load, is a motif for the colum. The not too exacting symmetry of the branches and leaves; the ornamentation and colouring, not too lavishly distributed, but enough to relieve mere construction, go to make natural objects appear correct. These considerations have led, says Ruskin, to architectural design and to recognisable schools of architecture. A load properly supported. A weight properly distributed. A structure properly balanced.

[13]

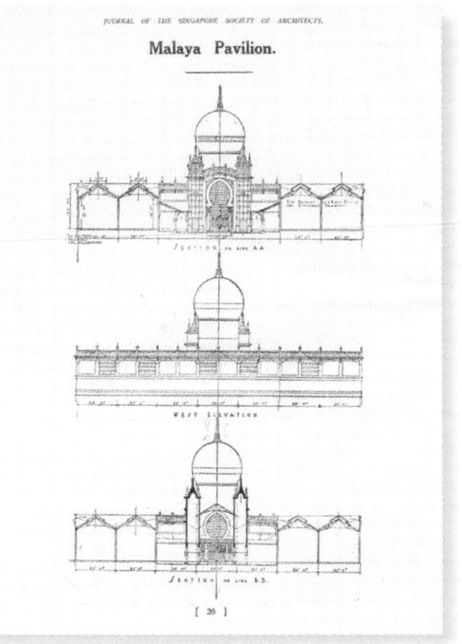

tectural profession. The first issue opened with an introductory piece by S. Douglas Meadows, then President of the society, who was also the Municipal Architect. In his essay, Meadows defined architecture as both an academic discipline and a profession. He asserted that architecture was a "cosmopolitan art" that was "linked up inseparably with the science of Engineering, Town Planning, Public Health, and a hundred [other] considerations". Not only must architects be well versed in the art and technique of designing and building, they also had to be "graduate[s] of the World's University of Experience".[3] In recognition of this all-encompassing nature of architecture, Meadows called it "The Mistress Art", which is also the title of his essay.[4]

[Top] The unique architectural features of the newly constructed Hong Kong and Shanghai Bank building **(left)**, as well as the 39,000-square-foot Malaya Pavilion with a central topping dome and two towering minarets **(right)**, are some of the highlights written about in the inaugural issue of the journal. The pavilion was an exhibition gallery that showcased the products and achievements of Singapore and the Federated Malay States in the British Empire Exhibition held in London from April 1924 to October 1925. *Courtesy of National Archives of Singapore.*

[Above] The first issue included an opening essay by S. Douglas Meadows titled "The Mistress Art" **(left)**, as well as elevation drawings of the Malaya Pavilion **(centre and right)**, which offer a flat representation of specific sides of the structure with vertical height dimensions provided.

Another interesting essay is by British architect Delissa Joseph, who criticised the height restriction laws imposed on buildings in London. He argued that the restrictions, which were put in place by archaic English law, impeded the urban and economic growth of London. Under the legislation, the construction of taller buildings that blocked natural light from streaming in through the windows was prohibited.[5] Joseph's essay was timely as there was an existing municipal by-law in Singapore that restricted the height of non-residential buildings in the business district to no more than one-and-a-half times the width of the street. Although exceptions were allowed, the by-law had prevented some new buildings at the time from reaching their intended height.[6]

Other essays in the journal showcase the unique architectural elements of buildings in Singapore. For example, the inaugural issue featured the "outstanding" stained glass window artwork of the soon to be completed Hong Kong and Shanghai Bank building at Collyer Quay. Designed by the famed British stained glass artist Leonard Walker, the windows depict allegorical figures of people from countries that the bank had worked with. The artwork was described as a masterpiece that "reflect[ed] the spirit of mediaeval craftsmanship", and "never wear[ied] the eye by monotonous repetition". It was deemed to be the "product of an inventive mind".[7]

Another structure featured in the same issue of the journal is the Malaya Pavilion, an exhibition gallery that showcased the products and achievements of Singapore and the Federated Malay States in the British Empire Exhibition held in London from April 1924 to October 1925. Through elevation drawings, the essay highlighted the grandiosity of the 39,000-square-foot (3,623 sq m) edifice, which was designed in the Indo-Saracenic[8] architectural style featuring a topping central dome flanked by two small corner minarets on either side. Another two imposing 75-ft (23-m) tall minarets marked the entrance to its courtyard.[9]

In subsequent issues of the journal, landmarks such as the second Ocean Building, the General Post Office building (The Fullerton Hotel Singapore since 2001) and the Eastern Extension Telegraph Company building (the Sofitel So Singapore hotel since 2013) were featured with in-depth discussions about their immersive architectural forms.[10] Large-scale infrastructure projects, such as the water supply development works in Seletar and the Singapore-Johor Causeway, were also highlighted to introduce the innovative construction methods used at the time.[11]

Other types of content that regularly found their way into the journal included essays relating to construction materials, and information about local architectural firms and projects approved by the municipality. Readers who wanted to trace the history of the society could peruse the organisational structure, membership rolls and minutes of meetings published in the journal. In addition, there were advertisements put out by construction companies, or those selling construction materials, building products and furniture. Some of the companies that had advertised prominently in the journal include John Little, Titan Cement, and Fraser and Chalmers Engineering Works.

The journal would continue its publication until 1931 when it was renamed *The Malayan Architect* following the reconstitution of the Singapore Society of Architects as the Institute of Architects Malaya in that year. *The Malayan Architect* was published until the outbreak of the war with Japan in 1941. Today, the official periodical of the Singapore Institute of Architects is *The Singapore Architect*, a quarterly publication. Previously, this periodical was known as *Rumah: Journal of the Singapore Institute of Architects* from 1958 to 1966, and *SIAJ: The Singapore Institute of Architects Journal* from 1966 to 1994. ♦ **Lim Tin Seng**

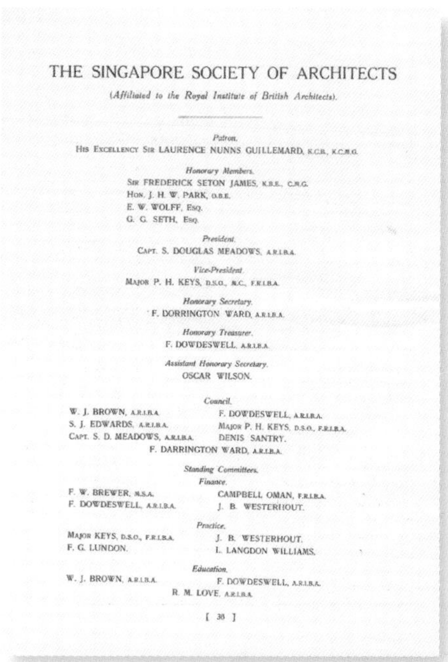

THE SINGAPORE SOCIETY OF ARCHITECTS

(Affiliated to the Royal Institute of British Architects).

Patron.
HIS EXCELLENCY SIR LAURENCE NUNNS GUILLEMARD, K.C.B., K.C.M.G.

Honorary Members.
SIR FREDERICK SETON JAMES, K.B.E., C.M.G.
HON. J. H. W. PARK, O.B.E.
E. W. WOLFF, ESQ.
G. G. SETH, ESQ.

President.
CAPT. S. DOUGLAS MEADOWS, A.R.I.B.A.

Vice-President.
MAJOR P. H. KEYS, D.S.O., M.C., F.R.I.B.A.

Honorary Secretary.
F. DORRINGTON WARD, A.R.I.B.A.

Honorary Treasurer.
F. DOWDESWELL, A.R.I.B.A.

Assistant Honorary Secretary.
OSCAR WILSON.

Council.
W. J. BROWN, A.R.I.B.A. — F. DOWDESWELL, A.R.I.B.A.
S. J. EDWARDS, A.R.I.B.A. — MAJOR P. H. KEYS, D.S.O., F.R.I.B.A.
CAPT. S. D. MEADOWS, A.R.I.B.A. — DENIS SANTRY.
F. DARRINGTON WARD, A.R.I.B.A.

Standing Committees.

Finance.
F. W. BREWER, M.S.A. — CAMPBELL OMAN, F.R.I.B.A.
F. DOWDESWELL, A.R.I.B.A. — J. B. WESTERHOUT.

Practice.
MAJOR KEYS, D.S.O., F.R.I.B.A. — J. B. WESTERHOUT.
F. G. LUNDON. — L. LANGDON WILLIAMS.

Education.
W. J. BROWN, A.R.I.B.A. — F. DOWDESWELL, A.R.I.B.A.
R. M. LOVE, A.R.I.B.A.

[38]

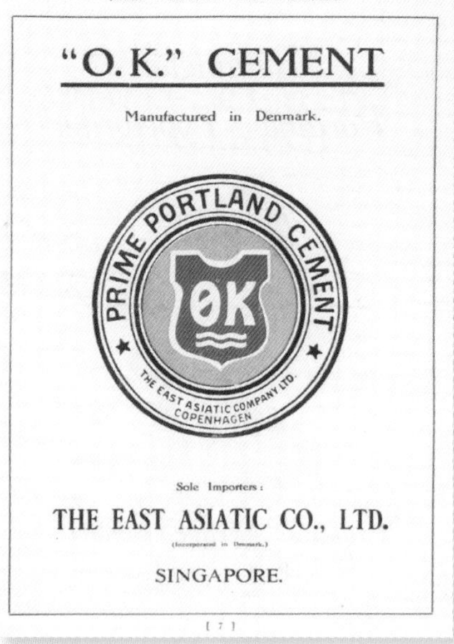

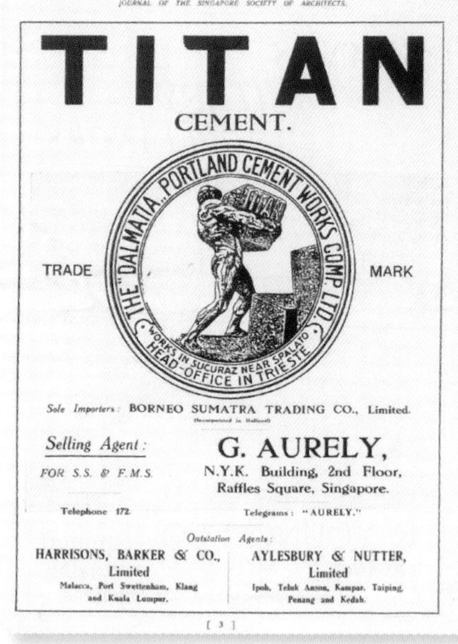

[Clockwise from top] The organisational structure of the Singapore Society of Architects, as well as advertisements, were published in the inaugural issue of the journal.

Notes

1 Society of Architects. (1924, January 3). *The Straits Times*, p. 8. Retrieved from NewspaperSG.

2 Singapore architects: Inaugural meeting at Raffles Museum. (1923, March 21). *The Straits Times*, p. 9. Retrieved from NewspaperSG.

3 Meadows, S. D. (1923, December). The Mistress Art. *The Journal of the Singapore Society of Architects* (p. 13). (Call no.: RRARE 720.95957 JSSA) (Microfilm no.: NL16646).

4 From the Renaissance (1300–1600) to the late 1930s, architecture was also referred to as the "Mistress Art". It describes the practice as a discipline that encompasses all forms of art and expression. See Farmer, B. et. al. (1993). *Companion to contemporary architectural thought.* (pp. 3, 21, 28, 36). London: Routledge. (Call no.: RART q720.1 COM)

5 Joseph, D. (1923, December). Building heights and ancient lights. *The Journal of the Singapore Society of Architects* (pp. 15–24). (Call no.: RRARE 720.95957 JSSA) (Microfilm no.: NL16646).

6 Hotel building. (1929, October 11). *The Malaya Tribune*, p. 2. Retrieved from NewspaperSG.

7 New Hongkong and Shanghai Bank Building, Singapore (December 1923). *The Journal of the Singapore Society of Architects* (p. 30). (Call no.: RRARE 720.95957 JSSA) (Microfilm no.: NL16646).

8 The Indo-Saracenic style originated in British India and combines aspects of Hindu and Islamic architecture with Western architectural elements. Buildings constructed in this style employed modern European structural engineering standards.

9 Malaya Pavilion (1923, December). *The Journal of the Singapore Society of Architects* (p. 30). (Call no.: RRARE 720.95957 JSSA) (Microfilm no.: NL16646).

10 Ocean Building. (1924, January). *The Journal of the Singapore Society of Architects* (pp. 22–25). (Microfilm no.: NL10188); New Post Office. (1924, April). *The Journal of the Singapore Society of Architects* (p. 23). (Microfilm no.: NL10188); New Telegraph Office. (1924, September). *The Journal of the Singapore Society of Architects* (pp. 34–35). (Microfilm no.: NL10188)

11 The Singapore water supply project. (1925, March). *The Journal of the Singapore Society of Architects* (pp. 15–18). (Microfilm no.: NL10188); Johore Causeway. (1924, April). *The Journal of the Singapore Society of Architects* (pp. 13–19). (Microfilm no.: NL10188)

A Colonial Gentleman's Collections

Title: Edwin A. Brown Collection photographs, circa 1900-1950
Compiler: Edwin Arthur Brown
Date: 1900s–1950s
Type: Photograph
Call no.: RRARE 959.5703 EDW
Accession no.: B20123853B
Donated by: Family of the late E.A. Brown

On 21 September 1955, an obituary on the front page of *The Straits Times* announced the death of Edwin A. Brown, aged 77, in Gloucester, England.[1] Barely 20 words in length, the inconspicuous notice belied the fascinating life of a man who was a prominent figure in colonial Singapore, and a pillar of its musical and theatrical scene.

Brown left a collection of about 170 photographs, which his family donated to the National Library in 2008. The images offer an insight into Brown's interests and social milieu as well as a glimpse of life in early 20th-century Singapore.

Sir Shenton Thomas (in dark uniform; standing on the podium) officiating the opening ceremony of King George VI Graving Dock.

Important events and celebrations feature prominently in Brown's collection. Take for instance a set of 18 photographs documenting the opening of the King George VI Graving Dock (KG6) at the Singapore Naval Base in Sembawang on 14 February 1938.

KG6 was the world's largest naval dock at the time of its unveiling, which also marked the official opening of the na-

Guests at the opening ceremony of King George VI Graving Dock (KG6), Singapore Naval Base, Sembawang. The two destroyers moored alongside where the guests were seated are H.M.S. *Duncan*, and on her right, H.M.S. *Diamond*. This print bears the stamp "R.A.F. Station. Seletar. Singapore, S.S. Photographic Section" on its back.

val base.[2] The base was the cornerstone of British strategic defences in the Far East. The ceremony was officiated by then Governor of the Straits Settlements, Sir Shenton Thomas, with over 11,000 guests witnessing the occasion. Brown was probably among them. The backs of these photographs bear the stamp of the Photographic Section of the Royal Air Force (RAF) station in Seletar.

What might appear at first glance to be a hodgepodge of old photographs becomes more meaningful when seen against the context of Brown's life. "I arrived in Singapore on Friday, January 4th, 1901 [...] I can remember to this day the lovely effect of the full moon on the entrance to the harbour, and on the Pasir Panjang coast-line," reminisced Brown in the opening pages of *Indiscreet Memories* (1935), a memoir of his first years here.

Brown was in his early 20s when he arrived here to join Brinkmann & Company, the Singapore branch of a Manchester shipping company where he had worked for five years.[3] Brown would go on to spend the better part of his life in Singapore, acquiring partnership in a brokerage and eventually establishing his own firm, E. A. Brown & Co in 1926.[4]

While the collection does not reveal much about Brown's private life or business, it does shed light on his work in the local musical and theatrical scene. Soon after his arrival here, Brown, who had acted semi-professionally in his native Manchester, was invited to join the cast of a musical.[5] He made his debut in the double bill, *Grass Widow* and *Charley's Aunt*, at the Town Hall in November 1901.[6] In 1906, Brown and six others formed the Singapore Amateur Dramatic Committee, which performed mainly Gilbert and Sullivan operas.[7] Brown lent his talents to numerous productions as actor, singer, stage-manager and voice-trainer – to the extent that he was said to have "put the Sing in Singapore".[8]

A highlight of the collection is a series of nine photographs depicting scenes from *The Pirates of Penzance*, a comic opera staged in 1937. These images are significant visual records of theatre performances in early Singapore, and also point to the cultural and recreational life of the European community here. Brown not only produced the 1937 show but also acted as the Pirate King, which he performed "with true piratical abandon and nautical swagger".[9] Coincidentally, the Pirate King was a part Brown had first played nearly 30 years earlier when *The Pirates of Penzance* was staged at the inauguration of Victoria Theatre in February 1909.[10]

Another notable set of photographs in the collection documents the royal visit by then Prince of Wales (later King Edward VIII, Duke of Windsor) in 1922. The two-day visit to Singapore at the end of March was part of the prince's eight-month tour of British colonies in the Far East.

Brown organised the "Children's Corner" programme for the prince's visit. There are 12 photographs, probably taken by Brown himself, of this event on 31 March 1922, which saw over 10,000 children assembled on the field in front of St Joseph's Institution, waving flags and handkerchiefs, to cheer and welcome the royal visitor.[11]

But that was not all. Brown served as a municipal commissioner from 1924–40, chairing the Parks and Open Spaces Committee and driving the development of

[Top] At the centre of this photo stands Brown, wielding a sword in his role as the Pirate King in *The Pirates of Penzance*.
[Above] The Prince of Wales (dressed in a white uniform with a sash) leads the party inspecting the guard of honour formed by the Girl Guides and Boy Scouts at the "Children's Corner" segment of his visit in 1922.

amenities like Katong Park, Jalan Besar Stadium, and Singapore's first public pool at Mount Emily.[12]

Brown also distinguished himself in the military service. He joined the Singapore Volunteer Corps (Rifles) in 1901, and in 1913, was given command of the Chinese Company. Two years later, he was commended for leading the armed civilian force that broke the siege of Alexandra Barracks during the mutiny of the 5th Light Infantry (known as the Singapore Mutiny).[13] Brown retired with the rank of Major in 1923.[14]

In recognition of his contributions, Brown was awarded the Order of the British Empire (OBE) by King George V in 1933.[15] Brown was later interned at Changi during the Japanese Occupation. After the war, he returned to England, where he spent his remaining years.

In writing his memoir, *Indiscreet Memories*, Brown had intended to give "a picture of the everyday life of an ordinary, unconsidered member of the resident public, a picture that may be taken as an epitome of the average life of most of the people out here".[16] As vignettes of European colonial life in Singapore, the photographs in Brown's collection may be read in the same light. ♦ **Janice Loo**

Notes

1 Broker dies. (1955, 21 September). *The Straits Times*, p. 1. Retrieved from NewspaperSG.
2 The biggest naval dock in the world. (1938, February 14). *The Singapore Free Press and Mercantile Advertiser*, p. 1; Features of Singapore base. (1940, December 4). *The Straits Times*, p. 12. Retrieved from NewspaperSG.
3 *Who's who in Malaya 1939* (p. 38). Singapore: Fishers Ltd. (Call no.: RCLOS 920.9595 WHO-[RFL]; Brown, E. A. (1935). *Indiscreet memories* (p. 6). London: Kelly & Walsh. (Call no.: RCLOS 959.51 BRO-[RFL])
4 *Who's who in Malaya 1939*, p. 38; Untitled. (1926, November 5). *The Straits Times*, p. 8. Retrieved from NewspaperSG.
5 Brown, 1935, pp. 25–26.
6 Makepeace, W., Brooke, G. E., & Braddell, R. St. J. (Eds.). (1991). *One hundred years of Singapore* (Vol. 2) (p. 396). Singapore: Oxford University Press (Call no. RSING 959.57 ONE)
7 Makepeace, Brooke, & Braddell, 1991, pp. 398–399; Old (77) Malayan dies in London. (1955, September 22). *Singapore Standard*, p. 8. Retrieved from NewspaperSG.
8 Makepeace, Brooke, & Braddell, 1991, p. 396; Brown, E. A. & Brown, M. (2015) *Singapore Mutiny: A colonial couple's stirring account of combat and survival in the 1915 Singapore Mutiny* (p. xxx). Singapore: Monsoon Books. (Call no.: RSING 959.5703 BRO)
9 Amateurs do well in "The Pirates of Penzance". (1937, December 3). *The Straits Times*, p. 14; Singapore amateurs revive Pirates of Penzance. (1937, December 3). *The Singapore Free Press and Mercantile Advertiser*, p. 7. Retrieved from NewspaperSG.
10 The Pirates of Penzance. (1909, February 9). *The Singapore Free Press and Mercantile Advertiser*, p. 5. Retrieved from NewspaperSG; Makepeace, Brooke, & Braddell, 1991, p. 396.
11 The Prince's visit. (1922, February 23). *The Singapore Free Press and Mercantile Advertiser*, p. 125; The royal visit. (1922, March 16). *The Singapore Free Press and Mercantile Advertiser*, p. 6; The children's cheers. (1922, April 1). *The Singapore Free Press and Mercantile Advertiser*, p. 7. Retrieved from NewspaperSG.
12 *Who's who in Malaya 1925* (p. 44). Singapore: J.S. Fisher. (Microfilm no.: NL 6705); Government house investiture. (1933, September 25). *The Straits Times*, p. 6; Municipal "old boys" who have retired. (1940, January 27). *The Straits Times*, p. 11. Retrieved from NewspaperSG.
13 Winsley, T. M. (1938). *A history of the Singapore volunteer corps*, 1854–1937 (p. 65). Singapore: G.P.O. (Call no.: RCLOS 355.23 WIN); Harper, R. W. E. & Miller, H. (1984) *Singapore mutiny* (pp. 156–157). Singapore: Oxford University Press. (Call. no.: RSING 355.1334095957 HAR); The Singapore Mutiny. (1915, April 21). *Manchester Guardian*. Reproduced in Brown, E. A. & Brown, M. (2015) *Singapore Mutiny: A colonial couple's stirring account of combat and survival in the 1915 Singapore Mutiny* (p. 81). Singapore: Monsoon Books. (Call no.: RSING 959.5703 BRO); Song, O.S. (1984). *One hundred years' history of the Chinese in Singapore* (p. 514). Singapore: Oxford University Press. (Call no.: RSING 959.57 SON-[HIS])
14 *Who's who in Malaya 1939*, p. 38.
15 Government house investiture. (1933, September 25). *The Straits Times*, p. 6; King's birthday honours. (1933, June 3). *The Straits Times*, p. 11. Retrieved from NewspaperSG
16 Brown, 1935, pp. xi–xii.

A Poetic Lament Translated

Title: *The Li Sao: An Elegy on Encountering Sorrows*
Translated by: Lim Boon Keng
Year published: 1929
Publisher: Commercial Press (Shanghai)
Language: English and Chinese
Type: Book; 238 pages
Call no.: RDTYS 895.11 CHU
Accession no.: B02862961A
Donated by: Tan Yeok Seong

Woodcut print of Qu Yuan and the title page of Lim Boon Keng's translation of Qu's poem.

Written more than 2,000 years ago, "Li Sao" ("离骚") is a major work in classical Chinese poetry. The 93-stanza poem[1] is attributed to Qu Yuan (屈原) (c. 340 BCE–278 BCE),[2] a poet and an official from the kingdom of Chu (楚国) who lived during the Warring States period (475–221 BCE).

The Li Sao: An Elegy on Encountering Sorrows is a translation by Dr Lim Boon Keng (1869–1957). An eminent figure in the Straits Chinese community in the first half of the 20th century, Dr Lim studied medicine at Edinburgh University on a Queen's Scholarship, then returned to Singapore to practice in 1893. He joined the Straits Settlements Legislative Council two years later, at the age of 26, and served a total of 14 years. A social reformer, he supported the education of women, helped set up the Singapore Chinese Girls' School in 1899, and campaigned against opium smoking.

During his busy career, Lim wrote numerous works. It was during his time as the president of Amoy University (now known as Xiamen University)[3] that his English translation of Qu Yuan's poem, together with accompanying essays written by him and prefaces from other prominent figures, was published in a 238-page hardcover book in 1929 by the Commercial Press in Shanghai. At the time, Lim was 60 years old.

The National Library's copy of the book was donated by Tan Yeok Seong and the book bears the rubber stamp of The China Society. Lim's translation is on the left-hand page, while corresponding Chinese text from Qu's poem is printed on the right-hand page. Together, they run to 38 pages.

The introduction was written by Sir Hugh Clifford, the Governor of the Straits Settlements between 1927 and 1929.[4] Professor Herbert A. Giles, the sinologist[5] from Cambridge who helped to develop the Wade-Giles romanisation system, wrote

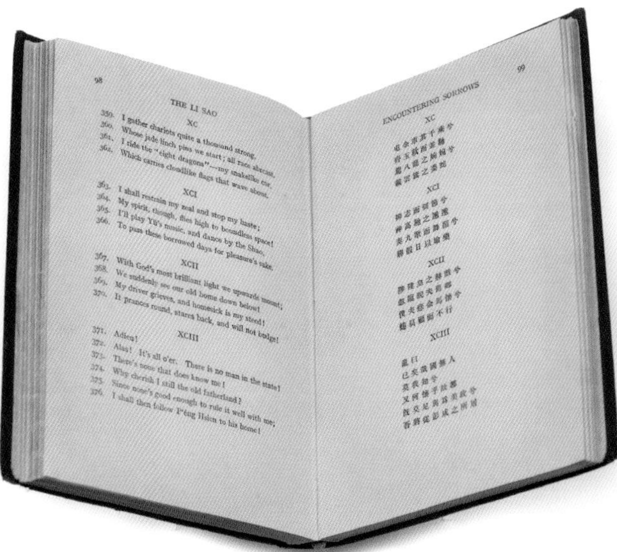

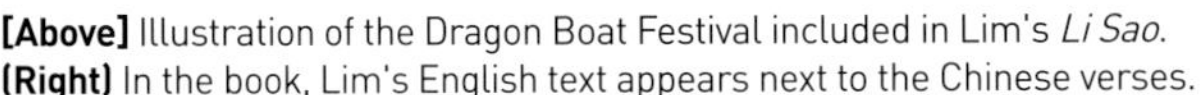

[Above] Illustration of the Dragon Boat Festival included in Lim's *Li Sao*.
(Right) In the book, Lim's English text appears next to the Chinese verses.

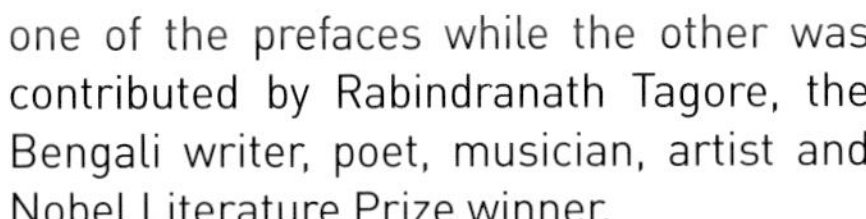

one of the prefaces while the other was contributed by Rabindranath Tagore, the Bengali writer, poet, musician, artist and Nobel Literature Prize winner.

The book also has Lim's 10-stanza ode to Qu Yuan, a synopsis of the poem, critiques – including the translation of an essay from the 6th century, the historical background, a biography of Qu Yuan, and an analysis of the significance of the poem and its style.

It ends with glossaries of words from the poem, these being "Special notes on plants and flowers", "Special vocabulary of names of persons, places, etc.", and a vocabulary list compiled by Lim's second wife, Grace Yin Pek Ha. Notes and commentaries analysing the poem, as well as a bibliography are included.[6]

A woodcut print of Qu Yuan, an illustration of the Dragon Boat Festival and a map of the Warring States of China further enrich the text. In the preface Lim wrote, he thanked numerous people, including his colleagues from Amoy University.[7]

Lim's motivations for producing the book can perhaps be gleaned from the same preface where he expressed the high esteem he held for Qu Yuan, whom he considered a "patriot":

> To-day, when the whole world is in chaos, and when men and women are on the verge of despair in search of the way to political salvation, this humble introduction to the feelings and aspirations of a great patriot whose ambition is "always to be pure and good," may help even the most timid to gain some self-confidence in fearlessly working for the welfare of society without the least desire for reward or recognition, in spite of popular misunderstanding, criticism, or attack.[8]

Lim also describes the poet as a "born leader, the aristocrat, who takes a share in establishing peace and order in the Empire. He is the prototype of the Nietzchean superman... The world to-day has need of a man like him to teach the rabble that human civilization has never benefitted from "the mob struggles for place and power"."[9]

Researchers have praised Lim's translation because he had the "proper representation of [background information about] the source text and extensive use of notes on difficult words and sentences with a strong Chinese cultural colour", which greatly enabled readers to appreciate the poem better.[10]

Qu Yuan had written "Li Sao" to protest against the injustice of his dismissal. He laments the King's folly, the corruption of the court, and despairs because of his estrangement from King Huai (楚怀王). Qu concludes the poem saying he would emulate Peng Xian (彭咸), a shaman from the Shang dynasty who drowned himself for his country.[11]

The poem foreshadows the death of the poet himself. In 278 BCE, Qu Yuan drowned himself in the Miluo River, in today's Hunan province. David Hawkes, a British sinologist and translator, explained that Qu Yuan thus came to be associated with the Dragon Boat Festival, which is celebrated in South China on the fifth day of the fifth month of the lunar calendar. It is a day on which rice dumplings are eaten and boat races are held.[12] Many believe that the dragon boat race originated from the act of villagers racing to save Qu Yuan while the rice dumplings were supposedly thrown into the water as food for fish so that the poet's body would be untouched.

♦ **Ang Seow Leng**

Notes

1 Chang, K.M. (1980, August 31). Voice of a master. *New Nation*, p. 9. Retrieved from NewspaperSG.
2 Singapore Federation of Chinese Clan Associations. (1989). *Chinese customs and festivals in Singapore* 《华人礼俗节日手册》 (p. 51). Singapore: Singapore Federation of Chinese Clan Associations. (Call no.: RSING 390.08995105957 CHI)
3 Lim was the president of Amoy University (now known as Xiamen University) for 16 years from 1921 till 1937. National Library Board. (2015, December 31). *Lim Boon Keng* written by Ang, Seow Leng and Lim, Fiona. Retrieved from *Singapore Infopedia*.
4 Encyclopaedia Britannica. (2019). *Sir Hugh Charles Clifford*. Retrieved from *Encyclopaedia Britannica* website.
5 Aylmer, C. (1997). Herbert Allen Giles (1845–1935). Abridged from East Asian History 13–14 (1997), pp. 1–7. Retrieved from the Cambridge University Library website.
6 Lim, 1929, pp. 100–200.
7 Lim, 1929, pp. xxx–xxxii.
8 Lim, 1929, pp. xxviii, xxix.
9 Lim, 1929, pp. xxvii–xxviii.
10 Hu, J. & Tian, C. (2017). Translation and dissemination of Chu Ci in the West. *IRA International Journal of Education and Multidisciplinary Studies, 8*(1), pp. 12–13. Retrieved from the Institute of Research Advances website.
11 Chang, K.M. (1980, August 31). Voice of a master. *New Nation*, p. 9. Retrieved from NewspaperSG; Ho, S.B. (1994, June 13); Watson, B. (Trans. & Ed.). (1984). *The Columbia book of Chinese poetry: from early times to the thirteenth century* (p. 56). New York: Columbia University Press. (Call no.: R 895.11008 COL)
12 Hawkes, D. (2011). *The songs of the south: an ancient Chinese anthology of poems by Qu Yuan and other poets* (p. 64). London; New York, N.Y.: Penguin Books. (Call no.: R 895.111 CHU)

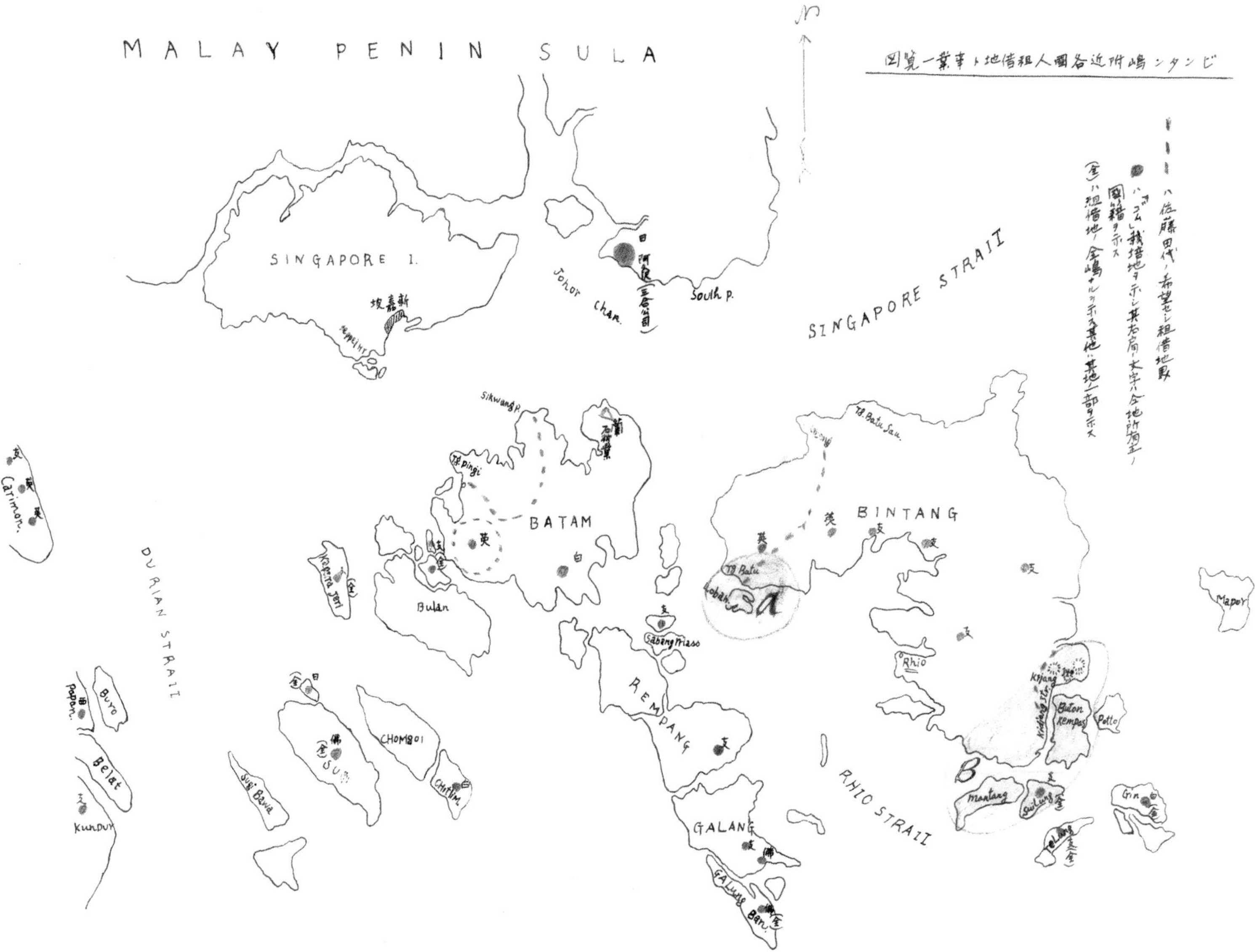

A 1910 Plan to Colonise Southeast Asia

Title: 南方経略ノ準備作業ニ就キ [On the Preparation for the Nanpō Operation]
Author: 宇都宮太郎 [Utsunomiya Tarō]
Year created: 1910
Language: Japanese
Type: Letter (3 pages); 1 map; Contract
Call no.: RRARE 952.03 LIM-[LSB]
Accession no.: B32428444I (Letter; map); B32428445J (Contracts)
Donated by: Lim Shao Bin

A hand-drawn map of the Riau Islands accompanying the letter dated 1 August 1910 that Utsunomiya Tarō sent to Army Reserve Colonel Koyama Shūsaku (小山秋作), with instructions on how to carry out the Nanpō Operation. These resulted in the signing of two land lease contracts in November 1910.

Details of covert land-leasing activities carried out by a few individuals within the Imperial Japanese Army suggest that there were plans to expand into Southeast Asia from as early as the 1910s, 30 years before the onset of the Japanese Occupation in the region. Primary sources attesting to this intent include a three-page letter dated 1 August 1910, a hand-drawn map of the Riau Islands with markings indicating where strategic locations are and copies of contracts. Termed Nanpō Operation by its mastermind, Major-General Utsunomiya Tarō (宇都宮太郎) (1861–1922), the land lease operation was, in fact, not sanctioned by the Japanese government.

The letter, titled 南方経略ノ準備作業ニ就キ (On the Preparation for the Nanpō Operation), was written by Utsunomiya, who was then Chief of the Second Division, Department of the Japanese Army General Staff. It outlines his plan to colonise Southeast Asia by leasing land in the Riau Islands to build military outposts. The letter was addressed to Koyama Shūsaku (小山秋作), a retired colonel who was a former colleague of Utsunomiya's and whom Utsunomiya had earlier persuaded to assist in the Nanpō Operation. The letter includes his instructions to Koyama, along with a map of the Riau Islands showing desirable locations for the military outposts.

In his letter, Utsunomiya identified the Dutch East Indies (present-day Indonesia) as the main target where future Japanese territories could be established. He believed that the Kapuas and Sambas river valleys in West Kalimantan were ideal due to their strategic location. First, both valleys were geographically close to the Crown Colony of North Borneo (present-day Sabah, Sarawak and Brunei), and he expected that the British would help Japan expand into West Kalimantan as the Anglo-Japanese Alliance (1902–23) bound Britain and Japan to protecting each other's interests then. Second, both valleys were located along the sea route between Japan and Europe.

To acquire these territories, Utsunomiya stressed that it was crucial for the Japanese army to establish military outposts near Singapore. As a first step, Utsunomiya suggested leasing land on the islands of Ayer Raja,[1] Kila, Momoi and Awi – all four are located near Pulau Batam and form part of the Riau Islands.[2] Interestingly, the four islands he mentioned are not marked on the map accompanying his letter. Instead, Tanjung Batu and its surrounds (labelled "a"), as well as a few islands along the Kijang Strait (labelled "B"), were shaded green on the map – these were the areas Utsunomiya hoped to lease, but as it turns out, did not manage to. Blue dots on Utsunomiya's map mark the locations of rubber plantations, with Japanese *kanji* characters indicating where their owners came from. For instance, "支" stands for China, "佛" means France, while "英" refers to Britain. Two other zones demarcated by red lines represent the areas that one of Utsunomiya's agents had identified.

Major-General Utsunomiya Tarō (宇都宮太郎). *Image reproduced from 宇都宮太郎関係資料研究会. (2007). 日本陸軍とアジア政策: 陸軍大将宇都宮太郎日記 第1巻 [Japanese Army and Asia Policy: Diary of Army General Utsunomiya Tarō Volume 1]. 東京: 岩波書店 (Tokyo: Iwanami Shoten).*

Utsunomiya had initiated his plan when he first received information from a civilian, Tashiro Kyohachi (田代強八), on 26 April 1910 about the possibility of leasing land on the Riau Islands. However, when Utsunomiya visited Army Minister Terauchi Masatake's (寺内正毅) office on 14 May 1910 to communicate his strategy, Terauchi did not share his conviction.[3] Another official with whom Utsunomiya discussed his plan and who also opposed the operation was Iwaya Jokichi (岩谷譲吉), the Japanese Vice-consul in Singapore.[4] Despite these objections, Utsunomiya pressed ahead with his land-leasing activities. This led to his letter to Koyama on 1 August 1910, in which he instructed the latter to head to Singapore to conclude land lease contracts with landowners on nearby islands.

Consequently, Koyama left Kobe, Japan on 6 August 1910, to carry out this task. He then orchestrated the signing of two land lease agreements on 1 November 1910. The first contract was signed between Uyeda Ushimatsu (上田丑松),[5] a Japanese permanent resident in the Dutch East Indies acting as Koyama's deputy, and Ki Hiong Tje (紀芝發), the Chinese landowner of Pulau Ayer Raja. Ki agreed to lease Pulau Ayer Raja to Uyeda for 2,500 Straits dollars, and received 500 Straits dollars as down payment.[6] But Ki later departed for China and did not return to the Riau Islands and, as a result, the transfer of surface rights[7] from Ki to Uyeda for the island was not completed.[8]

In contrast, the second contract was successfully concluded between Uyeda and Sultan Abdul Rahman Muazzam Shah of the Riau-Lingga Sultanate. It transferred surface rights to the islands of Kila, Momoi and Awi from the sultan to Uyeda,[9] and took effect after Uyeda had paid up 250 Straits dollars.[10] A possible reason why the sultan agreed to sign the contract was because he believed that the Japanese could help to free the region from Dutch rule.[11]

Subsequently, a contract signed between Uyeda and Koyama on 4 November 1910 transferred Uyeda's surface rights to the four islands unconditionally to Koyama after the latter had obtained the status of permanent residency in the Dutch East Indies. Koyama reserved the right to make decisions regarding the leasing of land and to retain all proceeds, and Uyeda promised not to intervene.[12]

In early 1911, the Ministry of Foreign Affairs in Japan carried out an inquiry into the Nanpō Operation following a report from Iwaya. The question of whether Koyama's land-leasing operation had received the army staff's informal consent was raised. Although Utsunomiya's letter clearly showed that he had instructed Koyama to proceed with the land leases, Utsunomiya managed to draft documents to prove that he had "nothing to do" with the Nanpō Operation.[13] For reasons unknown, Koyama was not punished for his involvement in Utsunomiya's plan.

After the inquiry in 1911, there was no further action on the leases and the islands remained as private property of individuals. When Utsunomiya died of cancer in 1922, the leases became meaningless to the Japanese government.[14] Although Utsunomiya's vision was not fulfilled, his letter, map and the contracts shed light on how meticulously he tried to carry out his plan. These form part of an intriguing set of Nanpō Operation documents donated by Lim Shao Bin to the National Library in 2018. ♦ **Yosuke Watanabe**

Notes

1 Spelt Pulau Airraja today.

2 宇都宮太郎 [Utsunomiya, T.]. (1910). 南方経略ノ準備作業ニ就キ. 明治43年8月1日. 辱知宇都宮太郎畏発小山秋作仁兄大人. [On the preparation for the Nanpō Operation. 1 August 1910. From Utsunomiya Tarō to Koyama Shūsaku]. Lim Shao Bin Collection, National Library, Singapore. (Accession no.: B32428444I)

3 宇都宮太郎 [Utsunomiya, T.]. (2007). 日本陸軍とアジア政策: 陸軍大将宇都宮太郎日記 1 [Japanese Army and Asia Policy: Diary of Army General Utsunomiya Tarō 1] (pp. 331, 336). 東京: 岩波書店. (Call no.: RSING 952.03092 UTS)

4 小山秋作の蘭領印度に於て土地租借に関する件. 機密第一号(明治44年1月7日). 在新嘉坡領事代理副領事岩谷譲吉外務大臣侯爵小村寿太郎殿. [Issue regarding Koyama Shūsaku's land lease in the Dutch East Indies. Secret No. 1 (7 Jan 1911). From Iwaya Jōkichi, Vice Consul in Singapore, to Marquis Komura Jutarō, Minister of Foreign Affairs.] Retrieved from Japan Center for Asian Historical Records website (Reference code: C03023033600).

5 His name on the contract appears as V. Vyeda; "Vyeda" is pronounced "Uyeda" in modern day context.

6 甲号訳文(上田と紀芝発の土地所有権移転契約). 1910年11月1日. [Contract of land ownership transfer between Uyeda and Ki Hiong Tje. 1 November 1910]. Lim Shao Bin Collection, National Library, Singapore. (Accession no.: B32428445J)

7 "Surface rights" refer to a landowner's right to use and modify the surface of the land. This does not necessarily include the rights to underground resources such as oil, gas and minerals.

8 千九百十二年十月某日に上田丑松がタンンピナン・リオ州付属地理事官に送った陳情書 [Petition sent by Uyeda Ushimatsu to the Resident of Tanjong Pinang, Riow State in October 1912]. Lim Shao Bin Collection, National Library, Singapore. (Accession no.: B32428445J)

9 乙号訳文(上田とサルタン・アブダル・ロッチマンシヤの土地買収契約). 1910年11月1日. [Contract of land purchase between Uyeda and Raja Abdul Rahman Shah. 1 November 1910]. Lim Shao Bin Collection, National Library, Singapore. (Accession no.: B32428445J)

10 乙号訳文(上田とサルタン・アブダル・ロッチマンシヤの土地買収契約). 1910年11月1日.

11 As Japan rose in power with its rapid military expansion during the Russo-Japanese War (1904–05), the Riau court tried to solicit Japanese assistance to oust the Dutch from the Riau Islands in as early as 1905. Andaya, B.W. (1977). "From Rūm to Tokyo: The search for anticolonial allies by the rulers of Riau, 1899–1914". *Indonesia*, *24*, 136, 148, 152. Retrieved from JSTOR.

12 明治四十三年十一月四日に小山秋作と上田丑松の間で結ばれた契約書 [Contract agreed between Koyama Shusaku and Uyeda Ushimatsu on 4 November 1910]. Lim Shao Bin Collection, National Library, Singapore. (Accession no.: B32428445J)

13 宇都宮, 2007, pp. 412–414.

14 宇都宮, 2007, p. ii.

A Scrapbook of Pre-war English Theatre

Title: *Repertory Players 1937–1948*
Compiler: Janet M.A. Lawson
Language: English
Type: Scrapbook
Call no.: RRARE 792.095957 SIN
Accession no.: B32410591C
Donated by: The Stage Club

One of the oldest scrapbooks in the National Library's collection, *Repertory Players 1937–1948* is important because of the light it sheds on Singapore's English language theatre scene before World War II.

This scrapbook of more than 100 pages includes newspaper clippings, photographs, programmes, notes from well-wishers, lists of cast members, details about the ticketing channel (usually via Robinsons department store) and prices of tickets, as well as the names of companies that sponsored props used in the Repertory Players' shows.

It also has some material on two other theatre groups: the Singapore Amateur Dramatic Club (S.A.D.C.)[1] as well as The Stage Club. The material is mostly arranged chronologically.

The scrapbook is very likely to have been compiled by Janet M.A. Lawson née Janet Marquerite Alexandrine Gow[2] whose name is handwritten on the inside front cover and dated 5 November 1937. In 1939, she married Carl Lawson, a well-known stage actor and producer, and took on his last name thereafter.

Despite its title, the scrapbook appears to cover Janet Lawson's involvement in Singapore's English language theatre scene during the period, which is why it mentions productions done by the S.A.D.C., the Repertory Players and The Stage Club. In the late 1930s, Carl Lawson played a key role in both the S.A.D.C. and the Repertory Players.[3]

From the scrapbook, we can see that the Repertory Players largely put up productions written in the 1930s, such as *Escape Me Never*, *George and Margaret*, *French Without Tears*, *On the Spot* and *Room for Two*.

On at least one rare occasion, the Repertory Players managed to stage the world premiere of a play in Singapore before it was due to be produced in London. This was so for *Curry Tiffin: A Comedy of Singapore*, which was staged in January 1940. The play was written by Thelma Faulkner (Mrs L.G. Hartmann), who was the wife of a military officer based in Singapore.[4]

The various cast lists give us a glimpse of Singapore's pre-war theatre scene. And if the names on the cast list of *Curry Tiffin* are any indication, even the Asian roles were played by non-Asians. In the play, Ah Foo was played by Alan D. Dant while Barbara Pyne was Amah.

Among the items in the scrapbook is a short note from the playwright Noel Coward to Carl Lawson, expressing Coward's regrets that he would not be able to attend the Repertory Players' staging of his play *Weatherwise* in Singapore on his return trip.

Programme sheets reveal that in addition to entertaining the paying public, the

Repertory Players also ran "camp tours", during which they presented shows to troops at the Singapore garrisons for free.[5] Servicemen were also given discounts when they watched the Repertory Players' shows at the theatres. Some performances for instance, the skit *Fifty-fifty*, were organised to raise funds for the troops.

The scrapbook is, unsurprisingly, silent during the period of the Japanese Occupation. The clippings end on 5 July 1941, and pick up again in 1945, when The Stage Club was formed.[6] Materials about The Stage Club dating from 1947 take up the remaining pages of Lawson's scrapbook.

The scrapbook also gives us a sense of Janet Lawson's professional life. She was involved in some of the early productions by The Stage Club, and in many plays put up by the Repertory Players. According to a cast list, for instance, she played the role of Monica Cole in their 1947 production *We Proudly Present*. Prior to that, she took on stage management responsibilities in the Repertory Players' *French Without Tears* (1939), as a programme sheet indicates.

It was during the Repertory Players' tour for *French Without Tears* in Kuala Lumpur that Janet and Carl Lawson got married on 29 June 1939. Their decision to wed was apparently a sudden one as Janet's parents were only informed by telegram after the fact.[7]

On 30 January 1940, while being sued for recovery of bills, Carl Lawson claimed in court that he had no monthly income and that he worked for his wife Janet. This is not documented in the scrapbook.[8] On 2 February 1940, two days after her husband lost the suit, Janet Lawson published a number of public notices in local newspapers identifying her as the "proprietress"[9] of the Repertory Players. The notice added that "(t)he performers who appear in the productions, or assist in any way, are amateurs, and receive no remuneration of any kind whatsoever for their services."

Further research indicates that after World War II, Janet Lawson continued to act with The Stage Club at least until the early 1950s.[10] Little is known about Carl Lawson in the post-war years.

This scrapbook, which was donated to the National Library in 2017 by The Stage Club, Singapore's oldest surviving amateur English language theatre group,[11] offers precious insights to pre-World War II English language theatre in Singapore. It is but one of five scrapbooks donated by The Stage Club that cover the period 1937 to 1964.

♦ **Kong Leng Foong**

[Facing page] Enclosed within the scrapbook is a copy of the manuscript for *Monkey's Paw*, one of the items performed at the Repertory Players' first presentation in September 1938 at the Victoria Theatre. The play was part of a larger vaudeville programme consisting of music and dance numbers, and *Planter's Paradise*, a comedy about life on rubber estates in Malaya, which was written by Carl Crawford Lawson.

[Clockwise below] Janet Lawson. *The Singapore Free Press and Mercantile Advertiser*, 29 June 1939, p. 1; Programme for the Repertory Players' first presentation in September 1938 at the Victoria Theatre; Photograph of the cast of *Curry Tiffin*, a comedy written by Thelma Faulkner, wife of Major L.G. Hartman, who was stationed in Singapore before he was appointed as military attache in Bangkok. The world premiere of *Curry Tiffin* was presented by the Repertory Players in January 1940 in Singapore. This was one of the few productions about life in Malaya staged by the company.

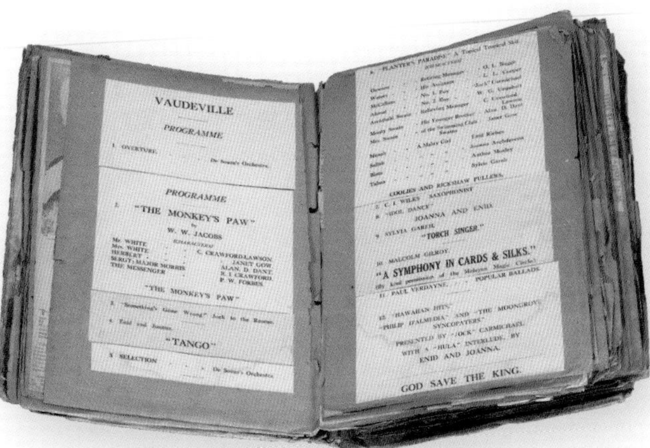

Notes

1 The Singapore Amateur Dramatic Club shares the same acronym as another group, the Singapore Amateur Dramatic Committee. It is not certain whether they are the same group.

2 As reported in the *Malay Mail* article "Stage wedding in Kuala Lumpur" (1939, June 29) kept in the scrapbook. External supporting sources include: Mr. Carl Lawson & Miss Gow wed at K.L. (1939, June 29). *Malaya Tribune*, p. 13. Retrieved from NewspaperSG.

3 Additional research shows that Carl Lawson was the secretary of the Singapore Amateur Dramatic Club. He resigned in mid-1938. See: New headquarters for the S.A.D.C., *Morning Tribune*, p. 8. Retrieved from NewspaperSG. Prior to that, at the Club's annual general meeting on 4 April 1938, it was suggested that the Club be renamed "Singapore Repertory Players". A majority of the Club's members did not support this suggestion though and to ensure that there was no further confusion, the Club clarified in a notice published in the *Morning Tribune* on 15 October 1938 that it was "not connected or associated in any way" to the Repertory Players. This notice came about soon after The Repertory Players presented their first stage presentation in September 1938, with an original work, *Planter's Paradise*, as part of a vaudeville showcase.

4 As indicated in the *Malaya Tribune* article "Singapore to see Curry Tiffin" (1939, November 16) kept in the scrapbook.

5 This was also reported in news articles not kept in the scrapbook. See, for instance: Free shows for services. *The Straits Times*, p. 5. Retrieved from NewspaperSG.

6 Stage Club for Singapore. (1945, December 1). *Malaya Tribune*, p. 2/3; Stage Club formed. (1945, December 2). *The Straits Times*, p. 3. Retrieved from NewspaperSG.

7 Carl Lawson springs surprise whirlwind K.L. wedding to stage assistant. (1939, June 29). *The Singapore Free Press and Mercantile Advertiser*, p. 1. Retrieved from NewspaperSG.

8 Civil suit against Mr. Carl Lawson. (1940, 30 January). *Malaya Tribute*, p. 3. Retrieved from NewspaperSG.

9 As captured in four published notices, dated 2 February 1940, kept in the scrapbook – *Morning Tribune*'s "Legal notice: Repertory Players"; *The Singapore Free Press and Mercantile Advertiser*'s "Public notices: Repertory Players"; *Malaya Tribune*'s "Legal notice: Repertory Players"; *The Straits Times*' "Public notices: Repertory Players".

10 Stage & Music. (1953, April 17). *The Straits Times*, p. 9. Retrieved from NewspaperSG.

11 The Stage Club, Singapore (2019). *About us: The Stage Club*. Retrieved from The Stage Club website.

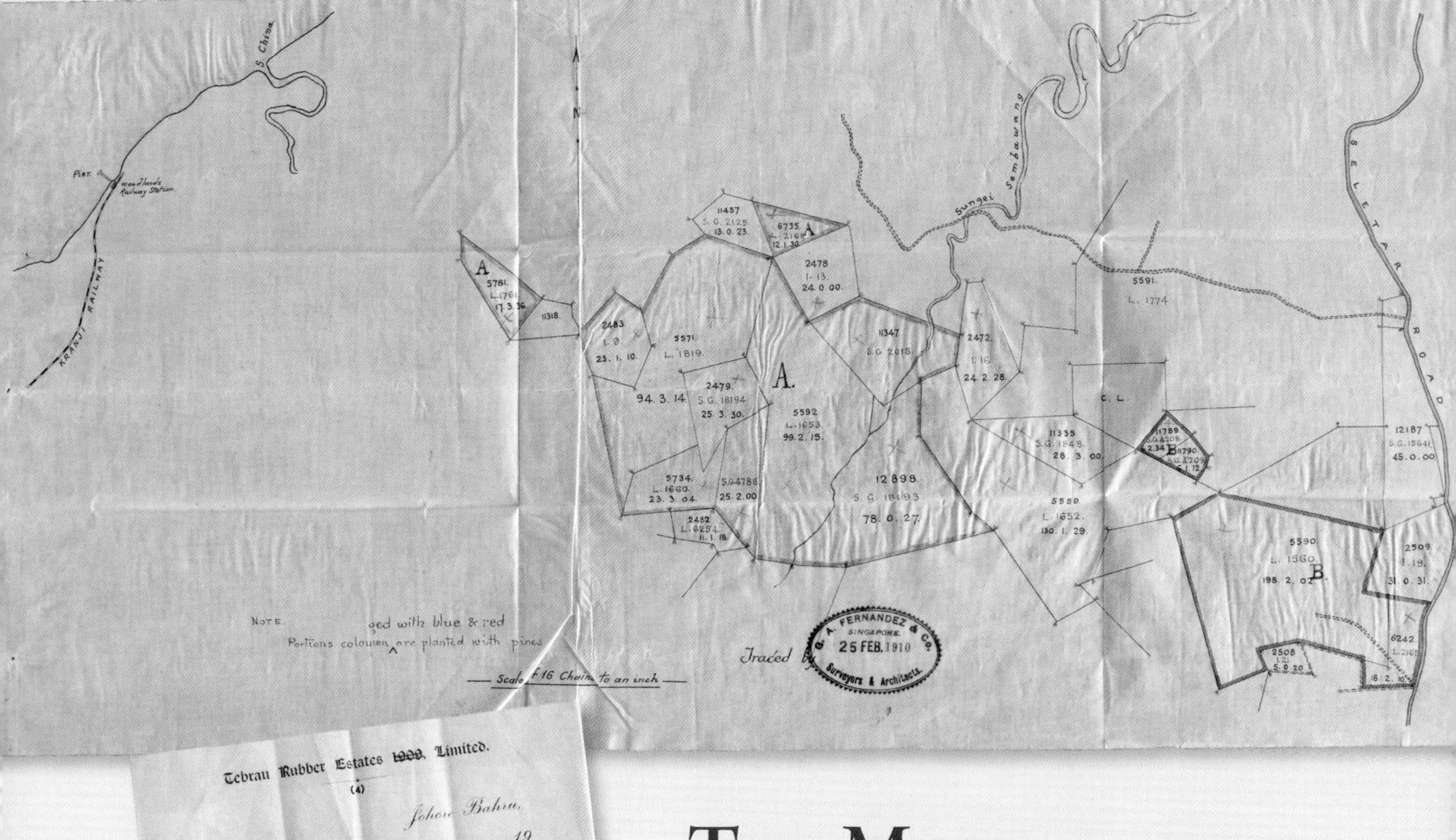

Tebrau Rubber Estates ~~1909~~, Limited.

(4)

Johore Bahru,

19

Report on Seletar Estate. Singapore.

Buildings. There are the usual Chinese coolie lines on the different blocks.

General Remarks. With regard to rubber properties of this description on Singapore Island there are four important points to be taken into consideration.

(1) Low rental and no export duty.

(2) A saving in freight owing to the proximity to the Port.

(3) A cheap and plentiful supply of labour.

(4) Absence of timber on the ground which eliminates any possibility of trouble from fungus "Fomes Semitostus" and minimizes loss from attacks by white ants.

I append a seven years' estimate of rubber production and a valuation which amounts to five years' purchase on the probable nett profit and I consider that at about this figure the estate will prove a profitable investment.

Edward C. Bagley
Manager Tebrau Rubber Estates Ltd

The Making of Seletar Rubber Estates

Title: (i) *Collection of Documents and Letters of the Seletar Rubber Estate*
(ii) *Plan of the Seletar Rubber Estate, Singapore*
Year published: 1909–21
Language: English
Type: Company documents
Call nos.: RRARE 338.476782 COL; RRARE 633.8952095957 PLA
Accession nos.: B29252088C; B30160375C

In 1910, Seletar Rubber Estates Limited was set up in London to invest in the new and booming rubber plantation sector of Southeast Asia. The aim was to buy over an existing pineapple estate in Sembawang owned by the Singaporean Chinese businessman Tan Kah Kee (see text box opposite), who as early as 1907 had already begun the process of interplanting lucrative rubber trees with pineapple plants.

Seletar Rubber Estates' collection of business papers, as well as a report and map related to the estate, reveal fascinating details of its business history, from the initial setting up of the company in London to its subsequent refinancing after it ran out of working capital during the post-World War I economic depression.

By the turn of the 20th century, rubber had become an increasingly sought after

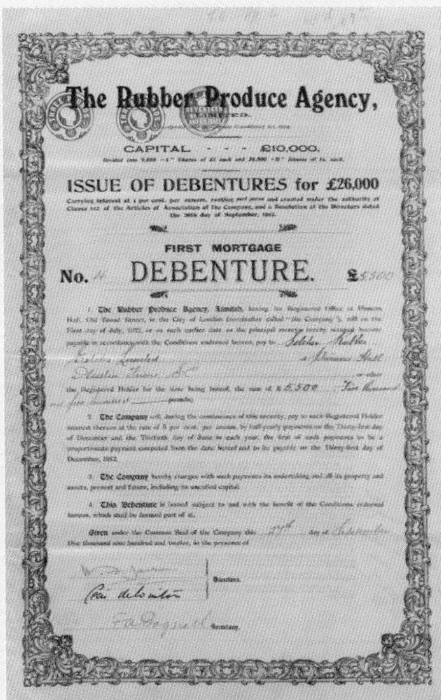
The Rubber Produce Agency,

CAPITAL - - - £10,000.

ISSUE OF DEBENTURES for £26,000

FIRST MORTGAGE

No. DEBENTURE. £5,500

The Enterprising Tan Kah Kee

A prominent businessman and philanthropist, Tan Kah Kee (1874–1961) contributed extensively to the financing of educational institutions in Malaya and China. Born in a village on the outskirts of Xiamen in China, Tan arrived in Singapore in 1890 to work for his father. In 1903, he took over his father's crumbling business and turned it around.

The plantation in Seletar was among Tan's first ventures, and its profitable sale in 1909 was a significant early success for him. He expanded into the manufacturing and processing of rubber goods and food products, and started the newspaper *Nanyang Siang Pau*. Along the way, Tan groomed several of his employees, including Lee Kong Chian, his son-in-law, into successful businessmen and community leaders. Although the 1920s saw Tan's fortunes decline, with his company Tan Kah Kee Ltd eventually folding in 1934, he remained a respected personality and was a seen as a formidable anti-Japanese patriot by the Chinese community.

Portrait of Tan Kah Kee, c. 1910. *Lee Brothers Studio Collection, courtesy of National Archives of Singapore.*

[Facing page] Documents which bear testimony to Seletar Rubber Estates Limited's establishment include a page from Edward Bryce's report on Tan Kah Kee's plantation. The report covers land area, number of trees planted and even anticipated crop yields till 1915. Of interest too is a map indicating the property lines of Tan Kah Kee's plantation (福山园), which was prepared as part of the report to London for the setting up of its purchase by Seletar Rubber Estates.

[Above] One of the debentures raised by Seletar Rubber Estates Limited in 1912, this one for £5,500. This was essentially a mortgage of Seletar Rubber's assets for the loan of money to the company at 5 percent interest. The money was raised to complete the planting of rubber trees on the estate and build a factory to process latex.

raw material for the manufacturing of tyres for bicycles and cars as well as insulation for electrical wiring invented in the 1800s.[1] Originally, latex was tapped from various tropical trees and vines but in time Brazil's Pará rubber tree (*Hevea brasiliensis*) became the dominant source.

In the mid-1890s, Chinese merchant Tan Chay Yan pioneered the successful commercial planting of the Pará rubber in Melaka on a commercial scale. In the first rubber boom of 1906, the Melaka Rubber Plantations Limited was formed in London to acquire Tan's plantations.[2] Investors were anxious to plough into the British Empire's latest growth industry and its financial capital, London, saw a proliferation of such rubber investment companies.

While most rubber plantations were found in Malaya and Sumatra, rural Singapore also hosted several plantations. The rubber boom inspired Tan Kah Kee, who had just started what would become a vast business empire, to almost double his pineapple estate[3] in Sembawang to 898 acres (3.6 sq km), and interplant it with rubber trees.

The resources needed to produce rubber – land, manpower and latex-processing machinery – all required sizable long-term capital investments that individual merchants in Malaya found difficult to finance (it takes almost a decade for rubber trees to start producing latex). London companies were thus created to invest in rubber plantations in faraway Malaya.

A 1909 report and map indicate that the nascent company had commissioned Edward Bryce, manager of another rubber estate in Johor, to look into the business prospects of Tan's Singapore plantation. The report included important information about the estate's condition, as well as its estimated production and revenue until 1915. In addition, the report contained a map of the estate and a listing of all the property deeds from the time of the original land grants until when the land was sold to Tan Kah Kee and his brother.

Seletar Rubber's initial flotation in 1910 raised £70,000 (600,000 Straits dollars) – a huge amount at the time – of which £17,000 (146,000 Straits dollars) was set aside as working capital after paying for the purchase of the estate in 1909 and other expenses. However, as Tan Kah Kee had not completed planting the estate with rubber trees, £15,000 more was raised through a debenture issue in 1912 for this task.

The 1910s proved to be a tumultuous decade for rubber plantations everywhere as worldwide demand and supply for the raw material fluctuated. The latex collecting industry in other parts of the world crashed, leaving British plantations in Asia as the main suppliers.[4]

Between 1914 and 1918, global trade suffered as a result of World War I. Unfortunately, yet another rubber market crash took place in 1920, and this time Seletar Rubber ran out of money. According to the papers in the Seletar Rubber Estates' collection, this resulted in the reorganisation and renaming of the company to Seletar Plantations in October 1921. Existing shareholders would be entitled to the same amount of shares they held in Seletar Rubber only if they agreed to increase the amount they had already invested by 37.5 percent.[5] Unsurprisingly, the smaller shareholders were unhappy and sent letters of objection. However, they had too few shares to stop the plan.

According to reports in local papers and directories, the refinanced Seletar Plantations survived the depression of 1920–21 and World War II, subsequently becoming Seletar Industrial Holdings. ♦ **Timothy Pwee**

Notes

1 Coates, A. (1987). *The commerce in rubber: the first 250 years* (p. 49). Singapore: Oxford University Press. (Call no.: RSING 338.1738952 COA)

2 Ward, A. H. C., Chu, R. W., & Salaff, J. (Eds., & Trans.). (1994). *The memoirs of Tan Kah-Kee* (p. 305). Singapore: Singapore University Press. (Call no.: RSING 338.04092 TAN); Malacca rubber flotation. (1906, February 5). *The Straits Times*, p. 8. Retrieved from NewspaperSG.

3 Ward, Chu, & Salaff, 1994, pp. 299, 302–303; 陈碧笙, & 陈毅明. (1986). 《陳嘉庚年譜》(p. 9). 福州：福建人民出版社. (Call no.: RSING 338.04092 TAN)

4 Coates, 1987, pp. 156–164.

5 Mincing Lane Tea & Rubber Share Brokers' Association. (1925). *Rubber producing companies–1925* (p. 461). London: The Financial Times (Not in NLB holdings); Seletar Rubber Estates. (1921, November 16). *The Straits Times*, p. 10. Retrieved from NewspaperSG.

THE MULTI-TALENTED MUHAMMAD ARIFF AHMAD

26.

BUDI

Pernahkah engkau menabor budi,
atau berqorban dermakan bakti ?
Kapada ibu ayah abdi :
selama umor mu dikurnia izzati ?

Kalau belum siap sekarang !
Ator hidupmu dalam budiman !!
agar tidak dichachi orang.
Tidak berakhlak, tiada beriman !

Ingat pepatah orang bijak !
dalam seni susunan sajak;
"Budi tidak dijual beli,
Payah didapat, sukar dichari !!"

Budi: bahasa ukuran hemah,
darjat insan kuat dan lemah;
sukatan harga jiwa sateria,
Tangga daki'an ka merchu bangsa.

Berbudilah, oh insan ! senyampang hidupmu,
bakal sahabat, tunggangan matimu;
balasan manusia usah diminta.
Berbudilah kerana Allah semata !!

Budi akhlakmu tunjok turunan,
Adakah engkau nisab beriman.
atau hanya chuchu Brahman :
Hidup jadi pengukor jalanan.

Mas 10hb.Nov: 1947.

Title: *Taman Puspa* (Garden)
Creator: Muhammad Ariff Ahmad (MAS) (1924–2016)
Dated: 1944–49
Language: Malay
Type: Manuscript; 62 pages
Call no: RCLOS 899.281 MUH
Accession no.: B26077962F
Donated by: The late Muhammad Ariff Ahmad

Title: *Nyanyi, Lakunan* (Sing, Act)
Creator: Muhammad Ariff Ahmad (MAS) (1924–2016)
Dated: 1946–48
Language: Malay
Type: Manuscript; 56 pages
Call no.: RRARE 781.62009595 NYA
Accession no.: B29242581K
Donated by: The late Muhammad Ariff Ahmad

[Top] Muhammad Ariff Ahmad, who enjoyed both writing and drawing, illustrated the cover of his notebook titled *Taman Puspa* (Garden) as well as the poems he wrote in it, such as "*Budi*" ("Contributions").

Ingat pepatah orang bijak!
dalam seni susunan sajak:
"Budi tidak dijual beli,
Payah didapat sukar dicari!"

Remember the words of the wise men!
in the art of poetry:
"You cannot buy or sell good deeds,
Difficult to obtain, hard to find!!" [1]

Muhammad Ariff Ahmad (1924–2016), who also went by the pseudonym MAS, was a prominent Malay language, literature and cultural expert and an activist. An award-winning writer, editor and lecturer too, the major awards he received include the prestigious Cultural Medallion in 1987, Tun Seri Lanang Award and the Southeast Asian Write Award in 1993, as well as the Bintang Bakti Masyarakat (Public Service Star) in 2000.[2]

Two of Muhammad Ariff's handwritten exercise books, titled *Taman Puspa* and *Nyanyi, Lakunan*, were donated by him to the National Library in 2014. These two compilations provide us with a rare glimpse into the creative works and inspiration of the young Muhammad Ariff. The 62-page *Taman Puspa*, which means "Taman Bunga" or "Garden", contains his earliest works of poetry. The second notebook, the 56-page *Nyanyi, Lakunan* (Sing, Act) contains songs he had collected and copied down between 1946 and 1948. Muhammad Ariff's drawings, which accompany the poems and songs, are a unique feature of both manuscripts.

Taman Puspa contains a collection of 67 poems Muhammad Ariff composed from 1944 to 1949. There are, however, some missing pages. Based on the dates written in the notebook, *Taman Puspa* was penned during the Japanese Occupation of Singapore and after the war when Muhammad Ariff was selected as a trainee teacher to study at Sultan Idris Training College (SITC) in Tanjung Malim, Perak. Most of the poems in *Taman Puspa* were subsequently published.

Muhammad Ariff's reflections on life – especially the concept of *budi* (contributions of good deeds) and patriotism – are the focus of the poems in *Taman Puspa*. The idea of *budi* was central to Muhammad Ariff's life and is evident in his work, particularly in his writings about Malay language, literature and culture. It is interesting to see that as early as 1949, he had already been composing works about *budi*, as exemplified by his handwritten poem of the same title. Dated 10 November 1949, "*Budi*" ("Contributions") illustrates his belief in selflessness, a trait he was respected for.

"*Budi*" expresses Muhammad Ariff's belief that one must "*berbudi*", that is, constantly do good deeds for the blessing of God (Allah) and altruistically for as long as one lives, as expressed in this verse:

Berbudilah, oh insan! Senyampang hidupmu,
Bekal sahabat, tunggangan matimu:
balasan manusia usah diminta.
Berbudilah kerana Allah semata!!

Translated, it reads:

Do good deeds, oh human! Just because it's your life,
Your offer as a friend, your foundation in death:
Do not ask for returns from humans.
Do good deeds solely for God!!

Many of his later works address *budi* as a theme as well. Muhammad Ariff himself wanted to live up to these standards, which is why he served in many organisations such as Asas '50, the Malay Language Council of Singapore and the Singapore Malay Teachers' Union. He was also a Board Member of Singapore Broadcasting Corporation.[3] His observations and reflections on humanity and community, which are some themes Muhammad Ariff covered in *Taman Puspa* too, were subsequently addressed in his novels, his play and works of non-fiction.

Nyanyi, Lakunan contains 60 children's songs, as well as the state anthems of Perak and Selangor. The children's songs have an educational focus, covering topics such as birds, fruits, and the natural environment, so that children could learn about these.

It was likely that Muhammad Ariff collected and copied these songs down between 1946 and 1948. Perhaps the compilation was part of his preparatory work to becoming a school teacher, since it was done during his teacher training days at SITC. It is not surprising to find the state anthems of Perak and the neighbouring state of Selangor included in *Nyanyi, Lakunan* as SITC was located in Perak.

Although Muhammad Ariff shared in his memoir, *Perjalanan Mas* (2003), that he had written children's songs which were used in schools in Singapore, it cannot be determined whether the songs in *Nyanyi, Lakunan* were authored by him. Nevertheless, the notebook offers a means to determine the approximate dating of some evergreen children's songs which continue to be popular today, for example, "*Bueh Sabun*" ("Soap Bubbles"). In *Nyanyi, Lakunan*, this song was copied down on 17 May 1948, suggesting that the song may have been composed earlier than 1948.

Muhammad Ariff's memoir also mentions that he enjoyed both drawing and writing. In fact, when he was a primary school student, he won many prizes for drawing.[4] It was only in later years that he shifted his focus to writing. As such, the two notebooks are even more precious as they showcase both of his artistic skills. The style of illustrations in *Nyanyi, Lakunan* is similar to those in *Taman Puspa*[5] – some of these are decorative borders, while others are coloured pen drawings that illustrate the subject of the songs, such as flowers.

These notebooks were just the beginning of Muhammad Ariff's long and illustrious contributions as a writer. His impressive oeuvre includes a wide range of works, such as Malay fiction and non-fiction, children's books, school textbooks, countless articles about Malay culture, tradition and language for magazines, journals and newspapers in Singapore and Malaysia, as well as scripts for Singapore Malay radio and television programmes.[6] Indeed, his works represent the titular *budi*, in that they are contributions which have truly enriched Singapore's literary heritage. ♦ **Juffri Supa'at**

Notes

1 Muhammad Ariff Ahmad. (2012). *Sumbangsih MAS: Koleksi puisi pilihan* (p. 33) (J. Supa'at, Trans.). Singapore: National Library Board. (Call no. RSING 899.281 MAS).
2 Muhammad Ariff first to win prestigious Malay literary award. (1993, February 22). *The Straits Times*, p. 22; Malay poet wins this year's SEA Write Award. (1993, October 1). *The Straits Times*, p. 30. Retrieved from NewspaperSG.
3 Muhammad Ariff Ahmad. (2003). *Perjalanan Mas – Memoir Muhammad Ariff Ahmad* (pp. 188–205). Singapore: Angkatan Sasterawan '50. (Call no. RSING q499.28092 MUH)
4 Muhammad Ariff Ahmad, 2003, p. 21.
5 A similar style appears in *Himpunan Kata .... Berjiwa*, which is another of Muhammad Ariff's notebooks.
6 Muhammad Ariff Ahmad, 2003, p. 21.

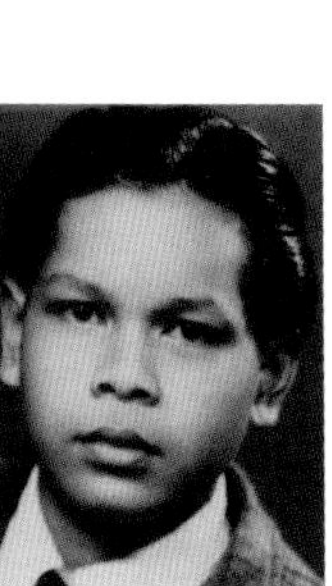

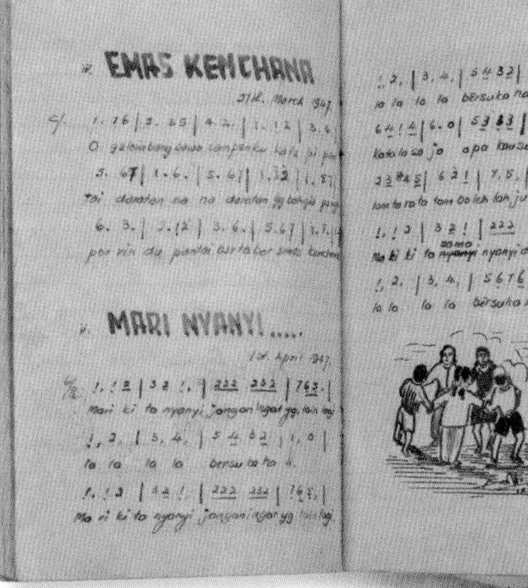

[Above] Portrait of MAS in 1945, sometime after he started working on the poems in *Taman Puspa* in 1944, and before he began compiling songs for *Nyanyi, Lakunan* in 1946. *Image reproduced from Muhammad Ariff Ahmad. (2003). Perjalanan MAS: memoir Muhammad Ariff Ahmad. Singapore: Angkatan Sasterawan '50.*
[Right] MAS' illustrations accompany the songs he had copied down in *Nyanyi, Lakunan* (Sing, Act).

SINGAPORE AS SEEN BY A CHINESE SCHOLAR

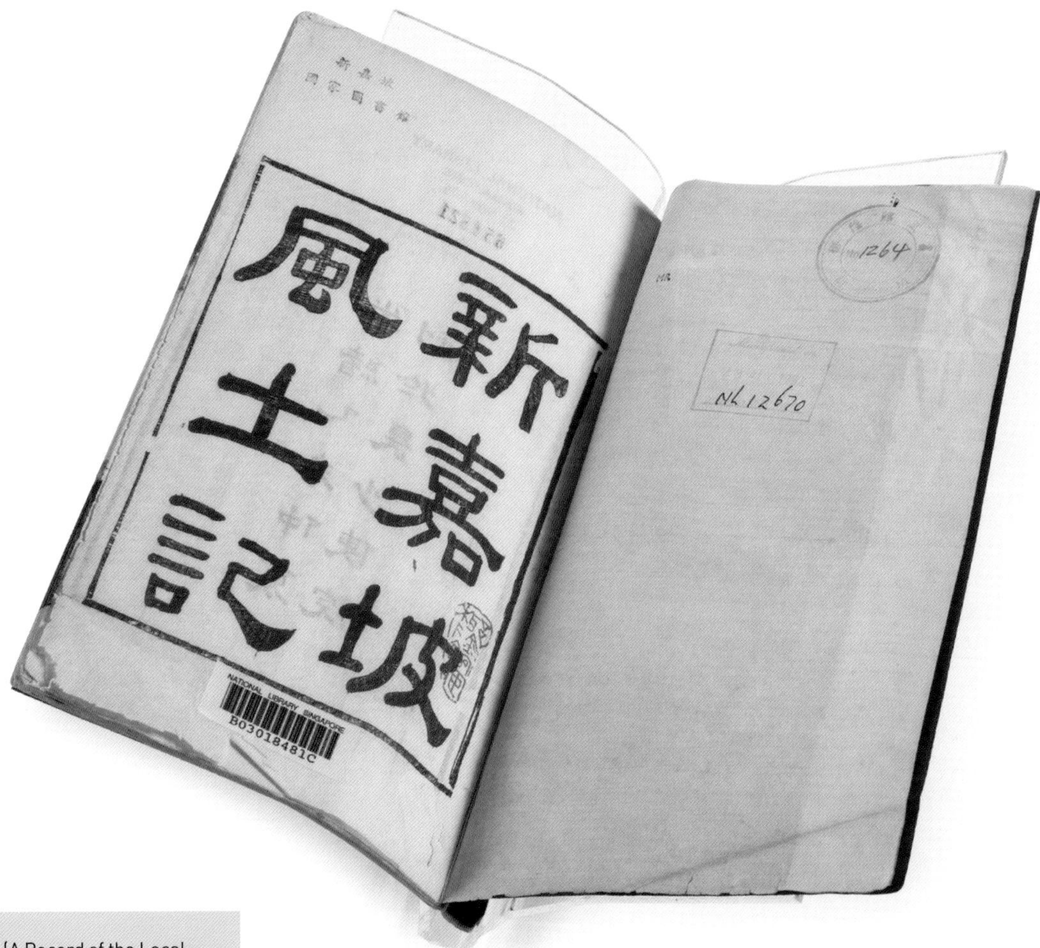

Title page of Li Zhongjue's travelogue. The book describes his observations of the conditions and life in Singapore in the 1880s.

Title: 《新加坡风土记》 (A Record of the Local Conditions of Singapore)
Author: 李钟珏 (Li Zhongjue)
Year published: 1895
Publisher: 长沙使院 (*Changsha shi yuan*)
Language: Chinese
Type: Book; 38 pages
Call no.: RRARE 959.5703 LCC
Accession no.: B03018481C
Donated by: Tan Yeok Seong

A slim 38-page thread-bound travelogue written by a scholar from China named Li Zhongjue (李钟珏) provides an interesting perspective of Singapore in the 1880s. Li visited Singapore at the invitation of Zuo Binglong (左秉隆), the first Chinese Consul to Singapore (1881–91)[1] appointed by the Qing government, and with whom Li enjoyed a close friendship. Li arrived in Singapore in late April 1887 and stayed here for two months.[2]

Li Zhongjue (1853–1927) was born to a family of physicians in Shanghai; his grandfather and father both practised Chinese medicine.[3] When Li was 24 years old, he travelled to Beijing to sit for the imperial examinations, where he met Zuo.[4] The two became firm friends and eventually sworn-brothers who pledged allegiance to each other.[5]

When Li returned to Shanghai after his studies, he took up the position of deputy editor-in-chief of a local newspaper in 1884, and one of his duties was to write daily articles about current affairs. This task piqued Li's interest in China's relations with foreign states as well as the state of affairs in other countries,[6] and explains why he decided to record his observations of Singapore on his visit here.

新嘉坡風土記
自暹羅直南伸如舌長如股中有山如脊斗入於海
由種人居之西人統名之曰下暹羅其國有十曰斜仔曰大
坤曰宋卡曰大年曰吉連丹曰丁噶奴曰彭亨曰柔佛在山
之東曰吉德曰沙剌我在山之西地至柔佛盡處畲衍一水
隔二三里而得一島西以蘇門答臘爲蔽南以爪亞爲屏東
以婆羅洲爲障四面環水如驪龍頷下珠即英人所謂新嘉
坡也舊名息力又稱石叻華人或稱新州府其地南距赤道
三百零四里
自香港乘輪船指西南行計程三千四百七十七里至越南
之西貢自西貢指南偏西行二千四百二十一里至新嘉坡

[Above] A page from Li's book where he described the areas surrounding Singapore (新嘉坡), stating that the Chinese referred to it as 新州府 (*xin zhou fu*, which means "new state").[7] Two other names for Singapore mentioned by Li were 息力 (*Xi li*) or 石叻 (*Shi le*), both of which were transliterations of the Malay word *selat* ("straits").
[Above right] This photo was likely staged to show a group of Chinese smokers in the 1880s – the men lying on the daybed are smoking opium, while those sitting in the foreground are smoking tobacco through a long-stemmed dry pipe or a water pipe (a Chinese hookah). One of the issues Li highlighted was how opium smoking ruined the lives of many Chinese coolies living in Singapore. *Courtesy of National Archives of Singapore.*

Li did not divide his travelogue into chapters, and the notes contained within are not organised in any thematic manner. In an almost diary-like style, he addressed topics such as population, government, legislation, trade, local produce, religion, language, leisure activities, modes of transport, places of interest, practices and customs of various ethnic groups, as well as the general lifestyle in the tropics.

The notes begin with an overview of Singapore's geographical position, with references to nearby places such as Pattani, Songkhla, Kelantan, Terengganu, Pahang, Johor, Kedah, Sarawak, Sumatra and Java. Li documented the details of his journey to Singapore, beginning with the first leg from Canton (present-day Guangzhou), with a stopover in Macau for a few weeks before he boarded the south-bound steamship in Hong Kong. According to Li, the steamship heading for Singapore would first travel in a south-westerly direction for 3,477 nautical miles (6,439 km) to Saigon (Ho Chi Minh City), and continue another 2,421 nautical miles (4,484 km) westward to reach Singapore.

Two interesting aspects of life in Singapore captured Li's attention. He noted that locals typically bathed in cold water, drenching themselves from head to toe to escape from the tropical heat. Li remarked that newcomers such as himself would hesitate to take a cold bath, but after sweating profusely from walking around in the midday heat, he quickly changed his mind, noting many visitors to Singapore often adopted the same practice.

The practice of raising a flag at Fort Canning Hill (formerly known as Government Hill) was mentioned by Li too. He explained that whenever a vessel entered the harbour, flags would be raised at the summit of Fort Canning Hill to alert the merchant community. Depending on the flag raised, merchants would be able to identify the vessel as well as the trading company and country she belonged to and where she was anchored.[8] Li also commented that a flag would be raised at Fort Canning Hill whenever a fire broke out in the city, with cannons fired to alert the people.

Additionally, Li wrote about the social ills that plagued Singapore, such as the trafficking of foreign labour, and the prevalence of gambling and opium-smoking among Chinese coolies. He reported that a rickshaw puller could earn around 1 Straits dollar after a hard day's work, out of which 40 cents would be used to pay his rent.[9] The remaining 60 cents was a sum that the rickshaw puller could live decently on, provided he did not spend it on opium. Unfortunately, almost 90 percent of the coolies were opium addicts. With each *qian* (钱, approximately 3 g) of opium paste costing 20 cents, most of the coolies' earnings would literally go up in smoke.

While Li's travelogue is not meant to provide a comprehensive account of life in Singapore in the mid-1880s, it is nonetheless a valuable resource as his detailed descriptions provide a glimpse into the lives of working-class Chinese through foreign eyes – in this case a visitor from China.

♦ **Jessie Yak**

Notes

1 Zuo Binglong served as the Chinese Consul from 1881 to 1891.
2 Zhu, J. (朱杰勤). (2008).《东南亚华侨史：外一种》(p. 338). 北京：中华书局. (Call no.: RSEA 959.004951 ZJQ)
3 Zhu, 2008, p. 334.
4 Zhu, 2008, p. 334.
5 Zhu, 2008, p. 334.
6 Zhu, 2008, p. 335.
7 Li, C. C. (C. C, Chang, Trans.). A description of Singapore in 1887. In *China Society of Singapore, 1949—1974: 25th Anniversary Journal* (1975). (p. 20). Singapore: China Society. (Call no.: RSING 301.20951 CHI)
8 Chang, 1975, p. 25.
9 It is unclear if Li was referring to rent for the coolie's lodgings or the rickshaw.

Writing off a Sultan's Debts

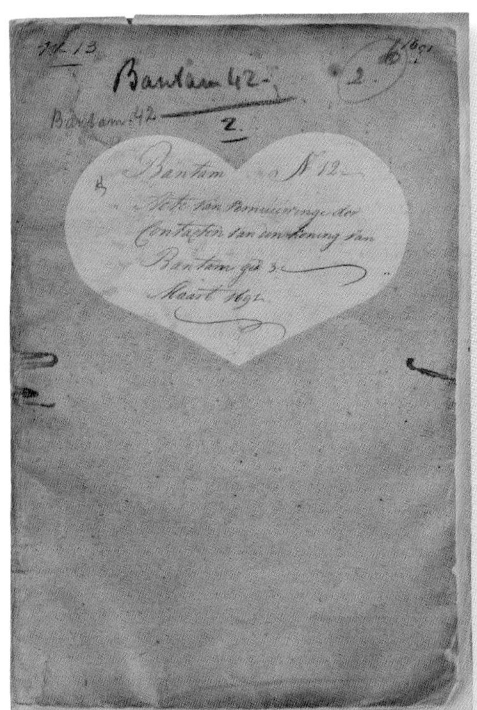

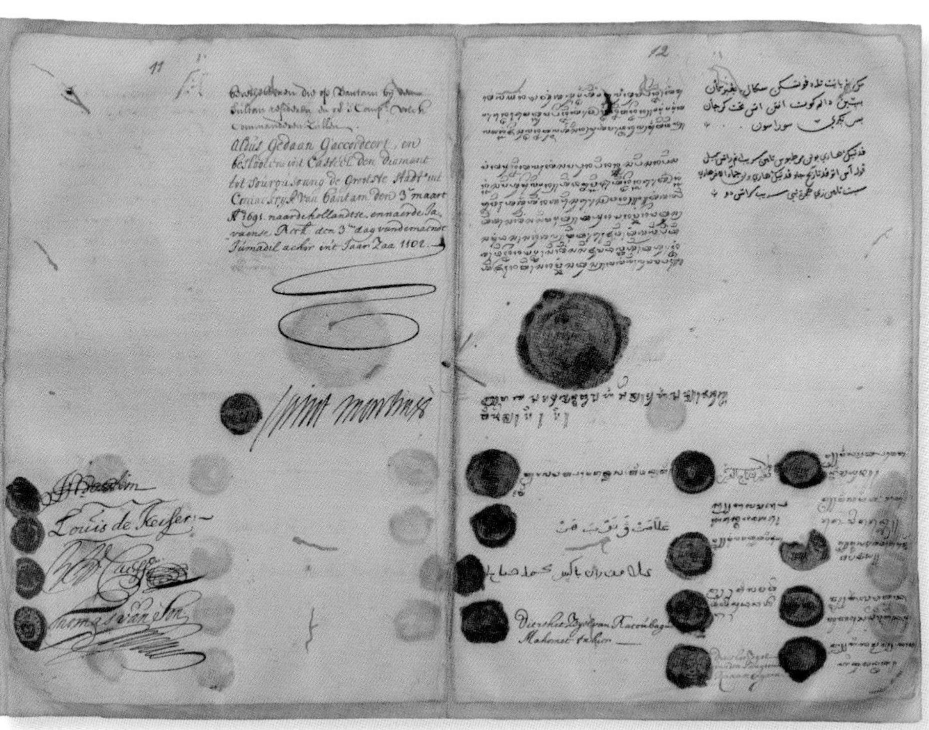

[Left] Front cover of *Acte van vernieuwinge der contacten van den koning van Bantam ged:3:e Maart 1691*. The word "*contacten*" (contacts) is likely an error and the correct word should be "*contracten*" (contracts). Written in Dutch with parallel translations in Javanese and Malay, the agreement was signed in Batavia in 1691.
[Right] The agreement bears the signatures and seals (with the exception of two headmen who apparently had no seals) of 20 signatories.

Title: *Acte van vernieuwinge der contacten van den koning van Bantam ged:3:e Maart 1691* (Deed of Renewal of the Contacts of the Sultan of Banten, Dated on 3rd of March 1691)
Date: 1691
Language: Dutch, Javanese and Malay
Type: Document; 17 pages
Call no.: RRARE 959.8021 NED
Accession no.: B32428986I

Acte van vernieuwinge der contacten van den koning van Bantam ged:3:e Maart 1691 (Deed of Renewal of the Contacts of the Sultan of Banten, Dated on 3rd of March 1691) is an agreement concluded in 1691 between the Vereenigde Oostindische Compagnie (VOC), or Dutch East India Company, and the ninth sultan of Banten, Abu al-Mahasin Muhammad Zainul Abidin in Batavia (present-day Jakarta). It bears the signatures and wax seals of five members of the Raad van Indië (Council of the Indies), the Sultan of Banten, his four brothers and 10 authorised headmen. The seals include the crowned monogram of Isaac de l'Ostal de Saint-Martin, head of the Raad van

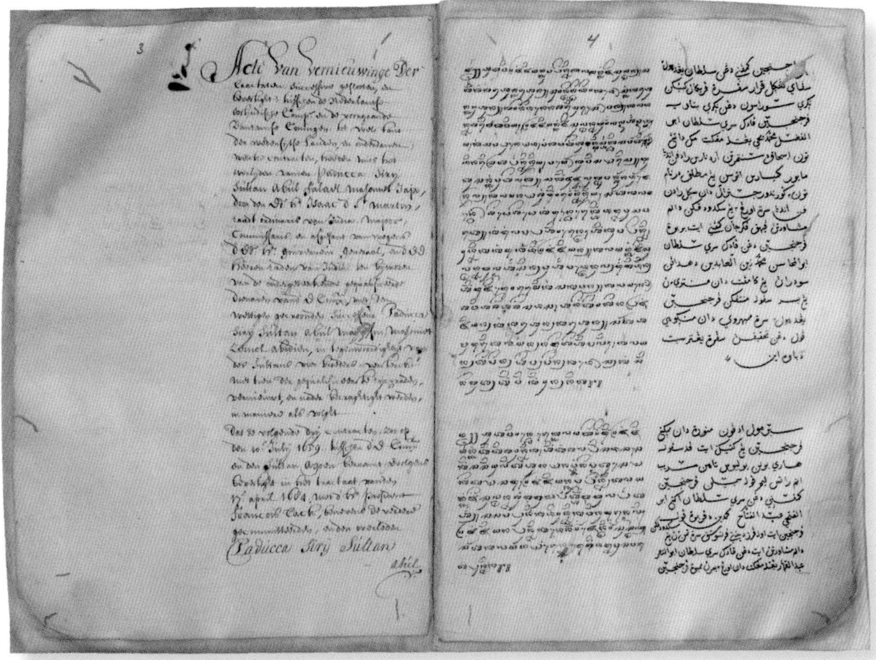

Key terms that wrote off the debts owed by the sultan, and gave the VOC monopoly of Banten's trading networks and the purchase of pepper in Banten, are stated towards the end of pages 3–4 **(top)** and on pages 5–6 **(above)** of the contract.

Indië;[1] the arms of council members such as Jan Franssen, Louis de Keyser, Willem Caef, and Thomas van Son, a junior official (*onderkoopman*); and the *tughra*[2] of the 18-year-old Sultan of Banten, Abu al-Mahasin Muhammad Zainul Abidin.

The 17-page contract is significant as it contains the agreement to write off the debts owed to the VOC by the sultan and his predecessors on condition that two earlier treaties signed in 1659 and 1686 – which had given the VOC economic superiority – were still in force. These treaties, along with *Acte van vernieuwinge der contacten van den koning van Bantam ged:3:e Maart 1691* and the co-opting of Banten as a protectorate of the Dutch in 1684, enabled the VOC to expand its control further westwards in Java and the region, at the expense of the once flourishing independent port city.[3]

Banten, also known as Bantam, is located on the northwest coast of Java, at the intersection of the maritime passageways connecting the Java Sea, the South China Sea and the Straits of Melaka. To understand Banten's development as an international trading port, it is important to trace its beginnings in the early 1500s.

In the early 16th century, the port of Banten was under the control of the Portuguese-allied Hindu Kingdom of Sunda, but it was captured at the behest of Sunan Gunung Jati,[4] the priest-king (*raja-pandita*) of Cirebon, a port city in Java, and who was largely known to be responsible for the Islamisation of Java. After his son Maulana Hasanuddin was installed as Sultan of Banten, the sultanate was expanded into former Sunda territories on the island of Sumatra, hence gaining control of the bulk of the East Indies pepper trade.[5]

By the late 1500s, Banten had become the leading port of the East Indies.[6] From the 1600s, Banten's strategic location and its monopoly of the pepper trade made it a site of contention among the British, Portuguese and Dutch.[7]

After the Portuguese, and then the Dutch, failed in their attempts to wrest control of Banten, the VOC succeeded in taking the city of Batavia (present-day Jakarta) in 1619.[8] As Banten came under intermittent Dutch blockades between 1619 and 1645, the huge international vessels heading there were diverted to Batavia instead.[9] This weakened Banten's trade although it did not severely undermine its dominance. The port continued to enjoy substantial profits well into the late 17th century by servicing other Dutch competitors such as the British.[10]

In 1645, a peace treaty was signed between the more conciliatory Sultan Abul Al Mafakhir Mahmud Abdulkadir (fourth Sultan of Banten) and the VOC. In 1656, the treaty was broken as Sultan Abu al-Fath Abdul Fattah (sixth Sultan of Banten, better known as Sultan Ageng Tirtayasa) strongly opposed the Dutch, resulting in war between both sides. Bantenese forces raided Dutch-controlled Batavian districts and VOC ships, and the Dutch retaliated by enforcing yet another blockade on Banten's ports.[11]

After the Bantenese defeat, a peace settlement was reached in 1659, giving the VOC control of Banten's trading networks.[12] This allowed the Dutch to take advantage of the internal rift between Sultan Ageng and his son, Abdul Kahar Abu al-Nasr (later known as Sultan Haji).[13] The VOC used the situation to gain leverage over the sultanate and the city. With the support of the VOC, Abdul Kahar Abu al-Nasr defeated his father in 1683 to become the seventh sultan. Banten's economic sovereignty was further weakened when Sultan Haji signed an

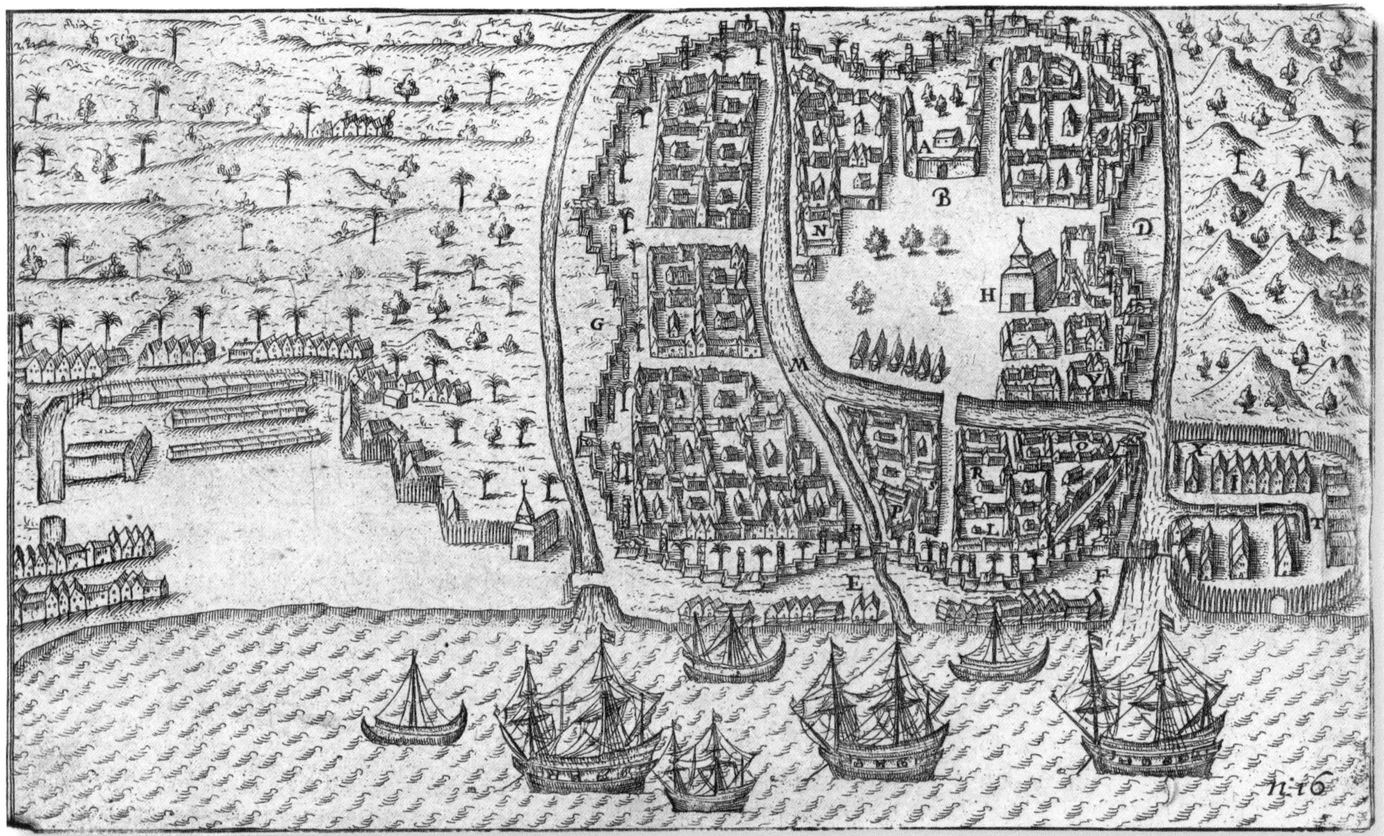

An illustrated map of Bantam (Banten) as shown in Volume 1 of Isaac Commelin's 1646 compendium *Begin ende Voortgangh, van de Vereenighde Nederlantsche Geoctroyeerde Oost-Indische Compagnie* (Origin and progress of the United Netherlands Chartered East-India Company).

economic treaty which gave the VOC complete monopoly of the pepper trade in Banten.[14]

Subsequently, the ongoing rivalry between the Dutch and the British for the control of trade and territories in the Malay Archipelago encouraged the VOC to re-visit past negotiations with Banten. This resulted in the signing of *Acte van vernieuwinge der contacten van den koning van Bantam ged:3:e Maart 1691*. By further thwarting the authority of the Banten sultanate, the VOC was able to exert its supremacy over Java on both the economic and political fronts. Thereafter, Banten's reputation as an independent and thriving port slowly declined. ♦ **Nadirah Norruddin**

Notes

1 Isaac de l'Ostal de Saint-Martin, ambassador to Banten, was also present during the installation of Sultan Abu al-Mahasin. His secretary, Thomas van Son, compiled a detailed report containing his observations of the ceremony. This report is one of the rarest documentation of the installation of kings in the region before the 19th century. It is now held at the VOC archives. See Talens, J. Ritual Power: The Installation Of A King In Banten, West Java, In 1691 (p. 336). *Bijdragen tot de Taal-, Land- en Volkenkunde, 1993, Deel 149, 2de Afl*, 333–335. Retrieved from JSTOR. The Raad van Indië comprised officials employed by the VOC. These officials served as advisers to the governor-general of the Dutch East Indies.

2 A sultan's calligraphic monogram, seal or signature, which is affixed to all official documents and correspondence.

3 Radical changes affected the Bantenese realm, some of these brought about by a war relating to a dynastic conflict between Sultan Ageng Tirtayasa (reigned 1651–82) and his son, Abdul Kahar Abu al-Nasr (reigned 1680–87). Under the command of Isaac de l'Ostal de Saint-Martin and Francois Tack, who intervened at the request of Abdul Kahar Abu al-Nasr, the VOC gained victory over the troops of Sultan Ageng. As a return favour for the military assistance, a treaty granting the VOC a number of privileges in Banten was concluded in 1684. The most important of these was a monopoly on the purchase of pepper, which formed the core of the economic relationship between Banten and Dutch-controlled Batavia. See Talens, 1993, p. 347.

4 It is believed that Sunan Gunung Jati was born Sharif Hidayatullah. See Ross, L. M. (2016). *The Encoded Cirebon mask: Materiality, flow and meaning along Java's Islamic northwest coast* (pp. 27–28). Leiden: Brill. (Call no.: RSEA 731.7509598424 ROS); Kersten, C. (2017). *History of Islam in Indonesia: Unity in diversity* (p. 33). Edinburgh: Edinburgh University Press. (Call no.: RSEA 297.09598 KER)

5 Hall, K. (2014). European Southeast Asia encounters with Islamic expansionism, circa 1500–1700: Comparative case studies of Banten, Ayutthaya, and Banjarmasin in the wider Indian Ocean Context. *Journal of World History, 25*(2/3), 233–4; Kathirithamby-Wells, J. (1987). Forces of regional and state integration in the Western Archipelago, c. 1500–1700. *Journal of Southeast Asian Studies, 18*(1), 29–31. Retrieved from JSTOR.

6 Kathirithamby-Wells, 1987, pp. 29–31.

7 Kathirithamby-Wells, 1987, p. 36.

8 Pigeaud, T. G. T. (1976). *Islamic states in Java 1500–1700: Eight Dutch books and articles by H.J. de Graaf* (p. 13). The Hague: Martinus Nijhoff. (Call no.: RCLOS 959.82 GRA-[GH])

9 Kathirithamby-Wells, J., & Villiers, J. (Eds.). (1990). *The Southeast Asian port and polity: Rise and demise* (p. 114). Singapore: Singapore University Press. (Call no.: RCLOS 959.82 GUI-[JSB]); Guillot, C. (1990). *The Sultanate of Banten* (p. 35). Jakarta: Gramedia Book Pub. Division. (Call no.: RCLOS 959.82 GUI-[JSB])

10 Hall, 2014, p. 233.

11 Ricklefs, M.C. (2008). *A history of modern Indonesia since c.1200* (pp. 97–98). Basingstoke: Palgrave Macmillan. (Call no.: 959.8 RIC)

12 Banten wanted to re-establish its right to sail to the Moluccas (Maluku islands) and to areas rich in tin in the Malay Peninsula, which the Dutch wanted to control. Under pressure, Banten accepted Batavia's terms in which all fugitives, whether Dutch or not, who were seeking sanctuary in Banten would be sent back to Batavia.

13 Ricklefs, 2008, p. 98.

14 The Dutch also demanded that they have a right to maintain a garrison in the town and palace.

INDEX

Page numbers in italics denote an image.